Seba Smith

My thirty years out of the senate

Seba Smith

My thirty years out of the senate

ISBN/EAN: 9783337173784

Printed in Europe, USA, Canada, Australia, Japan

Cover: Foto ©Suzi / pixelio.de

More available books at **www.hansebooks.com**

SOUTH CAROLINA NULLIFICATION.—[See Letter XXXIII.]

THIRTY YEARS

OUT OF THE SENATE.

BY

MAJOR JACK DOWNING.

ILLUSTRATED

WITH SIXTY-FOUR ORIGINAL AND CHARACTERISTIC ENGRAVINGS ON WOOD.

NEW YORK:
DERBY & JACKSON.
1860.

OAKSMITH & CO.
Printers and Stereotypers

WEEKS & CO
Binders.

PREFACE.

In January, 1830, the first Downing Letter ever written appeared in the Daily Courier, published in Portland, Maine. This paper had just been started by the author, and was the first daily paper published in the country north or east of Boston. The Courier was started as an independent paper, devoted to no political party—a position for a paper in those days likely to command but small support. The Maine Legislature met in Portland on the first of January, and the two political parties were so evenly balanced, and partizan feeling ran so high, that it was six weeks before they got fairly organized and proceeded with the business of legislation. The political papers were hot and furious, and there was no small excitement throughout the State, which even spread in a considerable degree to other portions of the country.

At this juncture of affairs, the author of these papers, wishing to show the ridiculous position of the legislature in its true light, and also, by something out of the common track of newspaper writing, to give increased interest and popularity to his little daily paper, bethought himself of the plan to bring a green, unsophisticated lad from the country into town with a load of axe-handles, hoop poles, and other notions, for sale, and while waiting the movements of a dull market, let him blunder into the halls of the legislature, and after witnessing for some days their strange doings, sit down and write an account of them to his friends at home in his own plain language. The plan was successful almost beyond parallel. The first letter made so strong a mark that others had to follow as a matter of course. The whole town read them and laughed; the politicians themselves read them, and their wrathful, fire-eating visages relaxed to a broad grin. The Boston papers copied them, and all Boston tittered over them. The series was inaugurated and must go on. The letters continued from time to time, and spread over the whole country, and were universally read.

The name of Downing was entirely original with the author, who had never heard or seen the name before, and did not then even know that there was a Downing street in London, or an oyster dealer by that name in New York. In a year or two the letters became national in their character, and young Mr. Downing repaired to Washington, where he became the right hand man and confidential adviser of President Jackson. The author continued the letters in the Portland Courier for seven years, when he sold that paper and removed to New York. After an interval of a few years he resumed the series again, publishing the letters in the National Intelligencer at Washington, and continuing them till near the close of the administration of President Pierce.

Thus these papers, begun and continued partly for emolument, partly for amusement, and partly from a desire to exert a salutary influence upon public affairs and the politics of the country, have grown up to their present condition. In presenting them in this collected form, with original illustrations, to render them more attractive, the author could not let them go out into the world to make new acquaintances, and possibly down to posterity to help furnish political lessons to "Young America" for generations yet to come, without a careful retrospection to consider their whole moral and political character and influence. For should they contain

"One line which, dying, he could wish to blot,"

he would certainly wish to blot it now. But, believing the work will be harmless, and, he hopes, salutary, he leaves it to his countrymen, praying for Heaven's blessing on our whole common country.

SEBA SMITH.

NEW YORK, February, 1859.

CONTENTS.

	PAGE
PUBLISHER'S PREFACE,	10
MAJOR DOWNING'S SKETCH OF HIS EARLY LIFE,	14

LETTERS AND "DOCKYMENTS."

LETTER.
1. HIS FIRST VISIT TO PORTLAND, ... 36
2. HE VISITS THE LEGISLATURE, ... 41
3. UNCLE JOSHUA GOES TO BOSTON, ... 46
4. COUSIN NABBY WRITES TO MR. DOWNING, ... 61
5. A DREADFUL SNARL IN THE MAINE LEGISLATURE, . . . 63
6. "BOTH LEGISLATERS SPLIT RIGHT IN TU," 67
7. AFFAIRS TAKE A MORE FAVORABLE TURN, ... 68
8. MRS. DOWNING URGES HIM TO COME HOME, ... 69
9. THE WHEELS OF GOVERNMENT TRIGGED, ... 71
10. THE LEGISLATURE "RIPPING UP THEIR DUINS," . . . 75
11. "QUEER DUINS," IN THE SENATE, ... 78
12. SETTING UP A CANDIDATE FOR OFFICE, ... 82
13. THE LEGISLATURE AND EDER HALL GO HOME, . . . 84
14. MR. DOWNING TALKED OF FOR GOVERNOR, ... 86
15. UNCLE JOSHUA'S GREAT SKILL IN POLITICS, ... 88
16. GIVES AN OPINION ABOUT NEWSPAPERS, ... 92
  DOCKYMENT—GRAND CAUCUS AT DOWNINGVILLE, . . 95
17. PORTLAND TOWN-MEETING—HOW THE VOTES STOOD, . 102
18. HOW THE VOTES STOOD IN DOWNINGVILLE, ... 105
19. MR. DOWNING DETERMINES TO GO TO WASHINGTON, . 106
20. TALKS WITH THE BOSTON EDITORS ON HIS WAY, . . 109
21. INTERVIEW WITH MAJOR NOAH AT NEW-YORK, . . . 113
22. MR. DOWNING'S HEROIC DEFENSE OF MR. INGHAM, . 119
23. RECEIVES A CAPTAIN'S COMMISSION FROM THE PRESIDENT, 127
24. DRAFTING THE MILITIA IN DOWNINGVILLE, ... 134
25. HIS FIRST MILITARY REPORT TO THE PRESIDENT, . . 148
26. HOW THE "LEGISLATERS SWALLOWED THE HEALING ACT." 152
27. OPPOSES THE SALE OF MADAWASKA TO THE BRITISH, . 159
28. A CONFIDENTIAL TALK WITH THE PRESIDENT, . . . 164
29. RUNS AN EXPRESS FROM BALTIMORE TO WASHINGTON, 168
30. RECEIVES A MAJOR'S COMMISSION TO PUT DOWN THE NULLIFIERS, 173
31. THE PRESIDENT'S PROCLAMATION AND THE FEDERALISTS, 177
32. THE DOWNINGVILLE MILITIA ARRIVE AT WASHINGTON, 180
33. THE EFFECTS OF NULLIFICATION ILLUSTRATED, . . . 183
34. POLITICS IN MAINE—POLITICAL PROMISES, ... 189
35. LISTENING FOR NULLIFICATION GUNS IN SOUTH CAROLINA, 191

36. THE SCIENCE OF LAND SPECULATION ELUCIDATED, ... 192
37. MR. CLAY PUTS A STOPPER ON NULLIFICATION, ... 194
38. WHETHER OLD HICKORY SHOULD SHAKE HANDS WITH THE FEDERALISTS, 207
39. THE PRESIDENT ASSAULTED BY LIEUT. RANDOLPH, ... 200
40. THE MAJOR SHAKES HANDS FOR THE PRESIDENT, ... 205
41. NARROW ESCAPE AT CASTLE GARDEN BRIDGE, ... 208
42. THE PRESIDENTIAL PARTY VISIT BOSTON, ... 212
43. THEY TURN A SHORT CORNER AT CONCORD, N. H., . . . 214
44. GREAT FUSS IN DOWNINGVILLE BECAUSE THE PRESIDENT DIDN'T COME, 215
    DOCUMENT—THE MAJOR NOMINATED FOR PRESIDENT, . . 220
45. MAKING OLD HICKORY A DOCTOR OF LAWS. 221
46. QUARREL BETWEEN THE MAJOR AND MR. VAN BUREN, . . . 225
47. HOW THE OLD DEMOCRATS ARE PUT OVER ON THE FEDERAL SIDE, . 232
48. ABOUT ME AND DANIEL WEBSTER, ... 234
49. DANIEL AND I, AND OLD HICKORY, ... 238
50. THE MAJOR PREVENTS A ROBBERY IN THE SENATE CHAMBER, . . 242
    DOCUMENT—A GAP IN HISTORY, ... 246
51. PRESIDENT POLK TRAVELS WITH THE MAJOR, ... 248
    DOCUMENT—FROM THE NATIONAL INTELLIGENCER, . . . 254
52. THE PRESIDENT AND THE MAJOR IN THE STATE OF MAINE, . . 255
53. MR. RITCHIE'S ENDLESS FIGHT WITH THE FEDERALISTS, . . . 260
    DOCUMENT—MR. RITCHIE'S COUNTERBLAST, ... 267
54. THE MAJOR POURS OIL ON MR. RITCHIE'S WOUNDS, ... 269
55. THE MAJOR'S FIRST DISPATCHES FROM MEXICO, ... 272
56. THE MAJOR'S ANNEXATION DREAM IN MEXICO, ... 278
57. PRIVATE DISPATCH AND GOOD ADVICE TO THE PRESIDENT, . . 285
58. THE MAJOR'S INTERVIEW WITH GENERAL SCOTT AND MR. TRIST, . 290
59. GENERAL SCOTT COURTMARTIALED IN MEXICO, ... 298
    DOCUMENT—BATTLE IN THE COURTMARTIAL, ... 302
60. RACE FOR THE PRESIDENCY—OLD ZACK AHEAD, ... 305
61. WRITING BY TELEGRAPH—THE TIDE TURNS FOR OLD ZACK, . . 309
62. CURIOUS NAVIGATION OF SALT RIVER, ... 315
63. KIND ADVICE TO MR. RITCHIE, ... 321
64. THE HIGH FENCE ON MASON AND DIXON'S LINE, ... 324
65. A FAMILY TALK ABOUT POLITICAL PARTIES, ... 335
66. THE NEW DOWNINGVILLE POLITICAL PLATFORM, ... 341
67. FRIENDLY EPISTLE TO GOVERNOR KOSSUTH, ... 349
68. GREAT CONVENTION IN DOWNINGVILLE, ... 357
69. ADJOURNED MEETING—GREAT SPEECHES, ... 365
70. THE GREAT PRESIDENTIAL *TUG* AT BALTIMORE, ... 376
71. DOWNINGVILLE RATIFICATION—TORCHLIGHT PROCESSION, . . 383
72. SARGENT JOEL HURRAHS FOR GEN. SCOTT, ... 391
73. PIERCE ELECTED—JOEL TURNS HIS TUNE, ... 398
74. PRIVATE ADVICE TO THE NEW PRESIDENT, ... 401
75. THE MAJOR'S VISIT TO THE FISHING SMACKS, ... 404
76. THE MAJOR'S MISSION TO EUROPE, ... 413
77. CONGRESS AT OSTEND—SOULE, SICKLES AND SAUNDERS, . . 419
78. THE SCHOONER TWO POLLIES SCUDDING ROUND CUBA, . . 426
79. THE TWO POLLIES BOMBARDING THE MORO, ... 436
80. THE TWO POLLIES AT ANCHOR, ... 447
81. A POSTSCRIPT, ... 457

PUBLISHERS' PREFACE

IT has been asserted, upon no less authority than the immortal Sam Patch, "that some things can be done as well as others." The veteran politician, Colonel Thomas H. Benton, has given to his countrymen a comprehensive and very valuable work entitled: "THIRTY YEARS IN THE UNITED STATES SENATE; Or, A History of the Working of the American Government for Thirty Years," &c.

Now, that other veteran politician, Major Jack Downing, who declares positively that there is an outside as well as an inside to everything, has prepared to lay before his countrymen his comprehensive and valuable work entitled: "THIRTY YEARS 'OUT' OF THE UNITED STATES SENATE; Or, A History of the Working of American Politicians for Thirty Years," &c.

Major Downing has been publishing this work for a couple of years in Emerson's Magazine and Putnam's Monthly; because, as he said, the work itself being of a strictly national character, he felt bound to select the most elevated and respectable channel for communicating it to the public. In commencing the preparation of his "Thirty Years" for publication, the Major said he would go clear back to his childhood, and give some account of his "ancestral posterity;" so far back as his old grandfather, Mr. Zebedee Downing, one of the early pioneers into the primeval "forests of Down East." He didn't know as he should make his work quite as long as Mr. Benton's two great big "vollums," but he would try to make it quite as interesting. He said he shouldn't interfere or encroach at all on Colonel Benton's ground. The Colonel's work was to show the working of the American Government for thirty years, and his work was to show the working of American politicians for thirty years. And, besides, the Colonel's stand-point was *inside* the Senate, and his stand-point was *outside* the Senate. So he didn't see as they ever need to clash, for in the worklngs of governments and politicians the last thing in the world to be apprehended was a clash between the *ins* and the *outs*.

Finally, we have made a satisfactory arrangement with the Major to produce his great work, his Thirty Years out of the Senate. It contains the whole batch of the Major's Letters and other "dockyments," from the year

1830, when he first struck out into public life, up to the present time. It will show the workings of politicians in the State of Maine in 1830, when "the wheels of Government got trig'd," and they had "such a tussle to get 'em agoing." It will then show how Mr. Downing went to Washington, and became "Gineral Jackson's right hand man;" and how he helped the old Gineral through with his fight against "Biddle's Bank," and how he settled the Madawaska Boundary difficulty, and how he put down and crushed out South Carolina Nullification. These letters and "dockyments" will show the workings of Politicians during the Mexican War, and how the Major helped President Polk along through those troublesome times; and how he and Mr. Trist went to Mexico, and held General Scott and General Taylor in check, and wouldn't let them run away with President Polk's thunder. They will show, also, how General Scott wasn't elected President, and how General Pierce was. They will describe the hard tug there was at Baltimore to get General Pierce nominated, and how at last the nomination was *ratified* at Downingville, and so secured his election. They will show how the Major and Mr. Buchanan and Mr. Souley got up that Ostend Convention, and laid the plan and made the agreement to "take Cuba if we have the power;" and how the Major fitted out a naval expedition in the schooner Two Pollies, and cruised about several months to effect that object. In short, the letters and other "dockyments" will show more things than you can shake a stick at, and of course more than can be alluded to here.

But besides the valuable political and historical information, interesting to the old and instructive to the young, that will be found embodied in this great work of Major Downing, there is another important reason why it should be given to the public, and why the publishers take pride and pleasure in presenting the work in a dress and with embellishments worthy of the subject—and that is, the universally admitted fact, that the writings of the genuine original Major Downing present the best and truest exposition of the peculiar Yankee dialect of the Anglo-Saxon language that there is extant. It may not be amiss to quote a few authorities in support of this opinion. A portion of the earlier part of this series of letters was published more than twenty years ago in a small volume in Boston, by Lilly, Waite & Co. On that occasion the late Major Noah, for many years known as an able and leading journalist in New-York, spoke of the book as follows, in his Evening Star:

"The Letters, which have obtained a circulation and celebrity more extended, perhaps, than any production that ever issued from the American press, are written with all the quaint simplicity of the style of Fielding, and abound in passages of infinite drollery and exquisite humor."

Robert Walsh, at that time, and for many years previous, editor of the

National Gazette, at Philadelphia, certainly one of the ablest journalists our country has produced, and the first American writer who compelled the English critics to respect American criticism, made the following remarks in his Gazette, in which he alludes to imitators who had unjustifiably adopted the Major's signature in writing in the newspapers:

"It has been the fate of all successful authors **to have** counterfeits, **who** deal with their originals, as Hamlet says that some players imitate **nature. The Rabelais,** the Swifts, the Voltairs, suffered **in their day by the productions** of interlopers of the sort. Mere bunglers attempted **to** personate them, and **confounded the** less discriminating or critical **part of** the reading public. Major Jack Downing has paid in like manner the penalty of genius and **popularity**; and he has complained of the hardship and injustice in a characteristic vein. We humbly advise him to write over the whole story of President **Jackson's late expedition.** It might confidently be predicted that a full narrative from his pen, duly authenticated, would obtain as much vogue in these United States as did Peter Plymley's Letters in Great Britain."

The old New York Mirror, March 23, 1839, speaking of some of the **writings** of Major Downing, said:

"**These are the most** graphic and really the best Yankee papers we have **ever seen, or ever** expect **to** see, let who will write them."

The New York Courier and Enquirer, July 3, 1839, **in speaking of the writings of the Major, used the following language:**

"There is no doubt that the author is *the best painter of Yankee peculiarities that ever wrote.* He is true to nature **and never** caricatures, but without caricaturing is most amusing."

The same paper, February 27, 1844, referring to Major Downing's Letters, said:

"Those letters were written in the true and genuine spirit of Yankeedom, and were clothed in the real vernacular of the land. Some of them deserve a much higher and more lasting reputation than seems to have awaited them; though we are very much mistaken if they do not hereafter take **the** place they so eminently merit. They ought **to** be considered standard exhibitions **of** New England **peculiarities** of style, feeling and sentiment at **the time, and** be cherished **as authentic mementoes** of the pilgrim opinions and pilgrim dialects of the generation in which they appeared."

The same leading New York journal, July 16, 1845, again referring to the author of these letters, said:

"He is, in point of fact, the only writer who has ever been entirely successful in the genuine dialect of Yankee land."

It becomes therefore, a matter of general interest in the history of the literature of the country, as well as of its politics and "the workings of politicians," that these papers should be preserved in an authentic form and attractive dress, corresponding in some degree with their intrinsic merits. To accomplish this important object the publishers have determined to spare no pains in their power to bestow. The Major's heart is very much given to the work, and he will superintend the management of the whole business, "picters" and all. For that purpose he has determined to let the "Two Pollies" lay off and on, or make short cruises under the command of Captain Jumper and Sargent Joel, while he devotes himself to the preparation of his "*Thirty Years' View*" for the press. We should explain what some of our readers, perhaps, may not recollect, that Sargent Joel Downing has command of the military force on board of the Two Pollies, consisting mainly of the Downingville militia, who were embarked on board in 1855, for the purpose of taking Cuba. The Major will not allow them to be disbanded or return to Downingville, for he says there is no knowing but what Mr. Buchanan may want their services before he gets through his Administration; and he never did leave a friend in the lurch yet, and, therefore, he shan't turn his back on Mr. Buchanan.

With these preliminary remarks and explanations, we will let the Major go straight ahead and tell his own story in his own way.

SKETCH OF MY EARLY LIFE.

IN WHICH I TELL CONSIDERABLE MORE ABOUT MY GRANDFATHER THAN I DO ABOUT MYSELF.

When we read about great men, we always want to know something about the place where they live; therefore I shall begin my history with a short account of Downingville, the place where I was born and brought up.

Downingville is a snug, tidy sort of a village, situated in a valley about two miles long, and a mile and a half wide, scooped out between two large rugged hills that lie to the east and west, having a thick forest of trees to the north, and a clear pond of water, with a sandy beach, to the south. It is about three miles from the main road, as you go back into the country, and is *jest about in the middle of Down East.* It contains by this time a pretty considerable number of inhabitants, though my grandfather Downing was the first person that settled there, jest after he got back from sogering in the Revolutionary war. It has a school-house and a tavern, and a minister, and a doctor, and a blacksmith, and a shoe-maker, and folks that work at most all sorts of trades. They haven't got any meeting house up yet, but the school-house is pretty large, and does very well to hold meetins in, and they have meetins **very regular every Sunday**—the men filling up all the seats **on one side of the school-house and the** women on the other.

They haven't got any lawyer in Downingville. There was one come once and sot out to settle there, and hired a room and put a sign up over the door with his name on it, and the word "office" in great large letters, so big you could read 'em clear across the road. A meeting of the inhabitants was called at the school-house the next day, and after chawing the matter over awhile it was unanimously agreed if the man wanted an office he should go somewhere else for it, for as for having an office-seeker in Downingville they never would. So they voted that he should **leave** the town in twenty-four hours, or they would **take him down to the** pond and duck him, and ride him out of town on a rail. A committee of twenty of the stoutest men in Downingville was appointed to carry the message to him, at which he prudently took the hint, and packed up and cleared out that afternoon. All the quarrels, and disputes and law-cases are always left out to Uncle Joshua Downing, and he settles them all, by and large, at two shillings a piece, except when **they** have come to blows, and then he charges two and sixpence a piece.

As I said afore, my grandfather, old **Mr. Zebedee Downing, was the first set**tler in Downingville. Bless his old heart, he's living yet [1834], **and,** although he is eighty-six years old, he attended a public caucus for the good of his country about two years ago, and made a speech, when I was nominated for Governor of the State of Maine.

As it is the fashion, in writing the lives of great folks, to go back and tell something about their posterity, I spose I ought to give some account of my good old grandfather, for he was a true patriot, and as strong a republican as ever Uncle Joshua was. He was born somewhere in the old Bay State, away back of Boston, and when the Revolutionary war come on he went a sogering. Many and many a time, when I was a little boy, I've sot in the corner till most midnight to hear him tell over his going through the *fatigue of Burgwine.* If one of the neighbors came in to chat awhile in an evening, my grandfather was always sure to go through the **fatigue of Burgwine ; and if a** stranger was traveling through Downingville and stopped at my grandfather's in a warm afternoon to get a glass of water, it was ten chances to one if he could get away till my grandfather had been through the whole story of the fatigue of Burgwine. He used to tell it the best to old Mr. Johnson, who used to come in regularly about once a week to spend an evening and drink a mug of my grandfather's cider. And he would set so patiently and hear my grandfather through from beginning to end, that I never could tell which took the most comfort, Mr. Johnson in drinking the cider, **or my** grandfather in going through the fatigue of Burgwine. After Mr. Johnson had taken about two or three drinks, he would smack his lips and say, "I guess, Mr. Downing, you would have been glad to get such a mug of cider as this in the battle of Burgwine."

"Why, yes," said my grandfather, "or when we was on the march from Cambridge to Peekskill either, or from Peekskill to Albany, or from Albany to Saratogue, where we went through the fatigue of Burgwine. Old Schuyler was our gineral," said my grandfather, bracing himself back in his chair, "and he turned out to be a traitor, and was sent for to go to

Gineral Washington to be court-martialed. Then Gineral Gates was sent to us to take command, and he was a most capital officer, every inch of him. He had his cocked hat on, and his regimentals, and his furbelows on his shoulders, and he looked nobly," said my grandfather. "I can see him now, as plain as if 'twas yesterday. He wore a plaguey great stub cue, as big as my wrist, sticking out at the back of his neck as straight as a handspike. We l, when Gates came we were all reviewed, and everything was put in complete order, and he led us on, ye see, to take Burgwine. By daylight in the morning we were called out by the sound of the drum, and drawn up in regiments, and the word was, 'on your posts, march.' And there we stood, marching on our posts without moving forward an inch; heads up, looking to the right. We didn't dare to move an eye, or hardly to wink.

"By and by along comes the old Gineral to inspect us, riding along so stately, and that old stub cue sticking out behind his head so straight, it seems as though I can see him now, right here before me. And then he addressed us, like a father talking to his children. 'Fellow soldiers,' says he, 'this day we are going to try the strength of Burgwine's forces. Now let every man keep a stiff upper lip, go forward boldly and attack them with courage, and you've nothing to fear.' O, he addressed us completely; and then we marched off to meet the inemy. By and by we begun to hear the balls whizzing over our heads, and the inemy's guns begun to roar like thunder. I felt terribly for a minute or two, but we kept marching up, marching up," said my grandfather, rising and marching across the floor, "for we had orders not to fire a gun till we got up so near we could almost reach them with our bagonuts; and there was a hundred drums all in a bunch, rattling enough to craze a nation, and the fifes and the bugles," continued my grandfather, still marching across the floor, " went tudle, tudle, tudle, tudle. O, I can hear that very tune ringing in my ears now as plain as if 'twas yesterday, and I never shall forget it to my dying day. When we got up so near the inemy that we could fairly see the white of their eyes, the word was 'halt,'" said my grandfather, suddenly

THE FATIGUE O. BURG.WINE.

halting in the middle of the floor, and sticking his head back as straight as a soldier, "'make ready;' 'twas did in a moment," continued my grandfather, throwing his staff up against his shoulder; "'take aim;' 'twas did in a moment," fetching his staff down straight before his eyes; "'fire!' then, O marcy, what a roar!" said my grandfather, striking his staff down upon the floor, "and such a smother and smoke you couldn't hardly see your hand afore you. Well, in an instant the word was, 'prime and load,' and as fast as we fired we fell back in the rear to let others come up and take their turn; so by the time we were loaded we were in front and ready to fire again, for we kept marching all the time," said my grandfather, beginning to march again across the floor. "But the inemy stood their ground, and kept pouring in upon us tremendously, and we kept marching up and firing, marching up and firing, but didn't gain forward an inch. I felt streaked enough, for the balls were whistling over our heads, and sometimes a man would drop down on one side of me, and sometimes on 'tother; but it wouldn't do for us to flinch a hair; we must march up and fire, and wheel to the right and left, and keep it going. By and by the word was, 'advance column,' then, heavens and earth, how light I felt," said my grandfather, quickening his march across the floor. "I knew in a moment the inemy was retreating, and it seemed to me I could have jumped over the moon. Well, we marched forward, but still kept firing, and presently we begun to come on to the inemy's ground; and then, O marcy! such a sight I never see before and never want to again—stepping over the dead bodies, and the poor wounded wretches wallowing in their blood, mangled all to pieces, and such screeches and groans, some crying out, 'don't kill me,' 'don't kill me,' and others begging us to kill 'em to put 'em out of misery. O, it was enough to melt the very heart of a stone!" said my grandfather, wiping the tears from his eyes.

"But they needn't have been afraid of being hurt, for our Gineral was one of the best men that ever lived. He had the carts brought up immediately, and all the poor wounded souls carried off as fast as possible where they could be taken good care of. He wouldn't let one of 'em be hurt any more than he would one of his own men. But it was a dreadful hot battle ; we fit and skirmished all the afternoon and took a good many prisoners, and some cannon and ammunition. When it came night the inemy retreated to their fortifications, and we camped all night on the ground with our guns in our hands, ready at a moment's warning to pitch battle again. As soon as it was daylight we were all mustered and paraded again, and round come the old Gineral to see how we looked. He held his head up like a soldier, and the old stub cue stuck out as straight as ever. I can see it now as plain as I can see my staff," said my grandfather. "And O, my stars, how he addressed us ; it made our hearts jump to hear him. 'Fellow-soldiers,' says he, 'this day we shall make Burgwine tremble. If you are only as brave as you were yesterday we shall have him and all his army before night.' But Burgwine had slipped away in the night, and got into a place stronger fortified. But he couldn't get away ; he was hemmed in all round ; so we got him before it was over. We were five or six days skirmishing about it ; but I can't tell you all, nor a quarter part on't."

"But how was it you took Burgwine at last?" said Mr. Johnson, taking another drink of cider. "O, he had to give it up at last," said my grandfather. "After we had skirmished a day or two longer, Gineral Gates sent word to Burgwine that if he had a mind to march his army back into Canada, and leave everything this side unmolested, he'd let him go peaceably. But Burgwine wouldn't accept it; he sent word back that 'he was going to winter with his troops in Boston.' Well, after we had skirmished round two or three days longer, and Burgwine got into such close quarters that he couldn't get away any how, he sent word to Gineral Gates that he'd accept the offer and march back to Canada; but Gates sent word back to him again, 'You said you meant to winter in Boston, and I mean to make you as good as your word.' At last Burgwine see it was no use for him to hold out any longer, so he give all his men up prisoners of war. Then we were all paraded in lines a little ways apart to see them surrender. And they marched out, and marched along towards us; and it was a most noble sight to see them all dressed out in their regimentals and their bagonuts glistening in the sun enough to dazzle anybody's eyes. And they marched along and stacked their arms, and marched through between our lines looking homesick enough. I guess we felt as well as they did, if our clothes wan't so good."

Mr Johnson handed me the mug and told me to run and get another mug of cider; for before my grandfather could get through the fatigue of Burgwine, Mr. Johnson would most always get to the bottom of the mug. When I brought in the second mug, Mr. Johnson took another sip and smacked his lips, and says he:

"Mr. Downing, I should like to drink a toast with you; so here's health and prosperity to the apple trees of Downingville. **Mr.** Downing, what will you drink to us !" said he, handing the mug to my grandfather.

"Why I don't keer about any cider," said my grandfather, (for he is a very temperate man, and so are all the Downings remarkably temperate,) "but I will jest drink a little to the memory of the greatest and the bravest Gineral that this world ever see yet ; so here's my respects to old Gineral Gates' stub cue."

By this time, my grandfather having poured out of him the whole fatigue of Burgwine, and Mr. Johnson having poured into him about three pints of cider, they would both of them feel pretty considerably relieved, and Mr. Johnson would bid us good night and go home.

I take it that it was hearing these stories of my grandfather's bravery told over so often in my younger days, that made me such a military character as to induce the President to appoint me to the command at Madawaska, and also to go to South Carolina to put down the Nullifiers. But I'm getting a little before my story, for I haven't got through with my grandfather yet, and my father comes before I do, too. As I said afore, my grandfather was the first settler in Downingville. When he got through sogering in the Revolutionary War, he took a notion he'd go and pick him out a good lot of land away Down East to settle on, where there was land enough to be had jest for whistling for it, and where his boys would have a chance to do something in the world. So he took grandmother and the two boys—for father and uncle Joshua were all the boys he had then, and packed them into a horse waggon, and took an axe, and a hoe, and a shovel, and some victuals, and a bed-tick to put some straw in, and a gun and some blankets and one thing another, and started off down East. He drove away into Maine till he got clear to the end of the road, and then he picked his way along through the woods and round the pond five miles further, till he got to the very spot where Downingville now is, and there he stopt and baited his horse, and while grandmother and the boys sot down and took a bit of a luncheon, grandfather went away up top of one of the hills to take a view of the country. And when he come down again says he, "I guess we may as well ontackle, for I don't believe we shall find a better place if we travel all Summer." So he ontackled the old horse, and took the waggon and turned it over against a great oak tree, and put some bushes up around it, and made a pretty comfortable sort of a house for 'em to sleep in a few nights, and then he took his axe and slashed away among the trees. But that old oak never was cut down; it's the very same one that stands out a little ways in front of grandfather's house now. And poor grandmother as long as she lived always made a practice once a year, when the day come round that they first camped under the old oak, to have the table carried out and set under the tree; and all hands, children and grandchildren, had to go and eat supper there, and the good old lady always used to tell over the whole story how she slept eight nights under the waggon, and how they were the sweetest nights' rest she ever had.

Well, grandfather, he smashed away among the trees, and he soon had half a dozen acres of 'em sprawling, and while they were drying in the sun he went to work and built him a snug little log house, and made two stools to set on, one for him and one for grandmother, and a couple of blocks for the

GRANDMOTHER'S ANNUAL DINNER.

boys. He made a stone fire-place in one corner of the house, and left a hole in one corner of the roof for the smoke to go out, and he got it all fixed as nice as a new pin, and then they moved into it; and I've heard grandmother say more than a hundred times that she believed she took more comfort in that log house than ever a queen took in a palace.

When the leaves and the twigs of the trees that grandfather had cut down had got considerable dry in the sun, he went out one warm clear afternoon and sot fire to 'em. The wind was blowing a considerable of a breeze from the southward, and the fire spread almost as fast as a horse could run. Grandmother used to say it was the grandest sight she ever see, to see them are six acres of trees all in a light flame at once, and the fire streaming up as high as the tallest pines, sometimes in a broad red sheet, and sometimes in narrow strips that went up rolling and bending like ten thousand fiery dragons' tongues. After the fire had gone through it, grandfather went to work to clear it up. He picked up the limbs and bits that were left, and threw 'em in heaps and sot fire to 'em again, and he laid sticks across the large logs that were too heavy to move, and *niggered* them off with fire, and then rolled them up in piles and sot fire to 'em again and burnt 'em all up smack smooth. Then he went to work and planted the ground all over to corn, and potatoes, and punkins, and beans, and squashes—and round near the house he planted water-millions and mush-millions, and cowcumbers, and beats, and carrots, and turnips; and grandmother carried out a whole apron full of seeds of all kinds of 'arbs that ever grew in old Massachusetts, and sowed 'em round, and they come up as thick as hops.

After this, the family of old Mr. Zebedee Downing always lived like heroes and never knew what it was to be in want. They had ten children, and a smart, likely set of boys and gals they were too, and they all lived to grow up, and were all married and well-to-do in the world. Father, whose name was Solomon, was the oldest boy, and as they grew up, the hardest of the work naturally fell upon him, and as grandfather begun to get along considerable in years, father had to take the principal care of the farm. So that he was always called a hard-working boy and a hard-working man. He had a quiet, peaceable disposition, and was never known to quarrel with anybody, and scarcely ever to speak **a** ha'sh word.

Uncle Joshua was the next oldest, and he was as different from father as a toad wants a tail. He was a clear shirk, and never would work if he could help it. But he was always good-natured, and full of his pranks, and kept his clack agoing the whole day long; so that the boys used to like him, and whenever they wanted to have any frolic or fun they always used to go to him to take the lead. As he grew up he took to reading considerable, and after they begun to have newspapers at Downingville he **was** a master-hand to read newspapers and talk politics, and by the time he was twenty-five years old he knew more about politics than any other man **in** Downingville. When he was thirty years old **he was chosen Moderator** of the town meeting, and has been chosen to that office every year since. He's been a Squire a good many years, and **has** held most **all** the offices in town, one after another, and is on the whole considered the foremost **man** in Downingville. He is now Postmaster of the United States for Downingville, an office which I was the means of helping him to by my acquaintance with the President. **But** it's time to begin to tell about myself.

Mother always said I was the smartest baby that she ever see. I don't speak of this by way of bragging, but as I am writing a history to go before the world, I'm bound to be impartial. She says before I was a week old I showed that I was real grit, and could kick and scream two hours upon the **stretch,** and not seem to be the least bit tired that ever was. **But** I don't remember anything about this. The first I remember, I found myself one cold November day, when I was about six years old, bareheaded and barefoot, sliding on the ice. It had been a snapping cold night, and all the boys in the neighborhood, and most all the gals turned out and had a fine frolic that day, sliding and running on the pond. Most of the larger boys had shoes, but we little fellers that wan't big enough to wear shoes had to tuff it out as well as we could. I carried a great pine chip in my hand, and when my feet got so cold I couldn't stand it no longer, I'd put the chip down and stand on that a little while and warm 'em, and then at it to sliding again.

WARMING HIS FEET.

When I got to be considerable of a boy I used to have to work with father on the farm. But it always seemed to go rather against my grain, and father used to say that I didn't love work a bit better than Uncle Joshua did, without he'd give me my stent, and then he said I would spring to it and get it done by noon, and go off round the pond in the afternoon fishing or hunting musquash. I think I took the most comfort in catching musquash of anything I used to do. There was a good deal of pleasure in catching pickerel—to take a long fishing pole and line, and go down to the pond in the morning, and stand on a log whose top limbs run away off into the water, and throw the hook off and bob it about on the top of the **water, and see** a great pickerel jump and catch it, and wait a minute or two for him **to** get **it well** into his mouth, and then pull him ashore, kicking and jumping and flouncing —this was most capital fun, but it wan't quite equal to musquashing. I had **a little** steel trap, and I used to go down at night to the bank of **a** brook that run into the pond, and set **the trap on** the bank just under water, and fasten it by a line **to** a stake or a tree, and put **a** bit of a parsnip on **a** stick and **place** it over the trap a little above the water, and then go home and sleep as well as I could for dreaming of musquashes, and as soon as it was cleverly light in the morning, go down to the pond and creep along where the trap was sot, with my heart in my mouth, wondering if it was sprung or **no,** and come along to the stake and see no trap, but the line drawn straight out into the water, then take hold of the line **and draw** up the trap, and see it rising up through the water fast hold of a great, plump musquash, as dead as a drowned **rat,** and full of fur as a beaver; this was fun alive; it made me feel as nicely as though I was hauling up a bucket of dollars. The summer I was fourteen years old I catched enough to buy me a fur hat and a pair of shoes, and a new jacket and trousers; and enough to buy me a pretty good new suit of clothes almost every summer after that till I was twenty.

We used to have a school in Downingville about three months in the Winter season and two months in the Summer, and I went to the Winter school three Winters, from the time I was twelve till I was fifteen. And I was called about the best scholar of my age that there was in school. But to be impartial, I must confess the praise didn't always belong to me, for I used sometimes to work headwork a little in order to get the name of being a smart scholar. One instance of it was in reading. I got along in reading so well, that the master said I read better than some of the boys that were considerable older than I, and that had been to school a dozen Winters. But the way I managed it was this. There was cousin Obediah was the best reader there was in school, and as clever a boy as one in a thousand, only his father hadn't got no orchard. So I used to carry a great apple to school in my pocket every day and give to him to get him to set behind me when I was reading, where he could peak into my book, and when I come to a hard word, have him whisper it to me, and then I read it out loud. Well, one day I was reading along so, pretty glib, and at last I come to a pesky great long crooked word, that I couldn't make head nor tail to it. So I waited for Obediah. But it proved to be a match for Obediah. He peaked, and squinted, and choked, and I was catching my breath and waiting for him to speak; and at last he found he could do nothing with it, and says he "skip it." The moment I heard the sound I bawled out, *skip it.* "What's that?" said the master, looking at me as queer as though he had catched a weazel asleep. I stopt and looked at the word again, and poked my tongue out, and waited for Obediah. Well, Obediah give me a hunch, and whispered again, "skip it." Then I bawled out again, *skip it*. At that the master and about one-half the scholars yaw-hawed right out. I couldn't stand that; and I dropt the book and streaked it out of school, and pulled foot for home as fast as I could go, and I never showed my head in school again from that day to this. But for all that, I made out to pick up a pretty good education. I got so I could read and spell like a fox, and could cypher as far as the rule of three. And when I got to be about twenty years old, I was strongly talked of one Winter for schoolmaster. But as a good many of the same boys and gals would go to me, that were in the school when I read "skip **it**," I didn't dare to venture it for fear there would be a sort of a snickering among 'em whenever **any of** them come to a hard word.

So I jogged along with father on the farm. But let me be doing what I would, whether it was hoeing potatoes, or pitching hay, or making stone wall, or junking and piling logs, I never could feel exactly easy. Something seemed to keep ringing in my ears all the time, and saying I was made to do something in the world besides this. And an old woman that come along and told fortunes, when she come to tell mine said that wherever I should go and whatever I should undertake to do, I should always get to the top of the ladder. Well, this made me keep a thinking so much the harder, and wondering what I should be in the world, and although I used to stick to my work as steady as any of the boys, yet I used to feel as uneasy as a fish out of water. But what made me think most about it was father. He always used to stand to it I was smarter than common boys, and used to tell mother she might depend upon it, if I lived and nothing didn't happen to me, I should some day or other raise the name of the Downings higher than it ever had been yet.

At last father dreampt a dream, that put the cap-stone upon the whole of it. He dreampt that I was out in the field hoeing potatoes, and he stood leaning over his staff, as he very often used to do, looking at me. By and by he said I stopped

MY FATHER'S DREAM.

hoeing, and stood up and leaned my chin on my hoe-handle, and seemed to look up toward the sky; and he said I looked as calm as the moon in a clear Summer night. Presently my hat began to rise up gradually and dropped off on the ground, but I stood still. Then he said the top of my head began to open, and a curious green plant began to sprout up out of it. And it grew up about two feet, and sent out ever so many young branches with broad green leaves, and then the little buds began to open and roll out great clusters of the most beautiful bright flowers, one **above another,** that ever he see **in all his life. He watched** 'em till they **all** got blowed out into a great **round** bunch, as big as a bushel basket, and then he waked **up, and** he **felt** so he got right out of bed and walked the floor till morning. And when we all got up he sot down and told the dream over to me and mother. Mother sot **with her** pocket-handkerchief wiping the tears out of her eyes **all** the time he was telling **of** it; and **I** felt as though my blood was running cold all over me. But from that time I always felt sure the time would come when Downingville wouldn't be big enough to hold me, and that I should do something **or** other in the world that would be worth telling of; but what it would be I couldn't think.

Well, I kept jogging along on the farm **after** the same old sort, year after year, so long, and there didn't nothing happen **to** me, that **sometimes** I almost begun to give it up, and think, sure enough, it was all nothing but a dream. Still I kept having spells **that** I felt terribly uneasy, and was tempted forty times to pack up and go and seek my fortune. I might **tell** a good deal more about **my** life, and my uncles **and aunts** and cousins, and the rest of the neighbors, but I begin to feel a most **tired of writing my** life, and I believe I shall have to **serve it** pretty much as I planted my watermillion seeds ; and that was this : When I was about six or seven years old our folks give me a pint of watermillion seeds and told me to go out into the field and plant **'em for** myself, **and** I might have all I could raise. So off I goes, tickled enough. And I went to work and punched little holes down in the ground and put in one seed to time along in a row, three or four inches apart, **till** I got about half the seeds planted. It was rather a warm afternoon, and I began to feel a little tired, so I took and dug a hole and poured the rest of the seeds all in together, and covered 'em up, and went into the house. **Well, mother** asked me if I planted **my seeds.** " Yes, **mam," says** I. "What, all of 'em ?" says she. "**Yes, mam," says** I. "But you've been very **spry,"** says she, "how did you get them done so **quick ?"** " O," says I, " easy enough ; I planted 'em in a *hill and a row.*" And when they begun to come up they found 'em in **a hill and a row,** sure enough. So I believe I shall have to pour the rest of my life into a hill and let **it** go.

To come, then, right to the pint—I don't mean the pint of watermillion seeds, but the pint **in my** life which seemed to be the turning pint. In the Fall of **the** year 1829, I took it into **my** head I'd go to Portland. So **one** day I up and told father, and says I, "I'm going to Portland, whether or no, and I'll see what this world's made of yet." Father stared a little at first, **and** said he was afraid I should get lost ; but when he see I was bent upon it he give it up, and he **stepped** to his **chist and opened the till, and took out a dollar and** give it to me, and says he, "Jack, this is **all I can do** for you ; but go, and lead an honest life, and I believe I shall hear good of you yet." He turned and walked across the room, but I could see the tears start into his eyes, and mother sot down and had a hearty crying spell. This made me feel rather bad for a minute or two, and I almost had a mind to give it up; and then again father's dream came into my mind, and I mustered up courage and declared I'd go. So I tackled up the old horse, and packed in a load of ax-handles and a few notions, and mother fried me some doughnuts and put 'em into a box along with some cheese and sassages, and ropped me up another shirt, for I told her I didn't know how long I should be gone; and after I got all rigged out I went round and bid all the neighbors good bye, and jumped in and drove off for Portland.

ON THE ROAD TO PORTLAND.

I hadn't been in Portland long before I happened to blunder into the Legislater; and I believe that was the beginning of my good luck. I see such queer kinds of carrying on there that I couldn't help setting down and writing to cousin Ephraim to tell uncle Joshua about it; because he always wanted to know everything that's going on in **Politics**. So I went to the editor of the Portland Courier and asked him if he would send it. So I let him have it, and fact, he went right to work and printed it in the Courier as large as life. He said he wouldn't let anybody else see it but cousin Ephraim; but somehow or other it leaked out, and was **all over the** Legislater the next morning, and everybody was inquiring for Mr. Downing. Well, this kind of got me right into public life at once; and I've been in **public life** ever since, and have been writing letters and rising up along gradually, one step after another, till I've got up along side of the President, and am talked of now pretty strong for President myself, **and have been nominated** in a good many of the first papers **of** the country.

My public life will be found in my letters, one after another, jest as they come, from the time I first sent that letter in the Portland Courier to cousin Ephraim till this time.

MAJOR JACK DOWNING.

Portland, Me., 1834.

POSTSCRIPT TO MY LIFE.

It will be seen by the date above that I wrote this little history of my life twenty odd years ago. It was the time the Boston folks published a little vollum of my first Letters, and the Life was writ to head the vollum with. But I've seen a great deal more of the world since then, and have writ a great many more Letters, and seen a great deal more of the workings of American Politicians. And they'll all have to come into my Thirty Years' View. But there'll be a kind of gap near the close of Gineral Jackson's time, and for awhile after, because a lot of my letters, written at that time, was lost in a fire some years afterward, and I don't suppose I can now find the papers they was published in. But I will bridge over the gap as well as I can, and there'll be a pretty long road to travel both sides of it. And this reminds me how strange the parallel runs between me and Colonel Benton; for he lost a lot of *his* letters and speeches and dockyments by fire, and had a good deal of a hard job to go over the ground again in getting up his work. But I and Colonel Benton are hard to beat. We generally go ahead, let what will stand in the way.

MAJOR JACK DOWNING.

New-York, 1858.

MY LETTERS AND OTHER DOCKYMENTS.

LETTER I.*

PORTLAND, Monday, Jan. 18, 1830.

To Cousin Ephraim Downing, up in Downingville:

DEAR COUSIN EPHRAIM :—I now take my pen in hand to let you know that I am well, hoping these few lines will find you enjoying the same blessing. When I come down to Portland I didn't think o' staying more than three or four days, if I could sell my load of ax handles, and mother's cheese, and cousin Nabby's bundle of footings; but when I got here I found Uncle Nat was gone a freighting down to Quoddy, and aunt Sally said as how I shouldn't stir a step home till he come back agin, which won't be this month. So here I am, loitering about this great town, as lazy as an ox. Ax handles don't fetch nothing; I couldn't hardly give 'em away. Tell Cousin Nabby I sold her footings for nine-pence a pair, and took it all in cotton cloth. Mother's cheese come to seven-and-sixpence; I get her half a pound of shushon,

---

* EDITORIAL NOTE.—The political struggle in the Legislature of Maine in the winter of 1830 will long be remembered. The preceding electioneering campaign had been carried on with a bitterness and personality unprecedented in the State, and so nearly were the parties divided, that before the meeting of the Legislature to count the votes for Governor, both sides confidently claimed the victory. Hence the members came together with feelings highly excited, prepared to dispute every inch of ground, and ready to take fire at the first spark which collision might produce. A fierce war commenced

and two ounces of snuff, and the rest in sugar. When Uncle Nat comes home I shall put my ax handles aboard of him, and let him take 'em to Boston next time he goes; I saw a feller tother day, that told me they'd fetch a good price there. I've been here now a whole fortnight, and if I could tell ye one half I've seen, I **guess you'd** stare worse than if you'd seen a catamount. I've been to meeting, **and to** the museum, and to both Legislaters, the one **they call the House, and** the one they call the Sinnet. I spose **Uncle** Joshua is in a great hurry to hear something about these Legislaters; for you know he's always reading newspapers, and talking politics, when he can get anybody to talk with him. I've seen him when he had five tons of hay in the field well made, and a heavy shower coming up, stand two hours disputing with Squire W. about Adams and Jackson—one calling Adams a tory and a fed, and the other saying Jackson was a murderer and a fool; so they kept it up, till the rain began to pour down, and about spoilt all his hay.

Uncle Joshua may set his heart at rest about the bushel of corn that he bet 'long with the postmaster, that Mr. Ruggles would be Speaker of that Legislater they call the House; for he's lost it, slick as a whistle. As I hadn't much to do, **I've**

---

at the first moment of the meeting, and continued for about six weeks without intermission, before they succeeded in organizing the government. It was during this state of things that **Mr.** Downing fortunately happened to drop into the Legislature. In explanation of the first letter, it may be remarked, that as soon as **the** Representatives **had** assembled, Albert Smith. Esq.. of Nobleborough, the then Marshal of Maine, called them to order, and nominated Mr. White, of Monmouth, Chairman, who was declared elected without ceremony, and took the chair. After he had occupied it two days Mr. Goodenow was elected Speaker.

been there every day since they've been a setting. A Mr. White, of Monmouth, was the Speaker the first two days ; and I can't see why they didn't keep him in all the time ; for he seemed to be a very clever, good-natured sort of man, and he had such a smooth, pleasant way with him, that I couldn't help feeling sorry when they turned him out and put in another. But some said he wasn't put in hardly fair ; and I don't know as he was, for the first day, when they were all coming in and crowding round, there was a large, fat man, with a round, full, jolly sort of a face, I suppose he was the captain, for he got up and commanded them to come to order, and then he told this Mr. White to whip into the chair quicker than you could say Jack Robinson. Some of 'em scolded about it, and I heard some, in a little room they called the lobby, say 'twas a mean trick ; but I couldn't see why, for I thought Mr. White made a capital Speaker, and when *our* company turns out, the cap'n always has a right to do as he's a mind to.

They kept disputing most all the time the first two days about a poor Mr. Roberts, from Waterborough. Some said he shouldn't have a seat because he adjourned the town meeting and wasn't fairly elected. Others said it was no such thing, and that he was elected as fairly as any of 'em. And Mr. Roberts himself said he was, and said he could bring men that would swear to it, and good men too. But, notwithstanding all this, when they came to vote, they got three or four majority that he should'nt have a seat. And I thought it a needless piece of cruelty, for they wan't crowded, and there was a number of seats empty. But they would have it so, and the poor man had to go and stand up in the lobby.

Then they disputed awhile about a Mr. Fowler's having a

seat. Some said he shouldn't have a seat, because when he was elected some of his votes were given for his father. But they were more kind to him than they were to Mr Roberts, for they voted that he *should* have a seat; and I suppose it was because they thought he had a lawful right to inherit whatever was his father's. They all declared **there was no party politics about it,** and I don't think there **was**; for I noticed that all who voted that Mr. Roberts *should* have a **seat,** voted that Mr. Fowler should **not;** and all who voted that **Mr.** Roberts should *not* have a seat, voted that Mr. Fowler *should.* So, as they all voted *both* ways, they must have been consciencious, and I don't see how there could be any party about it.

It's a pity they couldn't be allowed to have two Speakers, for they seemed to be very anxious to choose Mr. Ruggles **and** Mr. Goodenow. They two had every vote except one, **and if they had had** *that*, I believe they would both have been **chosen**; as it was, **however, they** both came within **a** humbird's eye of it. **Whether it was Mr** Ruggles voted for Mr. Goodenow, or Mr. Goodenow **for Mr.** Ruggles, I can't exactly tell; but I rather guess it was Mr. Ruggles voted for Mr. Goodenow, for he appeared to **be** very glad to see Mr. Goodenow in the chair, and shook hands with him as good-natured as could be. I would have given half my load of **ax** handles, if they could both have been elected and set up there together, they would have been so happy. But as they can't have but one Speaker at a time, and as Mr. Goodenow appears to understand the business very well, it is not likely Mr. Ruggles will be Speaker any this winter. So Uncle Joshua will have to shell out his bushel of corn, and I hope it will learn him better than to bet about politics again. Before

I came from home, some of the papers said how there was a majority of ten or fifteen *National Republicans* in the Legislater, and the other party said there was a pretty clever little majority of *Democratic Republicans*. Well, now everybody says it has turned out jest as that queer little paper, called the Daily Courier, said 'twould. That paper said it was such a close rub it couldn't hardly tell which side would beat. And it's jest so, for they've been here now most a fortnight acting jest like two boys playin see-saw on a rail. First one goes up, and then 'tother; but I reckon one of the boys is rather heaviest, for once in a while he comes down chuck, and throws the other up into the air as though he would pitch him head over heels. Your loving cousin till death.

JACK DOWNING.

OUT OF THE SENATE 41

DOWNINGVILLE TAVERN.

LETTER II.*

ABOUT POOR MR. ROBERTS HAVING TO STAND UP.

PORTLAND, Jan. 22, 1830.

To Uncle Joshua Downing, up in Downingville:

DEAR UNCLE JOSHUA :—I spose you learnt by my letter t'other day to cousin Ephraim, that you had lost the bushel

---

* EDITORIAL NOTE.—It was the rule at the meeting of the Legislature to admit all to a seat who could produce a certificate of their election, which cer-

2*

of corn you bet about the Speaker in the Legislater—I mean that Legislater they call the House—for Mr. White got it first, and then Mr. Goodenow got it, and he's kept it ever since. And they say he'll be Speaker all winter, although he don't *speak* near so much as some of the rest of 'em. There's lawyer Ruggles, of Thomaston, that used to be Speaker, and folks say he made a very smart one. And there's lawyer Boutelle, of Waterville, who's got eyes sharp enough to look through anybody, and who makes 'em all as still as mice when he speaks. And there's lawyer Smith, of Nobleborough; he looks very much like a man I saw in the museum, that they called Daniel Lambert, only he isn't quite so large. But my patience! he's a real peeler for speaking, and sometimes he pours out his voice so as to make me jump right up on my feet. If I was going to bet who would be Speaker next year, I should bet upon him before anybody else. And there's lawyer Bourne, of Kennebunk, and lawyer Kent, of Bangor, and lawyer Norton, of Milburn, and Dr. Burnham, of Orland, and Dr. Shaw, of Wiscasset, and Dr. Wells, of Freeport, and Parson Knowlton, of Montville, and Parson Swett, of Prospect, and some others, if I could only think of 'em. Now, most any of these speak more than Mr. Goodenow does;

---

tificate was considered *prima fccia* evidence that they were duly returned as members. The Portland Argus and Advertiser, were the leading papers of the two parties; and as matters began to grow worse and worse in the Legislature, the Argus constantly affirmed that the Democratic Republicans used every endeavor in their power to organize the government and proceed in the public business, but that the Huntonites would not let them. And the Advertiser as constantly affirmed that the National Republicans used their utmost endeavors to proceed in the public business, but the Jacksonites would not let them.

and still Mr. Goodenow **is called** the Speaker, **because they** voted that he should be.

They've disputed two days more **about that poor Mr. Roberts** having a seat. I can't see why **they need to make such a fuss about it.** As they've got **seats enough, why don't they** let him have **one, and not keep him standing up for three** weeks in the lobby and round the fire. It's a plaguey sight worse than being **on a standing committee, for they say the** standing committees **have a chance to set** most every day. But in the dispute about **Mr. Roberts last** Wednesday and Thursday, the difficulty seemed **to be** something or other about a *primy facy* case. I don't **know** what **sort of a** case 'twas, **but** that's what they called it. Some said he **hadn't got** any *primy facy* case, and he mustn't have a seat till he had one. The others stood to it that he *had* got one, and a very good one. Mr. **Ruggles said it was full as** good a one as the gentleman from Portland had. **And they read about twenty** papers that they called depositions, about **the town-meeting** of Waterborough ; but they didn't seem **to say anything** about the *primy facy* case. About one-half **of 'em said the** town-meeting was adjourned, and t'other half said 'twasn't. **And one** of the depositions said there **was** some of 'em at **the** meeting agreed **that** Mr. **Roberts** shouldn't be elected **at any rate ; and** if they **couldn't** prevent it any other way they agreed **to** keep up **a row till midnight. And when** they brought in candles in the **evening** they knocked 'em **all over** and put 'em out. So they all **had** to clear out ; and **some said** there was a vote to adjourn the meeting, and some said Mr. Roberts adjourned it alone, and some said 'twasn't adjourned at all. And one of the depositioners said Mr. Roberts offered to give him as much rum as he would drink if he would only say the meeting was fairly adjourned. But all the depositions didn't convince but sixty-nine members of the House that Mr. Roberts had a *primy facy* case, and there were seventy-five convinced t'other way. So, after they had disputed two days, they voted again that Mr. Roberts shouldn't have a seat yet.

Oh dear, Uncle Joshua, these Legislaters have got the State into a dreadful pickle. I've been reading the Portland Argus and the Portland Advertiser, and it's enough to scare a Bunker Hill soger out of his seven senses to see what we are all coming to. According to these papers there are two very clever parties in the State that are trying with all their might to save us from ruin. They are called *Democratic Republikins* and *National Republikins*—and you'd be perfectly astonished to see how hard they've worked, as these papers say, in both Legislaters, to set things right, and get business a-going on well, so that we can have a Governor, and live in peace and harmony, and not break out into civil war, and all be ruined in a bunch. But it's doubtful if they'll make out to save us after all ; for there is such a set of Jacksonites and Huntonites, that are all the time a-plotting to bring us to destruction, that I tell you what 'tis, if something isn't done pretty soon, it'll be gone goose with us.

These Jacksonites and Huntonites seem to have a majority in the Legislaters ; and they've been making a proper bother for a'most three weeks, so that the Democratic Republikins and the National Republikins couldn't do nothing at all. And sometimes I'm really afraid they'll have to break up and go home without doing anything ; and if they do, they say we shall all be afloat, and there's no knowing where we shall land. Tne Republikins appointed a committee to count the votes for Governor, and the committee told 'em t'other day there was thirty-nine majority for Mr. Hunton, and he was elected. But then these Jacksonites and Huntonites went to disputing about the matter, and some say they will dispute it this fortnight yet. What a blessing it would be if the Legislaters were all Democratic and National Republikins. The people are growing pretty mad at all this botheration, and I can't tell what'll be the end on't. But I shall write again to you or Cousin Ephraim pretty soon. So I remain your loving neffu till death.

JACK DOWNING.

LETTER III.

UNCLE JOSHUA TELLS HOW HE WENT TO BOSTON AND TOOK DINNER WITH THE GINERAL COURT.

BOSTON, January 25, 1830.

DEAR NEPHEW :—I left home just after your letter to your cousin Ephraim got there, and I didn't get a sight of your letter to me that you put into the Courier at Portland until I saw it in the Daily Advertiser in Boston, and I guess Mr Hale is the only person in Boston who takes that are little Courier, so you was pretty safe about the letter not being seen, as the printer promised you. How I happened to see it here you will find out before I have got through with this letter. I guess you won't be a little struck up when you find out that I'm in Boston. But I had best begin at the beginning, and then I shall get through quicker.

After seeing your letter to Ephraim, as I said before, I concluded it wouldn't be a bad scheme to tackle up and take a load of turkeys, some apple-sass, and other notions that the neighbors wanted to get to market, and as your Uncle Nat would be in Boston with the ax-handles, we all thought best to try our luck there. Nothing happened worth mentioning on the road, nor till next morning after I got here and put up in Elm street. I then got off my watch pretty curiously, as you shall be informed. I was down in the bar-room, and thought it well enough to look pretty considerable smart, and

UNCLE JOSHUA AND THE FOURTH STALLER.

now and then compared my watch with the clock in the bar, and found it as near right as ever it was, when a feller stept up to me and ask'd how I'd trade? and says I, for what? and says he, for your watch, and says I, any way that will be a fair shake; upon that says he, I'll give you *my* watch and five dollars; says I, it's done! He gave me the five dollars, and I gave him my watch. Now, says I, give me *your* watch; and, says he, with a loud laugh, I han't got none, and that kind a turned the laugh on me. Thinks I, let them laugh that lose. Soon as the laugh was well over the feller thought he'd try the watch to his ear; why, says he, it don't go; no, says I, not without it's carried; then I began to laugh. He tried to open it and couldn't start it a hair, and broke his thumb nail into the bargain. Won't she open, says he? Not's I know on, says I, and then the laugh seemed to take another turn.

Don't you think I got off the old Brittania pretty well, considerin? And then I thought I'd go and see about my load of turkeys and other notions. I expected to have gone all over town to sell my load, but Mr. Doolittle told me if I'd go down to the new market I should find folks enough to buy all I had at once. So down I goes, and a likely kind of a feller, with an eye like a hawk and quick as a steel trap for a trade, (they called him a fourth staller,*) came up to the waggon, and before you could say Jack Robinson we struck a bargain for the whole cargo; and come to weigh and reckon up I found I should get as much as 10s. 6d. more than any of us calculated before I left home, and had the apple-sass left be

* Fore-staller.

sides. So I thought I'd jest see how this fourth staller worked his card to be able to give us so good a price for the turkeys, and **I went** inside the market house, and a grander sight I never expect to see! **But it was the third** staller, instead of the fourth, had my turkeys all sorted and **hung up,** and looking so much better that I hardly should known 'em. Pretty soon a **gentleman** asked the third staller what he asked for turkeys? Why, says he, if **you** want something better than you ever saw before, there's some 'twas killed last night purpose for you. You may take 'em at 9d., [12½ cents Massachusetts currency,] being **it's you.** I'll give you 12 cents, said the gentleman, as I've got some of the General Court to dine with me, **and must treat well.** I shan't stand for half a cent with **an** old customer, **says** he. And so they traded; and in about the space of half an hour or more all my turkeys went into baskets at that rate. The fourth staller gave me 6d. a pound, and I began to think I'd been a little too much in a hurry for trade—but's no use to cry for spilt milk. Then I went up to the State House to see what was going on there; but I thought I'd get off **my apple-sass on** my way—and seeing a sign of old clothes **bartered, I stepped** in and made a trade, and got a whole suit of superfine black broadcloth from top to toe **for a firkin** of apple-sass (which didn't cost much I guess, at home.)

Accordingly I rigged myself up in the new suit, and you'd hardly known me. I didn't like the set of the shoulders, they were so dreadful puckery; but the **man** said that was all right. I guess he'll find the apple-sass full as puckery when he get's down into it—but that's between ourselves. Well, when I got up to the State House I found them at work on the railroad, busy enough I can tell you; they got a part of it made already. I found most all the folks kept their hats on except the man who was talking out loud and the man he was talking to; all the rest seemed to be busy about their own consarns. As I did't see anybody to talk to, I kept my hat on and took a seat, and look'd round to see what was going on. I hadn't been setting long before I saw a slick-headed, sharp-eyed little man, who seemed to have the principal management of the folks, looking at me pretty sharp, as much as to **say, who are you?** but I said nothing and looked tother way. At last he touched **me on** the shoulder; I thought he was feeling of the puckers. Are you a member? says he; sartin, says I; how long have you taken your seat? says he; about ten minutes, says I; are you qualified? says he; I guess not, **says I.** And then he left me. I didn't know exactly what this old gentleman was after, but soon he returned and said it was proper for me to be qualified before I took a seat, and I must go before the Governor! By Jing! I never felt so be**fore** in all my born days. As good luck would have it he was beckoned to come to a man at the desk, and as soon as his back was turned I give him the slip. Just as I was going off the gentleman who bought my turkeys of the fourth staller took hold of my arm, and I was afraid at first that he was **going to carry me** to the Governor; but he began to talk as sociable as if we had been old acquaintances. How long have you been in the house, Mr. Smith? says he. My name is Downing, said I. I beg your pardon, says he, I mean Downing. It's no offence, says I, I hav'nt been here long. Then, says he, in a very pleasant way, a few of your brother members are to take pot-lock with me to-day, and I should be happy to have you join them. What's pot-luck? said I. O, a family dinner, says he—no ceremony. I thought by this time I was well qualified for that without going to the Governor. So says I, yes, and thank ye too. How long before you'll want me, says I. At 3 o'clock, says he, and gave me a piece of pasteboard with his name on it, and the name of the street and the number of his house, and said that would show the way. Well, says I, I don't know of nothing that will keep me away. And then we parted. I took considerable liking to him.

After strolling round and seeing a great many things about the State House, and the marble image of Gineral Washington, standing on a stump in the porch, I went out into the street they call Bacon street, and my stars! what swarms of women folks I saw, all drest up as if they were going to meeting. You can tell cousin Polly Sandburn, who you know is no slimster, that she needn't take on so about being genteel in her shapes, for the genteelest ladies here beat her as to size all hollow. I don't believe one of 'em could get into our fore dore, and as for their arms, I shouldn't want better measure for a bushel of meal than one of their sleeves could hold. I shan't shell out the bushel of corn you say I've lost on Speaker Ruggles at that rate. But this puts me in mind of the dinner which Mr. ——— wanted I should help the Gineral Court eat. So I took out the piece of pasteboard and began to inquire my way and got along completely, and found the number the first time; but the door was locked, and there was no knocker, and I thumpt with my whip handle but nobody come. And says I to a man going by, don't nobody live here? and says he, yes. Well, how do you get in? Why, says he, ring; and says I, ring what? And says he, the bell. And says I, where's the rope? And says he, pull that little brass nub; and so I gave it a twitch, and I'm sure a bell did ring; and who do you think opened the door with a white apron afore him? You couldn't guess for a week a Sundays, so I'll tell you. It was Stephen Furlong,

UNCLE JOSHUA AND STEPHEN FURLONG.

who kept our district school last Winter, for five dollars a month, and kept bachelor's hall, and helped tend for Gineral Coombs a training days, and make out muster rolls. We was considerably struck up at first, both of us; and when he found I was going to eat dinner with Mr ——— and Gineral

Court, he thought it queer kind of doings; but says he, I guess it will be as well for both of us not to know each other a bit more than we can help. And says I, with a wink, you're half right, and in I went. There was nobody in the room but Mr. ——— and his wife, and not a **sign of** any dinner to be seen anywhere, though **I thought now and then** when a side door **opened I could smell cupboard, as they say.**

I thought I should be puzzled enough to know what to say, but I hadn't my thoughts **long to myself.** Mr. ——— has about **as nimble a** tongue as **you** ever heard, and **could say ten** words to my one, and I had nothing **to do in the way of** making talk. Just then I heard a ringing, **and Stephen was** busy opening the door and letting in the Gineral Court, who had all their hats off, **and looking** pretty scrumptious, you may depend. I didn't see but I could stand along side of 'em without disparagement, except to my boots, which had just got a lick of beeswax and tallow. Not a mite of dinner yet, and I began to feel as if 'twas nearer supper-time than dinner-time, when all at once two doors flew away from each other right into the wall, and what did I see but one of the grandest thanksgiving dinners you ever laid your eyes on, and lights on the table, and silver candlesticks and gold lamps **over** head—the window shutters closed. I guess more than one of **us** stared at first, but we soon found the way to our mouths. I made Stephen tend out for me pretty sharp, and he got **my** plate filled three or four times with soup, which beat all I ever tasted. I shan't go through the whole dinner again to you; but I am mistaken if it cost me much for victuals this week, if I pay by the meal at Mr. Doolittle's, who comes pretty near up to a thanksgiving every day. There was considerable **talk** about stock and manufactories, and lier bilities, and rimidies, and a great loss on stock. I thought this a good chance for me to put in a word, for I calculated I knew as much about raising stock and keeping over as any of 'em. Says I to Mr. ———, there's one thing I've always obsarved in **my** experience in stock—jest as sure as you try to keep over more stock than you have fodder to carry them well into Aperil, one half will die on your hands to a sartainty, **and there's no rimidy for it**; **I've** tried it out and **out**, and there's no law that can make a tun of hay keep over ten cows, unless you have more carrots and potatoes than you can throw **a stick at**. This made some of the folks stare who didn't know much about stock, and Steeve give me a jog, as much as to **say, keep** quiet. He thought I was getting into a quagmire, **and soon** after, giving me a wink, opened the door, and got me out of the room into the entry.

After **we** had got out of hearing, says I to Steve, how are you getting on in the world?—should you like to come back to keep our **school if I could** get a vote for you? Not by two chalks, **says Steve**, I know which side my bread is buttered better than that; I get twelve dollars a month and **found, and** now and then some old clothes, which is better than keeping school at five dollars and find myself, and work **out my highway tax** besides; then **turning** up the cape of **my** *new coat*, **says he, I guess I've** dusted that before now. Most likely, says I, but not in our district school. And this brings to mind to tell you **how** I got sight of your letter. They tell me here that everybody reads the Boston Daily Advertiser, because there is no knowing but what they may find out something to their advantage, so I thought I would be as wise as the rest of them, and before I got half way through, with it, what should I find mixed up with the news but your letter, that you put into that little paper down in Portland, **and I knew it was** your writing before I had read ten lines of it.

I hope I've answered it to your satisfaction.

Your respectful uncle,
JOSHUA DOWNING.

P. S.—Mr. Topliff says your **Uncle Nat is** telegraphed, but I'm afraid **the** ax handles won't **come to** much. I find the Boston **folks** make **of most anything** they can lay hold of, and jest as like as **not they'll make a handle of** our private letters **if they should see** them.

N. B.—You spell dreadful **bad,** according to my notion; and this proves what **I** always said, that our district has been going down hill **ever** since Stephen Furlong left it.

DOCKYMENTS.*

Extract from the Portland Courier, **January, 1830.**

Saturday forenoon, the house having adjourned at an early hour, we repaired to the Senate Chamber with a view of

---

* EDITORIAL NOTE.—In order that the reader may understand the progress of the war in the Maine Legislature, it should be remarked that the parties in the Senate were equally divided. There were eight Huntonites, or National Republicans, and eight Smithites or Democratic Republicans, and four vacancies. The battles, therefore, in the Senate, were more serious, obstinate and protracted than they were in the House. They balloted regularly for President every day for about a fortnight. To illustaate the state of affairs at that time, a couple of extracts from the Portland Courier in relation to the balloting in the Senate are subjoined.

standing watch awhile. We arrived just in the height of a spirited skirmish, or what might almost be called a battle; but the room was crowded and the doorway so impenetrably thronged that we could gain no entrance. There was scarcely room for a man to wedge his nose in, unless it were a remarkably thin and sharp one. From the subdued and regular hum within there was evidently a debate going on, but we being somewhat low in stature, and a solid **phalanx of** six-footers standing before us, we were left in the unpleasant predicament of stretching **up** on tip-toe without **catching a** single glimpse of the scene, **and** holding our hands behind our ears without distinguishing a syllable that was uttered.

The debate, however, soon subsided. We learned afterward, from inquiry, that it related to the subject of forming a convention with the House for the purpose of filling vacancies, before the Senate was organized; the eight Huntonites voting in favor of the proposition, and eight Smithites against it. A **vote** was then **passed to proceed to** ballot for President again, **and** luckily for us, **the** ballot-boxes were out in the lobby, **and** out came the messenger, cutting his way like a hero, (we like to have said hero of New Orleans, but happened to think some would say we were taking *sides*.) We simply say, then, he cut his way through the dense rank of **spectators like a** hero, and we crept in through the breach he **had** made. The committee collected the votes for President and retired. **In about** ten minutes they returned, and declared **the result—seven for** Mr. Dunlap, seven for Mr. Kingsbury, and two scattering.

They collected the votes again, and retired as before, and returned as before, and declared the same result. Again they proceeded in the same round, and came in the third time, and stood ready to declare. The spectators had become so accustomed to the report—for they had been listening to the same tune nearly three weeks—that they were whispering it off in advance of the committee, like a mischievous and sinful boy running ahead of some good old country Deacon, who always uses the same words in prayer. Judge then, ye readers of the Courier, what unspeakable astonishment prevailed, when from the lips of the chairman fell the startling words, eight for Sanford Kingsbury, six for Robert P. Dunlap, and two scattering.

The effect was like that of a clap of thunder in the dead of winter; some faces grew longer, and some grew shorter; in some eyes there was a look of **wildness**; in others a leering complacency, that seemed to say, " you're dished at last ;" while some confounded knowing glances from other quarters visibly replied, " not as you know on." And to be sure these last were in the right; for round they went the fourth time, collected the ballots, counted them, and came in again. Expectation was on tiptoe, and speculation was **very** busy. Some thought this ballot would settle the question, but others doubted. The committee declared, and the same old tune greeted the ears of the audience—seven for Mr. Dunlap, seven for Mr. Kingsbury, and two scattering.

Another extract from the same.

A NEW TUNE.—We have to pitch our pipe to a new tune this morning. The second great battle of the session was fought, or rather terminated yesterday afternoon. After a regular engagement for eight **days** in succession, during which time the regular armies of Huntonites and Smithites in the Senate were drawn up face to face, forenoon and afternoon, exchanging some half a dozen shots every day, and then retiring by mutual consent, and sleeping upon their arms, the conflict was ended yesterday afternoon by a *ruse de guerre* on the part of the Huntonites, which led them to victory without bloodshed. The Senate met in the afternoon at three o'clock, and proceeded to their usual round of duties. The committee received the votes for President, and retired, and came in again, and declared in the strains of the old tune, seven for Mr. Dunlap, seven for Mr. Kingsbury, and two scattering. They proceeded again, and came in as before. It was the *fiftieth* ballot since the commencement of the session ; and had a *fifty pounder* been unexpectedly discharged in the room, it would hardly have produced a stronger sensation, than the declaration of the committee, when they piped away in the following new tune : whole number of votes, 15 ; necessary to a choice, 8 ; Joshua Hall has 8, Robert Dunlap, 6 ; James Steele, 1 ; blank, 1. We shall not attempt to describe the coloring of faces, the wildness of eyes, or the biting of lips that ensued ; for, not arriving in season we did not see them. But we have no doubt, from the remarks of those who were present, that the occasion would have furnished a scene for painting, fully equal, if not surpassing that in the House on the choice of Speaker. After the first consternation had subsided, Mr. Hall was declared duly elected President of the Senate. Whereupon he rose in his place, and thanked the gentlemen of the Board for the confidence they had placed in him. He doubted his abilities to discharge properly the duties assigned him ; but under present circumstances he would accept the trust. He accordingly took the chair.*

---

* EDITORIAL NOTE.—Mr. Hall, or Elder Hall, as he was usually called, was a Democratic Republican, but chosen President exclusively by the National Republican votes, he throwing a blank vote himself. He was a short, fleshy, good-hearted old gentleman, a minister of the Methodist denomination, and knew much more about preaching than he did about politics. The Democratic Republicans after their first consternation at his election had subsided, fearing that he had actually gone over to the enemy, took measures to have a private consultation with him immediately after adjournment. This interview resulted in nailing the old gentleman to his former political faith, and he stuck to the party like wax during the remainder of the session. So the Senate was still divided, eight to eight, except when the four new Senators, elected by the National Republicans to fill the vacancies, attempted to act.

LETTER IV.

COUSIN NABBY ADVISES MR. DOWNING TO COME HOME.

Downingville, January 30, 1830.

Dear Cousin : If you were only here I would break the handle of our old birch broom over your back for serving me such a caper. Here I have been waiting three weeks for that cotton cloth you got for the footings ; and you know the meeting-house windows were to have been broke* a fortnight ago, if I had got it. And then I had to tell Sam I was waiting for some cotton cloth. He tried to keep in with all his might, but he burst out a laughing so, I'm a good mind to turn him off. But if I do, *you and he will be both in the same*

---

* Editorial Note.—The law " Down East" required that the intentions of marriage between a couple should be posted up at the meeting-house by the Town Clerk two or three weeks before the marriage ; and this was called breaking the meeting-house windows.

pickle. You had better let them *legislaters* alone ; and if you can't sell your ax-handles, take 'em and come home and mind your business. There is Jemime Parsons romping about with the school-master, fair weather and foul. Last Wednesday she went a sleigh-riding with him, and to-night she's going to the singing-school, and he is going to carry her. Last night she came over to our house, and wanted me to go to Uncle Zeke's to borrow their swifts, she said, when she knew we had some, and had borried them a dozen times. I said nothing, but went with her. When we got there who should we find but the school-master. I know Jemime knew it, and went there purpose to have him go home with her. She never askt for the swifts. Coming home the master askt her if she had seen your last letter. She said yes, and began to laugh and talk about you, just as though I was no relation. She said she guessed them legislaters would try to make a Governor out of *you* next, if you staid there much longer. One of them steers you sold to Jacob Small that week you went to Portland died t'other day ; and he says if we've no Governor this year he won't pay you a cent for 'em. So you have lost your steers and Jemime Parsons, jest by your dallying about there among them legislaters. I say you had better come home and see to your own business. I s'pose father and brother Ephraim would like to have you stay there all inter and tell 'em about the Governors and legislaters, but aunt wants her tea, and I want my cotton cloth, so I wish you'd make haste home and bring 'em.

     Your loving cousin,   NABBY

To Mr. JACK DOWNING.

LETTER V.

MR. DOWNING TELLS WHAT A HOBBLE THE LEGISLATURE GOT INTO IN TRYING TO MAKE SO MANY GOVERNORS.

PORTLAND, Feb. 1, 1830.

To Cousin Ephraim Downing, up in Downingville:

DEAR COUSIN EPHRAIM:—I spose you expected me to write to you agin long afore now and tell you something more about these Legislaters, and I meant to, but I couldn't very well; for I'll tell you jest how 'twas. Some days, when the Legislater would get into a plaguey hobble, I would think to myself, well, soon as they get out of this snarl, I'll write to cousin Ephraim and tell him all about it; but before they got fairly out of that, they'd be right into another; and if I waited till next day to see how that ended, my keesers! before night they'd all be higgledy piggle, in a worse hobble than they'd ever been in afore. So if I wait to tell you how it comes out, I believe I shall have to wait till haying time. Another thing I've been waiting for, was to tell you who was Governor. But, O dear, I can't find out half so much about it now, here in this great city of Portland, where all the Governors live, as I could six months ago among the bear-traps and log houses in our town, way back in the woods. Last August, you know, according to the papers, we were going to have two Governors right off, sure as rates—Mr. Hunton and Mr. Smith. Well, now it's got to be the first of February, and we haven't got *one* yet. And, although the Governor-makers have had four or five under way for a month past, some think it very doubtful whether they will get one done so as to be fit to use this year. There's Mr. Hunton, and Mr. Smith, and Mr. Cutler, and Mr. Goodenow, and Mr. Hall, have all been *partly* made into Governors ; but when in all creation any of 'em will be *finished*, I guess it would puzzle a Philadelphy lawyer to tell. I stated in my letter to Uncle Joshua, that there were two very clever parties in the Legislater, the Democratic Republikans and the National Republikans ; and they are so, and very industrious, and try to make things go on right ; and I really believe, if the confounded Jacksonites and Huntonites didn't bother 'em so, they'd make us a Governor as quick as I could make an ax handle. It is enough to do anybody's heart good to see how kind and obliging these Democratic Republikans and National Republikans are to each other, and how each party tries to help the other along ; and it's enough to make anybody's blood boil to see the Jacksonites and the Huntonites, jest like the dog in the manger, because they can't eat the hay themselves, snap at these two clever parties the moment either of 'em sets out to take a mouthful. I'll jest give you an instance of the kindness that these two clever parties show to each other. You know the Constitution says when we haven't any Governor the President of the Sinnet must be Governor, and when we haven't any President of the Sinnet, the Speaker of the House must be Governor. So when Governor Lincoln died Mr. Cutler was Governor for awhile, because he was last year President of the Sinnet. Mr. Goodenow is a National Republikan, and when he was elected Speaker of the House, the Democratic Republikans told him as there was no President of the Sinnet

elected yet, it belonged to him to be Governor, and tried as
hard as though he had belonged to their own party, to **encourage** him to go right into the Council Chamber and do the
Governor's business. But the National Republikans didn't
dare to let him go, for he **was** elected Speaker by only one
majority, and they said if he should leave the chair, it wouldn't
be five minutes before a Jacksonite would be whisked into it,
and then the two clever parties would all be up a tree. Well,
jest so 'twas in the Sinnet after Elder Hall was elected President, only the bread was buttered on t'other side. Elder Hall
is a Democratic Republikan, and there was a great deal
tougher scrabble to elect him than there was to choose the
Speaker of the House. But as soon as he was elected, the
National Republikans went to him very kindly, and said,
"Elder Hall, by the provisions of the Constitution you are
now fairly Governor of the State till another Governor is
qualified. Don't be bashful about it, but please to walk right
into the council chamber, and do the Governor's business."
But the Democratic Republikans said that would never do, for
if he should, the Sinnet Board would be capsized in an instant
and the Huntonites would rule the roast. So there was a pair
of Governors spoilt when they were more than half made,
jest by the mischief of the Jacksonites and Huntonites.
And the consequence is, that Mr. Cutler has to keep doing the
Governor's business yet, whether he wants to or not, and
whether it is right for him to or not. They say the poor man
is a good deal distressed about **it, and** has sent to the great
Judges of the Supreme Court **to know** whether it's right for
him to be Governor any longer or not. **If the Judges** should
say he mus'nt be Governor any longer, we shall be in a dread-

3*

ful pickle. Only think, no Governor, and no laws, but everybody do jest as they're a mind to. Well, if that should be the case, I know one thing, that is, Bill Johnson will get one good flogging for calling me a mean puppy and a coward last summer; I've longed to give it to him ever since; and if the Legislater don't make a Governor this winter, I shall come right home, and Bill must look out. What a pity 'tis they should waste so much time trying to make so many Governors; for, if they should make a dozen, we shouldn't want to use but one this year; and it is thought if they had all clapt to and worked upon one instead of working upon so many, they might have had him done more than three weeks ago.

Your lovin cousin,
JACK DOWNING.

LETTER VI.

MR. DOWNING DESCRIBES **A SAD MISHAP THAT** BEFELL THE HOUSE OF
REPRESENTATIVES *

PORTLAND, **Tuesday, Feb. 2, 1830.**

DEAR COUSIN EPHRAIM:—I have jest time to write you a short *postscript* to a letter that I shall send you in a day or two. We have had a dreadful time here to-day. You know the wheels of Government have been stopt here for three or four weeks, **and they** all clapt their shoulders under to-day and give 'em a lift; and they started so hard, **that as** true as you're alive *they split* **both** *Legislaters* **right** *in tu*. Some say they are split so bad they can't mend 'em again, but I hope they can though; I shall tell you all about how 'twas done, in a day or two. I've been expecting a letter from you, or some of the folks, sometime. Your hearty cousin,

JACK DOWNING.

---

* EDITORIAL NOTE.—After a stormy debate in the House in relation to forming a Convention of the two branches to fill **the** vacancies in the Senate, the National Republicans finally **carried the day;** whereupon the Democratic Republicans, **having remonstrated to the last, took their hats** and marched out of the House in a body, about sixty in number, headed by Mr. Smith, **of** Nobleborough. The **National Republicans** of the two branches, however, held the Convention, and filled **the vacancies in the Senate,** and the next day the Democratic Republicans returned to their seats.

LETTER VII.

AFFAIRS TAKE A MORE FAVORABLE TURN.

PORTLAND, Feb. 3, 1830.

COUSIN EPHRAIM:—I thought I would jest write you another little *postscript* to my letter that I was going to send you in a day or tu, and let you know that the Legislaters wan't split so bad as some folks tho't for. They've got 'em both mended agin, so that they set 'em agoing to-day afore noon. But in the afternoon, that Legislater they **call the Sinnet** got stuck, **and** in trying to **make it go, it rather** seemed to crack a little; so they stopt short **till to-morrow.** It's been jostled about so, and got so weak an' rickety, some are afraid it will give out yet, or *split in tu agin.*

JACK DOWNING.

LETTER VIII.

MRS. DOWNING URGES HER SON TO COME HOME.

DOWNINGVILLE, **Feb. 6, 1830.**

MY DEAR SON :—It's a good while since I writ a letter, and I almost forget how ; but you stay down there to Portland so long, I kind of want to say something to you. I have been churning this morning, and my hand shakes so I can't hardly hold my pen still. And then I am afraid the news I've got to tell will be such a blow to you, it makes me feel sort of narvous. Last Sunday the schoolmaster and Jemime Parsons had their names stuck up together in the meeting-house porch. Now I hope you won't take on, my dear Jack, for if I was you, I should be glad to get rid of her so. I guess she's rather *slack*, if the truth was known ; for I went in there one day, and she'd jest done washing the floor ; and I declare, it looked as gray as if she'd got the water out of a mud puddle. And then she went to making pies without washing her hands or shifting her apron. They made me stop to supper, but I never touched Jemime's pies. There's Dolly Spaulding, I'm sure she's likelier looking than Jemime Parsons, if 'twant for that habit she's got of looking two ways at once. If she's making a soup, one eye is *always* in the pot, if t'other *does* look up the chimney. She's as good a cook as ever was born, and neat as wax-work. Sally Kean was to our house spinning linen t'other day, because I burnt my hand so bad trying out lard I couldn't hold the thread, and she said Dolly had more sheets and pillow-cases than you could count for one while, and she is always making blankets and coverlids. She has sold footings enough to buy her half a dozen silver spoons and a case of knives. When I was young such a gal would had a husband long ago. The men didn't use to ask if a gal looked one way, or two ways with her eyes, but whether she was neat and smart; only if she had thin lips and peaked nose, they were sometimes a little shy of her.

O, Jack, I'm afraid these Legislaters will be the ruination of you! 'Twill make you jest like your Uncle Joshua. You know he had rather stand and dispute about politiks any time, than work on his farm, and talking will never build a stone wall or pay our taxes.

I don't care so much about the shushon as your poor cousin Nabby does about the cotton cloth. But your father has got the rumatiz dreadfully this winter; and it's rather hard for him to have to cut all the wood and make the fires this cold weather. I can't see what good 'twill do for you to stay in Portland any longer, and I think you had better come home and see a little to the work on the farm.

Your loving mother,
MARY DOWNING.

LETTER IX.

MR. DOWNING TELLS ABOUT TRIGGING THE WHEELS OF GOVERNMENT.

PORTLAND, Thursday, Feb. 11, 1830.

DEAR COUSIN EPHRAIM:—I've wrote you two *postscripts* since I wrote you a letter, and the reason is, these Legislaters have been carryin on so like all possest, and I've been in looking at 'em so much, I couldn't get time to write more than three lines at once, for fear I should be out of the way, and should miss seeing some of the fun But, thinkin you'd be tired of waiting, I tried to get the printer to send my letter yesterday; but he told me right up and down he couldn't. I told him he must, for I ought to sent before now. But he said he couldn't and wouldn't, and that was the upshot of the matter, for the paper was chock full, and more tu, of the Governor's message. Bless my stars, says I, and have we got a Governor done enough so he can speak a message? Yes, indeed we have, says **he,** *thanks be to the two great Republikin parties,* who have saved the State from the anarkee of the Jacksonites and Huntonites; the Governor is done, and is jest a going into the **Legislater, and if you'll** go right up there, you can see him. **So I pushed in among** the crowd, and I got a pretty good **squeezin tu ; but I** got a good place, for I could elbow it as **well as any on 'em.** And I hadn't been there five minutes, seemingly, before we had a Governor sure enough; and a good **stout,** genteel looking sort of **a man he was tu, as you** would see in a whole regiment, taking in captains and all. **Nobody** disputed that he was finished pretty workmanlike ; and he ought to be, for they'd been long enough about it. So they concluded to **swear him in, as they call it**, and he took a great oath to behave like a Governor a whole year. Some say the **wheels** of Government will go along smooth and easy now, as a wheelbarrow across a brick yard ; but some shake their heads, and say the wheels will be jolting over rocks and stumps all winter yet ; and I don't know but they will, for the Governor hadn't hardly turned his back upon 'em and gone out, before they went right to disputing agin as hard as ever. They took up that everlasting dispute about Mr. Roberts having a seat; for, if you'll believe **me**, they've kept that poor man standing there till this time.

I'll tell you how 'tis, Cousin Ephraim, we must contrive some way or other to keep these Jacksonites and Huntonites out of the Legislater another year, or we shall be ruin'd ; for they make pesky bad work, trigging the wheels of Government. They've trigged 'em so much that they say it has cost the State about *fifty thousand dollars* a'ready, more than 'twould if they'd gone along straight without stopping. So you may tell Uncle Joshua that **besides** that bushel of corn he lost in betting about the Speaker, he'll have to shell out as much as *two bushels more* **to pay the** cost of trigging the wheels. Jingoe ! **sometimes when I've** seen the wheels chocked with a little trig not bigger then a cat's head, and the whole Legislater trying with all their might two or three days, and couldn't **start it a** hair, how I've longed to hitch **on** my little speckled four-years-old, and give 'em a pull ; if they wouldn't make the wheels fly over the trigs in a jiffy, I won't guess agin. T'other day, in the great convention, when both Legislaters met together to chuse some Counsellors, Mr. Boutelle and Mr. Smith, of Nobleborough, tried to explain how 'twas that the wheels of Government were trig'd so much. **Mr.** Boutelle, as I have told you afore, is a National Republikan, and Mr. Smith is a Democratic Republikan. They differed a little in their opinion. Mr. Boutelle seemed to think the trigs were all put under by *one class of politicians*, and from what he said, I took it he meant the Jacksonites. He said ever since the Legislater began, the moment they started the wheels, that class of politicians would throw under a chock and **stop** 'em; and which ever way they turned, that class of politicians would meet 'em at every corner and bring 'em up all standin. Mr. Smith seemed to think *another* class of politicians had the greatest hand in it, and it was pretty clear that he meant the Huntonites. He said, when they first got here that class of politicians sot the wheels of Government rolling the *wrong way;* they put the big wheels forward, and the Legislater had been going backwards ever since, jest like a lobster. And the Huntonites not only trig'd the wheels, whenever they begun to roll the right way; but as soon as the "blessed Governor" was done they trig'd him tu; and though he had been done four days, they wouldn't let him come into the Legislater so that their eyes could be blest with the sight **of him.** So from what I can find out, the Jacksonites and Huntonites both are a troublesome, contrary set, and there must be some way contrived to keep 'em out of the Legislater in future.

It seems soon after you got my first letter, Uncle Joshua tackled up, and started off to Boston with a load of turkeys and apple-sass. I had a letter from him t'other day, as long as all out-doors, in the Boston Advertiser. He says he got more for the turkeys than he expected tu ; but I think it's a plaguey pity he didn't bring 'em to Portland. I know he'd got more than he could in Boston. Provision kind is getting up here wonderfully, on account of these Legislaters being likely to stay here all winter ; and some think they'll be here half the summer tu. And then there's sich a cloud of what they call lobby members and office-hunters that the butchers have got frightened, and gone to buying up all the beef and pork they can get hold on, far and near, for they are afraid a famine will be upon us next. Howsomever, Uncle Joshua did well to carry his " puckery apple-sass" to Boston. He couldn't get a cent for't here ; for everybody's puckery and sour enough here now.

Give my love to father and mother and cousin Nabby. I shall answer their letters as soon as I can.

Your lovin cousin,
JACK DOWNING.

LETTER X.

MR. DOWNING ADVISES UNCLE JOSHUA TO HOLD ON TO HIS BUSHEL OF CORN, BECAUSE THE LEGISLATURE HAD BEGUN TO "RIP UP THEIR DUINS."

PORTLAND, Friday, Feb. 12, 1830.

☞ *This with care and speed.*

DEAR UNCLE :—If you haven't paid over that are bushel of corn yet that you lost when you bet Mr. Ruggles would be Speaker, hold on to it for your life, till you hear from me agin, for I aint so clear but you may save it yet. They've gone to rippin up their duins here, and there's no knowing but they may go clear back to the beginning and have another tug about Speaker. At any rate, if your bushel of corn isn't gone out of your crib yet, I advise you by all means to keep it there.

Tell 'Squire N. the question isn't settled yet; and you won't shell out a single kernel till it is fairly nailed and clinched, so it can't be ript up agin. I'll tell you what 'tis, Uncle Josh, the Supreme Court beats the Jacksonites and Huntonites all hollow for trigging the wheels. You know, after they had such a tussle for about a week to choose Elder Hall President of the Sinnet, and after he come in at last all hollow, for they said he had a majority of eight out of sixteen, they went on then two or three weeks nicely, duin business *tie and tie*, hard as they could. Then up steps the Judges of the Supreme Court and tells Mr. Hall he was Governor, and ought to go into the Council Chamber. They seemed to be a little bit thunder struck at first. But they soon come to agin, and Elder Hall got out of the chair, and Mr. Kingsbury got into it, and they jogged along another week, duin business as hard as ever. They said all the chairs round the table ought to be filled, so they changed works with the House, and made four more Sinneters. So having four good fresh hands come in, they took hold in good earnest and turned off more business in two days than they had done in a month before.

Then up steps the Supreme Court agin, and tells 'em their cake is all dough; for they hadn't been duin constitutional. This was yesterday, and it made a dreadful touse. They went right to work rippin up and tarein away what they'd been duin; and before nine o'clock in the evening they turned out the four new Sinneters, out of their chairs, and appointed a committee to begin to make four more. They took hold so ha'sh about it, I s'pose some of the rest of the Sinneters begun to be afraid they should be ripped up tu; so they cleared out, I guess near about half on 'em, and haven't been seen nor heard of to-day. Some of 'em that had more courage went in and tried to du business; but there wasn't enough of 'em to start an inch. They sent a man all round town in the forenoon and afternoon to tell 'em to come in and go to work, but he couldn't find hide nor hair of one of 'em. Elder Hall said *he guessed they must be somewhere in a convention.*

Some say they'll rip up the new Counsellors next, and then the Governor, cause the new Sinneters helpt make 'em all. But there's one comfort left for us, let the cat jump which way 'twill; if Mr. Hunton is'nt a constitutional Governor, Elder

Hall is; the Judges have nailed that fast. So I think Bill Johnson will get off with a whole skin, for I shan't dare to flog him this year. If they go clear back to the Speaker and decide it in favor of your bushel of corn, I shall let you know as soon as possible. Your loving neffu,

JACK DOWNING.

LETTER XI.

MR. DOWNING DESCRIBES SOME QUEER DUINS IN THE SENATE.*

PORTLAND, Wednesday, Feb. 17, 1830.

To Cousin Ephraim Downing up in Downingville:

DEAR COUSIN EPHRAIM :—Here I am yet, and haven't much else to do, so I might as well keep writin to you ; for I s'pose Uncle Joshua's in a peck of trouble about his bushel of corn. I'm pesky 'fraid he'll lose it yet ; for they don't seem to rip up worth a cent since the first night they begun. The truth was, they took hold rather tu ha'sh that night ; and rippin up them are four new Sinneters so quick, they scart away four or five more old ones, so they didn't dare to come in again for tu days. And that threw 'em all into the suds, head and ears. It was worse than trigging the wheels, for it broke the Sinnet

---

* EDITORIAL NOTE.—The Democratic Republicans insisted that the Convention which filled the vacancies in the Senate was not constitutional, and refused to recognize the new members at the Board, and the President refused to count their votes. After considerable turmoil the four new Senators withdrew ; in consequence of which several others of the same party withdrew also, so that there was not a quorum left to do business. After two or three days, however, they returned, and the new Senators re-asserted their claims to a seat. Great confusion ensued ; the President refused to count their votes ; and taking the votes of the other members he declared the Senate adjourned. The National Republicans refused to consider it an adjournment, kept their seats, and began to talk of re-organizing the Senate by choosing a new President. Elder Hall, therefore, fearing the chair would be immediately filled again if he left it, kept his seat, but still repeatedly declared the Senate adjourned. The particulars of the scene are more minutely described in the Major's letter.

wheel right in tu, and left it so flat that all Job's oxen never could start it, if they hadn't got it mended again. They tried, and tried to keep duin something, but they couldn't du the leastest thing. One time they tried to du something with a little bit of a message that was sent to 'em on a piece of paper from the House. The President took it in his hand, and held it up, and asked 'em what was best to du with it. Some of 'em motioned that they'd lay it on the table; but come to consider on it, they found they couldn't according to the Constitution, without there was more of 'em to help; for they hadn't got a korum. They said they couldn't lay it on the table, nor du nothin at all with it. I was afraid the poor old gentleman would have to stand there and hold it till they got the wheel mended agin. But I believe he finally *let it drop* on the table; and I s'pose there was nothin in the Constitution against that.

They got the wheel mended Monday about eleven er clock, so they could start along a little. But them are four new Sinneters that they ript up Thursday night, come right back agin Monday, and sot down to the great round table; and stood tu it through thick and thin, that they wan't ript up and no such thing. Well, this kicked up a kind of a bobbery among 'em, so they thought they'd try to 'journ. The President counted 'em, and said they were 'journed, and might go out. One of the new Sinneters said the President didn't count right, and they wan't 'journed a bit; and they must set still and have an overhauling about it.

So they set down agin, all but four or five Democratic Republicans, that put on their hats and great coats and stood backside of the room. The room was chock full of folks looking on, and the President told 'em the Sinnet was 'journed and they might as well go out, but they did not seem to keer tu, and they put their hats on and began to laugh like fun. The President sot still in his cheer, for I s'pose he thought if he left it some of them are roguish fellers would be gettin' into it. The man that keeps order told the folks they must take

ELDER HALL ADJOURNING THE SENATE.

their hats off when they were in the Sinnet; but they said they wouldn't 'cause the Sinnet was ajourned. Then the man went and asked the President if the Sinnet was ajourned, and the President said 'twas, and there was no doubt about it. And the spectators felt so tickled to think they could wear their hats when the Sinneters were setting round the great table, that they kind of whistled a little bit all over the room.

Finally, after settin about half an hour, another man got up and motioned to adjourn, and the President got up and put it to vote agin. He told 'em if they wanted to ajourn they must say ah, and they all said ah this time, and cleared out in five minutes.

But about this rippin up business; instead of rippin up the Counsellors, as some thought they would, both Legislaters met together to-day, and called in four of the Counsellors, and nailed 'em down harder with an oath.

They've sot the committees to work like fun now, and it's thought they'll turn off business hand over hand; for you know it's almost March, and then the great Supreme Court meets here. And they say they have a grand jury that picks up all disorderly and mischievous folks, and carries 'em into court, and the court puts 'em in jail. These Legislaters have been cutting up such rigs here all winter, that they begin to look pretty shy when anything is said about the first of March, and I don't believe the grand jury'll be able to find a single mother's son of 'em when the court gets here.

From your cousin,
JACK DOWNING.

4

LETTER XII.

MR. DOWNING TELLS WHAT IT MEANS TO SET UP A CANDIDATE FOR OFFICE.

PORTLAND, Tuesday, March 16, 1830.

To Uncle Joshua Downing up in Downingville:

DEAR UNCLE JOSHUA :—There's a hot time ahead. I almost dread to think of it. I'm afraid there's going to be a worse scrabble next summer to see who shall go to the State husking than there was last. The Huntonites and Smithites are determined to have each of 'em a Governor agin next year. They've sot up their candidates on both sides; and who in all the world should you guess they are? The Huntonites have sot up Mr. Hunton, and the Smithites have sot up Mr. Smith. You understand what it means, I s'pose, to set up a candidate. It means the same as it does at a shooting match to set up a goose or a turkey to be fired at. The rule of the game is, that the Smithites are to fire at Mr. Hunton, and the Huntonites are to fire at Mr. Smith. They think it will take a pretty hard battle to get them both in. But both parties say they've got the constitution on their side, so I think likely they'll both beat.

They've been piling up a monstrous heap of ammunition this winter—enough to keep 'em firing all summer; and I guess it won't be long before you'll see the smoke rising all over the State, wherever there's a newspaper. I think these newspapers are dreadful smoky things; they are enough to blind anybody's eyes any time. I mean all except the Daily Courier, that I send my letters in; I never see much smoke in that. But take the rest of the papers that talk about politics, and patriotism, and Republikanism and Federalism, and Jacksonism, and Hartford Conventionism, and let anybody read in one of 'em half an hour, and his eyes will be so full of smoke he can't see better than an owl in the sunshine; he wouldn't be able to tell the difference between a corn-stalk and the biggest oak tree in our pasture.

Your neffu,
JACK DOWNING.

LETTER XIII.

MR. DOWNING TELLS HOW THE LEGISLATURE CLEARED OUT, AND HOW ELDER HALL WENT HOME.

PORTLAND, Monday, March 22, 1830.

To Cousin Ephraim Downing up in Downingville:

COUSIN EPHRAIM :—I kind of want to say a few more words to you about the Legislaters. You know they came together here in the first of the winter in a kind of a stew, and they had storms and tempests among 'em all the time they staid here, and finally they went off Friday in a sort of whirlwind or harricane, I don't know which. They were dreadful kind of snappish the last day they were here ; they couldn't hardly touch a single thing without quarreling about it. They quarreled about paying some of the folks they hired to work for 'em ; and they quarreled ever so long about paying them are four Sinneters that were chose in the convention ; and at last they got to quarreling like cats and dogs to see if they should thank the President and Speaker for all the work they've done this winter. But they had to thank 'em at last. And then Mr. Goodnow, the Speaker in that Legislater they call the House, got up and talked to 'em so pleasant, and kind, and scripture-like, it made 'em feel a little bad ; some of 'em couldn't hardly help shedding tears. I tho't them are, that had been quarreling so, must feel a little sheepish.

That are Elder Hall, that was President of the Sinnet, seemed to be the most poplar man in the whole bunch of both

Legislaters. There wasn't one of the rest of 'em that could work it so as to make both parties like 'em. But, some how or other, he did. The National Republikans liked him so well that they all voted for him for President ; and the Democratic Republikans liked him so well that they all voted to thank him when they went away. And I don't so much wonder at it, for he seemed to me to be about the cleverest, good-natured old gentleman that ever I see.

It's true the old gentleman had rather hard work to keep the wheels of Government going in the Sinnet this winter ; and they would get trig'd every little while in spite of all he could do. I s'pose this made him rather shy of all kinds of wheels ; for he wouldn't go home in a stage, nor a wagon, nor a shay. These kind of carts all have wheels, and I s'pose he thought they might get trig'd, and he wouldn't hardly get home all summer. So he concluded to go by water ; and he went aboard a vessel Saturday night. and sailed for Down East ; and as true as you are alive, before the next day noon the wheels of the vessel got trig'd ; though they said the vessel didn't go on wheels, but some how or other it got trig'd, and back they came next day into Portland again, and there they had to stay till Monday, because the wind didn't blow according to the constitution. But President Hall, you know, isn't the man to leave his post in time of difficulty ; so he never adjourned, nor came ashore, but stuck to the rack till Monday, when a good constitutional breeze sprung up, and they sot sail again. And I wish him a pleasant passage home, and peace and happiness after he gets there ; for, as I said afore, I don't think there's a cleverer man anywhere Down East. From your cousin,   JACK DOWNING.

LETTER XIV.

MR. DOWNING HINTS TO UNCLE JOSHUA THAT HE HAS A PROSPECT OF BEING NOMINATED FOR GOVERNOR.

PORTLAND, April 14, 1830.

To Uncle Joshua Downing, up in Downingville:

UNCLE JOSHUA :—There's one thing, uncle, that seems to wear pretty hard upon my mind, and plagues me a good deal; I haven't slept but little this tu three nights about it. I wish you wouldn't say anything about it up there amongst our folks, for if it should all prove a fudge, they'd be laughing at me. But I tell it to you, because I want your advice, as you've always read the papers, and know considerable about political matters ; tho', to be honest, I don't s'pose any one knows much more about politics by reading the papers, after all.

But what I was goin to tell you is—now, uncle don't twist your tobacco chaw over to t'other corner of your mouth, and leer over your spectacles, and say, Jack's a fool—what I was goin to tell you is this: I see by a paper printed down to Brunswick, that they talk of *nominating me for Governor* to run down Smith and Hunton. Think of that, uncle ; your poor neffu, Jack, that last summer was hoeing about among the potatoes, and chopping wood, and making stone walls, like enough before another summer comes about will be Governor of the State. I shall have a better chance to flog Bill Johnson then, than I should last winter, **if we hadn't had no** Governor nor no laws; for I s'pose a Governor has a right to flog anybody he's a mind to.

But that's nither here nor there, Uncle; I want your serious advice. *If they nominate me, had* I *better accept?* Sometimes I'm half afraid I shouldn't understand very well how to du the business; for I never had a chance to see any Governor business done, only what I see Elder Hall du in the Sinnet chamber last winter. Poor man, that makes me think what a time he had going home. I wrote to you before that he went by water, and that the vessel got trig'd by an unconstitutional wind the first day, and had to come back again. And he must have found a good many hard trigs after that, for he didn't get home till 2d day of April.

Where he was in that dreadful storm, the 26th of March, I have not heard. But I should think, after standing the racket he did last winter in the Legislater, and then this ere storm at sea, he need never to fear anything on land or water again in this world.

I wish you'd write me what you think about my being a candidate for Governor, and whether you think I could get along with the business. Considerable part of the business I shouldn't be a mite afraid but what I could du; that is *the turning out and putting in*. I know every crook and turn of that business; for I don't believe there's a boy in our county, though I say it myself, *that's turned out and tied up more cattle than I have*. And they say a Governor has a good deal of this sort of work to du.

No more at present from your loving neffu,
JACK DOWNING.

LETTER XV.

UNCLE JOSHUA SHOWS REMARKABLE SKILL IN THE SCIENCE OF POLITICS, AND ADVISES MR. DOWNING BY **ALL** MEANS TO STAND AS A CANDIDATE FOR GOVERNOR.

DOWNINGVILLE, April 18th, 1830.

To my neffu Jack Downing, at Portland:

DEAR JACK :—I never felt nicer in my life than I did when I got your last letter. I did think it was a kind of foolish notion in you to stay down there to Portland all winter, and then hire out there this summer. I thought you'd better be at home to work on the farm; for your father, poor old gentleman, is hauled up with the rheumatize so, he won't be able to du hardly a week's work this summer. But I begin to believe Jack knows which side his bread is buttered yet. For if you can only run pretty well as a candidate for Governor, even if you shouldn't be elected, it will be worth more to you than the best farm in this county. It will be the means of getting you into some good office before long, and then you can step up, ye see, from one office to another till you get to be Governor. But if the thing is managed right, I'm in hopes you'll get in this time, and the Downings will begin to look up, and be somebody. It's a very good start, your being nominated in that are paper down to Brunswick. But there's a good deal to be done yet, to carry it. I'm older than you are, and have seen more of this kind of business done than you, and of course ought to know more about it. Besides, you know I've always been reading the papers. Well, in the first place, you must fix upon the name of your party ; I'm thinking you better call it *the Democratic National Republican party,* and then, ye see, you'll haul in some from both of the two clever parties in the State. As for the Jacksonites and Huntonites, I wouldn't try to get any support from them ; for after the rigs they cut up in the Legislater last winter the people back here in the country don't like 'em very well. I think it would hurt you to have anything to do with 'em. Then you must get a few of your friends together in Portland, no matter if there ain't no more than half a dozen, and pass some patriotic resolutions, and then publish the duins of the meeting in the paper, headed, THE VOICE OF THE PEOPLE ; and then go on to say, "at a numerous and respectable meeting of Democratic National Republicans, held in Portland at such a time," &c.,

" Resolved, unanimously, That we have perfect confidence in the exalted talents, the unspotted integrity, and well-known patriotism of *Mr. Jack Downing,* [or perhaps it should be the Hon. Jack Downing,] and that we cheerfully recommend him to the people of this State as a candidate for the office of Governor.

" Resolved, That his well-known attachment to the interests, the principles, and usages of the Democratic National Republican party, eminently entitles him to their confidence and support.

" Resolved, As the sense of this meeting, that nothing short of the election of that firm patriot, the Hon. Jack Downing, can preserve the State from total, absolute, and irretrievable destruction

" Resolved, That a county convention be called to ratify

the doings of this meeting, and that the Democratic National Republicans in other counties be requested to call Conventions for the same purpose.

"Resolved, That the proceedings of this meeting be published in all the Democratic National Republican newspapers in the State."

We will then get up such a meeting in this town, and pass some more highly patriotic resolutions and send 'em down, and you must have 'em put into the paper, headed A VOICE FROM THE COUNTRY. And then we must get a few together somewhere, and call it a *County Convention*, and keep rolling the snow-ball over, till we wind up the whole State in it. Then, ye see, about the first of August we must begin to pin it down pretty snug in the papers. Kind of touch it up somehow like this : Extract of a letter from a gentleman of the first respectability in York County to the Central Committee in Portland. "The Democratic National Republicans here are wide awake ; York County is going for Mr. Downing, all hollow ; we shall give him in this county at least a thousand majority over both Smith and Hunton." Another from Penobscot : "Three quarters of the votes in this county will be given to Mr. Downing; the friends of Smith and Hunton have given up the question, so satisfied are they that there is no chance for them."

Another from Kennebec : "From information received from all parts of the State, upon which perfect reliance can be placed, we are enabled to state, for the information of our Democratic National Republican friends, that there is not the least shadow of doubt of the election of Mr. Downing. It is now rendered certain beyond the possibility of mistake, *that he will receive from five to ten thousand majority over both the other candidates."*

If this don't carry it, you'll have to hang up your fiddle till another year. And after the election is over, if you shouldn't happen to get hardly any votes at all, you must turn about with perfect indifference, and say the Democratic National Republicans *didn't try*—made no effort at all—but will undoubtedly carry the election next year all hollow.

P. S —If you get in I shall expect my son Ephraim to have the office of Sheriff in this county. The other offices we'll distribute at our leisure.

Your affectionate uncle,
JOSHUA DOWNING.

LETTER XVI.

MR. DOWNING GIVES HIS OPINION ABOUT NEWSPAPERS.

Extract of Letter to Uncle Joshua.

PORTLAND, March 30, 1830.

In one of my letters, you know, I said newspapers were dreadful *smoky* things, and anybody couldn't read in 'em half an hour without having their eyes so full of smoke they couldn't tell a pig-sty from a meeting-house.

But I'm thinking, after all, they are more like *rum* than smoke. You know rum will sometimes set quite peaceable folks together by the ears, and make them *quarrel* like mad dogs—so do the newspapers. Rum makes folks act very *silly*—so do the newspapers. Rum makes folks *see double*—so do the newspapers. Sometimes rum gets folks so they can't see at all—so do the newspapers. Rum, if they take tu much of it, makes folks *sick to the stomach*—so do the newspapers. Rum makes folks go rather *crooked*, reeling from one side of the road to t'other—and the newspapers make one half the politicians *cross their path* as often as any drunkard you ever see. It was the newspapers, uncle Joshua, that made you *bet* about the Speaker last summer, and lose your bushel of corn. Remember, that, uncle, and don't believe anything you see in the papers this summer, unless you see it in the Daily Courier.

RUNNING EXPRESS FROM DOWNINGVILLE TO PORTLAND.

DOCKYMENT.

GRAND CAUCUS AT DOWNINGVILLE—THE LONG AGONY OVER, AND THE NOMINATION OUT.

From the Portland Courier of July 21, 1830.

We delay this paper something beyond the usual hour of publication in order to lay before our readers the important intelligence received yesterday from Downingville. This we have been able to accomplish, tho' not without extraordinary exertions and extra help. But the crisis is important—we had almost said appalling—and demands of every patriotic citizen of Maine the highest sacrifices in his power to make. The important proceedings of the grand convention at Downingville reached here, by express, yesterday, about a quarter before 3 o'clock, P. M., having traveled the whole distance, notwithstanding the extreme high temperature of the weather, at the rate of thirteen and a half miles an hour. And but for an unfortunate occurrence, it would undoubtedly have reached here at least three hours earlier. *Capt. Jehu Downing*, who, with his characteristic magnanimity and patriotism volunteered to bring the express the whole way, having taken a very high spirited steed for the first ten miles, was unfortunately thrown to the ground in attempting to leap a barrier which lay across the road. Two of his ribs were broken by the fall, and his right arm so badly fractured that it is feared amputation must be resorted to, besides several other severe contusions on various parts of the body. We are happy to hear, however, that Dr. Zachariah Downing, who, on hearing the melancholy intelligence, very promptly repaired to the spot to offer his professional services, pronounces the Captain out of danger, and also that the Captain bears his misfortune with his accustomed fortitude, expressly declaring that the only regret he feels on the occasion is the delay of the express. Here is patriotism, a devotedness to the welfare of the country, and to genuine Democratic National Republican principles, worthy of the days of the Revolution.

 Lieut. Timothy Downing forwarded the express the remainder of the way with the utmost dispatch, having run down three horses, one of which died on the road. But we keep our readers too long from the gratifying intelligence received.

GRAND DEMOCRATIC NATIONAL REPUBLICAN CONVENTION.

DOWNINGVILLE, Monday, July 19, 1830.

 At a large and respectable meeting of the Democratic National Republicans of Downingville and the neighboring parts of the State, convened this day at the centre school-house, the meeting was called to order by the venerable and silver-haired patriarch, old *Mr. Zebedee Downing*, who had not been out to a political meeting before for the last twenty-five years. The venerable old gentleman stated, in a few feeling remarks, the object of the meeting ; that he had not meddled with politics since the days of Jefferson ; but that now, in view of the awful calamities which threatened to involve our country in total ruin, he felt it his duty, the little remaining time he might be spared from the grave, to lift up his voice and his example before his children, grand-children, and great grandchildren whom he saw gathered around him, and encourage them to serve the country for which he had fought and bled in his younger years. After the enthusiastic applause elicited by these remarks, the old gentleman called for the nomination of a chairman, and Joshua Downing, Esq., was unanimously called to the chair, and *Mr. Ephraim Downing* appointed Secretary.

On motion of Mr. Jacob Downing, voted, that a committee of five be appointed to draft resolutions to lay before this

GRAND CAUCUS AT DOWNINGVILLE.

meeting. Whereupon Mr. Jotham Downing, Ichabod Downing, Zenas Downing, Levi Downing, and Isaiah Downing were appointed said committee, and after retiring about five minutes, they returned and reported the following preamble and resolutions:

"Whereas, an awful crisis has arrived in the political affairs of our country, our public men all having turned traitors, and resolved to ruin the country, and make us and our children all slaves forever; and whereas, our ship of State and our ship of the United States are both driven with tremendous violence before the fury of the political tempest, and are just upon the point of being dashed upon the breakers of political destruction; and whereas, nothing short of the most prompt and vigorous exertions of the patriotic Democratic National Republicans of this State and of the United States can avert the impending danger,

"And whereas, the Jacksonites and Adamsites, and Huntonites, and Smithites, have so multiplied in the land, and brought things to such a pass, that our liberties are unquestionably about to receive their doom forever; therefore,

"Resolved, That it is the highest and most sacred duty of every patriotic Democratic National Republican in the State to arouse himself and buckle on his political armor, and make one last, one mighty effort to save the State and the country, and place the Constitution once more upon a safe and firm foundation.

"Resolved, That the awful crisis of affairs in this State requires a firm, devoted patriot, a high minded and gifted statesman, and a uniform, unwavering Democratic National Republikan for chief magistrate.

"Resolved, **That in this** awful crisis, we believe the **eyes** of all true **patriots are turned upon**

THE HON. JACK DOWNING,

late of Downingville, but since last winter a resident in Portland, the capital of the State.

"Resolved, That we have **the fullest confidence in the tal**ents, integrity, moral worth, **tried patriotism, and** unwavering and unchangeable sterling Democratic National Republicanism of the *Hon. Jack Downing*, **and that his election to the office of Governor in September next, and nothing else, can save the State from** total, unutterable, and irretrievable ruin.

"Resolved, therefore, That we recommend him **to the electors of this State as a** candidate for said office, and that we **will use all fair and honorable means,** and, if **necessary,** will **not stick** at some a little *dis*honorable, to secure his election.

"Resolved, That it be recommended to all the patriotic, Democratic National Republicans throughout the State, to be **up** and doing; **to** call county meetings, town meetings, school district meetings, and village and bar-room meetings, and proceed to organize the party as fast as possible, by appointing standing committees, and central committees, and corresponding committees, and bearers and distributors of hand bills, and, in short, by doing everything that the good of the cause and the salvation of **the country** requires.

"Resolved, conditionally, **That in case** General Jackson should be likely to be re-elected, we highly and cordially approve of his Administration, and believe him to be second to none but Washington; **but in case** he should stand no chance of re-election, **this resolve to be null** and void.

"Resolved, That the thanks of this Convention be presented to Miss Nabby Downing, for the use of her school-room this afternoon, she having with a generous patriotism dismissed the school for that purpose.

"Resolved, That the proceedings of this Convention, signed by the Chairman and Secretary, be published in the Portland Daily Courier, the official organ of the Hon. Jack Downing's correspondence, and any other genuine Democratic National Republican papers in the State.

"JOSHUA DOWNING, Chairman.

"Attest: EPHRAIM DOWNING, Secretary."

We are assured by Lieutenant Timothy Downing, with whom we had a short interview, that the best spirit prevailed in the Convention; not a dissenting voice was heard, and all the resolutions passed unanimously. We add an extract or two from private letters.

From Ephraim Downing to the Hon. Jack Downing.

"Well, Jack, if you don't acknowledge we've done the thing up in style, you're no gentleman and not fit for Governor. I wish you to be very particular to keep the Sheriff's office for me. Father says cousin Jeremiah has thrown out some hints that he shall have the Sheriff's office. But butter my ristbands, if you do give it to him, you'll go out of office again next year, that's positive. Jerry's a clear factionist, you may rely upon that. No, no, stick to your old friends, and they'll stick to you. I'm going to start to-morrow morning on an electioneering cruise. I shall drum 'em up about right. You only keep a stiff upper lip, and you'll come in all hollow."

From Joshua Downing, Esq., to the Hon. Jack Downing.

"Dear Jack, things look well here; with proper exertions I think you may rely upon success. I am in great haste, and write this jest to tell you to be sure and not promise a single office to any mortal living, till I see you. These things must **be managed very** prudently, and you stand in need of the counsel of your old uncle. I think I could **do** as much good to the State by being appointed Land Agent, as any way; but I'll determine upon that when I see you.

"N. B.—Make no promises.

"**Your** affectionate uncle,

JOSHUA."

LETTER XVII.

MR. DOWNING TELLS ABOUT THE PORTLAND TOWN-MEETING, AND HOW THE VOTES TURNED OUT.

PORTLAND, SEPT. 15, 1830.

DEAR UNCLE JOSHUA:—I suppose you would like to know something about how the election turned out down here. Soon as the bell rung, I sot out to go to the town hall, but before I got half way there, I met chaises, and wagons, and another kind of chaises, that went on four wheels, and was shut up close as a hen-coop, all driving *t'other way*, Jehu like. What is the matter? says I; who's beat? But along they went, snapping their whips without answering me a word, and by their being in such a terrible hurry I thought sure enough they had got beat, and the enemy was arter 'em. So I steered round into another street to get out of the way for fear they should get a brush at me; but there was as many more of 'em driving like split down that street tu. Where upon arth are they all going, says I to a feller that overtook me upon the full run. Going? says he; why to bring 'em to the polls, you goose; and away he went by me in a whisk. When he said poles, I thought that cousin Ephraim must have come in with a load, as they'd be likely to fetch a good price about this time, and I concluded all that running and driving was to see who should have the first grab at 'em. I called to him to tell me where Ephraim was, but he was out of hearing.

So I marched along till I got to the town hall, and they

were flocking in as thick as hops. When I got within two or three rods of the house a man come along and handed me a vote for Mr. Smith ; I stept on the side-walk and another man handed me a vote for Mr. Hunton ; and I went along towards the door and another man handed me a vote for Mr. Smith, and then another handed me one for Mr. Hunton. And then I went to go up stairs into the hall, and there was a row of about twenty men, and all of 'em gave me a vote, about one-half for Smith and one-half for Hunton. And before I got through the hall to the place where they were firing off their votes, they gave me about twenty more; so if I had been a mind to vote for Smith or Hunton I could have gin 'em a noble lift ; but that wasn't what I was arter. I was looking out for the interests of my constituents at Downingville. And when I come to see among so many votes not one of 'em had my name on it, I began to feel a little kind of streaked,

I went out again, and I see the chaises and wagons kept coming and going, and I found out that bringing of 'em to the polls meant bringing of 'em to vote. And I asked a feller that stood there, who them are men, that they kept bringing, voted for. Why, says he, they vote for whichever goes arter 'em, you goose-head you. Ah, says I, is that the way they work it? And where do they bring 'em from ? O, says he, down round the wharves, and the outskirts of the town and anywhere that they can catch 'em. Well, well, thinks I to myself, I've got a new rinkle, I see how this business is done now. So off I steered and hired a horse and wagon, and went to hunting up folks to carry to town meeting. And I guess before night I carried nearly fifty there, of one sort and another ; and I was sure to whisper to every one of 'em jest as they got out of the wagon, and tell 'em my name was Jack Downing. They all looked **very** good-natured when I **told 'em my** name, and I thought to be sure they would all vote for me. But how was I thunderstruck when the **vote was** declared, and there **was** 1,008 for Mr. Smith, **909 for Mr. Hun**ton, 4 for Mr. Ladd, and one or **two** for somebody else, and **not** *one* **for me.** Now was'nt that too bad, uncle? Them are faith**less** politicians that I carried up to the town meeting! **if I only knew who they were, they should pay for the horse** and wagon, **or we'd have a breeze about it.**

Write soon, for I am anxious to **know** how they turned out in Downingville

Your loving neffu,
JACK DOWNING.

LETTER XVIII.

RETURN OF VOTES FROM DOWNINGVILLE—THE SKIES LOOK BRIGHTER

DOWNINGVILLE, Monday Eve., Sept. 13, 1830.

To the Hon. Jack Downing, Portland:

DEAR JACK :—I have just returned, puffing and blowing from town meeting, and have only time to tell you that we gave you a confounded good run here. If your friends in the rest of the State have done their duty, you are elected by an overwhelming majority. The vote in this town for Governor stood as follows :

    Hon. JACK DOWNING..................................117
    Hon. Samuel E. Smith...............................000
    Hon. Jonathan G. Hunton............................000

Capt. Jehu Downing is elected Representative; it was thought to be due to him by the party for his magnanimous exertions in carrying the express to Portland at the time you were nominated by our grand convention.

    In great haste, your uncle,

              JOSHUA DOWNING.

LETTER XIX.

MR. DOWNING TELLS HOW HE GOT A NEW KINK INTO HIS HEAD, IN CONSEQUENCE OF THE BLOW-UP OF PRESIDENT JACKSON'S FIRST CABINET.

PORTLAND, April 26, 1831.

DEAR UNCLE JOSHUA:—I'm in considerable of a kind of a flusteration to-day, because I've got a new scheme in my head. New ideas, you know, are always apt to give me the agitations a little; so you mustn't wonder if my letter this time does have some rather odd things in it. I don't know when I've had such a great scheme in my head afore. But you know I was always determined to make something in the world, and if my friends 'll only jest stick by me, I shall make common folks stare yet. Some thought it was a pretty bold push my trying to get in to be Governor last year; and some have laughed at me, and said I come out at the little end of the horn about it, and that I'd better staid up to Downingville and hoed potatoes, than to be fishing about for an office and not get any more votes than I did. But they can't see through a millstone so fur as I can. Altho' I didn't get in to be Governor, its made me known in the world, and made considerable of a great man of me, so that I shall stand a much better chance to get an office if I try again. But I must make haste and tell you what I am at, for I am in a great hurry. I guess you'll stare when I tell you the next letter you'll get from me will be dated at Washington, or else somewhere on the road between here and there.

O, uncle, we have had some great news here from Washington; everybody's **up in arms** about it, and can't hardly tell what to **think** of it. They **say** the President's four great Secretaries **have all** resigned; only **think of** that, uncle. And they say their salaries were *six thousand dollars a-year;* only **jest** think of that, uncle. Six thousand dollars a year. Why, **a Governor's salary is a fool to it. On the** whole, I'm glad I didn't get the Governor's **office. I shall start** for Washington to-morrow morning ; **or I don't** know but I shall start to-night, if I can get ready, and travel all night. It's best to be in season in such things, and I shall have to go rather slow, for **I've got** pretty considerable short of money, and I expect I shall have to foot it part way. I shall get there in about a fortnight, and I'm in hopes to be in season to get one of them are offices. I think it's the duty of all true Republikans that **have the** good of the country at heart, to take hold and help **the** President along in these **trying** difficulties. For my part, I am perfectly willing to take one of the offices, and I hope some other **good** men **will** come right forward and take the others. What a shame 'twas that them are Secretaries should all clear out, and leave the poor old General to do all the work **alone.** Why, uncle, they had no more patriotism than your old hoss.

But I musn't stop to parley about it now; what I want to **say is, I** wish **you to write** a recommendation to the President for me to **have** one of his offices, and go round as quick as you can and get all our friends at Downingville to sign it, and send it on to Washington **as fast** as possible; for it would be no more than right that I should show the President some kind of recommendation before he gives me the office. I want you to tell the President that I've always been one of his strongest friends; and you know I always have spoke well of him, and *in fact he is the best President we ever had.* It might be well for you to quote this last sentence as an " extract from a letter of the Hon. Jack Downing." It would give the President some confidence in my friendship, and the " Hon." would convince him that I am a man of some standing in this State.

Now you keep up a good heart, uncle; you have always had to delve hard all your days up there on the old farm, and you've done considerable to boost me up into an office, and if I get hold of these six thousand dollars a year, you shall have a slice out of it that will make your old heart feel light again. I haven't named it to a single soul here except Aunt Sally, and I want it to be kept a profound secret till I get the office, so as to make them are chaps that have been a sneering at me here, stare like an owl in a thunder shower. And, besides, if it should leak out that I was going, I'm afraid somebody else might get the start of me, for there are always enough that have their mouths open when it rains such rich porridge. But it's like as not, the newspapers 'll blab it out before I get half way there. And you needn't think strange, if you see some of the Boston or New York papers in a few days saying, " The Hon. Jack Downing passed through this city yesterday, on his way to Washington. It is rumored that he is to be called upon to fill one of the vacant offices." But I must stop, for it is time I was picking up my duds for a start. Aunt Sally has been darning my stockings all the morning. Love to Aunt and cousin Nabby, and all of 'em. Good by.

  Your loving neffu,   JACK DOWNING.

LETTER XX.

MR. DOWNING TELLS ABOUT THE TALK HE HAD WITH THE BOSTON EDITORS ON HIS WAY TO WASHINGTON.

CITY OF NEW YORK, May 3, 1831.

DEAR UNCLE JOSHUA :—I have got so fur at last, and a pretty hard run I've had of it to get here, I can tell ye. This running after offices is pretty tuff work for poor folks. Sometimes I think there aint much profit in it after all, any more than there is in buying lottery tickets, where you pay a dollar and sometimes get four shillings back, and sometimes nothing. Howsomever I don't mean to be discouraged yet, for if I should give out now and go back again, them are sassy chaps in Portland would laugh at me worse than they did afore. What makes me feel kind of down-hearted about it, is because I've seen in the newspapers that tu of them are good offices at Washington are gone a-ready. One Mr. Livingston's got one of 'em, and Mr. Woodbury that lives up in New Hampshire's got tother, and I'm considerable afraid the others will be gone before I get there.

I want you to be sure and get my recommendation into the post-office as soon as you can, so it may get there as soon as I do. It's a week to-day since I started from Portland, and if I have good luck I'm in hopes to get there in about a week more. Any how, I shall worry along as fast as I can. I have to foot it more than three-quarters of the way, because the stage folks asks so much to ride, and my money's pretty near gone. But if I can **only jest get** there before the offices are gone I think I shall get one of 'em, for I got a good string of recommendations in Boston as I come along. I never thought of getting any recommendations of strangers, till a man I was traveling with kind of talked round and round, and found out what I was after. And then, says he, if you want to make out, you must get the newspaper folks to give you a lift, for they manage these matters. And he told me I better get some of the Boston editors to recommend me, or it would be no use for me to go.

I thought the man was more than half right, so when I got into Boston I called round to see the editors. They all seemed very glad to see me, when I told 'em who I was, and I never see a better set of true Republikans any where in the State of Maine. And when I told 'em that I was always a true Republikan, and my father and grandfather were Republikans before me, they all talked so clever about patriotism, and our Republikan institutions, and the good of the people, that I couldn't help thinking it was a plaguey shame there should be any such wicked parties as Federalists, or Huntonites, or Jacksonites, to try to tare the country to pieces and plague the Republikans so.

This don't include President Jackson. He isn't a Jacksonite, you know; he's as true a Republikan as there is in Downingville. I had a talk with the Boston Patriot man first. He said he would give me a recommendation with a good deal of pleasure, and when I got my office at Washington I must stick to the good old Republikan cause like wax; and if all true Republikans were only faithful to the country, Henry Clay, the Republikan candidate, will come in all hollow. He'll be the next **President, says he, jest as sure as your name is Jack** Downing.

Then I went to see the editor of the Boston Gazette. He said he certainly should be very happy to give me a recommendation; and he trusted when I got to Washington, where I should have considerable influence, I should look well to the interests of the Republikan party. He said there was an immense sight of intrigue and underhand work going on by the enemies of the country to ruin Mr. Calhoun, the Republikan candidate for President. But he said they wouldn't make out; Mr. Calhoun had found out their tricks, and the Republikans of old **Virginny and South Carolina** were all **up in arms** about it, and if we Republikans in the Northern States **would** only take hold and fight for the good cause, Mr. Calhoun would be elected as true as the sun will **rise** to-morrow.

The next I went **to see was the** editor of the Boston Statesman. He seemed to be a little shy of me at first, and **was** afraid I wasn't a true Republikan; **and wanted to** know if I didn't run against Governor **Smith last** year down there in Maine. I told him I had seen Governor Smith **a number of** times in Portland, but I was sure I never **run against him in my life,** and I didn't think I ever **come within a rod of him.** Well, he wanted to know if I wasn't **a candidate for Governor** in opposition to Mr. Smith. **I told him no, I was a candidate on the same side.** "Wasn't you," said he, looking mighty sharp at me, "*Wasn't you one of the Federal candidates for Governor?*" My stars, Uncle Joshua, **I never felt** my hair **curl quicker than it did then. My hand kind of drawed back, and** my fingers clinched as if I were jest agoing to up fist and knock him down. To think that he should charge **me** with being a *Federl Candidate!* it was too much for flesh and blood to bear. But I cooled down as quick as I could, for fear it might hurt me about getting my office. I told him I never was a Federal candidate, and there never was a drop of Federal blood in me; and I would run from a Federalist, if I should meet one, as quick as I would from *poison*. That's right, says he, I like that; that's good stuff, and he catched hold of my hand, and gave it such a shake, I didn't know but he'd a pulled it off.

He said he would give me the best recommendation he could write, and when I got to Washington I must stick to the old Gineral like the tooth-ache, for the Federalists were intriguing desperately to root him out of his office and upset the Republikan party. If the Republikans could only be kept together, he said, President Jackson, the Republikan candidate, could be elected as easy as a cat could lick her ear; but if we suffered ourselves to be divided it would be gone goose with us, and the country would be ruined. So you must stick to the re-election of Gineral Jackson, said he, *at all events*; and then he kind of whispered in my ear, and says he, in case Gineral Jackson should be sick or anything, you must remember that Mr. Van Buren is the *Republikan candidate.*

I told him he never need to fear me; I should stick to the Republikan party through thick and thin. So I took my recommendation and trudged along. I haven't time to-day to tell you how I got along with the rest of the editors, and a thousand other things that I met with along by the way, and all the fine things in this great city, and so on. But I shall write to you again soon.

Your loving neffu, JACK DOWNING

LETTER XXI.

MR. DOWNING RELATES HIS INTERVIEW WITH MAJOR NOAH AT NEW-YORK.

WASHINGTON CITY, May 30, 1831.

To the Portland Courier, if it ever gets there, away Down East in the State of Maine, to be sent to **Uncle** *Joshua Downing,* **up in** *Downingville, with care and speed.*

DEAR UNCLE JOSHUA :—I've got here at last, to this great city, where they make offices, and I'm determined not to leave it till I get one. It isn't sich a great city, after all, as New-York, though they do a great deal more business here than they do at New-York. I don't mean vessel business and trade, for there's no end to that in New-York, but in making offices and such like ; and they say it's the most profitable business in the country. If a man can get hold of a pretty good office, he can get rich enough by it in three or four years, and not to have to work very hard neither. I tell you what, uncle, if I make out to my mind here, I shall come back again one of these days in a rather guess way than what I come on. I don't have to foot it again, I'll warrant you, and I guess poor Aunt Sally won't have to set up all night to mend my coat and darn my stockings. You'll see me coming dressed up like a lawyer, with a fine carriage and three or four horses. And then them are chaps in Portland that used to laugh at me so about being Governor, may sneeze at me if they dare to, and if they don't keep out of my way I'll ride right over 'em. I had a pretty tuff time coming on here. It's a long, tiresome road through the Jarseys. I had to stop twice to get my shoes tapt, and once to get an old lady to sow up a rip in my coat while I chopped wood for her at the door to pay for it. But I shan't mind all the hard work I've had of it, if I can make out to come home rich.

MR. DOWNING EXCHANGING WORKS.

I got a pretty good boost in Boston, as I writ you in my last, by the editors giving me recommendations. But it was nothing at all hardly to what I got in New York, for they gave me a *public dinner* there. I can't think what's the matter that it hasn't been published yet. Major Noah promised me he'd have it all put into the New York Courier and Enquirer the very next day after I left New York, so that it should get to Washington as soon as I did; and now I've been here about a week and it hasn't come yet. If it doesn't come soon, I shall write an account of the dinner myself, and send it home and get it put in the Portland Courier. It was a most capital dinner, uncle; I don't know as I ever eat hartier in my life, for being pretty short of money I had pinched rather close a day or two, and, to tell the truth, I was as hungry as a bear. We had toasts and speeches, and a great many good things. I don't mean sich toast as they put butter on to eat, but toast to drink. And they don't exactly drink 'em neither; but they drink the punch and speak the toasts.

I can't think Major Noah meant to deceive me about publishing the proceedings of the dinner, for he appeared to be a very clever man, though he was the funniest chap that ever I see. There wasn't a man in New York that befriended me more than he did; and he talked to me very candidly, and advised me all about how to get an office. In the first place, says he, Mr. Downing, you can't get any kind of an office at Washington unless you are a true blue genuine Democratic Republikan. I told him I had recommendations coming to prove that I was all that. They are very strict, says he, in regard to that at Washington. If James Madison should apply for an office at Washington, says he, he couldn't get it. What, says I, him that was President! for it kind of startled me a little if such an old Republikan as he was couldn't get an office. It's true, says he, if James Madison should apply for an office he couldn't get it. Why not, says I? Because, says he, *he has turned Federalist*. It's melancholy to think, says he, how many good old Republikans at the South are turning Federalists lately. He said he was afraid there

MAJOR NOAH AND MR. DOWNING.

wasn't more than one true genuine old Democratic Republikan left in Virginny, and that was old Mr. Ritchie, of the Richmond Enquirer; and even he seemed to be a little wavering since Mr. Calhoun and some others had gone over.

Well, there's Mr. Clay, says I, of Kentucky, I don't think he'll ever flinch from the Republikan cause. Henry Clay, says he, turning up his nose, why he's been a Federalist this six years. No, no, Mr. Downing, if **you** think of going that gate, you may as well **turn** about and **go home** again before you go any further. What gate? says I. **Why to** join the Clay party, says he. I told him I never had sich a thought in **my** life; I always belonged to the Republikan party, **and always meant to.** He looked rather good-natured again when he heard that; and says he, do you know what the true **Republikan doctrine** is? I told him I had always had some kind of an idea of it, but **I** didn't know as I could explain it exactly. Well, says he, I'll tell you; it is to support Gineral Jackson for re-election, through thick and thin. That is the only thing that will save the country from ruin. And if Gineral Jackson should be unwell or any thing jest before election, so he could not be **a** candidate, the true Republikan doctrine is **to** support Mr. Van Buren. I told him very well, he might depend upon my sticking **to** the Republikan party, all weathers. Upon that he set down and wrote me a recommendation to the President for an office, and it almost made me blush to see what a master substantial genuine Republikan he made me. I had a number more capital recommendations at New York, but I haven't time to tell you about 'em **in this** letter. Some **were** to Mr. Clay, and some to Mr. **Van** Buren, **and** some **to Mr.** Calhoun. I took 'em all, for I thought it was kind of uncertain whose hands I might fall into hereafter, and it might **be** well enough to have two or three strings to my bow.

I haven't called on the President yet, though I've been here about a week. My clothes had got so shabby, I thought I better hire out a few days and get slicked up a little. Three of the offices that I come after are gone slick enough, and the other one's been given away to a Mr. White, but he wouldn't take it; so I'm in hopes I shall be able to get in. And if I don't get that, there's some chance for me to get in to be Vice President, for they had a great Jackson meeting 'tother day, and they kicked Mr. Calhoun right out doors, and said they wouldn't have him for Vice President no longer. Now some say they think I shall get it, and some think Mr. Van Buren 'll get it.

Howsomever, I feel pretty safe, for Major Noah told me if I couldn't get anything else, the President could easily make a foreign mission for me.

Oh dear! uncle, it makes me feel kind of bad when I think how fur I've got from home.

I shall call on the old Gineral in two or three days, and if I can make a dicker with him about the office I'll let you know

Your lovin neffu,
JACK DOWNING.

LETTER XXII.*

MR. DOWNING TELLS HOW HE STRIPT UP HIS SLEEVES AND DEFENDED MR. INGHAM ON **HIS** FRONT-DOOR-STEPS, DURING THE AFTER-CLAP THAT FOLLOWED THE BLOW-UP OF GINERAL JACKSON'S FIRST CABINET.

WASHINGTON CITY, June 21, 1831.

To Uncle Joshua Downing, up in Downingville, or **else to Cousin Nabby,** *it isn't much matter which, being that some of it is about the ladies :*

DEAR UNCLE JOSHUA :—It's pretty trying times here. They carry on so like the old smoker, I don't hardly know what to make of it. If I hadn't said I wouldn't leave Washington till **I got an office,** I don't know but I should come back to

---

*[EDITORIAL NOTE.—It will be remembered, by those whose political reminiscences extend back so far, that General Jackson's first Cabinet blew up. In other words, the whole Cabinet resigned **in a body.** This came upon the country something like a thunder-clap. **Very soon upon** the heels of the thunder-clap came **an** *after-clap,* which produced a sensation throughout the **country** scarcely inferior to that of the thunder-clap. The thunder-clap and **the after-clap** were believed to be intimately connected, and some even went **so far as to say** that the after-clap was the real cause of **the** thunder-clap. **Major** Downing's letter gives some of the exciting scenes of the after-clap, **and** perhaps a few words should be added here explanatory of the whole affair.

There was an inside view and an outside view to this Cabinet difficulty, as **well** as most other things **in the world.** The inside view, the Senatorial view, such as Colonel Benton would take **in his "Thirty Years,"** was something like this : Mr. Calhoun, the Vice-President, and Mr. Van Buren, the Secretary of State, were rival competitors for the successorship to the office of President. It came to the knowledge of the President that a proposition had been made in Mr. Monroe's Cabinet to punish General Jackson for his con**duct and** doings in Florida, in the Seminole War. For some time General

Downingville and go to planting potatoes. Them are Huntonites and Jacksonites down there in Maine last winter were pretty clever sort of folks to what these chaps are here. Cause down there if they got ever so mad, they didn't do nothing but talk and jaw one another; but here, if anybody doesn't do to suit 'em, fact they'll up and shoot him in a minute. I didn't think getting an office was such dangerous kind of business, or I don't know as I should have tried it. Howsomever, it's neck or nothing with me now, and I must do something to try to get some money here, for I about as lieves die as to undertake to foot it away back agin clear to the State of Maine. And as the folks have to go armed here,

Jackson believed that this proposition in the Cabinet came from Mr. Crawford, and that he was triumphantly defended by Mr. Calhoun and Mr. Adams, a statement having been published in a Western newspaper to this effect. Afterward the General learned, on the authority of Mr. Crawford and from other sources, that it was Mr. Calhoun who made the proposition to punish him, and that he was protected in the Cabinet by Mr. Crawford and Mr. Adams. And he believed, as did also Mr. Crawford, that the reverse and false statement in the papers had been published at the instigation of Mr. Calhoun. This, of course, produced a decided coolness, or rather a warm difficulty, between the President and the Vice-President. Mr. Calhoun thereupon published a pamphlet, addressed to the people of the United States, to explain the cause of the difficulty, and charging Mr. Van Buren with being at the bottom of all the mischief. The President and Vice-President were at sword-points, the members of the Cabinet were divided on the points of the quarrel—some of them were for Mr. Van Buren for the succession and some for Calhoun. An explosion was inevitable. The President had become attached to Mr. Van Buren, and was ready to do anything in the world for him.

It was finally determined that there must be a re-organization of the Cabinet. Mr. Ingham, Secretary of the Treasury, Mr. Branch, Secretary of the Navy, and Mr. Berrien, Attorney-General, were in favor of Mr. Calhoun; and Major Eaton, Secretary of War, and Mr. Barry, Postmaster-General, were in favor of Mr. Van Buren. In order to relieve the President from the necessity of dismissing any members of the Cabinet, Mr. Van Buren proposed

I want you to put my old fowling piece into the stage and send it on here as quick as possible. I hope you'll be as quick as you can about it, for if I get an office I shan't dare to take it till I get my gun. They come pretty near having a shooting scrape here yesterday. The Telegraph paper said something about Mr. Eaton's wife. It was nothing that I should think they need to make such a fuss about; it only said that some of the ladies here refused to visit her. But some how or other it made Mr. Eaton as mad as a March hair. He declared he'd fight somebody, he didn't care who.

The first man he happened to come at was **Mr.** Ingham. So he dared Mr. Ingham out to fight. Not to box, as they do sometimes up in Downingville, but to stand and shoot at

that the whole Cabinet should resign, which was promptly done. Their places were filled as follows: Edward Livingston, of Louisiana, Secretary of State; Louis McLane, of Delaware, Secretary of the Treasury; Lewis Cass, of Ohio, Secretary of War; Levi Woodbury, of New Hampshire, Secretary of the Navy; Amos Kendall, of Kentucky, Postmaster-General; Roger B. Taney, **of** Maryland, Attorney-General. **Mr. Downing,** who "footed it" from Portland to Washington for the express purpose of filling one of these offices, was a little too late, it seems, as other people are sometimes who go to Washington on a similar errand. So much for the inside view.

The outside view of this matter, such as Mr. Downing would take in his "Thirty Years," and such as a good many outside folks took at the time, showed "a lady in the case." Mr. Eaton had married Mrs. Timberlake, widow of **an** officer of the navy, and Mr. Eaton and his wife were pets and **protegés** of President Jackson. But, in consequence of certain gossip or slanders about this lady, the wives of the other members of the Cabinet refused to visit or associate with her. Then, of course, "the fat was all in the fire." No Cabinet could **stand an ordeal like** that without an explosion. General Jackson was furious as a roaring lion, and Major Eaton a little more so. He challenged Mr. Ingham to a duel, but Ingham would not fight. Then followed the scenes of attempted redress with canes and bowie-knives, and an assault upon Mr. Ingham's house at night, which was so bravely defended by Mr. Downing, and so graphically described in his letter, and, we may add, so well delineated by our artist.

each other. But Mr. Ingham wouldn't touch to, and told him he was crazy. That made Mr. Eaton ten times more mad than he was before; and he declared he'd flog him anyhow, whether he was willing or not. So he got a gang of gentlemen yesterday to go with him to the Treasury Office, where Mr. Ingham does his writing, and waited there and in a grog shop close by as much as two hours for a chance to catch him and give it to him. Mr. Ingham was out a visiting in the city, and when he got home his folks told him what was going on, and begged him not to go to the office, for he would certainly be killed. "Poh," says he, "do you think I'm afraid of them are blustering chaps? There's more smoke than fire there, I can tell ye; give me my pistols, it is time for me to go to the office." Some of the ladies cried, and some almost fainted away. But he pacified 'em as well as he could, and then set out for the office, and three or four men went with him, and I guess they carried something under their arms that would make daylight shine through a feller pretty quick. And I guess the gang of gentlemen waiting for him begun to smell a rat, for they cleared out pretty soon and never touched him. But their courage came again in the evening, and this same gang of gentlemen turned out and marched up to Mr. Ingham's house, and threatened to burst the doors open and drag him out by the hair of the head and skin him alive. I thought this was carrying the joke rather too far, so I tho't I'd put in my oar; for when I see any body run upon too hard I can't help taking their part.

So I stepped up to Mr. Ingham's front door steps, and threw my hat down, and rolled up my sleeves, and spit on my hands; and by that time the chaps began to stare at me a little. And

THE BATTLE OF THE AFTER-CLAP.

[123]

now says I, "Major Eaton, this is quite too bad. A man's house is his castle. Here's Mr. Ingham in his house as peaceable as a lamb; he isn't a meddling with nobody, and you needn't think to drag him out here to-night, I can tell ye. If you really want to take a bit of a box, just throw away your powder and ball and here's the boy for you. I'll take a fist or two with you and glad of the chance."

"You impudent scoundrel," says he, "who are you? what business is it to you what I *done*? Clear out, or I'll send you where you ought to have been long ago."

"Well, then, you'll send me into some good office," says I, for there's where I ought to have been more than two years ago."

"Well," says he, "clear out;" and up he come blustering along toward the steps. But I jest put my foot down, and doubled up my fist, and now, says I, "Major Eaton, it won't be healthy for you to come on to these steps to-night."

Says he, "I'm going through that door whether or no." Says I, "you don't go through this door to-night, without you pass over the dead body of *Jack Downing*, of the State of Maine." My stars, when they heard that, they dropt their heads as quick as though they had been cut off, for they didn't know who I was before. Major Eaton and the whole gang of gentlemen with him turned right about and marched away as whist as mice. They were afraid I should have 'em all before the President to-day, and have 'em turned out of office; for it's got whispered round the city that the President sets a great deal by me, and that I have a good deal of influence with him.

This morning Mr. Ingham started for Philadelphy. Before he left, he thanked me a thousand times for defending his house so well last night, and he wrote a letter to the President, telling him all about the scrape. I went a piece with him to see him safe out of the city on the great road toward Baltimore.

About my prospects for an office, I can't tell you yet how I shall come out. I've been in to see the President a number of times, and he talks very favorable. I have some chance to get in to be Secretary of War, if old Judge White don't take it ; and if I don't get that the President says he'll do the best he can for me.

I never had to be so strict a Republikan before in my life as I've had to be since I've been here, in order to get the right side of the President. I'll tell you something about it in my next, and about my visits to the President, and a good many other famous things here.

P. S.—Be sure and send the old gun as quick as possible.

Your loving neffu,

JACK DOWNING.

LETTER XXIII.

Mr. Downing receives a Captain's commission in the United States Army, with orders to go and protect the inhabitants of Madawaska.

Washington City, the 20th day of October, 1831.

To Uncle Joshua Downing, *up in Downingville*, State of Maine, *this with care and speed:*

Dear Uncle Joshua :—I've got it at last, as true as you're alive, and now I don't keer a snap for the fattest of 'em. I'll teach them are young chaps down to Portland that used to poke fun at me so because I didn't get in to be Governor, that they must carry a better tongue in their heads, or they'll find out who **they are** talking to. **I guess they'll find out** by and by it won't be healthy for 'em **to poke fun at an officer of** my rank. And as for **Jemime** Parsons, that married the schoolmaster winter before last, **when she** had promised as fair as could be **that she would have** me, she may go to grass for what I keer; **I wouldn't** have her now no more than I'd **have a** Virginny nigger. And I guess when she comes to **see me with my regimentals on** she'll feel sorry enough, **and wish her** cake was dough **again. Now** she's tied down **to that** clodpole of a schoolmaster, that wasn't fit for a schoolmaster neither, for **he** has had to go to hoeing **potatoes for** a living, and much as ever he can get potatoes **enough to keep 'em** from starving, **when** if she had only done as she had promised, she might **now be the** wife **of Captain Jack Downing, of** the United

States Army. But let her go; as I said afore, I don't care a snap for her or all old White's cattle. I'll tell you what 'tis, uncle, I feel about right now. It seems to me I could foot it home in two days, for my feet never felt half so light before. There's nothing like trying, in this world, uncle; anybody that tries can be something or other, if he don't get discouraged too soon. When I came on here, you know, I expected to get one of the great Secretaries' offices; but the good old President told me they had got him into such a hobble about them are offices that he couldn't give me one of 'em if he was to die. But he treated me like a gentleman, and I shall always vote for him as long as I live, and I told him so. And when he found out that I was a true genuine Republikan, says he, "Mr. Downing, you must be patient, and I'll bear you in mind, and do something for you the very first chance. And you may depend upon it, Mr. Downing," he added with a good deal of earnestness, "I never desert my friends, let that lying Stephen Simpson, of Philadelphy, say what he will about it—a good-for-nothing, ungrateful dog." And he fetched a stomp with his foot, and his eyes kind of flashed so fiery that I couldn't help starting back, for I didn't know but he was going to knock me over. But he looked pleasant again in a minute, and took me by the hand, and now, says he, "Mr. Downing, I give you my honor that I'll do something for you as soon as I possibly can." I told him I hoped he would be as spry as he could about it, for I had but jest ninepence left, and I didn't know how I should get along very well, in a strange place, too. But he told me never to mind that at all; I might come and eat my meals at his house whenever I'd a mind to or he would be bondsman for my board where I put up. So I've worked along from that time to this, nearly four months, as well as I could—sometimes getting a little job of garden-work, and sometimes getting a little wood to saw, and so on, nearly enough to pay my expenses. I used to call and see the President once in a while, and he always told me I

GENERAL JACKSON SENDS FOR MR. DOWNING.

must be patient and keep up a good heart—the world wasn't made in one day—and something would turn up for me by and by. But fact, after digging and sawing, and waiting four months, my patience got most wore out, and I was jest upon the point of giving up the chase, and starting off for Downingville with the intention of retiring to private life, when, last night, about seven o'clock, as I sot eating a bowl of bread and milk for my supper, a boy knocked at the door and wanted to see Mr. Downing. So they brought him into the room where I was, and says he, " Mr. Downing, the President wants to see you for something very particular, right away this evening." My heart almost jump'd right up in my mouth. My spoon dropt out of my hand, and to eat another mouthful I couldn't if I was to starve. I flew round, and washed my face and hands, and combed my head, and brushed up as well as I could, and should have looked tolerable spruce if it hadn't been for an unlucky hole in the knee of my trouses. What to do I did not know. It made me feel bad enough I can tell you. The woman where I boarded said she would mend them for me if I would take them off, but it would take her till about nine o'clock, and the President was waiting for me, and there 'twas. Such a hobble I never was in before. But this woman is a kind, good creature as ever was; she boards me for four and sixpence a week, considering that I split wood for her, and bring water, and do all sich kind of chores. And she always had some contrivance to get out of every difficulty; and so she handed me a neat little pocket handkerchief and told me to tie that round my knee. Being thus rigged out at last, I started off as fast as I could go for the President's.

When I went into his room the old gentleman was sitting by a table with his spectacles on, and two great lamps burning before him, and a bundle of letters and papers in his hand. He started up and took me by the hand, and says he, " good evening, Mr. Downing, I'm very glad to see you; you are the very man I want now, above all others in the world. But now is this," says he, looking at my knee; "not lame, I hope? That would be a most unfortunate thing in this critical moment. It would knock my **plan** in the head at once." I felt kind of blue, and I guess I blushed a little; but I turned it off as well **as I could**; I told **him** I wasn't lame **at** all; it was **nothing but** a slight scrach, and by to-morrow morning I should **be as well as ever** I was in my life. " Well then," says he, " **Mr.** Downing, sit **down** here and see what I have got to tell **you.**" The old gentleman set himself back in his chair and pushed his spectacles up on his forehead and held **up** the letter in his hand, and says he, "Mr. Downing, here is a letter from Governor Smith, of Maine, and now, Sir, I've got something for you to do. You see now that I was sincere when I told you if you would be patient and stick to the Republikan text, I would look out for you one of these days. I'm always true to my friends; that lying Stephen Simpson might have had an office before now if he had behaved himself."

"Well, dear Sir," said **I**, for I felt in such a pucker to know what I was going to get that I couldn't stand it any longer, so says I, "what sort of business is it you've got for me to do?" Says he " Mr. Downing, I take it you are a man of courage; I have always thought so ever since you faced Mr. Eaton so boldly on Mr. Ingham's door-steps. Tho' I was sorry **your courage was** not displayed in a better cause, for that Ingham is a rascal after all." I told him as for courage I believed I had some of the stuff about me when there was any occasion for it, and that I never would stand by and see anybody abused. "Well," says he, " we must come to the point, for the business requires haste. Governor Smith writes me that there are four of your fellow-citizens of Maine in a British jail at Fredericton, who have been taken from their farms by British constables and sheriffs and other officers and carried off by force to prison."

By this time my very hair begun to curl, I felt so mad, and I couldn't help jumping up and smiting my fists together, and saying pretty hard things about the British.

"Well," says the President, "I like your spunk, Mr. Downing ; you're jest the man I want in this business. I'm going to give you a captain's commission in the United States army, and you must go down there and set that business right at Madawaska. You must go to Maine and raise a company of volunteers as quick as possible; tell 'em I'll see 'em paid ; and you must march down to Fredericton and demand the prisoners, and if they are not given up you must force the jail, and if the British make any resistance you must fire upon them and bring the prisoners off at some rate or other. Then write me and let me know how affairs stand, and I'll give you further orders. At any rate you must see that the rights of Maine are well protected, for that State has come round so in my favor since last year I'm determined to do everything I can for them; I tell you, Mr. Downing, I never desert my friends."

So, after he gave me the rest of my orders and my commission, and a pocket full of money, and told me to be brave and if I wanted anything to let him know, he bid me good night, and I went home. But I couldn't sleep a wink all night. I was up before day-light this morning, and I've got two women to work for me to-day fixing up my clothes, and I shall be ready to start to-morrow morning. I want you to keep this matter pretty still till **I get there,** except that you may let cousin **Ephraim know it and get him** to volunteer some of the **Downingville boys for my company.** I want to get them **pretty much all there if I can, for I know what** sort of stuff **the** Downingville **boys are made** of, and shall know what I've **got to depend** upon.

In haste, **your** loving neffu,

CAPTAIN JACK DOWNING.

LETTER XXIV.

UNCLE JOSHUA DESCRIBES TO PRESIDENT JACKSON HOW THEY DRAFTED THE MILITIA COMPANY IN DOWNINGVILLE TO GO WITH CAPT. JACK DOWNING TO THE MADAWASKA WAR.

DOWNINGVILLE, Nov. 6, 1831.

GENERAL JACKSON—*Dear Sir:* I hope you'll excuse me, my makin' bold to write to you, bein' you are President of the United States and I only a humble farmer in the back-woods down here in Maine; but I'm a Republikan to the back-bone, so I kind of think you'll take it in good part. My neffu, Captain Jack Downing, has been here and got his company and started off for Madawaska. He said he ought to write to you before he started, but he was so arnest to get down there and give them New Brumzickers a thrashin' he didn't know how to stop. So I told him to go ahead, and I'd write and tell you all about it arter he was gone. We had the company all drafted and cut and dried for him when he got here, for the Governor of the State had given orders to draft the militia all over the State to be ready for the war down in the disputed territory.

My son Joel has gone down to the boundary war along with the rest of 'em, and we feel bad enough about it, I can tell you. He's too young to go, I know; he's a mere striplin' of a boy yet; he won't be seventeen years old till the fifth day of next May, if he should live to see it. But the poor boy may not live to see that day now; for he's taken his life in his hands, and gone to fight for his country like a man and a hero, live or die. It was a tryin' time to us, Gineral; it was a tryin' time—but I may as well tell you the story, and then you'll know.

After we heard the British had taken our land agent, and carried him off to New Brumzick, we begun to look out for a squall. It was about dark when the post brought the papers that had the account of it; so, arter supper, we all went into father's to talk the matter over. For father knows more about sich matters than anybody else in Downingville—he was out three years in the Revolution, and was in the battle of Lexington before he 'listed, and had the fore-finger of his right hand shot off in the battle of Bunker Hill, jest as he was pulling trigger, and aiming at a British officer that was hurrying up the hill, and driving his soldiers up like a fury. But father always says he didn't lose his shot by it; fur when he found that finger was gone, and wouldn't pull, he tried the next finger, and the old gun went without losing his aim, and the British officer fell; and he always believed it was his shot brought him down. Though father is eighty-five years old now, and is so lame he can't walk about much, yet his mind holds out remarkably, and he can talk about these things as smart as ever he could. His house stands right aside of mine, only fur enough apart for a long shed between 'em, and he used to live in the same house with me, or rather, I lived in the same house with him, till I had so many children, and my family got so large 'twas rather worrisome to the old gentleman, and we was rather scant of room, so I built another house and moved into it, and got cousin Debby to live with the old folks and take care of them.

So, as I said afore, arter supper we took the papers and went into father's, and I sot down and read it all over to him—how a parcel of the British come over into our disputed territory and went to cutting down our timber like smoke, so as to steal it, and carry it off in the spring when the rivers open, away down to New Brumzick; and how our Governor, as soon as he heard about it, sent Mr. McIntire, the land agent, and a hundred and fifty men to put a stop to that stealin' business, and ketch the fellers if he could, and bring 'em off; and how Mr. McIntire took his men and marched off down there into the woods, ever so fur, into our disputed territory, and got all ready and was jest a going to ketch the fellers and bring 'em off up to Augusta, when the thieving chaps turned about and *ketched him,* and put him on a sled and hauled him off down to Fredericton, in New Brumzick, and put him in jail.

When I got along so fur, father couldn't hold still no longer; he struck his staff down on the floor, jest as if it had been a training-gun, and says he:

"Joshua, there'll be trouble; you may depend upon't, there'll be trouble. If our people will stand that, they ain't made of such kind of stuff as the old Revolution folks was made of, nor nothing like it. In them days, if the British had took one of our men and hauled him off to Fredericton, and put him in jail, every man in the old Bay State, and every boy tu, that was big enough to carry a gun, would a shouldered it, and marched to New Brumzick, and Fredericton jail would a been stripped down in no time, and Mr. McIntire brought home agin."

Says I, "father, you mistake; your Revolution folks

couldn't a brought Mr. McIntire home again, for he **was not** there in them days; it's Mr. McIntire that's in jail now."

"Yes they **would**," said the old gentleman, rising out of his chair, and striking his staff down on the floor harder than he did afore; "they'd a gone **after Mr.** McIntire, or any other **man living**, that had American blood in his veins, and they'd **a brought him back**, if they'd had to fit their way through **forty New** Brumzicks for him. Ain't the people waking up **about it no** where? ain't they going down to give them New Brumzicks **a** thrashing?"

I looked **at my son Joel**, and I see his face was all of **a** blaze; and **he looked** as if he was jest a going to burst out

Says I, "Joel, my boy, what's the matter?"

His face grew redder, and the tears came into his eyes, and he struck his fists together, hard enough to crack a walnut.

"By king," says he, "father, I wish I was old enough to train; I want to go down there, and help **give** them are British what they deserve."

"**By the** memory of George Washington!" said my father, "I wish I was young enough to train; I should like to shoulder my gun agin, and go and teach them New Brumzickers better manners. But what are they doing at Augusta? Ain't there no stir about it yet?"

Says I, "we'll read on and see." So I looked over the **papers a little** more, and found the Governor had ordered ten thousand **of the militia** to be drafted to go down and keep the British out of our disputed territory, and prevent their stealing our pine timber.

"That looks something like it," said my father; "that's **a** little like the spunk of old seventy-six. The British 'll have to let our disputed territory alone now, or else they'll have to come to the scratch for it. I wish I was twenty years younger, I'd go down as a volunteer."

"I wish I was only two years **older," said my son** Joel, "then I should stan' a chance to be drafted; and if I wasn't drafted, I'd go, whether or no."

At that my wife and mother both fetched a heavy sigh. Mother said **she** thought father had been through wars enough in his day to rest in his old age, and let sich things alone. My wife, she wiped her eyes, for they was full of tears, and begged Joel not **to talk** so, for he was too young ever to think of sich things. And then she turned to father, and asked him if he really thought there was going to be any war.

"Yes," said father, **"jest as true as** the sun will rise to-morrow, there'll be a **war,** and that pretty **soon tu,** unless the New Brunzickers back out, and give up Mr. McIntire, and let the timber on our disputed territory alone. The orders will be up here to draft the militia within two days, and I shouldn't be surprised if they should be called out before to-morrow morning."

At that my wife and the gals had a **pretty considerable of a** crying spell.

After we'd talked the matter all over, we went home, and went to bed; but we didn't any of us rest very well. My wife she sighed herself to sleep arter awhile; and I heard my son Joel, arter he got to sleep, muttering about guns and the British, and declaring he would go. I had jest got into a drowse, about midnight, when I heard **a heavy** knock at the door. I sprung out of bed, and went and looked out of the window, and asked who was there.

"Sargent Johnson," was the reply. "We've got to stan a draft to-night. The Governor's orders got here about an hour ago. We're sending round to warn our company to meet up here, to Mr. Wilson's tavern, at two o'clock this morning; it's near about one now, and the Captain wants Squire Downing to come over and help see about making the draft. He wants to get through with it as soon as he can, so them that's drafted may be getting ready, for they've got to set out to Bangor at eight o'clock this morning."

I told him I would come right over; and so I lit a candle and dressed myself as quick as I could, and come out into the kitchen to put on my boots, and who should I find there but my son Joel all dressed, and his cap on, ready for a start. He had heard what had been said, and it put the fidgets right into him.

Says he, "Father, I want to go over and see 'em draft." I told him he better be abed and asleep by half. But he said he couldn't sleep; and I found the boy was so arnest to go, that I finally told him he might.

We hadn't more than got dressed, before we heard the drum beat over to Mr. Wilson's tavern; so we started off and went over. When we got there, they had a fire in the large hall, and the company was most all there. The Captain had got a bowl and some black beans and white beans all ready, and he wanted me to draw for them, so they might all feel satisfied there was no partiality. There was one sargent to be drafted, and we drew him first; and it fell to Sargent Johnson. He stood it like a man; I didn't see as he trembled or turned pale a bit. He looked a little redder if anything, and kind of bit his lip as he took his gun and marched into the middle of the floor, and he turned round and looked at the company, and says he,

"I'm ready to go and fight for our country to the last drop of my blood but what we'll make the British back out of our disputed territory, and stop their thieving."

The company gave three cheers for Sargent Johnson, and then we went to drafting the privates. There was eighty in the company, and twenty was to be drafted. So they took sixty white beans and twenty black ones, and put 'em into the bowl, and held it up, so nobody couldn't look into it, and I was to draw 'em out as the orderly sargent called out the names. So when we got ready to begin, the sargent sung out,

"William Jones."

I put my had into the bowl and drawed, and sung out,

"White bean."

"Peter Livermore," cried the sargent.

Peter Livermore started, as if he'd had a shock from an electrical machine; his legs shook a little, and he looked in the face as if he felt rather bad. I put my hand in and drawed, and sung out,

"White bean."

Peter looked better in a minute. He's a great, tall, six-foot chap, and looks as if he could almost whip a regiment of common fellers himself; and although he's something of a brag, it's generally thought, when you come right up to the pinch of the game, he's a little cowardly. Peter stretched his head back, and straddled his legs a little wider, and looked round on the company, and says he,

"I swow, I thought I should a been drafted, and I almost

wish I had. It would a been fun alive to a gone down there, and had a brush 'long with them are New Brumzickers. My old fowling-piece would a made daylight shine through fifty of 'em in half an hour's fighting. I swow I'm disappinted—I was in hopes I should been drafted."

The company knew Peter too well to mind much what he said; they only laughed a little, and the Sargent went on, and called out,

"John Smith, the third."

I drawed to it, and says I,

"White bean."

The Sargent called out again,

"John Downing, the second."

That was the oldest son of Uncle John Downing, the blacksmith, a smart boy, and twenty-three years old. Somehow, as soon as I heard his name, I kind of felt as if he was going to be drafted; and I put in my hand and drawed, and sure enough, I sung out,

"Black bean."

John shouldered his gun in a minute, and marched out into the middle of the floor, and took his stand beside Sargent Johnson. He looked so resolute, and marched so quick, that the company at once gave three cheers for John.

"David Sanborn," cried the Sargent.

"White bean," said I.

"Ichabod Downing," said the Sargent.

I drawed, and answered the same as before,

"White bean."

"Jeremiah Cole," called out the Sargent.

"Black bean," said I; "black bean for Jerry."

After waiting a minute, the Captain called out, "Where's Jerry Cole? Isn't Jerry here?"

"Yes, setting down behind here on a bench," answered half a dozen at once.

"Come Jerry, come forward," said the Captain; "let us see your spunk."

By and by Jerry come creeping out from behind the company, and tried to get across the floor; but his face was as white as a cloth, and he shook and trembled so he couldn't scarcely walk. He let his gun fall on the floor, and sot down in a chair that stood by the side of the room, and boo-hoo'd out a crying like a baby.

"Well done," said the Captain; "there's spunk for you. What's the matter, Jerry—can't you go?"

"Booh-hoo," said Jerry, "I aint well—I'm very sick, Captain; I don't think I could go any way in the world."

"Well, well," said the Captain, "leave your gun, and you may run home as fast as you can go, and see your mother, and we'll get somebody else to go in your room."

At that, Jerry darted out of the door, and pulled foot for home, like a streak of lightning.

"Where's Peter Livermore," said the Captain; "he may take Jerry's place, being he was disappointed at not being drafted." And he called Peter, and told him to take Jerry's gun and stand up in the floor with the drafts. Peter colored as red as you ever see, and begun to sweat. At last, says he:

"Captain, I don't see how I can go any way in the world, my family's out of wood and meal, and a good many other things, and I couldn't leave home."

"Oh," says the Captain, "we'll take care of your family

while you are gone, Peter. Come, take the gun; don't stop **to parley."**

"But, Captain," said Peter, the sweat beginning to roll off his face, "if **I'd** been drafted, Captain, I'd **a** gone with the greatest pleasure in the world, and shouldn't wanted no better fun. But somehow or other, it seems to me like presumption, to go throwing myself into danger, when it wasn't my lot to go. I shouldn't like to go, Captain, without I **was** drafted."

"Well, well," said the Captain, "you needn't go; we want no cowards to go. But who is there here, among the spectators, or among the men whose names have been called, that isn't afraid to take Jerry's gun and fill Jerry's place. If there's any one here that's willing to go, let him come forward."

At that, my son Joel sprung like a young tiger, and seized Jerry's gun, and jumped into the middle of the floor and stood up by the side of Sargent Johnson, and shouldered his gun with so much eagerness, and looked so fierce and determined, although nothing but a striplin' of a boy, that the whole company burst out in three tremendous cheers for Joel Downing. The Captain asked me **if** I was willing he should go. I was never so tried in my life. For my own part, bein' the boy was so brave and wanted to go so much, I should a said yes. But then I knew it would almost kill his mother. So, what to do I didn't know. But I found the boy had got his mind so fixed upon going, that if **he didn't go it** would about kill him. So, on the whole, I told the Captain yes, he might put his name down.

Then we went on with the drafting again and got all through without any more trouble, and got ready to go home about three o'clock. The Captain told them that was drafted that they must all **be ready** to march at eight o'clock in the morning, and they must be in front of the tavern at that hour, and start together for Bangor. My son Joel and I then went home, and made up a fire and routed the folks all out, and told 'em Joel was listed, and got to start at eight o'clock, to fight for our disputed territory. Sich an outcry as there was for about a half an hour I guess you never heard. My wife couldn't a cried harder if Joel had been shot dead there before her feet, though she didn't make much noise about it, for she always cries to herself. The older gals, they cried considerable louder; and some of the younger children, that didn't hardly understand what the trouble was about, sot in and **screamed as loud as** they could bawl.

At last says I, "There's no use in this noise and fuss; the boy's got to go, and he's got to be off at eight o'clock tu, and the sooner we set ourselves to work to get him ready the better." That seemed to wake 'em up a little. My wife went to work and picked up his clothes, and she and the gals sot down and mended his shirts and stockins, and **fried** up a parcel of doughnuts for him to put in his knapsack, and got him all fixed up and breakfast ready about six o'clock. We hadn't waked up old father in the night, bein' he's so old; but in the morning we let him know about it, and he wanted my son Joel to come in and see him before he went; so we went into the old gentleman's room.

"Now, Joel, my boy," said the old gentleman, "I feel proud to hear sich a good report of you. You'd a made a good soldier in the days of the Revolution. 'Twas such boys as you that drove the British from Lexington, and mowed 'em down on Bunker Hill, and went through the fatigue of Burgoine. You'll feel a little queer at first, when you see the enemy coming up to you with their guns pinted right at you; and, brave as you are, you'll feel a little streaked. But you mus'n't mind it; as soon as they've fired once, you wont feel any more of it, and wont keer any more about 'em than you would about a flock of sheep. But don't be in a hurry to fire—mind that— don't be in a hurry to fire; they told us at Bunker Hill not to fire till the enemy got up so near we could see the whites of their eyes. And 'twas a good rule; for by that means we let 'em get up so near, that when we did fire, we mowed 'em down like a field of clover, I can tell you. Be a good boy, Joel, and don't quit our disputed territory as long as there is any dispute about it."

By this time we see 'em begin to gather in the road up by the tavern, and I told Joel it was time to be off; so he took his gun, and his knapsack, which was pretty well stuffed, for each of the children had put in a doughnut or an apple, or a piece of cake, after their mother had crammed in as much as she thought he could carry, and then he marched away like a soldier up to the tavern. When they started they had to come down again by our house and go up over a rise of land t'other way about half a mile, before they got out of sight. So we all stood out in a row along by the side of the road to see 'em as they went by. Father got out as fur as the door-step and stood leaning on his staff, and mother stood behind him with her specs on, looking over his shoulder; and the rest of us, with the children, and cousin Debby, and all, went clear out to the side of the road. Pretty soon they come along by, my son Joel at the head, and the rest marching two and two.

When they got along against us, little Sally run up and tucked another great apple into Joel's pocket, and my wife called out to him, "Now do pray be careful, Joel, and not get shot."

THE DOWNINGVILLE COMPANY STARTING FOR THE WAR.

Then grandfather raised his trembling voice, and says he: "Now Joel, my boy, remember and don't be in a hurry to fire."

And the children called out all together, "good-by, Joel, good-by, Joel," each repeating it over three or four times. Joel looked round and nodded once, when his mother called out to him, but the rest of the time he held his head up straight and marched like a soldier. We stood and watched 'em till they got clear to the top of the hill and was jest a going out of sight, when all to once Joel stepped out one side, where we could see him, and let his old gun blaze away into the air, and in a minute more they were out of sight.

"Ah," said old father, "that sounds like Bunker Hill; that boy 'll do the business for them New Brumzickers, if they don't let our disputed territory alone."

The company had not been gone more than half an hour when my neffu, Captain Jack Downing, arrived with his commission in his pocket. Jack hadn't been in Downingville before for two years, and if there wasn't a time of it among our folks I'll never guess agin. Nabby, she hopped right up and down, like a mouse treed in a flour barrel. Ephraim snapped his thumb and finger, and spit on his hands, as though he had a cord of wood to chop. Aunt Keziah, (that's my wife) she put her apron up to her eyes and cried as much as half an hour, as hard as she could cry. I found I was rather choky, but I took down my pipe and rolled out a few whifs, and so made out to smoke it off. As soon as Jack had a chance to shake hands all round and get a little breakfast, he started off like a streak of chalk to overtake the company and take command.

So I remain your true friend and fellow-laborer in the Republikan cause.

JOSHUA DOWNING.

LETTER XXV.

CAPTAIN DOWNING'S FIRST MILITARY REPORT TO THE PRESIDENT.

MADAWASKA, November 15, 1831.

To His Excellency, Gineral Jackson, President of the United States, &c.

DEAR GINERAL:—The prisoners are out and no blood spilt yet. I had prepared to give the British a most terrible battle if they hadn't let 'em out. I guess I should made 'em think old Bonapart had got back among 'em again, for a keener set of fellows than my company is made up of never shouldered a musket or trod shoe leather. I was pesky sorry they let 'em out quite so soon, for I really longed to have a brush with 'em; and how they come to let 'em go I don't know, unless it was because they heard I was coming. And I expect that was the case, for the prisoners told me the British Minister at Washington sent on some kind of word to Governor Campbell, and I suppose he told him how I had got a commission, and was coming down upon New Brunswick like a harrycane.

If I could only got down there a little sooner and fit such a great battle as you did at New Orleans, my fortune would have been made for this world. I should have stood a good chance then to be President of the United States one of these days. And that's as high as ever I should want to get. I got home to Downingville in little more than a week after I left you at Washington—for having a pretty good pocketfull of money, and knowing that my business was very important, I rid in the stage most all the way. I spose I needn't stop to **tell you how** tickled all my folks were to see **me**. I didn't know for awhile but they'd eat **me up.** But **I** s'pose that's neither here nor there in making military **reports,** so I'll go **on.** I found **no** difficulty in getting volunteers. **I believe I** could have got nearly half the State **of** Maine **to march if I had wanted 'em.** But as I only had **orders to list one good** stout company, **I took** 'em all in Downingville, for **I rather trust myself with one hundred** genuine Downingville boys than five hundred of your common run. **I took** one supernumerary, however, when I got to Bangor. The editor **of the** Bangor Republican was so zealous to go, and said he'd fight so to the last drop of his blood, that I couldn't help taking him, so I appointed him supernumerary corporal. Poor fellow, he was so disappointed when he found the prisoners were out that he fairly cried for vexation. He's for having me go right on now and give all **New** Brunswick a real thrashing.

But I know what belongs to gineralship better than that; I haven't had my orders yet. Well, after we left Bangor, we had a dreadful rough and tumble sort of a journey, over rocks, and mountains, and rivers, and swamps, and bogs, and meadows, and through long pieces of woods, that I didn't know as **we** should find the way out of. But we got through at last, and arrived **here at** Madawaska day before yesterday. I thought **I better come this** way and make a little stop at Madawaska **to see if** the prisoners' **wives and** little ones were in want of anything, and then go down to Fredericton and blow the British sky-high.

When **our** company first came out in sight in Madawaska,

they thought it was the British coming to catch some more of 'em; and such a scattering and scampering I guess you never see. The men flew into the woods like a flock of sheep with forty dogs after 'em, and the women catched their babies up in their arms and run from one house to another, screeching and screaming enough to make the woods ring again. But when they found out we were United States troops come to help 'em, you never see anybody so glad. They all cried for joy then. The women run into the woods and called for their husbands to come back again, for there was nobody there that would hurt them, and back they came and treated us with the best they had in their houses. And while we sot chatting, before the women hardly got their tears wiped up, one of 'em looked up toward the woods and screamed out *there comes the prisoners.* Some turned pale a little, thinking it might be their ghosts, but in a minute in they come, as good flesh and blood as any of us, and then the women had another good crying spell.

I asked one of the prisoners how they got away, for I thought you would want to know all about it; and says he, "we come away on our legs." "Did you break out of jail," said I? "I guess there was no need of that," said he, "for we wa'nt locked in half the time." "Did you knock down the guard," said I, "and fight your way out?" "Humph!" said he, "I guess we might have hunted one while before we could find a guard to knock down. Nobody seemed to take any care of us; if we wanted a drop of grog we had to go out and buy it ourselves." "Well, but" said I, "if you were left in such a loose state as that, why did you not run away before?" "Tut," said he, shrugging up his shoulders, "I guess we knew what we were about; the longer we staid there the **more** land the State of Maine would give us to pay us **for** being put in jail; but when they turned us out of jail, **and** wouldn't keep us any longer, we thought we **might as well come home."**

And now, dear Gineral, since matters are **as they are, I shall** take up **my** headquarters here **at Madawaska for the present, and** wait **for further orders.** I shall take good care **of** the people here, and **keep everything in good order and not allow** a single New Brunswicker to come anywhere within gun-shot. **As** for that Leftenant-Governor, Mr. Archibald **Campbell,** he better keep himself scarce; if he shows his head here again, **I shall jest** put him into **a meal bag and** send him to Washington. I shall expect to **hear from you** soon; and as I shall have to be **here sometime, I don't** know but you **had** better send me on a little more money. My uniform got rather shattered **coming through the woods, and it** will cost me something to get it fixt up again.

This, from your old friend and humble servant,

CAPTAIN JACK DOWNING.

LETTER XXVI.*

MR. DOWNING TELLS HOW THE JACKSONITES IN THE LEGISLATURE HAD A DREADFUL TUSSLE TO POUR A "HEALING ACT" DOWN THE THROATS OF THE HUNTONITES.

Portland, Feb. 4, 1831.

Dear Uncle Joshua :—There's terrible times here again, and I'm half afraid it's going to be worse than it was last winter. The Legislater's been all in the wind this two or three days, pulling and hauling and fighting like smoke. The wheels of Government are all stopt; I can't say as they are *trigged*, as they used to be lyst winter, but they are fairly stopped, because nobody don't pull 'em along ; for when the members are

---

* Editorial Note.—The bitterness of feeling occasioned by the struggle for the ascendency between the two parties in 1830, still rankled in the breasts of the members of the Legislature in 1831. The Huntonites had acquired the ascendency the preceding session, but now the Jacksonites were in power, and they contended that the acts of the Huntonites in 1830 were unconstitutional and void. They therefore set about preparing a "healing act" to declare all the doings of the preceding Legislature *valid* in the lump. When this bill was brought forward, it produced a storm in the Legislature, almost unparalleled. The Huntonites considered it altogehter a useless, provoking piece of political trickery. They contended that if the acts of the former Legislature were in fact unconstitutional, no law passed by this Legislature could make them constitutional, and considering it a wanton attempt to heap insult and odium upon them, they fought against it almost while life and breath remained. A fierce debate on the passage of this bill was carried on for several days. But the Jacksonites had the power in their own hands, and the bill was finally passed. The scene is somewhat minutely described in the accompanying letter.

all pulling each other's caps, how can they pull the wheels of
Government? My heart's been up in my mouth a dozen times
for fear the State would go to ruin before I could get out of
it; and I've scratched round and picked up what few bean-
poles and ax-handles I had left, and got all ready to set sail
to Boston, for I'm determined to be off before the State goes to
rack. And I advise you and all our friends at Downingville
to pack up as soon as you get this letter, and be all ready as
soon as you hear a cracking down this way to fly for your
lives away back into New-Hampshire or Vermont. The
trouble, as near as I could understand it, begun in this way:
The Jacksonites said the Huntonites worked so hard last winter in trying to trig the wheels of Government, and tear the
Constitution to pieces, that they made themselves all sick,
dreadful sick, and hadn't got well yet; and it was time to do
something to try to cure 'em; for their sickness was so catching that all the State would be taken down with it in a little
while, if they want cured.

But the Huntonite said they want sick abit; they never
was better in their lives; and moreover, it was false that they
had tried to trig the wheels of Government last winter; or tear
a single leaf out of the Constitution; if anything of that kind
was done, they said the Jacksonites did it, and as for taking
doctor's stuff they'd no notion of it. But the Jacksonites said
'twas no use, the Huntonites were all sick, and they must take
some doctor stuff, and if they wouldn't take it willingly they
must be *made* to take it. So they went to work and fixed a dose
that they called a *healing act*, that they said would cure all the
Huntonites and anybody else that had catched the sickness of
'em. The Huntonites declared 'twas no use for 'em to fix it,

for they never would take it as long as they lived, that's what they wouldn't; they were as well as anbody, and they'd fight it out till next June before they'd take it. Howsomever, the Jacksonites got their dose ready, and yesterday they carried it into the House of Representatives and told the Huntonites they must take it, and 'twould do 'em good. As soon as the Huntonites smelt of it, they turned up their noses, and said no, before they'd take that are plaguy dirty stuff they'd fight 'em all over the State, inch by inch. But the Jacksonites said 'twas no use—they might sniff as much as they pleased—it was the only thing that would cure 'em, and they must take it, and more than all that, they was the strongest and they *should* take it. The Huntonites see how 'twas gone goose with 'em, and they thought the on'y chance left was to put their hands over their mouth and fight and kick and scrabble with all their might, and keep it out of their throats as long as they could. Still they tried to talk and reason with the Jacksonites about it. They asked 'em to let 'em have time to examine the medicine carefully and see what it was made of, or that they would tell 'em what it was made of, or why they thought it would do any good to take it. But the Jacksonites said they shouldn't tell 'em anything about it, it would be " casting pearls before swine," and the good book said they musn't do so.

The men who had fixed the dose knew what they were about, they had fixed it right, and the Huntonites must open their mouths and take it, and not parley any more about it. Well, the Jacksonites took the dose in one hand, and grab'd the Huntonites with the other, and tipped their heads back, and were jest agoing to pour it down their throats, when the Huntonites fetched a spring and kicked it away to the fourth day of April. But the Jacsonites run after it and got it back again in about half an hour, and clinched 'em again, and got all ready to pour it down ; but jest as they got it almost to their lips, the Huntonites fetched another spring, and kicked it away to the fourth of March. Away went the Jacksonites after it again, and brought it back, and clinched the Huntonites in the same manner as before, and they kicked it away again, but they didn't kick this time quite to the end of February. Well, after the Jacksonites, had tried nearly twenty times to pour down the bitter dose, and the Huntonites had kicked it away as many times, both parties seemed to be nearly tired out, and so they finally agreed to adjourn till nine o'clock next morning. I thought the Huntonites, if they once got out, would cut and run home and get clear of the plaguy stuff. But instead of that they all come in again next morning. When I got there the Jacksonites were holding the Huntonites by the hair of the head with one hand and trying to cram the healing plaster down their throats with t'other, and the Huntonites were kicking and scrabbling, and gritting their teeth together with all their might, and doubling up their fists and stamping, and declaring up hill and down that they would never take it. And they were so upstropulous about it for awhile, I didn't know as they ever would swallow it. But the Jacksonites were the stoutest, and held on to 'em like a dog to a root, and kept 'em there all day and all the evening till about midnight, and then the poor Huntonites seemed to be a most dragged out. I fairly pitied 'em. Along in the first of it they threatened pretty stoutly, and declared by everything that's black and blue, if they had to take this dirty dose, and should happen to be strongest next year, they'd make the Jacksonites take a dose worth two of this. But all the threatening didn't do any good; and then they fell to begging and coaxing, and that didn't do any good nuther. The Jacksonites said they should not only take it, but they should take it that night before they slept. At last they got their hands

FORCING THE "HEALING-ACT" DOWN THE THROATS OF THE HUNTONITES.

and feet tied, and kept bringing it up a little nearer and little nearer to their mouths, and the Huntonites got so they couldn't do nothing but *spit*. But the Jacksonites didn't mind the spitting, for you know it isn't for the doctor to stand about being spit upon a little, when he's giving medicine. Just before the last on't, the poor Huntonites rolled their eyes dreadfully, and I believe some on 'em lost their senses a little; one of 'em took a notion that they were agoing to make him swallow a whole live goose, feathers and all; and he begged of 'em, if they wouldn't take out the gizzard and t'other inside things, that they'd jest pull out the pin feathers, so that it wouldn't scratch his throat going down. But they didn't pay no attention to him, and just before the clock struck twelve they grabbed 'em by the throat, and pried their mouths open, and poured it in. The Huntonites guggled a little, but they had to swallow it.

Some thought this healing dose would make the Huntonites worse, and some thought it would make 'em better. I've watched 'em ever since they took it, whenever I dared to go near the Legislater, and I can't see much alteration in 'em. But that, or something else, has kicked up a monstrous dust among other folks all over the world amost. I've been looking over the newspapers a little, and I never see the world in such a terrible hubbub before in all my life. Everybody seems to be running mad, and jest ready to eat each other up. There's Russia snapping her teeth like a great bear, and is jest agoing to eat up the Poles—I don't mean Ephraim's bean poles—but all the folks that live in Poland; not that are Poland up there where Mr. Dunn lives, but that great Poland over alongside of Russia. And there's the Dutch trying to eat up Holland, and the Belgians are trying to eat up the Dutch, and there's "five great powers" trying to pour a healing dose down the throat of the King of the Netherlands; and there's Mr. O'Connell trying to make the King of

England and Parliament take a healing dose, and there's Ireland jest ready to eat up Mr. O'Connell, and all the kings of Europe are trying to eat up the people, and the people are all trying to eat up the kings.

And our great folks in this country, too, away off there to Washington, have got into such a snarl, I guess it would puzzle a Philadelphy lawyer to get 'em out of it. There's the President, and Mr. Calhoun, and Mr. Van Buren, and the two great Republikan papers, and half a dozen more of 'em, all together by the ears; but which of 'em will eat up the rest I don't know. I've heard a good many guess that Mr. Van Buren would eat up the whole toat of 'em; for they say, although he's a small man, there isn't another man in the country that can eat his way through a political pudding as slick as he can. These are dreadful times, uncle; I don't know what'll become of the world if I don't get an office pretty soon. But a faint heart never won fair lady, and I shall stick to it like a dog to a root.

Your loving neffu,

JACK DOWNING

LETTER XXVII.*

CAPTAIN DOWNING IS IN A PECK OF TROUBLE ABOUT THE LEGISLATURE'S SELLING MADAWASKA TO THE GENERAL GOVERNMENT, TO BE GIVEN UP TO THE BRITISH, AND SITS DOWN AND FIGURES UP THE PRICE.

> MADAWASKA, State of Maine, *or else* Great
> Britain, I don't know which,
> March 12, 1832.

To the Editor of the Portland Courier—this with care and speed:

MY DEAR OLD FRIEND :—I cleared out from Augusta in such a kind of a whirlwind that I hadn't time to write you a single word before I left. And I feel so kind of crazy now, I don't know hardly which end I stand upon. I've had a good many head-flaws and worriments in my lifetime, and been in a great many hobbles, but I never, in all my born days, met with anything that puzzled me quite so bad as this ere *selling*

---

* EDITORIAL NOTE.—Captain Downing went to Madawaska with his company in November, 1831, and remained there till the Spring of 1832, when he returned to Washington. He had visited the Legislature, at Augusta, twice during the winter, and came about as near being lost among the cold, snowy mountains around Moosehead Lake as Colonel Fremont did in crossing the Rocky Mountains. He published, in the Portland Courier, some account of these perilous journeys back and forth between Augusta and Madawaska, and also various proceedings of the Legislature during the winter. While taking an active part in the proceedings of the lobby, he learned that the General Government had agreed with England to refer this question of disputed territory to the King of the Netherlands, and to abide by his decision. Instead of deciding that the disputed territory belonged to either party, the King of the Netherlands concluded to split the difference, and run a new

out down here. I fit in the Legislater as long as fighting would do any good—that is, I mean in the caucus, for they wouldn't let me go right into the Legislater in the day time and talk to 'em there, because I was only a lobby member. But jest let them know it, lobby members can do as much as any of 'em on sich kind of business as this. I laid it down to 'em in the caucus as well as I could. I asked 'em if they didn't think I should look like a pretty fool, after marching my company down there, and standing ready all winter to flog the whole British nation the moment any of 'em stept a foot on to our land, if I should now have to march back again and give up the land, and all without flogging a single son-of-a-gun of 'em. But they said it was no use—it couldn't be helped; Mr. Netherlands had given the land away to the British, and the President had agreed to do jest as Mr. Netherlands said about it, and all we could do now was to get as much pay for it as we could.

So I sot down and figured it up a little, to see how much it would come to, for I used to cypher to the rule of three when I went to school, and I found it would come to a pretty round sum. There was, in the first place, about two millions of

---

boundary line. This would transfer to the British Provinces some two millions of acres of land, that was resolutely claimed by the State of Maine. The matter was warmly discussed in the Legislature, and a strong party was violently opposed to giving up the territory—they would rather fight for it; they contended that the General Government had no authority to cede away the territory of a sovereign State. It was understood, however, that the General Government would pay a fair indemnity for the land to Maine and Massachusetts (for it was undivided land, belonging to the two States), and this consideration finally reconciled a majority of the Legislature to the arrangement. What Captain Jack Downing and his brave Downingville boys thought of the matter will be learned from the accompanying letter, from the Captain to the Portland Courier.

acres of land. This, considerin' the timber there was on it, would certainly be worth a dollar an acre, and that would be two millions of dollars. Then there was two or three thousand inhabitants, say twenty-five hundred; we must be paid for them, too; and how much are they worth? I've read in the newspapers that black slaves, at the South, sell for three or four hundred dollars apiece. I should think, then, that white ones ought to fetch eight hundred. This, according to the rule of three, would be two hundred thousand dollars. Then there's the pretty little town of Madawaska, that our Legislater made last winter, already cut and dried, with **town** officers all chosen, and everything ready for the British to use without any more trouble. We ought to have pay for this, too, and I should think it was worth ten thousand dollars.

And then the town of Madawaska has chosen Mr. Lizote to be a representative in the Legislater, and as the British can take him right into **the** Parliament, without choosing him over again, they ought to pay us for that, too. Now, I have read in the newspapers that it sometimes costs, in England, two hundred thousand dollars to choose a representative to Parliament, reckoning all the grog they drink and all the money **they** pay for votes. But I wouldn't be screwing about it, so I **put** Mr. Lizote down at one hundred thousand dollars. And then I footed up, and found it to be:

For land, including timber............................	$2,000,000
For inhabitants, including women and children........	200,000
For the town of Madawaska, officers **and all**............	10,000
For Mr. Lizote, **all** ready **to go to** Parliament.........	100,000
Total...	$2,310,000

This was a pretty round sum, and I begun to think, come

to divide it out, it would be a slice apiece worth having, especially if we didn't give the Feds any of it; and I supposed **we shouldn't**, as there **wasn't** any of 'em there in the caucus to help see about it.

In this view of the subject, I almost made up my mind that we ought to be patriotic enough to give it up, and help the General Government out of the hobble they had got into. And I was jest agoing to get up and make a speech, and tell 'em so, when Mr. McCrate, of Nobleborough, and Captain Smith, of Westbrook, two of the best fellers in our party, came along and see what I was figuring about, and says they, "Captain Downing, *are you going to sell your country?*" In a minute I felt something rise right up in my throat, that felt as big as an ox-yoke. As soon as I got so I could speak, says I, "*No, never,* while my name is Jack Downing, or my old rifle can carry a bullet." They declared, too, that they wouldn't *sell out* to the General Government, nor the British, nor nobody else. And we stuck it out most of the evening, till we found out how it was going, and then we cleared out; and as soon as the matter was fairly settled, I started off for Madawaska, for I was afraid, if my company should hear of it before I got there, it would make a blow up among 'em, and I should have to court-martial 'em.

When I first told 'em how the jig was up with us, that the British were going to have the land without fighting about it, I never see fellows so mad before in my life, unless it was Major Eaton, at Washington, when he sot out to flog Mr. Ingham. They said, if they could only have had one good battle, they wouldn't care a snap about it, but to be played tom-fool with in this way, they wouldn't bear it. They were so mad they hopped right up and down, and declared they never would go back till they had been over to Fredericton and pulled the jail down, or thrashed some of the New Brunswick boys. But, after awhile, I pacified 'em by telling 'em if we didn't get a chance to fight here, I rather thought we might away off to Georgia, for there was something of a bobbery kicking up ; and if the President should want troops to go on there, I was very sure my company would be one of the first he would send for.

So here we are, lying upon our arms, not knowing what to do. I have written to the President, and hope to hear from him soon. If the land is to go, I want to know it in season to get off before it's all over ; for I'll be hanged if ever I'll belong to the British.

   Your distrest friend,

      CAPTAIN JACK DOWNING.

LETTER XXVIII.

CAPTAIN DOWNING RELATES A CONFIDENTIAL CONVERSATION WITH PRESIDENT JACKSON WHILE ON A JOURNEY TO TENNESSEE.

WASHINGTON CITY, October 20, 1832.

To the Editor of the Portland Courier, away Down East, in the State of Maine: [O, dear! seems to me I never shall get there again.]

MY DEAR OLD FRIEND :—I haven't done anything this three months that seemed so natural as to set down and write to you. To write the name of the Portland Courier raises my sperits right up. It makes me feel as if I was again talking with you, and Uncle Joshua, and Cousin Ephraim, and Cousin Nabby, and Ant Sally, and all of 'em. I and President Jackson got back here yesterday from Tennessee, where we've been gone most all summer. And a long journey we've had of it, too. I thought that from here to Portland was a dreadful ways, but it's a great deal further to Tennessee. I didn't think before that our country was half so large as I find it is. It seems as if there was no end to it; for when we got clear to Tennessee the President said we wan't half way across it. I couldn't hardly believe him; but he stood tu it we wan't. "Why," says he, "Jack, I've got the largest country in the world, and the hardest to govern tu. Say what you will of free Governments, where folks will act pretty much as they are a mind to, it's the hardest work to administer it that ever

I did. I had rather fight forty New Orleans battles than to govern this everlasting great country one year. There are so many, you see, who want to have a finger in the pie, it's the most difficult business you can imagine. You thought you had a tough time of it, Jack, to take care of them are small matters down to Madawaska last winter, with your brave company of Downingville boys. But that's no more than a drop in the bucket to being President one month. I tell you, Jack, there isn't a monarch in Europe who has so hard a time of it as I have. There are so many cooks, the broth most always comes out rather bad. If I have to write a message, one must put in a sentence, and another a sentence, and another, till it gets so at last I can't hardly tell whether I've written any of it myself or not. And sometimes I have a good mind to throw it all in the fire and say nothing at all. But then, again, that won't do, for since I've undertaken to be President, I must go through with it. And then there was such a pulling and hauling for offices along in the outset, it seemed as though they would pull me to pieces. If I gave an office to one, Mr. Ingham or Mr. Branch would be mad, and if I gave it to another, Mr. Van Buren wouldn't like it, and if I gave it to another, perhaps Mrs. Eaton would make a plaguy fuss about it. One wanted me to do this thing, and another wanted me to do that; and it was nothing but quarrel the whole time. At last Mr. Van Buren said he'd resign if I would turn the rest out. So I made a scattering among 'em, and turned 'em all out in a heap—all but Mr. Lewis and Mr. Kendall, who staid to give me their friendly advice and help me through my trying difficulties.

"And then, again, to be so slandered as I have been in the

papers, it is enough to wear the patience of Job out. **And if
I got a little angry at the contrariness of the Senate, they
must needs call me a 'roaring lion,' the rascals. But that
Senate did use me shamefully. The very best nominations I
made,** they always rejected. **To think the stupid heads should
reject** Mr. Van Buren—decidedly the greatest man in the
country—it was **too provoking.** Yes, Mr. Van Buren is the
first man in this country ; and jest between you and me, Jack,
he's the only man in it that is **well qualified to succeed me in
the government of this great nation of twenty-four republics.
And he must come in, too, or the country won't be worth a
stiver much longer. There's Clay, he would make pretty
work of it, if he should come in. Why, Jack,** he would
**gamble one-half of the country away in two years, and spend
the other half in digging canals** and building **railroads ; and
when the** funds **in the Treasury** failed, **he would** go **to the
United States Bank and get more.**

" Calhoun would break the Union to pieces in three months
if he was President. **He's** trying all he can now **to tear off
something of a slice from it at the South. And** as for Wirt,
he's a fiddling away with **the Anti-Masons.** Letting Anti-
Masonry alone, he's **a pretty good sort of** a man ; but he
hasn't energy enough to steer **our crazy ship of state** in these
stormy times. I would **sooner trust it in** the hands of **Mrs.
Eaton** than him. There's no **one** fit for it but Mr. **Van Buren** ;
and if it was not for getting him in, I wouldn't have consented
to stand for another term.

But, my dear friend, by stopping to tell you some of the
conversation I and the President had along the road, I have
almost forgot to tell you anything about myself and the thou-

sand things I met with on my journey. But I cannot write any more to-day. I expect to start from here Monday, **on my way to Portland. You may hear from me a few times** before **I get** there, as I shall stop along by **the way some, to see** how **matters go** in Pennsylvany **and New York.**

If you have a chance, send my love to all my folks **up at** Downingville, and tell 'em old Jack **is** alive and hearty.

I remain your loving friend,

CAPTAIN JACK DOWNING.

LETTER XXIX.*

CAPTAIN DOWNING RUNS AN EXPRESS FROM **BALTIMORE TO WASHINGTON, AND FOOTS IT THROUGH PENNSYLVANIA AVENUE TO THE PRESIDENT'S HOUSE.**

WASHINGTON CITY, Nov. 5, 1832.

To the Editor of the Portland Courier, in the Mariner's Church Building, second story, eastern end, Fore street, Portland, away Down East, in the State of Maine:

MY DEAR OLD FRIEND:—Here I am, back again to Washington, though I've been as far as Baltimore, on my way Down East, to see you and the rest of my uncles, and aunts, and cousins. And what do you think I posted back to Washington for? I can tell you. When I got to Baltimore I met an *express* coming on, full chisel, from Philadelphia, to carry the

---

* EDITORIAL NOTE.—The second election of General Jackson to the Presidency, November 4, 1832, was a marked era in American politics. The great questions in issue before the country were a re-charter of the United States Bank, a high tariff for the protection of manufactures, distribution among the States of the proceeds of the sales of public lands, and a general system of internal improvements by the Federal Government. Mr. Clay was the leader of the party in favor of these measures, and their candidate for the Presidency. Mr John Sergeant, of Pennsylvania, was placed on the same ticket for Vice-President. On the opposite side, General Jackson was the candidate for a second term, and Mr. Van Buren for Vice-President. It will be remembered, that after the blow-up or resignation of General Jackson's first Cabinet, Mr. Van Buren had been sent, by the President, as Minister to England, but, on the meeting of Congress, his nomination was rejected by the Senate—much to the chagrin of General Jackson; whereupon he was taken

news to Washington that Pennsylvany had gone all hollow for Old Hickory's second election. The poor fellow that was carrying it had got so out of breath, that he declared he couldn't go no further if the President never heard of it.

Well, thinks I, it will be worth a journey back to Washington, jest to see the old Gineral's eyes strike fire when he hears of it. So says I, "I'll take it, and carry it on for you, if you are a mind to." He kind of hesitated at first, and was afraid I might play a trick upon him; but when he found out my name was Jack Downing, he jumped off his horse quick enough. "I'll trust it with you," says he, "as quick as I would with the President himself." So I jumped on, and whipped up. And sure enough, as true as you are alive, I did get to Washington before dark, though I had but three hours to go it in, and it's nearly forty miles. It was the smartest horse that ever I backed, except one that belongs to the President. But, poor fellow, he's so done tu I guess he'll never run another express. Jest before I got to Washington, say about two miles from the city, the poor fellow keeled up,

up by the "unterrified Democracy" to run as Vice-President on the ticket with "Old Hickory;" and both were triumphantly elected. Out of two hundred and eighty-eight votes, Mr. Clay received but forty-nine. South Carolina refused to vote for either party, and threw away her vote on Governor Floyd, of Virginia. Vermont voted for Mr. Wirt, the Anti-Masonic candidate, and the rest voted for "Old Hickory." Mr. Van Buren received the same vote, with the exception of Pennsylvania, whose vote for Vice-President was cast for one of her own sons, Mr. Wilkins, then a Senator in Congress. In that election there was intense anxiety throughout the country in regard to the vote of Pennsylvania, as was recently the case in the election of Mr. Buchanan, for it was thought the main question would turn on the result in that State. This state of things accounts for the running of the express from Baltimore to Washington by Major Downing, and other curious matters related in the two accompanying letters.

and couldn't go another step. I had lost my hat on the way, and was too much in a hurry to pick it up, and he had thrown me off twice and torn my coat pretty bad, so that I didn't look very trig to go through the city, or go to the President's fine

CAN'T STOP FOR YOUR OLD STAGE—GOT AN EXPRESS FOR THE GINERAL.

house. But, notwithstanding, I knew the President would overlook it, considering the business I was coming upon; so I catched the express, and pulled foot right through Pennsylvany Avenue, without any hat, and torn coat sleeves and coat-tail flying. The stage offered to carry me, but I thought I wouldn't stop for it.

Almost the first person I met was Mr. Duff Green. Says he, "Captain Downing, what's the matter?" I held up the express and shook it at him, but never answered him a word, and pulled on. He turned and walked as fast as he could without running, and followed me. Pretty soon I met Mr. Gales, of the Intelligencer, and says he, "For mercy sake, Captain Downing, what's the matter? Have you been chased by a wolf, or Governor Houston, or have you got news from Pennsylvania?" I didn't turn to the right nor left, but shook the express at him and run like wildfire.

When I came up to the President's house, the old gentleman was standing in the door. He stepped quicker than I ever see him before, and met me at the gate. Says he, "My dear friend Downing, what's the matter? Has the United States Bank been trying to bribe you, and you are trying to run away from 'em? They may buy over Webster and Clay and such trash, but I knew if they touched you they would get the wrong pig by the ear." As he said this, Duff Green hove in sight, puffing and blowing at full speed.

"Oh," said the President, "Duff Green wants to have a lick at you, does he? Well, don't retreat another step, Mr. Downing; I'll stand between you and harm." Upon that he called his boy, and told him to bring his pistols in a moment. By this time I made out to get breath enough jest to say Pennsylvany, and to shake the express at him. The old man's color changed in a minute. Says he, "Come in, Mr. Downing, come in—set down—don't say a word to Duff." So we went in, and shut the door. "Now," says the President, looking as though he would route a regiment in five minutes, " now speak, and let me know whether I am a dead man or alive."

"Gineral," says I, "it's all over with "———. "I won't hear a word of it," says he, stomping his foot. His eyes flashed fire so that I trembled and almost fell backward. But I see he didn't understand me. "Dear Gineral," says I, "it's all over with Clay and the Bank." At that he clapt his hands and jumpt like a boy. I never see the President jump before, as much as I've been acquainted with him. In less than a minute he looked entirely like another man. His eyes were as calm and as bright as the moon jest coming out from behind a black thunder-cloud.

He clenched my hand, and gave it such a shake I didn't know but he would pull it off. Says he, "Jack, I knew Pennsylvany would never desert me, and if she has gone for me I'm safe. And now if I don't make them are Bank chaps hug it, my name isn't Andrew Jackson. And after all, Jack, I aint so glad on my own account that I am re-elected as I am for the coutry and Mr. Van Buren. This election has all been on Mr. Van Buren's account, and we shall get him now to be President after me. And you know, Jack, that he's the only man, after me, that's fit to govern this country."

The President has made me promise to stop and spend the night with him, and help him rejoice over the victory. But I haven't time to write any more before the mail goes.

Your loving friend,

CAPTAIN JACK DOWNING.

LETTER XXX.

CAPTAIN DOWNING RECEIVES A MAJOR'S COMMISSION, AND IS APPOINTED TO MARCH AGAINST THE NULLIFIERS.

WASHINGTON CITY, Dec. 8, 1832.

To the Editor of the Portland Courier, in the Mariners' **Church** *Building, second story,* **eastern** *end,* **Fore** *street, Portland,* **away** *Down East, in the State of Maine.*

MY DEAR OLD FRIEND :—I believe the last time I wrote to you was when I come back with the express from Baltimore, and Duff Green chased me so through the streets **to** find out what **I was bringing, and the** President thought he was running to **get a lick at me, and** called for his pistols to stand between **me** and harm, **you know.** Well, I intended to turn right about again after I had made the old gentleman's heart jump up by telling **him** that he had got Pennsylvany, and would be elected as sure as eggs was bacon, and make the best of my way toward Portland. For you can't think how I long to see you **and** Uncle Joshua and Ant Keziah and Cousin Ephraim and Cousin Nabby and all the rest of the dear souls up in Downingville. It seems as though it was six years instead **of six** months since **I left that part of the** country, and when I shall be able to get back again is more than I can tell now ; **for I** find when a man once gets into public life he can never say his time is his **own** ; he must always stand ready to go where **his country calls.** The long and the short of it is, the President has got so many other fish for me to fry, it's no use for me to think of going home yet. That evening, after I got back with the express, the President said we must honor this

REJOICING OVER THE VICTORY IN PENNSYLVANIA.

victory in Pennsylvany with a glass of wine. "I am sure," said he, "Captain Downing, you will have no objection to take a glass with me on this joyful occasion." I told him as for that matter, I supposed I could take a glass of wine upon a pinch, even if the occasion was not half so joyful. So we had two or three bottles full brought in, and filled up the glasses. "And now," says the President, "I will give you a toast. The State of Pennsylvany—the most patriotic State in the Union; for though I go against all her great public interests, still she votes for me by an overwhelming majority."

He then called for my toast. And what could I give but my dear native "Downingville—the most genuine, unwavering Democratic Republikan town in New England."

"Good," said the President; "and that Downingville has never been rewarded yet. You shall have a Post-Office established there; and name to me which of your friends you would like should be Postmaster, and he shall be appointed."

The President then gave his second toast: "Martin Van Buren, the next President of the United States, and the only man in the country that is fit for it. Captain Downing, your toast if you please."

So I gave, "Uncle Joshua Downing, the most thorough-going Republikan in Downingville."

"Good," said the President; "I understand you, Captain Downing; your Uncle Joshua shall have the Post-Office."

His third toast was the "Editor of the Washington Globe;" and mine was the "Editor of the Portland Courier." But I told him he musn't ask me for any more toasts, for that was as fur as I could go.

The President toasted some more of his friends, sich as Major Eaton, and Mr. Kendall, and Mr. Lewis, and the Hon. Isaac Hill, and so on, 'til it got to be pretty late in the evening; and I told the President I would be glad if he would excuse me, for

I wanted to start early in the morning on my way Down East, and I thought I should feel better if I could get a little nap first. And, besides, I had got to go and get the old lady that used to do my washing and mending to patch up my coat, that got such a terrible shipwreck by being thrown off the horse with the express.

"Start Down East to-morrow morning, Captain Downing," said he; "you must not think of it. I have an important and delicate job on hand, which I can't get along with very well without your assistance. There's that miserable, ambitious Calhoun has been trying this dozen years to be President of the United States, but he can't make out; so now he is determined to lop off a few of the Southern States and make himself President of them. But if he don't find he's mistaken, my name isn't Andrew Jackson."

As he said this, he started up on his feet, and begun to march across the floor with a very soldier-like step, and his eyes fairly flashed fire.

"No," said he, "Captain Downing, he must wait till somebody else is President besides me before he can do that. Let him move an inch by force in this business, if he dares. I'll chase him as far beyond Tennessee as it is from here there but what I'll catch him, and string him up by the neck to the first tree I can find. I must send some troops out there to South Carolina to reconnoiter and keep matters strait, and your gallant defense of Madawaska last winter points you out as the most suitable man to take the command. I shall give you a major's commission tomorrow, and wish you to enlist two or three companies of brave volunteers and hold yourself in readiness to obey orders. In case we should have to come to a real brush," said the President, "I shall take command myself, and make you lieutenant-general. But I wish you to bear in mind, let what will come, never to shoot that Calhoun. Shooting is too good for him. He must dance upon nothing, with a rope round his neck. As for your coat, Captain Downing, don't trouble the old lady with it. I'll give you one of mine to wear 'til you get a suit of regimentals made."

I told him I felt a little uneasy about taking command among strangers, unless I could have my Downingville company with me.

"Send for them," said the President ; "by all means, send for them. There are no troops equal to 'em, except it is the Tennessee boys." So I shall forthwith send orders to Sargent Joel to march 'em on here. As I am to have my commission to-morrow, I shall venture to subscribe myself your friend,

MAJOR JACK DOWNING.

LETTER XXXI.

UNCLE JOSHUA TELLS WHAT A TUSSLE THEY HAD IN DOWNINGVILLE TO KEEP THE FEDERALISTS FROM PRAISING THE PRESIDENT'S PROCLAMATION AGAINST THE NULLIFIERS.

DOWNINGVILLE, State of Maine, Dec. 27, 1832.

To Major Jack Downing, at Washington City, or if he has gone to South Carolina, I want President Jackson to send this along tu him.

MY DEAR NEFFU :—We had almost gin you up for dead, you had been gone so long before we got your letter in the Portland Courier, telling how you had been away to Tennessee along with President Jackson. Your poor mother had pined away so that she had nothing left, seemingly, but skin and bones, and your Cousin Nabby had cried her eyes half out of her head, poor girl. But when the Portland Courier came, bringing that are letter of yourn, Downingville was in a complete uproar all day. Sargent Joel had come home from Madawaska and dismissed your company, and gone to work in the woods chopping wood. But as soon as he heard your letter had come, he dropped his ax, and I don't think he's touched it since; and he put on his regimentals, and scoured up the old piece of a scythe that he used to have for a sword and stuck it into his waistband, and strutted about like a major-gineral Your mother begun to pick up her crumbs immediately, and has been growing fat ever since. And Nabby run about from house to house, like a crazy bed-bug, telling 'em Jack was alive, and was agoing to build up Downingville and make something out of it yet.

We got your last letter and the President's proclamation both together, though I see your letter was written two days first. You know I've made politics my study for thirty years, and I must say it's the most ginuine Republikan thing I ever come acrost. But what was most provoking about it was, all the old Federalists in town undertook to praise it tu. Squire Dudley, you know, was always a Federalist, and an Adams man tu. I met him the next day after the proclamation come, and he was chock full of the matter. Says he, "Mr. Downing, that proclamation is jest the thing. It's the true constitutional doctrine. We all support the President in this business through thick and thin."

My dander began to rise, and I could not hold in any longer. Says I, "Squire Dudley, shet up your clack, or I'll knock your clam-shells together pretty quick. It's got to be a pretty time of day indeed, if after we've worked so hard to get President Jackson in, you Federalists are going to undertake to praise his proclamation as much as though he was your own President. You've a right to grumble and find fault with it as much as you like ; but don't let me hear you say another word in favor of it, if you do I'll make daylight shine through you." The old man hauled in his horns and meeched off, looking shamed enough.

The next day we concluded to have a public meeting to pass resolutions in favor of the proclamation. I was appointed chairman. The Federal party all came flocking round and wanted to come in and help praise the President. We told 'em no ; it was our President and our proclamation, and they must keep their distance. So we shut the doors and went on with our resolutions. By and by the Federal party begun to hurra for Jackson outside the house. At that I told Sargent Joel and your Cousin Ephraim, and two or three more of the young Democrats, to go out and clear the coast of them are fellers. And they went out, and Sargent Joel drew his piece of a scythe and went at 'em, and the Federalists run like a flock of sheep with a dog after 'em. So we finished our resolutions without getting a drop of Federalism mixed with 'em, and sent 'em on to the President by Sargent Joel. He got his company together last week, and they filled their knapsacks with bread, and sausages, and doe-nuts, and started for Washington according to your orders.

I was glad to see that hint in your letter about a Post-Office here. We need one very much. And if the President should think I ought to have it, being I've always been such a good friend to him, why you know, Jack, I'm always ready to serve my country.

So I remain your loving uncle,

JOSHUA DOWNING.

P. S.—If the President shouldn't say anything more about

the Post-Office, I think you had better name it to him again before you go to South Carolina ; **for if anything** should happen to you there, he might never do any more about it.

LETTER XXXII.

MAJOR DOWNING DESCRIBES THE ARRIVAL OF SARGENT JOEL **WITH THE** COMPANY AT WASHINGTON.

WASHINGTON CITY, Jan. 4, 1833.

To my dear Cousin Ephraim Downing, what watches the Legislater at Augusta, away **Down** *East, in the State of Maine, while I stay here and look arter Congress and the President*

DEAR COUSIN :—Sargent Joel got here day before yesterday, with my hearty old company of Downingville boys, that went down to Madawaska with me last winter. They cut rather a curious figure marching through Pennsylvany Avenu. One half of 'em had worn their shoes out so that their toes stuck out like the heads of so many young turtles, and t'other half had holes through their knees or elbows, and Sargent Joel marched ahead of 'em, swinging his piece of an old scythe for a sword, and inquiring of every one he met for Major Jack Downing. They all told him to keep along till he got to the President's house, which was the biggest house in the city except the Congress house, and there he would find me. I and the President were taking a little walk out, and talking about Mr. Calhoun and so on, when the President begun to stare as though he saw a catamount.

He started back, and says he, "Major Downing, if my eyes don't deceive me, there's nullification now, coming up Pennsylvany Avenu." He begun to call for his pistols, and to tell his men to fasten up the doors, when I looked round, and I knew

Joel's strut in a minute. Says I, "Dear Gineral, that's no nullification, but it's what 'll put a stopper on nullification pretty quick if it once gets to South Carolina. It's my Downingville company, commanded by Sargent Joel." At that

ARRIVAL OF THE DOWNINGVILLE COMPANY AT WASHINGTON.

the President looked more pleased than I've seen him before since he got the news of the vote of Pennsylvany. He ordered 'em into the east room, and gave 'em as much as they could eat and drink of the best the house affords. He has found quarters for 'em in the neighborhood, and says we must be ready to march for South Carolina whenever he says the word.

But I'll tell you what 'tis, Cousin Ephraim, I begin to grow a little kind of wamble-cropt about goin' to South Carolina, arter all. If they've got many such fellers there as one Gineral Blair there is here from that State, I'd sooner take my chance in the woods, forty miles above Downingville, fighting bears, and wolves, and catamounts, than come within gun-shot of one of these Carolina giants. He's a whaler of a feller—as big as any two men in Downingville. They say he weighs over three hundred pounds. About a week ago he met Gineral Duff Green in the street, and he fell afoul of him with a great club and knocked him down, and broke his arm, and beat him almost to death, jest because he got mad at something Mr. Green said in his paper. And what makes me feel more skittish about getting into the hands of such chaps is, because he says he couldn't help it. He says all his friends persuaded him not to meddle with Gineral Green, and he tried as hard as he could to let him alone, but he "found himself unequal to the effort." So Green like to got killed.

The folks here sot out to carry him to court about it, but he said he wouldn't go, and so he armed himself with four pistols, and two dirks, and a great knife, and said he'd shoot the first man that touched him. Last night he went to the theater with all his arms and coutrements about him. And after he sot there a spell, and all the folks were looking to see the play go on, he draws out one of his pistols and fires it at the players. Then there was a dreadful uproar. They told him he must clear out about the quickest. But he said if they'd let him alone he'd behave like a gentleman. So they went on with the play again.

By and by he draws out another pistol, and points it towards the players. At that there was a whole parcel of 'em seized him and dragged him out into another room, big as he was. But pretty soon he got upon his feet, and begun to rave like a mad ox. He pulled off his coat and threw it down, and declared he'd fight the whole **boodle of 'em.** The constables were all so frightened they **cut and run,** and nobody dared to go a near him, till he got cooled down a little, when some of his friends coaxed him away to a tavern. Now, as for going to South Carolina to fight such chaps as these, I'd sooner let nullification go to grass and eat mullen.

Sargent Joel told me, when he left Downingville, you had **jest** loaded up with apples **and one** thing or another to go down to Augusta to peddle **'em** out ; **and** that you was agoing to stay there **while** the Legislater folks were there. So I thought it would be a good plan for you and I to write to one another about once a week, or so, how matters get along.

So I remain your loving cousin,

MAJOR JACK DOWNING.

LETTER XXXIII.

MAJOR DOWNING GIVES HIS OPINION ABOUT NULLIFICATION AND ILLUSTRATES IT WITH A LUCID EXAMPLE.

WASHINGTON CITY, **Jan.** 17, 1833.

To the Editor of the Portland Courier, in the Mariners' Church Building, second story, eastern end, Fore street, away Down East, in the State of Maine.

MY KIND AND DEAR OLD FRIEND :—The President's message to Congress **makes cracking work** here. Mr. Calhoun shows his teeth like **a lion.** Mr. McDuffie **is** cool as a cowcumber,

---

* EDITORIAL NOTE.—South Carolina took very violent ground against Mr. Clay's American system, and especially against the tariff for the protection of manufactures, threatening to nullify the tariff law, and in case an attempt

though they say he's got a terrible tempest inside of him, that he'll let out before long. For my part, I think the President's message is about right. I was setting with the President in the east room last night, chatting about one thing and another, and the President says he, "Major Downing, have you read my message that I sent to Congress to-day." I told him I

was made to enforce it, to secede from the Union. And notwithstanding the triumphant election of General Jackson, in 1832, gave ample assurance that all she had asked and desired would soon be accomplished, she refused to be pacified, and, like a rowdy in a passion, declared she'd have a fight anyhow. Accordingly, in less than three weeks after the triumph of her principles in the overwhelming re-election of General Jackson, on the 24th of November, she issued her famous *Nullification Ordinance*, under the following title: "An ordinance to nullify certain acts of the Congress of the United States, purporting to be laws laying duties and imposts on the importation of foreign commodities."

This ordinance, after enumerating the grievances complained of under the acts of Congress, and requiring all the officials of the State to take an oath, "well and truly to obey, execute and enforce this ordinance, and such act or acts of the Legislature as may be passed in pursuance thereof," goes on to say:

"And we, the people of South Carolina, to the end that it may be fully understood by the Government of the United States and the people of the co-States, that we are determined to maintain this, our ordinance and declaration, at every hazard, do further declare that we will not submit to the application of force, on the part of the Federal Government, to reduce this State to obedience," &c.; and, finally, that any attempt to enforce these acts of Congress shall be considered "inconsistent with the longer continuance of South Carolina in the Union; and that the people of this State will henceforth hold themselves absolved from all further obligation to maintain or preserve the political connection with the people of the other States, and will forthwith proceed to organize a separate Government, and do all other acts and things which sovereign and independent States may of right do."

This ordinance was the act of a State Convention, held at Columbia, and was signed by more than a hundred of the most prominent and influential men of the State. It was to take effect on the first day of February following, and placed the State in open rebellion to the General Government. The ordinance was officially communicated to President Jackson early in December, and on the 10th of that month the President issued his famous *proclamation against Nullification*. This was an able and patriotic document, and added

hadn't. "Well," says he, "I should like to have you read it and give me your opinion upon it." So he handed it to me, and I sot down and read it through.

And when I got through, "Now," says I, "Gineral, I'll tell you jest what I think of this ere business. When I was a youngster, some of us Downingville boys used to go down to

much to the popularity of the President among all conservative citizens throughout the country ; so much so that, according to the testimony of Major Downing and Uncle Joshua, the Democrats of Downingville had the greatest difficulty imaginable to keep the Federal party from praising it.

After an elaborate constitutional argument upon the subject, in which South Carolina is shown to be clearly and grossly in the wrong, the President makes a touching and forcible appeal to the feelings and patriotism of the citizens of that State, from which we make some brief quotations :

"Fellow-citizens of my native State, let me not only admonish you, as the first Magistrate of our common country, not to incur the penalty of its laws, but use the influence that a father would over his children whom he saw rushing to certain ruin," &c.   *   *   *   *   *

"You are free members of a flourishing and happy Union. There is no settled design to oppress you. You have, indeed, felt the unequal operation of laws which may have been unwisely, not unconstitutionally, passed ; but that inequality must, necessarily be removed. At the very moment when you were madly urged on to the unfortunate course you have begun, a change in the public opinion had commenced."   *   *   *

"I adjure you, as you value the peace of your country, the lives of its best citizens, and your own fair fame, to retrace your steps. Snatch from the archives of your State the disorganizing edict of its Convention ; bid its members to re-assemble, and promulgate the decided expressions of your will to remain in the path which alone can conduct you to safety, prosperity and honor. Tell them that, compared to disunion, all other evils are light, because that brings with it an accumulation of all. Declare that you will never take the field unless the star spangled banner of your country shall float over you ; that you will not be stigmatized when dead, and dishonored and scorned while you live, as the authors of the first attack on the Constitution of your country. Its destroyers you cannot be. You may disturb its peace ; you may interrupt the course of its prosperity ; you may cloud its reputation for stability, but its tranquility will be restored, its prosperity will return, and the stain upon its national character will be transferred, and remain an eternal blot on the memory of those who caused the disorder."

Sebago Pond every spring and hire out a month or two rafting logs across the pond. And one time I and Cousin Ephraim, and Joel, and Bill Johnson, and two or three more of us had each a whopping great log to carry across the pond. It was rather a windy day, and the waves kept the logs bobbing up and down pretty considerable bad, so we agreed to bring 'em along side-and-side and lash 'em together and drive some thole-pins in the outermost logs and row 'em over together. We went along two or three miles pretty well. But by and by Bill Johnson begun to complain. He was always an uneasy, harum-scarum sort of a chap. Always thought everybody else had an easier time than he had, and, when he was a boy, always used to be complaining that the other boys had more butter on their bread than he had. Well, Bill was rowing on the leward side, and he begun to fret and said his side went the hardest, and he wouldn't give us any peace till one of us changed sides with him.

The proclamation then closes with an appeal to the citizens of the United States. We make a brief extract or two:

"Fellow-citizens of the United States:—The threat of unhallowed disunion, the names of those, once respected, by whom it is uttered, the array of military force to support it, denote the approach of a crisis in our affairs on which the continuance of our unexampled prosperity, our political existence, and perhaps that of all free Governments may depend. Having the fullest confidence in the justness of the legal and constitutional opinion of my duties which has been expressed, I rely with equal confidence on your undivided support in my determination to execute the laws—to preserve the Union by all constitutional means—to arrest, if possible, by moderate, but firm measures, the necessity of a recourse to force."

"Fellow-citizens:—The momentous case is before you. On your undivided support of your Government depends the decision of the great question it involves, whether your sacred Union will be preserved, and the blessings it secures to us as one people shall be perpetuated. No one can doubt that the unanimity with which that decision will be expressed will be such as to inspire new confidence in republican institutions, and that the prudence, the wisdom and the courage which it will bring to their defense will transmit them, unimpaired and invigorated, to our children."

SOUTH CAROLINA NULLIFICATION.

"Well, Bill hadn't rowed but a little ways on the winward side before he began to fret again, and declared that side went harder than t'other, and he wouldn't touch to row on that side any longer. We told him he had his choice, and he shouldn't keep changing so. But he only fretted the more, and begun to get mad. At last he declared if we didn't change with him in five minutes, he'd cut the lashings and take his log and paddle off alone. And before we had hardly time to turn round, he declared the five minutes were out, and up hatchet and cut the lashings, and away went Bill on his own log, bobbing and rolling about, and dancing like a monkey, to try to keep on the upper side. The rest of us scrabbled to as well as we could, and fastened our logs together again, though we had a tough match for it, the wind blew so hard. Bill hadn't gone but a little ways before his log begun to roll more and more, and by and by in he went splash, head and ears. He came up puffing and blowing, and got hold of the log and tried to climb up on to it, but the more he tried the more the log rolled; and finding it would be gone goose with him pretty soon if he staid there, he begun to sing out like a loon for us to come and take him. We asked him which side he would row if we would take his log into the raft again. 'Oh,' says Bill, 'I'll row on either side or both sides if you want me to, if you'll only come and help me before I sink.'"

"But," said the President, "I hope you didn't help the foolish rascal out till he got a pretty good soaking." "He got soaked enough before we got to him," says I, "for he was just ready to sink for the last time, and our logs come pesky near getting scattered, and if they had, we should all gone to the bottom together. And now, Gineral, this is jest what I think: if you let South Carolina cut the lashings you'll see such a log-rolling in this country as you never see yet." The old Gineral started up and marched across the floor like a boy.

Says he, "Major Downing, she shan't cut the lashings while my name is Andrew Jackson. Tell Sargent Joel to have his company sleep on their arms every night." I told him they should be ready at a moment's warning.

I wish you would jest give Cousin Ephraim, up to Augusta, a jog to know why he don't write to me and let me know how the Legislater is getting along.

I remain your loving friend,

MAJOR JACK DOWNING.

LETTER XXXIV.

COUSIN EPHRAIM TELLS THE MAJOR HOW MATTERS GET ALONG AT AUGUSTA, AND GIVES A SPECIMEN OF THE VALUE OF POLITICAL PROMISES.

AUGUSTA, State of Maine, Jan. 30, 1833.

To Major Jack Downing, at Washington.

DEAR COUSIN JACK :—I got your letter some time ago, but I hadn't time to answer it afore now, because I had to go back up to Downingville to get another load of apples. These Legislater folks cronch apples down by the wholesale between speeches, and sometimes in the middle of speeches tu. That afternoon that Mr. Clark spoke all day, I guess I sold nigh upon a half a bushel for cash, and trusted out most three pecks besides. The folks up to Downingville are all pretty well, only your poor old mother; she's got the reumatics pretty bad this winter. She says she wishes with all her heart Jack would come home, and not think of going to South Carolina. Ever since she heard about Gineral Blair she can't hardly sleep nights, she's so fraid you'll get shot. I tell her there's no danger of you as long as you have President Jackson one side of you and Sargent Joel t'other.

The Legislater is jogging along here pretty well ; I guess they'll get through about the first of March, if they don't have too many boundary questions come along. We made some major-ginerals here t'other day, and I tried to get you elected. Not because I thought you cared much about the office now, but jest for the honor of Downingville. I tried most all the members, and thought to be sure you would come in as slick as grease ; for about forty of 'em told me they thought it *belonged* to you. They said it was against their principles to pledge their votes to anybody ; but they whispered in my ear that they would *do what they could*, and they hadn't *scarcely* a doubt but what you'd be elected. Sixty-eight of 'em told me you was the *best man for it*, and would undoubtedly be chosen as a matter of course. And twenty-five of 'em promised me right up and down, by the crook of the elbow, that they *would vote* for you. Well, Jack, after all this, you didn't get but *two votes*. By that time I begun to think it wasn't so strange that it took you two years hard fishing before you could get an office.

This is the most Democratic Legislater that they have ever had in this State yet. They are most all real ginuine Demokrats, and they have give Mr. Holmes and Mr. Sprague a terrible basting for turning Federalists, and they have turned Mr. Holmes out and put Mr. Shepley in.

The Legislater is talking of moving the seat of government back to Portland again. They say it will be better all round. They won't have to go so fur through the snow-drifts to their boarding-houses, and won't have to pay much more than half so much for their board. And here they have to pay fourpence apiece every time they are shaved ; but in Portland they can get shaved by the half dozen for three cents apiece. I hope they will go, for I can get more for my apples in Portland than I can here.

P. S.—Bill Johnson was married last week, and he quarreled with his wife the very next day. So you see he is the same old sixpence he used to be. He says he'll send a petition to the Legislater to be divorced, and he declares if they don't grant it he'll cut the lashings as he did once on the raft on Sebago Pond, sink or swim.

N. B.—Uncle Joshua wished me to ask you to ask the President about that Post-Office again, as his commission hasn't come yet.

I remain your loving cousin,

EPHRAIM DOWNING.

LETTER XXXV.*

MAJOR DOWNING GOES UP TOP THE CONGRESS HOUSE AND LISTENS TO SEE IF HE CAN HEAR THE GUNS IN SOUTH CAROLINA, AND ALSO HAS A TALK WITH THE PRESIDENT ABOUT THE SLANDER OF THE NEWSPAPERS.

WASHINGTON CITY, Feb. 1, 1833.

To the Editor of the Portland Courier, in the Mariners' Church Building, second story, eastern end, Fore street, away Down East, in the State of Maine.

MY DEAR FRIEND:—This is nullification day, and it's most night, and I aint dead yet, and haint been shot at once to-day. I got up this morning as soon as it was light, and went out, and looked away toward South Carolina, and listened as hard as I could to see if I could hear the guns crackin' and the

---

* EDITORIAL NOTE.—The 1st of February, 1833, was the day appointed by South Carolina for putting in force her nullifying ordinance.

cannons roarin'. But it was all still as a mouse. And I've been up top the Congress house five or six times to-day, and listened and listened; but all the firing I could hear was inside the Congress house itself, where the members were shooting their speeches at each other. I had my company all ready this morning, with their dinners in their 'napsacks, to start as

LISTENING FOR THE GUNS IN SOUTH CAROLINA.

quick as we heard a single gun. We shan't go till we hear something from these nullifiers, for the President says he aint agoing to begin the scrape; but if the nullifiers begin it, then the hardest must fend off.

Yesterday a friend handed me a couple of papers printed at Hallowell, away down pretty near to Augusta, in the State of

Maine, called the American Advocate, and I found something in 'em that made me as mad as a March hair. The first one mentioned that Captain Dow was chosen Mayor of Portland, and then said: "He is the reputed author of the Jack Downing letters that have been published in the Portland Courier." The other paper, that was printed two or three days afterward, said: "Mr. Dow, the new Mayor of Portland, is not the author of Jack Downing's letters; they are written by the editor of the Portland Courier." Now, Mr. Editor, my good old friend, isn't this too bad? I haven't come acrost any thing that made me feel so wamble-cropt this good while. Jest as if Major Jack Downing couldn't write his own letters.

I've been to school, put it altogether, off and on, more than six months; and, though I say it myself, I always used to be called the best scholar among all the boys in Downingville, and most always used to stand at the head of my class. I'd been through Webster's spelling book before I was fifteen, and before I was twenty I could cypher to the rule of three. And now to have it said that I don't write my own letters is too bad. It's what I call a rascally shame. I was so boiling over with it last night, that I couldn't hold in; and so I took the papers, and went in and showed them to the President. I always go to the President when I have any difficulty, and when he has any he comes to me; so we help one another along as well as we can. When the President had read it, says he:

"Major Downing, it's strange to see how this world is given to lying. The public papers are beginning to slander you jest as they always do me. I haven't written scarcely a public document since I've been President but what it's been laid off to Mr. Van Buren, or Mr. McLane, or Mr. Livingston, or Mr. Taney, or somebody or other. And how to help this slanderous business I don't know. But it's too provoking, Major, that's certain. Sometimes I've a good mind to make

Congress pass a law that every editor who says I don't write my proclamations and messages, or that you don't write your letters, shall forfeit his press and types; and, if that don't stop him, that he shall be strung up by the neck without judge or jury."

And now, Mr. Editor, I wish you would jest give that Hallowell man a hint to mind his own p's and q's in future, and look out for his neck. And as you know very well that I do write my own letters, I would thank you jest to tell the public so.

I remain your sincere and loving friend,

MAJOR JACK DOWNING.

LETTER XXXVI.

COUSIN EPHRAIM EXPLAINS THE SCIENCE OF LAND SPECULATON.

AUGUSTA, State of Maine, March 4, 1833.
To Major Jack Downing, at President Jackson's house, in Washington City.

DEAR COUSIN JACK :—The Legislater folks have all cleared out to-day, one arter t'other, jest like a flock of sheep; and some of 'em have left me in the lurch tu, for they cleared out without paying me for my apples. Some of 'em went off in my debt as much as twenty cents, and some ninepence, and a shilling, and so on. They all kept telling me when they got paid off they'd settle up with me. And so I waited with patience till they adjourned, and thought I was as sure of my money as though it was in the bank.

But, my patience, when they did adjourn, such a hubbub I guess you never see. They were flying about from one room to another, like so many pigeons shot in the head. They run into Mr. Harris' room, and clawed the money off his table, hand over fist. I brustled up to some of 'em, and tried to settle. I come to one man that owed me twelve cents, and he had a ninepence in change; but he wouldn't let me have that, because he should lose half a cent. So, while we were bothering about it, trying to get it changed, the first I knew the rest of 'em had got their money in their pockets, and were off lik a shot—some of 'em in stages, and some in sleighs, and some footing it. I out and followed arter 'em, but 't was no use; I couldn't catch one of 'em. And as for my money, and apples tu, I guess I shall have to whistle for 'em now. It's pesky hard, for I owe four and sixpence here yet for my board, and I've paid away every cent I've got for my apples, and don't know but I shall have to come down with another load to clear out my expenses. Howsomever, you know Uncle Joshua always told us never to cry for spilt milk, so I mean to hold my head up yet.

I don't know but I shall have to give up retailing apples, I meet with so many head flaws about it. I was thinking that, soon as the Legislater adjourned, I'd take a load of apples and apple-sass, and a few sassages, and come on to Washington, and go long with your company to South Carolina. But they say Mr. Clay has put a stopper on that nullification business, and it's ten chanches to one you won't have to go.

I don't care so much about the apple business after all, for I've found out a way to get rich forty times as fast as I can by retailing apples, or as you can by hunting after an office. And I advise you to come right home, as quick as you can come. Here's a business going on here that you can get rich by ten times as quick as you can in any office, even if you should get to be President. The President don't have but twenty-five thousand dollars a year; but in this 'ere business that's going on here, a man can make twenty-five thousand dollars in a week if he's a mind to, and not work hard neither.

I s'pose by this time you begin to feel rather in a pucker to know what this business is. I'll tell you; but you must keep it to yourself, for if all them are Washington folks and Congress folks should come on here and go dipping into it, I'm afraid they'd cut us all out. But between you and me, it's only jest buying and selling land. Why, Jack, it's forty times more profitable than money digging, or any other business that you ever see. I knew a man here t'other day from Bangor, that made ten thousand dollars, and I guess he wan't more than an hour about it. Most all the folks here, and down to Portland and Bangor, have got their fortunes made, and now we are beginning to take hold of it up in the country.

They've got a slice up in Downingville, and I missed it by being down here selling apples, or I should had a finger in the pie. Uncle Joshua Downing—you know he's an old fox, and always knows where to jump; well, he see how everybody was getting rich, so he went and bought a piece of township up back of Downingville, and give his note for a thousand dollars for it. And then he sold it to Uncle Jacob, and took his note for two thousand dollars; and Uncle Jacob sold it to Uncle Zackary, and took his note for three thousand dollars; and Uncle Zackary sold it to Uncle Jim, and took his note for four thousand dollars; and Uncle Jim sold it to Cousin Sam, and took his note for five thousand dollars; and Cousin Sam sold it to Bill Johnson, and took his note for six thousand dollars. So you see there's five of 'em, that wan't worth ninepence apiece, (except Uncle Joshua,) have now got a thousand dollars apiece clear, when their notes are paid. And Bill Johnson's going to logging off of it, and they say he'll make more than any of 'em.

Come home, Jack; come home by all means, if you want

to get rich. Give up your commission, and think no more about being President, or anything else, but come home and buy land before it's all gone.

Your loving cousin,

EPHRAIM DOWNING.

LETTER XXXVII.

MAJOR DOWNING TELLS HOW MR. CLAY PUT A STOP TO THAT FUSS IN SOUTH CAROLINA, BESIDES HUSHING UP SOME OTHER QUARRELS.

WASHINGTON CITY, March 10, 1833.

To Cousin Ephraim Downing, up in Downingville.

DEAR COUSIN EPHRAIM :—I got your letter this morning. It was a shame for them are Legislater folks to skulk off without paying you for your apples. But they are the worst folks about standing to their word that I know of. They've promised me an office more than twenty times, but some how or other, come to the case in hand, their votes always went for somebody else. But I don't care a fig for 'em as long as I've got the President on my side, for his offices are as fat again as the Legislater offices are. The President's offices will support a man pretty well if he doesn't do anything at all. As soon as Mr. Clay's tariff bill passed, the President called me into his room, and says he, "Major Downing, the nullification jig is up. There'll be no fun for you in South Carolina now, and I guess you may as well let Sargent Joel march the company back to Downingville, and wait till somebody kicks up another bobbery somewhere, and then I'll send for 'em, for they are the likeliest company I've seen since I went with my Tennessee Rangers to New Orleans. And as for you, Major Downing, you shall still hold your commission, and be under half pay, holding yourself in readiness to march at a moment's warning, and to fight whenever called for."

So you see, Cousin Ephraim, I am pretty well to live in the world, without any of your land speculations or apple-selling Down East. I can't seem to see how 'tis they all make money so fast in that land business down there that you tell about. How could all our folks, and Bill Johnson, and all of 'em there in Downingville make a thousand dollars apiece, jest a trading round among themselves, when there ain't fifty dollars in money, put it all together, in the whole town. It rather puzzles me a little. As soon as I see 'em all get their thousand dollars, cash in hand, I guess I'll give up my commission, and come home and buy some land tu.

But at present I think I rather have a bird in the hand than one in the bush. Our Congress folks here cleared out about the same time that your Legislater folks did, and I and the President have been rather lonesome a few days. The old gentleman says I must n't leave him on any account; but I guess I shall start Joel and the company off for Downingville in a day or two. They've got their clothes pretty much mended up, and they look quite tidy. I should n't feel ashamed to see 'em marched through any city in the United States.

It isn't likely I shall have anything to do under my commission very soon. For some say there'll be no fighting in the country while Mr. Clay lives, if it should be a thousand years. He's got a master knack of pacifying folks and hushing up quarrels as you ever see. He's stopt all that fuss in South Carolina, that you know was just ready to blow the whole country sky-high. He stept up to 'em in Congress, and told 'em what sort of a bill to pass, and they passed it without hardly any jaw about it. And South Carolina has hauled in her horns, and they say she'll be as calm as a clock now. And that isn't the only quarrel Mr. Clay has stopt. Two of the Senators, Mr. Webster and Mr. Poindexter, got as mad as March hairs at each other. They called each other some pesky hard names, and looked cross enough for a week to bite a board nail off. Well, after Mr. Clay got through with South Carolina he took them in hand. He jest talked to 'em about five minutes, and they got up and went and shook hands with each other, and looked as loving as two brothers.

Then Mr. Holmes got up and went to Mr. Clay, and, almost with tears in his eyes, asked him if he wouldn't be so kind as to settle a little difficulty there was between him and his constituents, so they might elect him to come to Congress again. And I believe some of the other Senators asked for the same favor.

So as there is likely to be peace now all round the house for some time to come, I'm in a kind of a quandary what course to steer this summer. The President talks of taking a journey Down East this summer, and he wants me to go with him, because I'm acquainted there, and can show him all about it. He has a great desire to go as fur as Downingville, and get acquainted with Uncle Joshua, who has always stuck by him in all weathers, through thick and thin.

The President thinks Uncle Joshua is one of the Republikan pillars of New England, and says he shall always have the Post-Office as long as he lives, and his children after him.

I rather guess, on the whole, I shall come on that way this summer with the President. But wherever I go I shall remain your loving cousin,

MAJOR JACK DOWNING

LETTER XXXVIII.

MAJOR DOWNING GIVES THE RESULT OF A CONSULTATION AMONG THE GOVERNMENT ON THE QUESTION WHETHER THE PRESIDENT SHOULD SHAKE HANDS WITH THE FEDERALISTS DURING HIS JOURNEY DOWN EAST.

WASHINGTON CITY, April 20, 1833.

To the Editor of the Portland Courier, in the Mariners' Church Building, second story, eastern end, Fore street, away Down East, in the State of Maine.

MY DEAR OLD FRIEND :—Bein' I haint writ to you for some time, I am afraid you and our folks up in Downingville will begin to feel a little uneasy by and by, so I'll jest write you a little, if it aint but two lines, to let you know how we get on here. I and the President seem to enjoy ourselves pretty well together, though it's getting to be a little lonesome since the Congress folks went off, and Sargent Joel cleared out with my Downingville company. Poor souls, I wonder if they have got home yet. I haven't heard a word from 'em since they left here. I wish you would send up word to Sargent Joel to write to me and let me know how they got along. He can send his letter in your Currier, or get Uncle Joshua to frank it—either way it won't cost me anything. Now I think of it, I wish you would jest ask Cousin Nabby to ask Uncle Joshua to frank me on two or three pair of stockings, for mine have got terribly out at the heels. He can do it jest as well as not; they make nothing here of franking a bushel basket full of great books to the Western States. And they say some of the members of Congress frank their clothes home by mail to be washed.

I and the President are getting ready to come on that way this summer. We shall come as far as Portland, and I expect we shall go up to Downingville, for the President says he must shake hands with Uncle Joshua before he comes back—that faithful old Republikan, who has stood by him through thick and thin, ever since he found he was going to be elected President. He will either go up to Downingville, or send for Uncle Joshua to meet him at Portland.

There is some trouble among us here a little, to know how we shall get along among the Federalists when we come that way. They say the Federalists in Massachusetts want to keep the President all to themselves when he comes there. But Mr. Van Buren says that'll never do; he must stick to the Demokratic party; he may shake hands with a Federalist once in a while if the Demokrats don't see him, but whenever there's any Demokrats round he musn't look at a Federalist. Mr. McLane and Mr. Livingston advise him t'other way. They tell him he'd better treat the Federalists pretty civil, and shake hands with Mr. Webster as quick as he would with Uncle Joshua Downing. And when they give this advice Mr. Lewis and Mr. Kendle hop right up as mad as March hairs, and tell him if he shakes hands with a single Federalist while he is gone, the Demokratic party will be ruined. And then the President turns to me and asks me what he had better do. And I tell him I guess he better go straight ahead, and keep a stiff upper lip, and shake hands with whoever he is a mind to.

Mr. Van Buren staid with us awhile at the President's, but he's moved into a house now on Pennsylvany Avenue. He's a fine, slick man, I can tell you, and the President says he's the greatest man in America.

Your old friend,

MAJOR JACK DOWNING.

LETTER XXXIX.

MAJOR DOWNING DEFENDS THE PRESIDENT FROM THE ASSAULT OF LIEUTENANT RANDOLPH, ON BOARD THE STEAMBOAT CYGNET.

> ON BOARD THE STEAMBOAT CYGNET, near the City of Alexandria, down a little ways below Washington, May the 6th, 1833.

To the Editor of the Portland Courier, in the Mariners' Church Building, second story, eastern end, Fore street, away Down East, in the State of Maine.

MY DEAR OLD FRIEND :—We've had a kind of a hurly-burly time here to-day. I didn't know but we should bust the biler one spell; and some of us, as it was, got scalding hot. You see, I and the President and a few more gentlemen got into the steamboat this morning to go round into old Virginny to help lay the foundation of a monument, so they shouldn't forget who Washington's mother was.

When we got down along to Alexandria, the boat hauled up to the side of the wharf awhile to let some more folks get in, and while she lay there, I and the President and a few more of 'em sot in the cabin reading and chatting with one another. The President had jest got through reading a letter from Uncle Joshua Downing, urging him very strongly to come up as fur as Downingville when he comes on that way. And says he, "Major Downing, this Uncle Joshua Downing of yours is a real true blue Republikan as I know of anywhere. I wouldn't miss seeing him when I go Down East for anything."

Says I, "Your honor, Downingville is the most thorough-going Republikan town there is anywhere in the eastern country; and you ought not to come back till you have visited it." Jest as I said that, there was a stranger came into the cabin and stept along up to the President, and begun to pull off his glove. I thought there was some mischief bruing,

ASSAULT OF LIEUTENANT RANDOLPH ON GENERAL JACKSON.

for his lips were kind of quivery, and I didn't like the looks of his eyes a bit. But the President thought he was trying to get his gloves off to shake hands with him, and the good old man is always ready to shake hands with a friend; so he reached out his hand to him and smiled, and told him never to stand for the gloves, and the words wan't hardly out of his mouth when dab went one of the fellow's hands slap into the President's face.

In a moment I leveled my umbrella at the villain's head, and came pesky near fetching him to the floor. Two more gentlemen then clenched him by the collar and had him down as quick as ever you see a beef ox knocked down with an ax. In a minute a crowd was round him thick as a swarm of bees.

But, my stars, I wish you could have seen the President jest at that minute. If you ever see a lion lying down asleep and a man come along with a great club and hit him a polt with all his might, and then see that lion spring on his feet, and see the fire flash in his eyes, and hear him roar and gnash his teeth, you might guess what kind of a harrycane we had of it.

The old gineral no sooner felt the fellow's paw in his face than he sprung like a steel trap, and catched his cane and went at him. But there was such a crowd of men there in an instant, that it was as much impossible to get through 'em as it was for the British to get through his pile of cotton wool bags at New Orleans. If it hadn't been for that, I think he would have kicked the feller through the side of the steamboat in two minutes.

However, somehow or other, the rascal got hussled out of the boat on to the wharf, and fled. They have sent some officers after him, but where they will overtake him nobody knows. I don't know exactly what the trouble begun about, but I believe Leftenant Randolf (that was his name) got terrible mad with the President somehow about his commission.

The President has got cleverly cooled down again, and we are going on to lay the foundation of the monument.

In haste, your old friend,

MAJOR JACK DOWNING.

LETTER XL.

MAJOR DOWNING SHAKES HANDS FOR THE PRESIDENT AT PHILADELPHIA, WHILE ON THE GRAND TOUR DOWN EAST.

PHILADELPHIA, June, 10, 1833.

To Uncle Joshua Downing, Postmaster, *up in* Downingville, *in the State of* Maine, *with care and speed.*

DEAR UNCLE JOSHUA :—We are coming on, full chisel. I've been trying, ever since we started, to get a chance to write a little to you; but when we've been on the road I couldn't catch my breath hardly long enough to write my name, we kept flying so fast; and when we made any stop, there was such a jam round us there wasn't elbow room enough for a miskeeter to turn round without knocking his wings off.

I'm most afraid now we shall get to Downingville before this letter does, so that we shall be likely to catch you all in the suds before you think of it. But I understand there is a *fast mail* goes on that way, and I mean to send it by that, so I'm in hopes you'll get it time enough to have the children's faces washed and their heads combed, and the gals get on their clean gowns. And if Sargent Joel *could* have time enough to call out my old Downingville company and get their uniforms brushed up a little, and come down the road as fur as your new barn to meet us, there's nothing that would please the President better. As for victuals, most anything won't come amiss; we are as hungry as bears after traveling a hundred miles a day. A little fried pork and eggs, or a pot of baked beans and an Indian pudding would suit us much better than the soft stuff they give here in these great cities.

The President wouldn't miss of seeing you for anything in the world, and he will go to Downingville if he has legs and arms enough left when he goes to Portland to carry him there. But, for fear that anything should happen that he shouldn't be able to come, you had better meet us in Portland, say about the 22d ; and then you can go up to Downingville with us.

This traveling with the President is capital fun, after all, if it wasn't so plaguy tiresome. We come into Baltimore on a railroad, and we flew over the ground like a harrycane. There isn't a horse in this country that could keep up with us, if he should go upon the clean clip. When we got to Baltimore, the streets were filled with folks as thick as the spruce trees down in your swamp. There we found Black Hawk, a little, old, dried up Indian king. And I thought the folks looked at him and the prophet about as much as they did at me and the President. I gave the President a wink that this Indian fellow was taking the shine off us a little ; so we concluded we wouldn't have him with us any more, but go on without him.

I can't stop to tell you, in this letter, how we got along to Philadelphy, though we had a pretty easy time some of the way in the steamboats. And I can't stop to tell you of half of the fine things I have seen here. They took us up into a great hall this morning, as big as a meeting-house, and then the folks begun to pour in by thousands to shake hands with the President—Federalists and all, it made no difference. There was such a stream of 'em coming in that the hall was full in a few minutes, and it was so jammed up around the door that they couldn't get out again if they were to die. So they had to knock out some of the windows, and go out t'other way.

The President shook hands with all his might an hour or two, 'till he got so tired he couldn't hardly stand it. I took hold and shook for him once in a while to help him along, but at last he got so tired he had to lay down on a soft bench, covered with cloth, and shake as well as he could; and when he couldn't shake, he'd nod to 'em as they come along. And at last he got so beat out, he couldn't only wrinkle his forehead and wink. Then I kind of stood behind him, and reached my arm round under his, and shook for him for about half an hour as tight as I could spring. Then we concluded it was best to adjourn for to-day.

MAJOR DOWNING SHAKING HANDS FOR THE GINERAL.

And I've made out to get away up into the garret in the tavern long enough to write this letter. We shall be off to-morrow or next day for York; and if I can possibly get breathing time enough there, I shall write to you again.

Give my love to all the folks in Downingville, and believe me your loving neffu,

MAJOR JACK DOWNING.

LETTER XLI.*

THE PRESIDENT AND MAJOR DOWNING HAVE A VERY NARROW ESCAPE AT THE BREAKING DOWN OF THE CASTLE GARDEN BRIDGE IN NEW YORK.

NEW YORK CITY, Friday Evening, June 14, 1833.

To Uncle Joshua Downing, Postmaster up in Downingville, State of Maine.

DEAR UNCLE JOSHUA :—Here we are, amongst an ocean of folks, and cutting up capers as high as a cat's back. I s'pose you will see by the papers how we like to got drowned yester-

---

* EDITORIAL NOTE.—Here we come to an important point—an era in the Downing literature, which requires special notice. It was now about three years and a half that Major Downing had been serving and enlightening his countrymen. In all that time his fame had steadily increased. His letters were copied into almost every paper all over the land, and his name was in everybody's mouth. Next to General Jackson, he was decidedly the most popular man in the United States. Perhaps nothing is more calculated to excite a feeling of envy than great popularity. The popular man is like the child who holds a nice stick of candy in his hand; all the children around are on tiptoe to get a nibble. It is not strange, therefore, that many in different parts of the country, endeavored to get a taste of Major Downing's popularity by attempting to imitate his writings.

But one individual, at this time, made a bold and systematic rush at the Major, and attempted to strip his well-earned laurels from his brow, and entwine them around his own head. This was a respectable merchant, a heavy iron dealer in New York. Violently seized with a literary mania, he sat down and wrote a Downing letter, giving an account of the arrival of the Presidential party in New York, signed it with the Major's name, and published it in the old Daily Advertiser.

As the letter of the genuine Major, giving an account of the same affair, was sent to his Uncle Joshua, through the Portland Courier, it took several days for it to make the journey Down East and back again to New York. In

day crossing the bridge between the castle and the garden.† It was a pesky narrow squeak for me and the President. He was riding over on a great fine hoss, and I was walking along by the side of him, and trying to clear the way a little, for they crowded upon us so there was no getting along, and hardly a chance to breathe. When we got under the arch, we stopped a little bit for the crowd to clear away, when all at the meantime, the letter of the iron dealer made its appearance, with Major Downing's signature, and was seized upon by the greedy multitude, and passed about as the true coin. The thousands and tens of thousands who had been hurrahing for Major Downing for weeks and months, and some of them for years, of course raised their voices again as loud as ever.

"God bless me!" said the iron merchant; "why, I've electrified the world! I had no idea I was such a great writer before. I must go into this business deep; who cares for trade when he can get popularity and literary fame?"

Henceforth the merchant became a man of *letters*, and the iron business was turned over to the other members of the firm. For months afterward he earnestly applied himself to writing Downing letters; and as he could always get them to the New York market before the letters of the true Major, who was riding about with the "Gineral," and sending his epistles through the Portland Courier, could arrive there, the merchant thought the run of the trade was all in his favor. And whenever the voice of public applause, in all parts of the country, pealed forth the name of Major Downing, "God bless me!" said the merchant, "Don't you hear my thunder!"

Even to this day it is said, the New York iron merchant enjoys the secret satisfaction of occasionally meeting with an individual so benighted in literary history as to look up to him with awe and admiration, regarding him as the great, the distinguished Major Downing.

† EDITORIAL NOTE.—The Presidential party landed at Castle Garden, the ancient, heavy old fort standing in the harbor, six or eight rods from the shore, at the southern point of the city. A bridge connected Castle Garden with the green public park, called the Battery. The Major speaks of the bridge "between the castle and the garden," by which it would seem that he supposed the old fort was the *castle*, and the green Battery the *garden*. In the facts of the breaking down of the bridge, and the narrow escape of some of the Presidential party, the Major is strictly accurate, as he always is on all historical points. His remark to the President, that "Mr Van Buren wasn' in the company," when the bridge gave way, will be explained by the fact that Mr. Van Buren joined the President's traveling party at New York.

9*

once I thought I heard something crack. Says I, "Gineral, you better go ahead, I'm afraid there's mischief bruin' here." At that he gave his hoss a lick and pushed through the crowd; but we hadn't got more than a rod, before crash went the bridge behind us, all down in a heap, and two toll-houses on

ESCAPE OF PRESIDENT JACKSON AT CASTLE GARDEN BRIDGE.

top of it, and as many as a hundred folks splashed into the water, all mixed up together, one top of t'other. The President looked over his shoulder, and seeing I was safe behind him, called out for Mr. Van Buren, and asked me to run and see if he was hurt. I told him he had forgot himself, for Mr. Van Buren wasn't in the company; but Mr. Woodbury and Mr. Cass were in for it, for I could see them floundering about in the water now. "Run, Major," said the President, "run and give them a lift. Take Mr. Woodbury first; you know I can't spare him at any rate."

So there was a parcel of us took hold and went to hauling of 'em out of the water, like so many drownded rats. But we got 'em all out alive, except a few young things they called dandies; they looked so after they got wet all over that we couldn't make out whether they were alive or dead. So we laid 'em up to dry, and left 'em; and I went on to help the President review the troops on the Battery, as they call it; and a grand place it is tu. I've seen more fine shows here, it seems to me, than ever I see before in my life. Such a sight of folks, and fine ladies, and fine houses, and vessels, and steamboats, and flags a flying, and canons firing, and fireworks a whisking about, I never see the beat of it. I didn't think there was so much fun in this world before, for all I've been about so much at Madawaska, and among the nullifiers, and all round.

But I can't tell you much about it till we get there, for I can't find any time to write. I've only catched a few minutes this evening, while the President is gone into Mr. Niblo's garden. One of the master sights that I've seen yet was that balloon that went up this afternoon, carrying a man with it.

All these sights keep us back a little longer than we expected. I don't think now we shall be in Portand before the 28th or 29th of this month. So I thought I'd jest write you a line that you might be down there about that time.

In haste, your loving neffu,

MAJOR JACK DOWNING.

LETTER XLII.*

MAJOR DOWNING DESCRIBES THE VISIT OF THE PRESIDENT AT BOSTON, AND ALSO COMPLAINS OF THE RASCALLY COUNTERFEITERS THAT WRITE LETTERS IN HIS NAME FOR THE NEWSPAPERS.

Boston, Tuesday, June 25, 1833.

To the Editor of the Portland Courier.

My Dear Old Friend:—I'm keeping house with the President to-day, and bein' he's getting considerable better, I thought I'd catch a chance when he was taking a knap, and write a little to let you know how we get along. This ere sickness of the President has been a bad pull-back to us. He hasn't been able to go out since Sunday afternoon, and I've been watchin' with him this two nights, and if I wasn't as tough as a halter, I should be half dead by this time.

And if the President wan't tougher than a catamount, he'd kick the bucket before he'd been round to see one half the notions there is in Boston. Poor man, he has a hard time of it; you've no idea how much he has to go through. It's worse than being dragged through forty knot-holes.

To be bamboozled about from four o'clock in the morning till midnight, rain or shine—jammed into one great house to eat a breakfast, and into another great house to eat a dinner, and into another to eat supper, and into two or three others between meals, to eat cooliations, and to have to go out and review three or four regiments of troops, and then to be jammed into Funnel Hall two hours, and shake hands

---

* Editorial Note.—It will be recollected that the President, while in Boston, was for a few days seriously ill.

with three or four thousand folks, and then to go into the State House and stand there two or three hours, and see all Boston streaming through it like a river through a saw-mill, and then to ride about the city awile in a fine painted covered wagon, with four or five horses to draw it, and then ride awhile in one without any cover to it, finney-fined off to the top notch, and then get on to the horses and ride awhile a horseback, and then run into a great picture-room and see more fine pictures than you could shake a stick at in a week, and then go into some grand gentleman's house, and shake hands a half an hour with a flock of ladies, and then after supper go and have a little still kind of a hubbub all alone with three or four hundred particular friends, and talk an hour or two, and take another cooliation, and then go home, and about midnight get ready to go to bed, and up again at four o'clock the next morning and at it. And if this aint enough to tucker a feller out, I don't know what is. The President wouldn't have stood it till this time, if he hadn't sent me and Mr. Van Buren to some of the parties, while he staid at home to rest

The President's got so much better, I think we shall be able to start for Salem'to-morrow, for we must go through with it now we've begun, as hard work as 'tis. I think we shall get to Portland about the 4th of July ; so, if you get your guns and things all ready, you can kill two birds with one stone. I hope you'll be pretty careful there how you point your guns. They pointed 'em so careless at New York that a wad come within six inches of making daylight shine through the President.

Now I think on't, there is the most rascally set of fellers skulking about somewhere in this part of the country that ever I heard of, and I wish you would blow 'em up. They are worse than the pickpockets. I mean them are fellers that's got to writing letters and putting my name to 'em, and sending of 'em to the printers. And I heard there was one sassy feller last Saturday, down to Newburyport, that got on to a horse, and rid about town calling himself Major Jack Downing, and all the soldiers and the folks marched up and shook hands with him, and thought it was me. Isn't it Mr. Shakespeare that says something about "he that steals my munnypus steals trash, but he that steals my name ought to have his head broke?" I wish you would find that story and print it.

  Your old friend,   MAJOR JACK DOWNING.

LETTER XLIII.

THE PRESIDENT AND THE REST OF 'EM **TURN A SHORT** CORNER AT CONCORD, AND SET THEIR FACES TOWARD WASHINGTON.

     CONCORD, Nu Hamsheer, June 30, 1833.

To the Editor of the Portland Courier.

MY DEAR OLD FRIEND:—The jig is all up about our going to Portland and Downingville. I've battled the watch with the President this two days about it, and told him he must go there if he had the breath of life in him; and he kept telling me he certainly would, if horses could carry him there.

But the President isn't very well, and that aint the worst of it; there's been a little difficulty bruin' among us, and the President's got so riled about it, that he's finally concluded to start on his way back to-morrow. I can't help it; but I feel bad enough about it to cry a barrel of tears.

I don't know how they will stan' it in Downingville, when they come to get the news. I'm afraid there will be a master uproar there, for you know they are all great Demokrats. But the stage is jest agoing to start.

    In haste, from your friend,

      MAJOR JACK DOWNING.

LETTER XLIV.

COUSIN NABBY DESCRIBES THE **UNUTTERABLE DISAPPOINTMENT AT DOWNINGVILLE** BECAUSE THE **PRESIDENT DIDN'T COME, AND** TELLS **WHAT A TERRIBLE PUCKER ANT KEZIAH WAS IN ABOUT IT—GREAT UPROAR IN DOWNINGVILLE.**

DOWNINGVILLE, July 8, 1833.

To the Editor of the Portland Courier.

RESPECTABLE SIR :—As Cousin Jack is always so mity budge in writing letters to you, and as he and the President showed us a most provoking trick, and run off like **a** stream of chalk, **back to** Washington, without coming **here, after** they had promised **over and over** again that they would come, and we had got all slicked up and our clean gowuds on, and more good victuals cooked than there ever was in all Downingville before—I say, Mr. Editor, I declare it's too bad ; we are all as mad as blazes about **it,** and I mean to write and tell you all **about it,** if I live ; and if Cousin Jack don't like it, he may lump it ; so there now.

Ye see Cousin Jack writ to us that he and the President **and** some more gentlemen should be here the 4th of July, and **we must** spring to it and brush up and see how smart we **could look, and how many** fine things we could show to **the President.** This was a Saturday before the 4th of July come a Thursday. The letter was to Uncle Joshua, the Postmaster. Most all the folks in Downingville were at the Post-Office waiting when the mail come in, for we expected to hear **from** Jack.

Uncle **Joshua** put on his spettacles and opened the mail,

and hauled out the papers and letters in a bunch. In a minute I see one to Uncle Joshua with the President's name on the outside ; so I knew it was from Jack, for the President always puts his name on Jack's letters. We all cried out to Uncle Joshua to open it, and let us know what was in it. But he's such a provoking odd old man, he wouldn't touch it 'till he got every one of the papers and letters sorted and put up in their places. And then he took it and set down in his armchair, and took out his tobacker box and took a chaw of tobacker, and then he broke open the seal and sot and chawed and read to himself. We all stood tiptoe, with our hearts in our mouths, and he must needs read it over to himself three times, chawing his old quid, and once in a while giving us a knowing wink, before he would tell us what was in it. And he wouldn't tell us arter all, but, says he, "You must all be ready to put the best side out Thursday morning ; there'll be business to attend to, such as Downingville never see before."

At that we all turned and run, and such a hubbub as we were in from that time 'till Thursday morning, I guess you never see. Such a washing and scrubbing, and making new clothes and mending old ones, and baking and cooking. Every thing seemed to be in a clutter all over the neighborhood. Sargent Joel flew round like a ravin' distracted rooster. He called out his company every morning before sunrise, and marched 'em up and down the road three hours every day. He sent to the store and got a whole new set of buttons, and had 'em sowed on to his regimental coat, and had a new piece of red put round the collar. And had his trowses washed and his boots greased, and looked as though he might take the shine off of most anything. But the greatest rumpus was at Uncle Joshua's ; for they said the President must stay there all night. And Ant Keziah was in such a pucker to have everything nice, I didn't know but she would fly off the handle.

She had every part of the house washed from garret to cellar, and the floors all sanded, and a bunch of green bushes put into all the fire places. And she baked three ovens-full of dried punkin pies, besides a few dried huckleberry pies, and cake, and a great pot of pork and beans. But the worst trouble was to fix up the bed so as to look nice; for Ant Keziah declared the President should have as good a night's lodging in her house as he had in New York or Boston. So she put on two feather beds on top the straw bed, and a brannew calico quilt that she made the first summer after she was married, and never put it on a bed before. And to make it look as nice as the New York beds, she took her red silk gown and ripped it up and made a blanket to spread over the top. And then she hung up some sheets all round the bedroom, and the gals brought in a whole handful of roses and pinks, and pinned 'em up round as thick as flies in August.

After we got things pretty much fixed, Uncle Joshua started off to meet Cousin Jack and the President, and left Sargent Joel to put matters to rights, and told us we must all be ready and be paraded in the road by nine o'clock Thursday morning. Well, Thursday morning come, and we all mustered as soon as it was daylight and dressed up. The children were all washed, and had their clean aprons on and their heads combed, and were put under the care of the schoolmarm, to be paraded along with her scholars.

About eight o'clock, all the village got together down the road as fur as Uncle Joshua's new barn; and Sargent Joel told us how to stand, as he said, in military order. He placed Bill Johnson and Cousin Ephraim out a little ways in front, with each of 'em a great long fowling piece with a smart charge in to fire a salute, and told 'em as soon as the President hove in sight to let drive, only to be careful and pint their guns up, so as not to hurt anybody. Then come Sargent

Joel and his company ; and then come the schoolmarm and the children ; and then come all the women and gals over sixteen with Ant Keziah at their head ; and then come all the men in town that owned horses riding on horseback ; and all the boys that Sargent Joel didn't think was large enough to walk in the procession got up and sot on the fences along by the side of the road.

There we stood 'till about nine o'clock, when, sure enough, we saw somebody come riding out of the woods down the hill. The boys all screamed, ready to split their throats, "Hoorah for Jackson," and Bill Johnson fired off his gun. Cousin Ephraim, who aint so easily fluttered, held on to his and didn't fire, for he couldn't see anybody but Uncle Joshua on his old gray horse. Along come Uncle Joshua, on a slow trot, and we looked and looked, and couldn't see anybody coming behind him.

Then they all begun to look at one another as wild as hawks, and turn all manner of colors. When Uncle Joshua got up so we could see him pretty plain, he looked as cross as a thunder-cloud. He rid up to Sargent Joel, and says he, "You may all go home about your business, for Jack and the President are half way to Washington by this time."

My stars ! what a time there was then. I never see so many folks boiling over mad before. Bill Johnson threw his gun over into the field as much as ten rods, and hopped up and down, and struck his fists together like all possessed. Sargent Joel marched back and forth across the road two or three times, growing redder and redder, till at last he drew out his sword and fetched a blow across a hemlock stump, and snapped it off like a pipe-stem. Ant Keziah fell down in a conniption fit ; and it was an hour before we could bring her tu and get her into the house. And when she come to go round the house and see the victuals she had cooked up, and go into the bedroom and see her gown all cut up, she went into conniption fits again. But she's better to-day, and has gone to work to try to patch up her gown again.

I thought I would jest let you know about these things, and if you are a mind to send word on to Cousin Jack and the

THE DISAPPOINTMENT AND UPROAR IN DOWNINGVILLE.

President, I'm willing. You may tell 'em there aint five folks in Downingville that would hoorah for Jackson now, and hardly one that would vote for him, unless 'tis Uncle Joshua, and he wouldn't if he wasn't afraid of losing the Post-Office.

Your respected friend,

NABBY DOWNING.

DOCKYMENT.

NOMINATION FOR THE PRESIDENCY.

From the National Intelligencer.

We do not know whether it be necessary, in copying the subjoined effusion, to enter into a protest against misinterpretation of our motives. We should be sorry to be understood, while humoring a jest, as meaning to burlesque so serious an action as the choice of President of the United States. We copy the following for the sake of its moral, as well as its wit, and we do not like the moral the less for being taught with a smiling countenance:

From the Mauch Chunk (Pa.) Courier.

OUR NEXT PRESIDENT.

Many of the papers in the United States have already manifested a disposition to agitate the subject of the next Presidency, and several distinguished individuals have been informally named for that office, amoug whom are Mr. Van Buren, Mr. M'Lean, Mr. Cass, Mr. Clay and Mr. Webster. As we are opposed to a premature discussion of this ticklish question, we have not hitherto committed ourself in favor of either of these individuals. Indeed, we have considered it very imprudent, in these times, for any one who wishes to be an orthodox politician, to "come out" for anybody until he can ascertain who will be most likely to succeed. Accordingly, we have stood upon our "reserved rights" of neutrality, to watch the signs of the times, and see who would probably be the most popular candidate. Recent indications have satisfactorily convinced us on that point, and as we wished to be considered among the "originals"—the *real Simon Pures*—we would lose no time in nominating, for President,

MAJOR JACK DOWNING, OF DOWNINGVILLE.

In recommending this distinguished personage to our fellow citizens, it will be scarcely necessary to enumerate his various claims to their suffrages. Suffice it to say, his military renown, his valuable public services in assisting President Jackson to put down the nullifiers, especially in shaking hands with the Yankees "Down East," and last, though not least, the fidelity with which he and his Uncle Joshua stuck to the old hero after he found he was going to be President, eminently qualify him for that exalted station.

LETTER XLV.

MAJOR DOWNING TELLS ABOUT GOING TO CAMBRIDGE AND MAKING THE PRESIDENT A DOCTOR OF LAWS.

On Board the Steamboat,
Going from Providence to York, July 2, 1833.

To my old friend, the Editor of the Portland Courier, in the Mariners' Church Building, second story, eastern end, Fore street, away Down East, in the State of Maine.

My Dear Friend :—We are driving back again full chisel, as fast as we come on when we were on the railroad between Washington and Baltimore. And we've been drivin' so fast on a round turn in all the places we've been, and have had so much shaking hands, and eating and one thing another to do, that I couldn't get time to write to you at half the places where I wanted to, so I thought I'd set down now, while the President's laid down to rest him awhile, and tell you something about Cambridge and Lowell. Ye see when we were at Boston they sent word to us to come out to Cambridge, for they wanted to make the President a doctor of laws. What upon airth a doctor of laws was, or why they wanted to make the

President one, I couldn't think. So when we come to go up to bed I asked the Gineral about it. And says I, "Gineral, what is it they want to do to you out to Cambridge?" Says he, "They want to make a doctor of laws of me." "Well," says I, "but what good will that do?" "Why," says he, "you know, Major Downing, there's a pesky many of them are laws passed by Congress, that are rickety things. Some of 'em have very poor constitutions, and some of 'em haven't no constitution at all. So that it is necessary to have somebody there to doctor 'em up a little and not let 'em go out into the world, where they would stand a chance to catch cold and be sick, without they had good constitutions to bear it. You know," says he, "I've had to doctor the laws considerable ever since I've been at Washington, although I wasn't a regular bred doctor. And I made out so well about it, that these Cambridge folks think I better be made into a regular doctor at once, and then there'll be no grumbling and disputing about my practice." Says he, "Major, what do you think of it?" I told him I thought it an excellent plan; and asked him if he didn't think they would be willing, bein' I'd been round in the military business considerable for a year or two past, to make me a doctor of war. He said he didn't know, but he thought it would be no harm to try 'em. "But," says he, "Major, I feel a little kind of streaked about it, after all; for they say they will go to talking to me in Latin, and although I studied it a little once, I don't know any more about it now than the man in the moon. And how I can get along in that case, I don't know." I told him my way, when anybody talked to me in a lingo that I didn't understand, was jest to say nothing, but look as knowing as any of 'em, and then they ginerally thought I knew a pesky sight more than any of 'em. At that the Gineral fetched me a slap on my shoulder, and haw-hawed right out.

Says he, "Major Downing, you are the boy for me; I don't know how I should get along in this world if it wasn't for you."

So when we got ready we went right to Cambridge as bold as could be. And that are Cambridge is a real pretty place; it seems to me I should like to live in them colleges as well as any place I've seen. We went into the libry, and I guess I stared a little, for I didn't think before there was half so many books in the world. I should think there was near about enough to fill a meetin'-house. I don't believe they was ever all read, or ever will be to all ages.

When we come to go in to be made doctors of, there was a terrible crowding around; but they give us a good place, and sure enough, they did begin to talk in Latin or some other gibberish; but whether they were talking to the Gineral, or who 'twas, I couldn't tell. I guess the Gineral was a little puzzled. But he never said a word, only once in a while bowed a little. And I s'pose he happened sometimes to put the bows in the wrong place, for I could see some of the sassy students look up one side once in a while, and snicker out of one corner of their mouths. Howsomever, the Gineral stood it out like a hero, and got through very well. And when 'twas over, I stept up to Mr. Quincy and asked him if he wouldn't be so good as to make me a doctor of war, and hinted to him a little about my services down to Madawaska and among the nullifiers. At that he made me a very polite bow, and says he, "Major Downing, we should be very happy to oblige you if we could, but we never give any degrees of war here; all our degrees are degrees of peace." So I find I shall have to practice war in the natural way—let nullification or what will come. After 'twas all over, we went to Mr. Quincy's and had a capital dinner. And, on the whole, had about as good a visit to Cambridge as most anywhere.

I meant to a told you considerable about Lowell, but the steamboat goes so fast I shan't have time to. We went all over the factories, and there!—I wont try to say one word about 'em, for I've been filled with such a wonderment ever since that my ideas are all as big as hay-stacks, and if I should try to get one of 'em out of my head, it would tear it all to pieces. It beat all that ever I heard of before, and the Gineral said it beat all that ever he heard of. But what made the Gineral hold his head up, and feel more like a soldier than he had before since he was at New Orleans, was when we marched along the street by them are five thousand gals, all dressed up, and looking as pretty as a million of butterflies. The Gineral marched along as light as a boy, and seems to me I never see his eyes shine so bright afore. After we got along to about the middle of 'em, he whispered to me, and says he, "Major Downing, is your Cousin Nabby here among 'em? If she is, I must be introduced to her." I told him she was not; as they were expecting us to come to Downingville, she staid to home to help get ready. "Well," says he, "if any thing should happen that we can't go to Downingville, you must send for your Cousin Nabby and Uncle Joshua to come on to Washington to see me. I will bear all the expenses, if they will only come," says he. "These Northern gals are as much afore our Southern and Western gals as can be, and I've thought of your Cousin Nabby a great deal lately." He looked as though he was going to say something more, but Mr. Van Buren and the rest of 'em crowded along up so near that it broke it off, and we had to go along.

I see we've got most to York, and shall have to go ashore in a few minutes, so I can't write any more now, but remain

Your sincere and loving friend,

MAJOR JACK DOWNING.

LETTER XLVI.

MAJOR DOWNING TELLS ABOUT THE QUARREL THAT HE AND MR. VAN BUREN HAD AT CONCORD AFTER THEY WENT UP CHAMBER TO BED; AND ALSO DECLARES HIS INTENTION TO RUN FOR THE PRESIDENCY.

WASHINGTON CITY, July 20, 1833.

To my old friend, the Editor of the Portland Courier, away Down East, in the State of Maine.

MY DEAR OLD FRIEND :—I don't know but **you might think** strange on't, that I should be back here to Washington more than a fortnight, and not write to you. But I hant forgot you. You needn't never be afraid of that. We aint very apt to forget our best friends; and you may depend upon it, Jack Downing will never forget the editor of the Portland Courier any more than **Andrew** Jackson **will** forget Jack Downing. You **was the** first person that ever **give** me a lift **into** public life, and you've **been a** boosting me along ever since. And jest between you and me, I think **I'm** getting into a way now where I shall be able, by and **by, to** do something to pay you for it. The reason that I haven't **writ** to you before is, **that** we have had pretty serious business to attend to since we **got** back. **But** we've jest got through with it, and Mr. Van **Buren has cleared out** and gone back about the **quickest to New York, and** I guess with a flea **in his ear.** Now, **jest** between you and me, in **confidence,** I'll **tell you how** 'tis; but, pray, don't let on about **it to anybody else for** the world. Didn't you think plaguy strange **what made us** cut back so quick from Concord, without going **to** Portland, or Portsmouth, or Downingville? You know the papers have said it was because the President want very well, and the President had to make that excuse himself, in some of his letters; but it was no such thing. The President could a marched on foot twenty miles a day then; and only let him been at the head of my Downingville company, and he'd make a whole British regiment scamper like a flock of sheep.

But you see the trouble on't was, there was some difficulty between I and Mr. Van Buren. Some how or other, Mr. Van Buren always looked kind of jealous at me all the time after he met us at New York; and I couldn't help minding every time the folks hollored, "Hoorah for Major Downing!" he would turn as red as a blaze of fire. And wherever we stopped to take a bite, or to have a chat, he would always work it, if he could, somehow or other, so as to crowd in between me and the President. Well, ye see, I wouldn't mind much about it, but would jest step round t'other side. And though I say it myself, the folks would look at me, let me be on which side I would; and after they'd cried "Hoorah for the President," they'd most always sing out, "Hoorah for Major Downing." Mr. Van Buren kept growing more and more fidgety till we got to Concord; and there we had a room full of sturdy old Democrats of New Hampshire; and after they had all flocked round the old President and shook hands with him, he happened to introduce me to some of 'em before he did Mr. Van Buren. At that the fat was all in the fire. Mr. Van Buren wheeled about and marched out of the room, looking as though he could bite a board nail off. The President had to send to him three times before he could get him back into the room again. And when he did come in, he didn't speak to me for the whole evening. However, we kept it from the company pretty much; but when we come to go up to bed that night, we had a real quarrel. It was nothing but jaw, jaw, the whole night. Mr. Woodbury and Mr. Cass tried to pacify us all they could, but it was all in vain—we didn't one of us get a wink of sleep, and shouldn't if the night had lasted a fortnight. Mr. Van Buren said the President had dishonored the country, by placing a military major on half pay before the second officer of the Government. The President begged him to consider that I was a very particular friend of his; that I had been a great help to him at both ends of the country; that I had kept the British out of Madawaska, away down in Maine, and had marched my company clear from Downingville to Washington, on my way to South Carolina, to put down the nullifiers; and he thought I was entitled to as much respect as any man in the country.

This nettled Mr. Van Buren peskily. He said he thought it was a fine time of day if a raw jockey from an obscure village away Down East, jest because he had a major's commission, was going to throw the Vice-President of the United States and the heads of Departments into the back-ground. At this my dander began to rise, and I stept right up to him; and says I, "Mr. Van Buren, you are the last man that ought to call me a jockey. And if you'll go to Downingville, and stand up before my company, with Sargent Joel at their head, and call Downingville an obscure village, I'll let you use my head for a foot-ball as long as you live afterwards. For if they wouldn't blow you into ten thousand atoms, I'll never guess again." We got so high at last that the old President hopt off the bed like a boy; for he had laid down to rest him, bein' it was near daylight, though he couldn't get to sleep. And says he, "Mr. Donaldson, set down and write Mr. Anderson at Portland, and my friend Joshua Downing, at Downingville, that I can't come; I'm going to start for Washington this morning." "What!" says Mr. Cass, "and not go to Portsmouth, and Exeter, and round there!" "I tell you," says the President, "I'm going to start for Washington this morning, and in three days I'll be there." "What!" says Mr.

Woodbury, "and not go to Portland, where they have spent so much money to get ready for us?" "I tell you," says the President, "my foot is down: I go not a step further, but turn about this morning for Washington." "What!" says I, "and not go to Downingville: what will Uncle Joshua say?" At this the President looked a little hurt; and says he, "Major Downing, I can't help it. As for going any further with

THE QUARREL BETWEEN MAJOR DOWNING AND MR. VAN BUREN.

such a din as this about my ears, I cannot and will not, and I am resolved not to budge another inch." And, sure enough, the President was as good as his word, and we were all packed up by sunrise, and in three days we were in Washington.

And here we've been ever since, battling the watch about

the next Presidency. Mr. Van Buren says the President promised it to him, and now he charges me and the President with a plot to work myself into it and leave him out. It's true I've been nominated in a good many papers: in the National Intelligencer, and in the Mauch Chunk Courier, printed away off among the coal-diggers in Pennsylvany, and a good many more. And them are Pennsylvany chaps are real pealers for electing folks when they take hold; and that's what makes Mr. Van Buren so uneasy. The President tells him as he has promised to help him, he shall do what he can for him—but if the folks *will* vote for me, he can't help it. Mr. Van Buren wanted I should come out in the National Intelligencer and resign, and so be put up for Vice-President under him. But I told him no; bein' it had gone so fur, I wouldn't do nothing about it. I hadn't asked for the office, and if the folks had a mind to give it to me, I wouldn't refuse it So, after we had battled it about a fortnight. Mr. Van Buren found it was no use to try to dicker with me, and he's cleared out and gone to New York to see what he can do there.

I never thought of getting in to be President so soon, though I've had a kind of hankering for it this two years. But now, seeing it's turned out as it has, I'm determined to make a bold push; and if I *can* get in by the free votes of the people, I mean to. The President says he rather I should have it than anybody else; and, if he hadn't promised Mr. Van Buren before hand, he would use his influence for me.

I remember when I was a boy, about a dozen years old, there was an old woman come to our house to tell fortunes. And after she'd told the rest of 'em, father says he, "Here's Jack, you haven't told his fortune yet, and I don't 'spose it's worth a telling, for he's a real mutton-headed boy." At that the old woman catched hold of my hair, and pulled my head back and looked into my face, and I never shall forget how she looked right through me as long as I live. At last, says she, and she gin me a shove that sent me almost through the side of the house, "Jack will beat the whole of you. He'll be a famous climber in his day ; **and wherever** he sets out to climb, you may depend upon it, he will go to the top of the ladder." Now, putting all these things together, and the nominations in the papers, and the " hoorahs for Major Downing," I don't **know what it** means, unless it means that I must **be President.** So, as I said afore, I'm determined to make a bold push. I've writ to Colonel Crockett to see if I can get the support of the Western States, and his reply is, "*Go ahead.*" I shall depend upon you and Uncle Joshua to carry the State of Maine for **me ; and, in** order to secure the other States, I 'spose it will be **necessary** to publish my life **and writings.** President Jackson had his life published before he was elected, and when Mr. Clay was a candidate he had his'n published. **I've talked with the** President about it, and he says publish it by all means, and set the printer of **the** Portland Courier right about it.

So I want you to go to work as soon as you get this, and pick up my letters, and begin to print 'em in a book ; and I'll set down and write a history of my life to put into it, and send it along as fast as I can get it done. But I want you to be very careful not to get any of them are confounded counterfeit letters, that **the rascally fellers have been sending to** the printers, mixed **in 'long with mine.** It would be as bad as breaking **a rotten** egg in 'long with **the** good ones ; it would spile the whole pudding. You can tell all my letters, for **they** were all sent to you first.

The President says I must have a picter of me made and put into the book. He says he had one put into his, and Mr. Clay had one put into his. These things, you know, will all **help** get the free votes of the people, and **that's** all I want.

For I tell you now, right up and down, I never will take any office that doesn't come by the free votes of the people. I'm a genuine Demokratic Republikan, and always was, and so was my father before me, and Uncle Joshua besides.

There's a few more things that I want to speak to you about in this letter, but I'm afraid it will get to be too lengthy. That are story that they got in the newspapers about my being married in Philadelphy is all a hoax. I ain't married **yet**, nor shan't be till a little blue-eyed gal that used to run about with me, and go to school and slide down hill in Downingville, is the wife of President Downing. And that are other story, that the President gave me a curnel's commission jest before we started Down East, isn't exactly true. The President did offer me one, but I thanked him, and told him if he would excuse me, I should rather not take it, for I had always noticed that majors were more apt to rise in the world than curnels.

I wish you would take a little pains to send up to Downing**ville and get Uncle Joshua to** call a public meeting, and have me nominated there. I'm so well known there, it would have **a** great effect in other places. And I want to have it particularly understood, and so stated in their resolutions, that I am the genuine Demokratic Republikan candidate. I know you will put your shoulder to the wheel in this business, and do all you can for me, for you was always a friend to me, and **just** between you and me, when I get in to be President you may depend upon it you shall have as good an office as you want.

But **I see it's time for** me to end this letter. The President is quite comfortable, and sends his respects to you and Uncle Joshua. I remain your sincere friend,

MAJOR JACK DOWNING.

LETTER XLVII.

COUSIN EPHRAIM DESCRIBES THE METHOD OF PUTTING "DIMOKRATS" OVER ON TO THE FEDERAL SIDE, AND LAYS A PLAN TO GET THE DOWNINGVILLE POST-OFFICE.

DOWNINGVILLE, State of Maine, August 12, 1833.

To Cousin Major Jack Downing, at Washington City.

DEAR COUSIN JACK :—I've got something pretty heavy on my mind that I want to tell ye about, and ask your advice, and may be I shall want you to lend me a hand a little. I've been watching politics pretty snug ever since I was a little boy, and that's near about thirty years; and I believe I know most as much about it as Uncle Joshua, although he's twenty years older than I be. Now about this Republikanism and Federalism, I've minded that it always keeps changing, and always has, ever since I can remember. And I've minded, tu, it most always keeps going round one way; that is, *the young Federalists keep turning Dimokrats, and the old Dimokrats keep turning Federalists*. What it's for I don't exactly know, but that's the way it goes. I s'pose a man, on the whole, isn't hardly fit to be a Dimokrat after he gets to be fifty years old. And here is old Uncle Joshua in the Post-Office, he's got to be about fifty, and he's hanging on to the Dimokratic side yet, like the toothache; and it begins to worry me a good deal. I think it's high time he went over. You know Downingville has always been a genuine Republikan town, and I want it should always go according to the *usages* (I think that's what they call it) of the Dimokratic party.

When it gets to be time for an old Dimokrat to go over on

the Federal side, I believe the Argus always put's em over. You remember there was old Mr. Insley in Portland, and old Gineral Wingate in Bath, as much as a dozen years ago, were some as big Republikans as there was anywhere about. Well, they got to be considerable old, and had been in office some time, so the Argus took and clapt 'em right over on to the Federal side. And you know there was Mr. Holmes, he was a whapping great Republikan. But he begun to grow old, and so the Argus put him over.

And this summer the Argus is putting of 'em over considerable younger on to the Federal side. It has put Judge Preble over, and Judge Ware, and Mr. Mitchell, the Postmaster at Portland, and he isn't near so old as Uncle Joshua; and it has put Mr. Megquier over—only think, such a young man as Mr. Megquier, that's only been in the State Sinnet three or four years. Now don't you think, according to Dimokratic usage, it's high time old Uncle Joshua was put over? I wish you would jest write to the Argus and have it done, for I feel a good deal worried about it.

And as soon as it comes out in the Argus that he is fairly over, I want you to tell the President that Uncle Joshua is a Federalist, and have him removed from the Post-Office, for it would be an everlasting shame to have the Post-Office in Downingville kept by a Federalist.

N. B.—If Uncle Joshua should be removed, I wish you would use your influence to get the President to give the office to me; for, next to Uncle Joshua, I s'pose I've done more for the Republikan party than any man in Downingville. I can have a recommendation from Sargent Joel and all the company. By attending to this, you will much oblige

Your friend and cousin,

EPHRAIM DOWNING.

LETTER XLVIII.

IN WHICH THE PRESIDENT BEGUN TO SAY SOMETHING ABOUT ME AND DANIEL.

WASHINGTON CITY, Sept. 14, 1833.

To the Editor of the Portland Courier, away Down East, in the State of Maine.

MY DEAR OLD FRIEND :—It's got to be a pretty considerable long while now since I've writ to you ; for I never like to write, you know, without I have something to say. But I've got something on my mind now that keeps me all the time a thinking so much that I can't hold in any longer. So, jest between you and me, I'll tell you what 'tis. But I must begin a little ways beforehand, so you can see both sides of it, and I'll tell you what 'tis as soon as I get along to it.

You see I and the President has been down to the Rip Raps a few weeks, to try to recruit up a little ; for that pesky tower away Down East like to did the job for the old Gineral. So, after we got things pretty much to rights here, we jest stepped aboard the steamboat and went down to the Rip Raps. That are Rip Raps is a capital place ; it is worth all the money we ever paid for it, if it was for nothing else only jest to recruit up the Government. It is one of the most coolest places in the summer time that you ever see. Let a feller be all worn out and wilted down as limpsy as a rag, so that the doctors would think he was jest ready to fly off the handle, and let him go down to the Rip Raps, and stay there a fortnight, and he'd come home again as smart as a steel-trap. The President got recruited up so nicely, while we were down to the Rip Raps, that ever since we got back, till two or three days ago, he has been as good-natured and sociable as ever I should wish to see a body. And now I'm coming, pretty soon, to what I was going to tell you about, that bears so heavy on my mind.

You see the President likes, every morning after the breakfast is out of the way, to set down and read over the newspapers, and see what is going on in the country, and who's elected, and so on. So, when we've done breakfast, we take the letters and papers that come from the Post-Office, and go away by ourselves into the great East Room, where we can say jest what we've a mind to, and nobody not hear us, and the President sets down in his great arm rocking-chair and smokes his cigar, and I set down by the table and read to him. Last Monday morning, as I was reading over the papers, one arter another, I come to a Pennsylvany paper, and opened it, and says I, "Hullow, Gineral, here's a speech of Mr. Webster, at Pittsburgh, as large as life."

"Ah," said he, "well, let us hear what Daniel has been talking to them are Pennsylvany and Ohio chaps about."

So, I hitched back in my chair, and read on. And by and by I begun to get into the marrow of the story, where he told all about nullification, and what a dark time we had of it last winter, and how the black clouds begun to rise and spread over the country, and the thunders of civil war begun to roll and rumble away off to the South, and by and by how the tempest was jest ready to burst over our heads, and split the country all into shivers, and how, in the very nick of time, the President's proclamation came out and spread over the whole country like a rainbow, and how everybody then took courage and said the danger was all over. While I had been reading this, the President had started up on his feet, and walked back and forth across the room pretty quick, puffing away and making the smoke roll out of his mouth like a house a fire; and by the time I had got through, he had thrown his cigar out of the window, and come and sot down, leaning his elbow on the table, and looking right in my face. I laid the paper down, and there he sot looking right at me as much as five minutes, and never said a word; but he seemed to keep a thinking as fast as a horse could run. At last, said he,

THE MAJOR READING THE NEWS IN THE EAST ROOM.

"Major Downing, were you ever told that you resembled Daniel Webster?"

"Why, Gineral," says I, "how do you mean—in looks or what?"

"Why, perhaps a little of both," says he, "but mostly in looks."

"Bless my stars," says I, "Gineral, you don't mean to say that I am quite so *dark* as he is?"

"Perhaps not," says he, "but you have that sharp, knowing look, as though you could see right through a millstone. I know," says he, "that Mr. Webster is rather a dark-looking man, but there isn't another man in this country that can throw so much *light* on a dark subject as he can."

"Why, yes," says I, "he has a remarkable faculty for that; he can see through most anything, and he can make other folks see through it, too. I guess," says I, "if he'd been born in old Virginny, he'd stood next to most anybody."

"A *leetle* afore 'em," says the Gineral, "in my way of thinking. "I'll tell you what 'tis, Major, I begin to think your New Englanders ain't the worst sort of fellows in the world, after all."

"Ah, well," says I, "seeing is believing, and you've been down tnat way now, and can judge for yourself. But if you had only gone as fur as Downingville, I guess you would have thought still better of 'em than you do now. Other folks may talk larger and bluster more," says I, "but whenever you are in trouble, and want the real support in time of need, go to New England for it, and you never need to be afraid but what it will come."

"I believe you are right," says the Gineral; "for, notwithstanding all I could do with my proclamation against nullification, I believe I should have rubbed hard if there had been no such men in the country as Major Downing and Daniel Webster. But this nullification business isn't killed yet. The tops are beat down, but the roots are alive as ever, and spreading under ground wider and wider; and one of these days, when they begin to sprout up again, there'll be a tougher scrabble to keep 'em down than there has been yet; and I've been thinking," says he, and he laid his hand on my shoulder, and looked very anxious—" I've been thinking," says he, *"if you and Daniel "*—

And here the door opened, and in come Amos Kendil with a long letter from Mr. Van Buren about the Bank, and the Safety Fund, and the Government Deposits, and I don't know what all; and the President's brow was clouded in a minute; for he always feels **kind of pettish when** they plague him about the Safety Fund. I haven't had any chance to talk with him since, there's so many of 'em round him; and I'm as uneasy as a fish out of **water,** I feel so anxious to know what the President was going to say about me and Daniel. I shall watch the first chance when I think it will do to talk with him, and find out what he was going to say. I can't hardly sleep a nights, I think so much about it. When I find out I'll write to you **again.**

Send my love to **the folks** up in Downingville when you have a chance.

I remain **your sincere** friend,

MAJOR JACK DOWNING.

LETTER XLIX.

IN WHICH THE PRESIDENT FINISHED WHAT HE WAS GOING TO SAY ABOUT ME AND DANIEL.

WASHINGTON CITY, Sept. 30, 1833.

To the Editor of the Portland Courier, away **Down** *East, in the State of Maine.*

MY DEAR FRIEND:—Haven't you been in a terrible kind of a pucker ever since my last letter to you, to know what the President was going to say about me and Daniel? If you haven't I have. I never felt so uneasy for a fortnight hardly in my life. If I went to bed I couldn't sleep, and I've got up and walked the floor as much as half the night almost every night since. I've wished the bank to Guinea more than fifty times, for there's been such a hubbub here about the bank this fortnight past, that I couldn't get a moment's chance to talk with the President about anything else. We'd have cabinet meetings once in a while to see about moving the deposits, and Mr. Duane, and Mr. Cass, and Mr. McLane would talk up to the President so about it, that he'd conclude to let 'em alone and do nothing about it, and let Congress manage it jest as they'd a mind to. And then we'd go home, and Mr. Kendil would come in and talk the matter over, and read some great long letters from Mr. Van Buren, and get the President so confused that he would lose all patience a'most.

But Mr. Kendil is the master feller to hang on that ever I see; he's equal to the toothache. And he talked and palavered with the President till he finally brought him over, and then the President put his foot down, and said the deposits should be moved, whether or no. And then the botheration was to see who should move 'em. The President told Mr. Duane to do it; but he said his conscience wouldn't let him. Then the President told Mr. Taney to take Mr. Duane's place, and see if his conscience would let him. Mr. Taney tried it, and found his conscience went easy enough; so Mr. Duane packed up and went home to Philadelphy. We were all dreadful sorry to lose Mr. Duane, for he was a nice man as you will see one in a thousand. It's a pity he had such a stiff conscience; he might have staid here in the Treasury jest as well as not, if it hadn't been for that.

But this storm about the bank begins to blow over, and the President's got, in a manner, cooled down again. This morning, after breakfast, we took the papers and letters jest as we used to, and went away into the East Room to read the news and chat awhile ; and it really did my heart good to see the President set down once more looking so good-natured in his great arm-chair smoking his cigar. After I had read over the news to him awhile, and got him in pretty good humor, I made bold to out with it, and says I, " Gineral, there's one question I want to ask you." And says he, " you know, Major, I always allow you to ask me anything you're a mind to ; what is it ? " " Well," says I, " when we had that talk here, about a fortnight ago, you begun to say something about me and Daniel ; and jest as you got into the middle of it, Mr. Kendil come in, and broke it right off, short as a pipe-stem. It's been running in my head ever since, and I've been half crazy to know what it was you was going to say." " Well, let us see," says the Gineral, " where was it I left off ? for this everlasting fuss about the bank has kept my head so full I can't seem to remember much about it."

" Why," says I, " you was talking about nullification ; how the tops were beat down a little, but the roots were all running about under ground as live as ever, and it wouldn't be long before they'd be sprouting up again all over the country, and there'd be a tougher scrabble to keep 'em down than ever there had been yet ; and then you said *if I and Daniel* ——, and there that plaguy Kendil came in—I've no patience with him now when I think of it—and broke it right off." " Ah, now I remember," says the Gineral, " how 'twas. Well," says he, " Major Downing, it is a solemn fact, this country is to see a blacker storm of nullification, before many years comes about, than ever it has seen yet ; the clouds are beginning to gather now ; I've seen 'em rolling over South Carolina, and hanging about Georgia, and edging along into old Virginny, and I see the storm's a gathering ; it must come ; and if there isn't somebody at the helm that knows how to steer pretty well, the old ship must go down. I an't afraid," says he, " but what I can keep her up while I have the command, but I'm getting to be old, and must give up soon, and then what'll become of her I don't know. But what I was going to say was this : I've been thinking if you and Daniel, after I give up, would put your heads together, and take charge of her till the storm has blown over, you might save her. And I don't know who else can."

"But how do you mean, Gineral ?" says I. " Why, to speak plain," says he, " if nullification shows its head, Daniel must talk and you must fight. There's nothing else will do the job for it that I know of. Daniel must go into the Presidential chair, and you must take command of the army, and then things will go straight." At this I was a little struck up ; and I looked him right in the eye, and says I, " Gineral, do you mean that Daniel Webster ought to be President after you give up ?" " Certainly," says he, " if you want to keep the country out of the jaws of nullification." "But," says I, " Gineral, Daniel is a Federalist, a Hartford Convention Federalist ; and I should like to know which is worst, the jaws of nullification, or the jaws of Federalism ?" " The jaws of a fiddlestick !" said the President, starting up and throwing his cigar out of the window as much as two rods ; " but how do you know, Major Downing, that Daniel is a Federalist ?" "Because," says I, " I've heard him called so Down East more than a hundred times." " And that's jest all you know about it," says he. " Now, I tell you how 'tis, Major Downing, Daniel is as thorough a Republican as you be, or as I be, and has been ever since my proclamation came out against nullification. As soon as that proclamation came out, Daniel came right over on to the Republican ground, and took it upon his shoulder, and carried it through thick and thin, where no other man in the country could have carried it." Says I, " Gineral, is that a fact ?" And says he, " Yes, you may depend upon it, 'tis every word truth." "Well," says I, "that alters the case a little, and I'll write to Uncle Joshua and the editor of the Portland Courier, and see what they think of it; and if they think it's best to have Daniel for President we'll have him in, and I'll take my turn afterward; for, seeing the people are bent upon having me for President, I won't decline; though if it is thought best that I should wait a little while, I won't be particular about that. I'm willing to do that which will be best for the country."

So I remain your loving friend,

MAJOR JACK DOWNING.

LETTER L.

MAJOR DOWNING PREVENTS A ROBBERY IN THE SENATE CHAMBER.

WASHINGTON CITY, Dec. 28, 1833.

To the Editor of the Portland Courier, in the Mariners' Church Building, second story, eastern end, Fore street, Porland, away Down East, in the State of Maine.

MY DEAR OLD FRIEND :—We've been in a kind of harrycane here, and I and the Gineral has had to hold on so tight, to keep things from blowing away, that I couldn't hardly get a chance to write to you afore now, though I have wanted to twenty times.

It seems as if this Congress come together determined to have a real whirlwind all winter. Mr. McDuffie raves like a mad lion; I thought when he was making a speech t'other day that he would stave his bench all to pieces, he slat things round so. And Mr. Clay is as full of mischief as he can live. He's been bothering us with some pesky thing or other the whole time since he has been here. When the Senate sent to the President for that document that he read to the Cabinet last September, about removing the deposites, I didn't know one spell but the old Gineral would a took his cane and gone right into the Senate room, and drove 'em all out together, and told 'em to go home about their business. But I talked to him and pacified him, and got him pretty well cooled down at last. And then says he, "Major, what would you do about it?" "Well," says I, "Gineral, supposin' the Senate should ask you to send 'em one of my letters, what would you tell 'em?" "Why," says he, "I would tell 'em that they had no business with it." "Well," says I, "Gineral, what is the difference between one of my letters to you and one of your letters to the Cabinet?" "None at all," says he, "and I'll be hanged if they get it;" and he sot right down and wrote to 'em and told 'em so.

Well, then we sot and smoked a little while, talking about one thing or another, and at last the President broke out again about the Senate sending to him for that document that he read to the Cabinet; and all at once he started up and catched his hat and cane, and says he, "Major, if I don't put a veto upon them chaps, my name isn't Andrew Jackson;" and he whisked out of doors before I had time to think. I had my shoes off, and my feet up against the jam, but I slipped 'em on as quick as I could, and out after him. But by the time I got out he was away down Pennsylvany avenu ever so far, pulling for the Congress house as fast as he could go. I pulled on after him, and overtook him jest as he was going into the Senate room. And I took hold of his arm, and says I, "Gineral, haven't I always advised you well?" And he stopt and looked round at me, and the rinkles begun to smooth out of his face, jest as they always do when he looks at me, and says he, "Yes, Major, I must say that." "Well," says I, "Gineral, then my opinion is, that you better stop and think of this business a little before you go into the Senate to kick up a bobbery. There's Mr. Clay making a speech now; and if you should make a drive right in among 'em, it would be like going into a hornet's nest. The opposition, you

OLD HICKORY AT THE SENATE DOOR.

know, have the majority, and they'd flock round Clay as thick as though he was the queen bee in a beehive, and they might be too many for you." Says he, "Major, I shouldn't be afraid of 'em if there was five times as many; but I never did know your advice to prove wrong yet, so, if you think it's best, I'll stop and consider of it a little." After a while I got him to go back to the house again, and be contented with sending the letter that they shouldn't have the document. But it was a good while before I could get him entirely calmed down, and he seemed to be considerably riled about my telling him the Senate might be too much for him if he went right in among 'em. He declared if they sent to him for any more of his private papers, he'd pull the ears of some of 'em, if he didn't cut 'em off. "Why, Major," says he, "I shouldn't be afraid to meet a whole regiment of 'em."

I'll write to you again pretty soon, and let you know something more about matters and things here.

Your faithful friend,

MAJOR JACK DOWNING.

THE GAP IN HISTORY.

EDITORIAL NOTE.—Here occurs a deplorable hiatus in Major Downing's "Thirty Years out of the Senate," occasioned by one of those inevitable catastrophes to which literature, as well as everything else connected with human labors, is sometimes exposed. In consequence of the loss of a large mass of letters and "Dockyments," the Major has to make a clean jump from Jackson to Polk, as is more fully explained in his own "Dockyment," on the following page. The world must bear the loss as well as it can.

DOCKYMENT.

In the little Postscript to my Life, that heads "My Thirty Years Out of the Senate," I said, "There'll be a kind of gap near the close of Gineral Jackson's time, and for a while after, because a lot of my letters written at that time was

MAJOR DOWNING GETTING OVER A GAP IN HISTORY.

lost in a fire some years afterward, and I don't suppose I can now find the papers they was published in. But I will try to bridge over the gap as well as I can."

Well, I've got to the gap now, and must try to make a clean jump of it, from Old Hickory to Young Hickory. I must bid good-by to my dear old friend, the Gineral, and put my shoulder to the wheel to help Colonel Polk along through the Mexican war. I feel bad to part with the old Gineral—a true man and a true Dimokrat as ever lived—and I am sure he feels bad to part with me. We worked hard together; we could conquer nullification, and conquer Biddle's Bank, but we couldn't head off old Father Time, who conquers us all, sooner or later. The best friends in the world must part, so in the nature of things the time must come when Old Hickory and Major Downing must bid each other farewell. I am sorry the world has lost them letters of mine that was burnt, for they contained a good many interesting things, and described some very pleasant times that the Gineral and I had together. They told all about cutting off the "figger head" of "Old Ironsides," (the frigate Constitution,) in Boston harbor, and about me and the Gineral going a skating in a bright moonlight night away down on the Potomac, and a hundred other matters, that's lost now with the things before the flood. But Ant Keziah always used to say, "It's no use to cry for spilt milk;" so I hope the world will dry up its tears, and not worry any more about my lost letters than it does about that great library that was burnt in Alexandria two thousand years ago. The artist has gi'n me a good lift in jumping over.

From the National Intelligencer.

We were thrown quite into a flutter yesterday by receiving in our bag from the Post-Office the following letter from the public's old friend, Major Jack Downing, who seems to have written to us for the purpose of communicating to the public, in his plain way, some views of President Polk—Young Hickory, as he delights to call him—which that distinguished functionary had not thought necessary to confide to his most confidential friends before he met with the Major:

LETTER LI.

PRESIDENT POLK ON HIS TOUR DOWN EAST—HIS INTERVIEW WITH MAJOR DOWNING.

On Board the Steamboat on Long Island Sound,
Bound to Connecticut and Down East, June 28, 1847.

Mr. Gales & Seaton—

My Dear Old Friends :—I and Mr. Buchanan, and the rest of us, overtook the President last night at York, where we found him pretty well tuckered out, having got through with all his birds-egging in that everlasting great city, and ready to push on this morning Down East. I was going to write a line to friend Ritchie, as he's the Government editor, as soon as I could ketch up with the President, and let him know how the old gentleman stood the journey. But I happened to look into your paper, and I see brother Ingersoll, of Philadelphy, sends his letters to you. This puzzled me a little at first, because I knew he was on Mr. Ritchie's side. But I looked along, and I see he called your paper a "powerful journal," and then the thought struck me that I had read somewhere that "there's a power behind the throne greater than the throne itself." Well, thinks I, that Ingersoll is a cunning feller, but he ain't agoin' to get ahead of me. If he writes to the power behind the throne I will, too. So, if Mr. Ritchie complains, and says I ought to wrote to him, I wish you would just smooth it over to him, and tell him the reason of it, and tell him when the old ship gets on t'other tack, and his paper gets on behind, I'll write to *him*.

As I had come right on from Mexico, the shortest cut, and

had brought a letter from Ginera. Scott to the President, as soon as we got to York I run right up to the tavern where he stopped to give him the letter. Folks told me he was at the Astor House—that great tavern made out of hewed stone. So I went up and went in, and asked one of the waiters if Colonel Polk put up there.

"Is it Jemmy Polk ye mane; Young Hickory, the President?"

"Sartin," says I.

THE MAJOR'S ARRIVAL AT THE ASTOR HOUSE.

"Yes," says he; "he's here, up stairs in his room."

Says I, "Show me his chamber as quick as you can; I must see him."

"You can't see him to-night," says he; "Young Hickory is tired out, and can't see nobody at all. Why wan't ye on hand in the Governor's room if ye wanted to see him? All the boys had a chance there."

Says I, "That's nothing to the pint; I was on the road from Washington then, and I'm going to see the President to-night if I have to go through the stone walls of this house for it."

Then along come Mr. Stutson, and says he, "Patrick, what's the row here?"

"Here's a feller getting wrathy," says Patrick, "because I won't let him go up to the President's room."

At that Mr. Stutson turned round to me, and as soon as he see me, he ketched hold of my hand, and says he, "Major Downing, I am very happy to see you. I'll show you right up to the President's room myself. I'm sorry you wan't here before. We've had some very pleasant tea parties since the President's been here."

When I got into the President's chamber he was laying down on the bed to rest, and looking as tired as a rat that had been drawed through forty knot-holes. But, as soon as he see me, he jumped up, looking rather wild, and says he, "Major Downing, how are ye? I didn't think of seeing you back from Mexico so soon as this. How does things go on there now?"

Says I, "Colonel, they don't go on hardly at all. They are waiting for more help. Scott and Taylor both are growing rather red and angry to think you should chuck 'em away into the middle of Mexico there, and then not send 'em help to fight the way out again. And it seems to me, Colonel, you do hold back in this business a little too much. If you don't send 'em help pretty soon, them guerillas will eat our little armies all up. Why Colonel," says I, "if this war had come on in the time of the old Gineral, my old friend Hickory, he would a had them Mexicans half whipped to death by this time. But here's a letter from Scott, to tell ye what he thinks about the business. I come on post-haste to bring it. He says he won't stir from Puebla till you send on more men to take the place of all them that's coming home."

The President took the letter and read a few lines, and threw it down upon the table; **and** says he, "It's no use; Scott may grumble and growl as much as he's a mind to, but **it's no use.** This war is a concern of my own getting up—for **my own** use; and I shall manage it **jest** as I please." Says he, "Major Downing, there's reason **in** all **things.** I **don't want them** Mexicans whipped too fast, especially when them upstart generals get all the glory of it. When I found that Taylor was swellin' **up** too large, I meant to a stopped him at Monterey, and draw off a part of his glory on to Scott. But that Taylor is a headstrong chap—a dangerous man. **He overstept his duty, and** blundered on to that victory at Buena Vista, that sot everything in a blaze. I shan't overlook it in him very soon. If the selfish creature had only let Santa Anna given him a handsome licking there, we might a had peace in a little while, for I had things all arranged with Santa Anna to wind the business right up in such a way that **we** might each of us have made a handsome plum out of it. **But that unpardonable Taylor must cut and** slash round with his handful of men, untutored volunteers, that I thought were as harmless as a flock of sheep, and contrive, by that awful blunder at Buena Vista, to pour all the fat into the fire.

"Well, then, Scott hasn't behaved much better. **He's licked** the Mexicans too fast by a great sight, and is swellin' himself up in the eyes of the people shamefully. **I** thought if I **could a sent** Colonel Benton on there, he would a squeezed the glory **out of both** of 'em in a little while, and settled 'em down **so they wouldn't a** been dangerous. But that vagabond Senate **wouldn't let me** do it. That was too bad, Major, when them two generals were attracting all the glory that belonged to me, that the Senate wouldn't let me do anything to offset them. But I'll let 'em know that Young Hickory isn't to be beat any more than Old Hickory was. I've sent

Mr. Trist on to look after matters, and to see that the armies don't go too fast; for I'm determined Scott and Taylor shan't whip the Mexicans any faster than is prudent. All the glory of this war fairly belongs to me, **and I'll have it."**

"But," **says** I, "Colonel, you **are** agoing to send on more men, an't you? Or what are you going to do? How are you going to wind the business up?"

Says he, "**I'm too** tired to talk over my plans **to-night.** But there's no need of your going right back to Mexico yet. Mr. Trist is there, and I can trust him to look after matters, and you had better jump into the boat with us in the morning and take a trip Down East, and we can talk on the way."

About five o'clock in the morning the President rattled away at my door, and waked me **out of a sound sleep; and** when he found I wasn't up, says he, "Major, you must be spry, or you'll be too late, for we're off at six."

I was up and dressed about the quickest, and went out, and **fact,** there was a quarter of a mile of soldiers all ready to escort us to the boat. And down **we** went, through whole streets full of men and women, and boys and gals, of all sorts and sizes, some running and crowding, and some hollering and hurrahing, and in a few minutes we were aboard the steamboat, and the bell rung, and the steamer puffed, and off we went on the Sound toward Connecticut.

The President had a little room all to himself, **and he** made me go right into it with him, and **he** sat down in an easy chair, and put his feet upon another, and says he, "Major, I'm glad to get out of the crowd again; we'll take a few hours of rest and comfort on this voyage. This being President, Major, is mighty hard work; but, after all, I like it. I've had a glorious time of it in New York. Everybody was running after me, and it seems as though I had seen everything. I feel as though I had lived through a whole year in these three days ; and I don't believe anybody ever received more honors in so short a space of time in this country."

"Well," says I, "Colonel, it seems to me a pity you told the folks at Baltimore, the other day, that you should retire when this term was up. You might go two terms, as Old Hickory did, jest as well as not, you are so popular."

At that he gave me a tuck in the ribs and a sly wink, and says he, "Major, don't you understand that? Telling of 'em I shouldn't stand another term is jest the way to make 'em the more fierce to have me. Don't you know Anthony said Cæsar refused the crown three times, jest so as to be more sure of having it placed on his head. And just see how Santa Anna is working it now in Mexico. When he gets pretty near run down, and shivering in the wind, and nothing to stand upon, he sends in his resignation, with a long patriotic speech about shedding the last drop of blood for his country, and all that, and the people refuse to receive his resignation, and cry out, 'Long live Santa Anna!' and away he goes again, and drums up another army of soldiers.

"But, to tell the truth, Major," says he, "when I made that remark at Baltimore, I had some little notion of retiring. Our party was so cut up, things looked rather dark ahead, and I find this Mexican war something of a bother after all. Taylor and Scott commit so many blunders, I had really then some notion of retiring when this term is up. But, since I got along to New York, things seem to look brighter. I'm popular, Major, I know I am. I shouldn't be surprised if the Whigs made a demonstration in my favor yet. They seemed very fond of me in New York ; and so did everybody—everybody you could mention ; even the market-women took me by the hand and called me Young Hickory, and gave me lots of fruit. There, do you see that pineapple on the table, there?" says he. "That was given to me at the Fulton Market, as we were going over to Brooklyn on Saturday.* Cut away, Major, and help yourself to it; it's a nice one. And here's a paper of most excellent tobacco," says he, " that was presented to me at the same time. You go into the pineapple and I'll go into the tobacco, and then we'll have a little more talk about the war."

Jest as we got cleverly under way, they sung out aboard the boat for the passengers to get ready for landing. So I must cut my yarn off here for the present; but likely as not you'll hear from me again.

Your old friend,
MAJOR JACK DOWNING.

DOCKYMENT.

From the National Intelligencer.

It was with real satisfaction that we recognized again, yesterday, among our letters from the Post-Office, the handwriting of our friend, Major Jack Downing. His personal associations, as our readers know, have always been with those who have made it a mortal offense in us—even to the extent of denouncing it as moral treason—that we have not always approved of their principles or their measures; but, somehow or other, our feelings have always yearned to the Major. There is such a transparent honesty in all his thoughts, and such a kindness of heart perceptible in all his motions, that we would rather at any time receive even a rebuke from him

---

* EDITORIAL NOTE.—This is no embellishment of the Major's, but a literal fact. When the procession was moving down Fulton street, to go to Brooklyn, a market-woman presented the President a pineapple, and another person a paper of choice tobacco.

than the praise of some folks. If it be a pleasure to us, as it is, to be able to differ from public men, to canvass their measures, and even to censure them where censure is deserved, without cherishing anything like personal malice toward them, the reader may imagine what value we place upon the correspondence of a true-hearted man like Major Downing, who has not suffered his friendship for us to be sundered, or even shaken, by the many differences of opinion about men and measures that have grown up between us for the last dozen or fifteen years.

We are right glad to understand, from what he says at the close of the following letter, that it is not the last we may expect from the Major :

LETTER LII.

PRESIDENT POLK AND MAJOR DOWNING IN THE STATE OF MAINE.

DOWNINGVILLE, in the State of Maine, **July 6, 1847.**

MR. GALES & SEATON—

MY DEAR OLD FRIENDS :—My letter to you on board the steamboat on Long Island Sound, was cut off so short by the bell's ringing for us to get ready to go ashore, that I didn't get half through telling you the talk I had with the President that day ; and we've had so much talk since, and seen so much on the journey, that I shan't be able to tell you one-half, nor a quarter on't, in a letter. It would take a whole book to give you a good notion of the whole story. But the President will be back to Washington before you can get this letter, for he started to go back last Saturday ; so you can get the whole account of the journey from him. He'll be delighted to set down and tell you all about it ; for he's been amazingly pleased with the whole journey, from top to bottom. He's been on his high-heeled **boots all the way.** Instead of growin' more stoopin' by bowing so much, it seems as if he stood straighter than ever. He told the Governor, in his speech at Augusta, Saturday :. " It seldom happens that the course of any man's life is marked by so distinguished a reception as has been accorded to me to-day." Well, so it has been all the way along ; hurrahing, and complimenting, and firing, and speeches, and dinners, and suppers, and shaking hands. On board the steamboat, from Portland to Augusta, we got a little breathing time, and had a good long talk.

Says the President to me : " Now, Major," says he, " I want you to be candid. No one is a true friend to one in a high station unless he will be candid and speak the truth. And now, Major, I don't want you to flatter me ; I want you to be candid, and tell me jest what you think. You went along with President Jackson when he made his tour Down East, and had a chance to see the whole operation ; and now I want you to tell me candidly, if you think the people was any more fond of him than they are of me."

" Well, now, Colonel," says I, " not wishing to hurt your feelins at all, but seein' you've asked my candid opinion, I won't deny but what the people are very fond of you, amazingly fond, perhaps as fond as they can be. But, after all, these times ain't exactly equal to Old Hickory's times."

" But what do you mean ?" says he.

" Well," says I, " the people all seem to be amazing fond, but somehow it seems to have a sort of *mother-in-law show* about it ; it don't seem to be so real hearty as they showed to Old Hickory "

" Well, now, Major," says he, and he reddened a little when he said this ; says he, " that only shows how strong your prejudices set in favor of the old Gineral. But I thought you was a man of a stronger mind and sounder judgment. I can't agree with you against the evidence of my own senses. Did you notice all the way along how thick the crowds flocked around me to shake hands with me?"

"Yes," says I; "but they didn't go it with such a rush as they did when my old friend, the Gineral, come this way. They jammed around *him* so that they had to climb over each other's heads to get at him. And I had to take hold sometimes by the hour together and help him shake hands, or he never would have got through with one-half of 'em."

"Well, then," says he, "did you mind how loud they cheered and hurraked wherever we come along?"

"Yes, Colonel," says I; "I heard all that; but, my gracious! wherever Old Hickory made his appearance, the crowd roared right out like thunder."

"Well, Major," says he, "they couldn't beat them cheers that the Democrats and Captain Rynders give me at Tammany Hall, I know; thunder itself couldn't beat that. It's no use, Major, for you to argue the pint; no President ever received such marks of honor from the people before—I am sure of that; I mean the whole people, Federalists as well as Democrats—that is, if there is any such people as Federalists now days, and Mr. Ritchie says there is. Only think, the old Federal State of Massachusetts did the business up as handsome and seemed to be as fond of me as Governor Hill's State; I couldn't see any difference. You must confess, Major, that even your old friend Hickory didn't receive so much honor in Massachusetts as I have."

"Well, now," says I, "Colonel, I don't want to hurt your feelin's, but you are just as much mistaken as you was when you sent old Rough and Ready into Mexico. Have you forgot how they took the old Gineral into Cambridge College and made a doctor of him?"

"Who cares for that?" says the Colonel; says he, turning

up his nose, "Didn't the Democrats and Captain Rynders take me into Tammany Hall, and make a Tammany of me?* No, no, Major Downing, it's no use for you to argue the pint against my popularity, for I've got eyes, and I can see; and I tell you, and I want you to mark my words, I tell you I'm more popular with the whole people than ever old Hickory was in all his life. He was very popular with the Democratic party, but I am fully persuaded he hadn't such a hold upon the affections of the whole people as I have."

Here the President got up and walked about the floor, and seemed in a deep study. At last says he: "Major, I missed a figger in my speech at Baltimore t'other day; and I don't know exactly how to get over it."

"How so?" says I.

"Why," says he, "I ought not to have said, right up and down, pint blank, that I should retire when this term is up. I should only talked about my desire to retire to private life. I was too hasty, and committed myself too soon. There never was a better chance for anybody to be elected than there is for me now, if I hadn't made that unfortunate remark. Jackson stood twice, and Jefferson stood twice, and I suppose it is really my duty to serve my country as long as they did. But if I should undertake to run agin, I s'pose they would be throwing that Baltimore speech in my teeth."

"Well, now," says I, "Colonel, can't you see your way out of that? You wasn't born Down East so fur as I was. It's no great of a job to get over that trouble."

At that the President brightened up a good deal, and says he, "Well, Major, I'll tell you what 'tis, if you'll get me over that difficulty handsomely, when we come to have another

---

* EDITORIAL NOTE.—While in New York, President Polk was initiated into the Order of St. Tammany.

shuffle for the offices, you may choose any card in the pack, and you shall have it."

"Well, says I, "Colonel, about that remark of yourn at Baltimore, that you should give up when this term is out, all you've got to do is to get Mr. Ritchie to take it back in the Union; let him declare that it was only a sort of speculation, hastily thrown out, without much consideration, and that, so far as he understands, neither the President nor any of his Cabinet entertains any such views. Then you can go along just as smooth and safe as if nothing had happened."

"Fact, that's it," says the Colonel, snapping his fingers; "strange I didn't think of that before. Major, you do beat all for working out of difficulties! I believe I'll make up my mind to go ahead another term; I don't see anything in the way. I'll tell you how I think of working it. I've been reading over this letter of Taylor's to the Cincinnati Signal. He's an old head, but he an't agoing to come another Bona Vista blunder over me. If I don't take the wind out of his sails before long, I'll engage to make him King of Mexico. And I'll try him on his own tack, too. I'll come out and declare that I won't be the candidate of no party neither, and throw myself upon the people. I'm convinced, from what I've seen on this journey, that the Whigs will go for me almost to a man. Van Buren and Wright, who say I'm not the man for the Northern Democrats, may go to grass. I go for the people, the whole people, and nothing but the people."

"Well," says I, "Colonel, that's the road; and I wish you a pleasant and prosperous journey."

We had some more talk about the war before we reached Augusta, but I haven't got time to explain to you the President's views about it in this letter. He says he means to keep a tight rein over Taylor, and not let him do much; and when he does do anything, make him report it to the Government, through Scott. I asked him if he wasn't afraid of making too tall a man out of Scott by placing him on Taylor's shoulders; and he said no—he should look out for that; and if he see any danger of it, he should make Scott report to the Government through Mr. Trist.

After we visited Augusta, and Hallowell, and Gardiner, I tried to get the President to go out to Downingville, but he said he didn't think it would do for him to stop any longer this time, though there was no place in the country that he was more anxious to see; and he promised, the first leisure time he could get, to make a flying visit there. I asked him if he didn't think it would do for me to go out and stop a day or two, as I hadn't seen Uncle Joshua, or Aunt Keziah, or any of 'em there for a long time. He said certainly, by all means, and he would hurry back to Washington and have things all cut and dried by the time I got back along, so that we could make up our minds at once what is best to be done, in order to keep Scott and Taylor in the traces, and curb 'em in.

Your old friend,
MAJOR JACK DOWNING.

LETTER LIII.

MAJOR DOWNING, ON THE ROAD TO THE WAR, SITS DOWN BY THE ROADSIDE AND WRITES TO THE EDITORS OF THE NATIONAL INTELLIGENCER AN ACCOUNT OF HIS INTERVIEW WITH PRESIDENT POLK AND OLD MR. RITCHIE, EDITOR OF THE GOVERNMENT ORGAN.

ON THE ROAD TO THE WAR, August —, 1847.

MR. GALES & SEATON—

MY DEAR OLD FRIENDS:—I s'pose you'll be amazinly disapinted to find I'm away off here, pushin' on to the seat of war, and didn't call to see you when I come through Washington.

But you musn't blame me for it, for I couldn't help it; the President wouldn't let me call; he said I was getting quite too thick with you, writing letters to you and all that. And when he spoke about the letters, he looked a kind of red and

ON THE ROAD TO THE WAR.

showed considerable spunk. But now I am away off here where the President won't see me, so I'll set right down by the side of the road and write you a good long letter. The President was a little touched at first, when I see him.

Says he, "Major Downing, I have put a good deal of confidence in you as a friend of my Administration; and if you are a friend to it, you must let Gales and Seaton alone; keep out of their way, and have nothing to do with them; they are dangerous, mischief-making fellers, eternally peckin' at my Administration, all weathers. Let me try to keep things ever so snug, and lay my plans ever so deep, they are sure to dig them all up, lug them into the Intelligencer, and blaze 'em all over the country. Confound their picturs, they are the most troublesome customers an Administration ever had; they've come pretty near swamping me two or three times. So, if you are my friend, I warn you not to be so thick with Gales and Seaton."

"Well," says I, "Colonel, you know I am a friend to you and your Administration, as much as I ever was to the old Gineral and his Administration; and I shall stand by you and do everything I can to help you out of this scrape you've got into about the war. But I don't know as that need to make me break with Gales and Seaton. We've been old friends so long, it would be kind of hard for me to give 'em up now; and I don't hardly think they are quite so bad as you think for. They may not mean to do you so much hurt when they put these things into their paper, and only put them in because they think folks want to know what's goin' on. Mr. Ritchie sometimes puts things into *his* paper that folks think don't do you no good."

The President give two or three hard chaws upon his cud of tobacco, and says he: "Yes, Major, that's too true, it must be confessed; and it annoys me beyond all patience. But then I have to forgive it, and overlook it, because Mr. Ritchie don't mean it. The old gentleman is always sorry for it, and always willing to take it back. And then he's such a tuff old feller to fight the Federalists, I can't have a heart to scold at him much about his mistakes and blunders."

"Well," says I, "Colonel, being you've named Federalists, I want to know if any of them animals is really supposed to be alive anywhere in the country, now-a-days. Seeing sich awful accounts about 'em in the Union paper all the time, I inquired all the way along through New England, where they used to be the thickest, and I couldn't get track of one; and when I asked the folks if there was any Federalists anywhere in them quarters, they all stared at me, and said they didn't know what sort of critters they was. When I got to Downingville, I asked Uncle Joshua about it. He said, in his younger days there used to be considerable many of 'em about, but they wasn't thought to be dangerous, for they never was much given to fighting. But he said he guessed they'd all died out long ago, for he hadn't come across one these twenty years. So now, Colonel," says I, "how is it they are so thick in Mr. Ritchie's paper all the time?"

At that he give me a very knowing kind of a look, and lowered his voice down almost to a whisper; and says he, "Major, I'll tell you how that is. When Mr. Ritchie was a young man, he used to fight a good deal with the Federalists, and took a good deal of pride in it; and now the fancies and scenes of his youth all seem to come back fresh to his mind, and he can't think or talk about anything else. You know that's oftentimes the way with old people. As he always used to have the name of a smart fighter, I give him the command of the newspaper battery here to defend my Administration. But 'twas as great a mistake as 'twas when I sent Taylor into Mexico; I didn't know my man. No matter what forces was gathering to overthrow my Administration, Mr. Ritchie somehow didn't seem to see 'em; no matter how hard they fired at me, he didn't seem to hear it; and when I called to him to fire back, he would rouse up and touch off a few squibs with about as good aim as the boys take when they fire crackers on the 4th of July, and did about as much execution. At last I found out a way that I could make the old veteran fight like a Turk, and hold on like a bull-dog. It was by giving him a notion at any time that he was fighting with Federalists. Since I made that discovery, he's been more help to me. Whenever I see the enemy intrenching himself around me, and bringing up his batteries to fire into my Administration, all I have to do is to whisper in Mr. Ritchie's ear and say, 'Mr. Ritchie, the air smells of Federalism; you may depend upon it there is Federalists abroad somewhere.' In a minute, you've no idea with what fury the old gentleman flies round, and mounts his heaviest guns, and sets his paper battery in a roar. His shots fly right and left, and sometimes knock down friends as well as foes. To be sure, they don't make a very great impression upon the enemy; but then there's this advantage in it: if he don't kill or beat off the enemy, he keeps the Administration so perfectly covered up with smoke that the enemy can't see half the time where to fire at us. On the whole, Mr. Ritchie is a valuable man to my Administration, notwithstanding all his mistakes and blunders."

Jest then the door opened, and who should come in but Mr. Ritchie himself. As he opened the door he ketched the sound of the two last words the President was saying.

"Mistakes and blunders!" says Mr. Ritchie; says he, "What, have you got something more of Scott and Taylor's blundering in Mexico?"

"Nothing more, to-day," says the President; "I was only telling Major Downing how their blunders there have come pretty near ruining the country, and how it is absolutely necessary to get the staff out of their hands, somehow or other, before they quite finish the job. I'm going, now, to try one more plan, Mr. Ritchie; but be careful that you don't say anything about it in the Union and blow it all up. I tried once to send Colonel Benton on for the same purpose, and Congress blowed that up. Then I sent Trist on for the same purpose, and Scott has blown him up. Now, I'm agoing to send Major Downing, not as a regular open ambassador, but as a sort of watch upon them, you know, to work round and do the business up before anybody knows it. He isn't to go to Scott nor Taylor, nor have anything to do with 'em, but work his way into Mexico, and go right to Santa Anna and knock up a

THE MAJOR, THE PRESIDENT AND MR. RITCHIE.

bargain with him. I don't care what he gives. The fact is, Mr. Ritchie, the country needs peace, and I'll have peace, cost what it will."

"An excellent idea," says Mr. Ritchie; "an excellent plan, sir. I'm for peace at all hazards, if it is to be found anywhere in Mexico—that is, if we can get hold of it before Scott or Taylor does. And I think Major Downing is just the man for it—a true, stanch Democratic Republikan ; and whatever he does will go for the benefit of the Administration. Now the country's shins are aching pretty bad with the war, if we can fix up a good smooth peace right off, and not let Scott nor Taylor have any hand in it, who knows, Mr. President, but it might make our Administration so popular that you and I might both be elected to serve another four years ? But when is the Major to start ?"

" Right off, to-night," says the President, " or rather, in the morning, before daylight—before anybody in Washington finds out that he has got back from Downingville. I have forbid his calling at the Intelligencer office, and I don't want they should find out or mistrust that he's been here. If they should get wind of the movement, they would be sure to throw some constitutional difficulty in the way, and try to make a bad botch of the business."

The President shet me into his room and charged me not to leave the house, while he sent for Mr. Buchanan and Mr. Marcy to fix up my private instructions. While he was gone Mr. Ritchie fixed me up a nice little bundle of private instructions, too, on his own hook, moddled, he said, on the Virginia Resolutions of '98. Presently the President came back with my budget all ready, and give me my instructions, and filled my pockets with rations, and told me how to draw whenever I wanted money ; and before daylight I was off a good piece on the road to the war.

To-day I met a man going on to carry letters to the Government from Gineral Scott's side of the war, and I made him stop a little while to take this letter to you ; for I was afraid you might begin to think I was dead. He says Scott is quite wrathy about the Trist business, and wants to push right on and take the city of Mexico, but Mr. Trist is disposed to wait and see if he can't make a bargain with Santa Anna's men.

I shall push along as fast as I can, and get into the city of Mexico, if possible, before Scott does ; and if I only once get hold of Santa Anna, I have no doubt I shall make a trade.

I don't know yet whether I shall take Scott's road or Taylor's road to go to the city of Mexico ; it will depend a little upon the news I get on the way. Two or three times, when I have been stopping to rest, I have been looking over my private instructions. They are fust rate, especially Mr. Ritchie's.

I remain your old friend, and the President's private Embasseder,

MAJOR JACK DOWNING.

DOCKYMENT.

A day or two after the foregoing letter was published in the Intelligencer, the following belligerent editorial appeared in the *Government organ*, the Washington Union, then edited by the veteran and venerable Thomas Ritchie :

"JACK DOWNING.—We enjoy wit, and have no objection to waggery. We can excuse it, even when the joke is made at our own expense. But then we have a right to ask if the wit be 'good,' and the waggery 'genuine?'

"To this issue we are brought by a letter in Wednesday's National Intelligencer, headed, 'Another Letter from Major Downing,' and signed ostensibly by 'Major Jack Downing.' The question with us is, is this the veritable Major Jack Downing? or is it some inferior wag, some 'counterfeit presentment,' who assumes the mask and name of the true Jack Downing, and passes off his spurious coin for the solid bullion of that original wit and wag, Jack Downing? It is not because its writer makes fun of us that we raise the question. It is not because he jeers at our blunders, or our Republican principles of yore, that we doubt his identity. To some blunders we cannot but plead guilty, though they have been excessively magnified by the scribblers of the day, and though they are generally, by some extraordinary cross purposes, more the work of others than of our own. Of the firmness of our opinions, indorsed, as they have been, by the principles of Jefferson and the 'resolutions' of Madison, we have no reason to be ashamed. But if there was any very extraordinary humor in the letters of this fictitious 'Jack Downing'—if there was any of the wit and *naivete* of the original Jack Downing—the worthy C. A. D., of New York, the one who universally passes as the author of the *Downing Letters*—we should give him the credit he deserves. It is not because we happen to be the subject of his last letter that we protest against his pretensions ; but because we happen to know that the present Jack Downing, who has written three letters in a mask for the National Intelligencer, is not the Simon Pure, but a counterfeit presentment—in other words, something of the literary 'jackdaw in the peacock's plumes.' And we fear that our friends of the National Intelligencer knew that they were palming off this amusing trick upon their readers when they hailed, with such cordial acclamation, the receipt of the two first letters of 'Jack Downing,' and when they introduced the letter of Wednesday as 'Another Letter from Jack Downing.' We undertake to say positively that these letters in the Intelligencer are something of humbugs ; that they are not written by the original Jack Downing, of New York ; that he has not employed that signature since the days of Old Hickory ; and that he would be the last man to satirize the President or his administration. Therefore, we strip the mask off from the counterfeit, and repeat the motto of the Intelligencer—' *Ridentem, dicere verum quid vetat* ?'

"We seize the same opportunity to say that we, too, may have done unconscious injustice to Jack Downing himself when, mistaking one person for another of similar name, we asked whether any of the blood of Jack Downing could flow in the veins of the author of the letters of the 'Genevese Traveler,' in the London Times. The very question was calculated to mislead our readers, as we find upon better information; but we correct our blunder, at the hazard of provoking the laughter even of this mock Jack **Downing**."

LETTER LIV.

As soon as Major Downing received the Union containing the editorial outburst of Mr. Ritchie, he replied to the veteran politician, through the Intelligencer, in the following conciliatory and soothing terms:

———, September, 1847.

To Mr. Ritchie, Editor of the Government Organ, Washington.

My Dear Old Friend :—I've jest got the Union, containing the broadside you fired at me, and I'm amazingly struck up, and my feelins is badly hurt, to see that you've got so bewildered that you seemingly don't know me. It's a melancholy sign when old folks get so bewildered that they mistake their oldest and best friends, one for t'other. Why, your head is turned right round. How *could* you say that I was "a fictitious Major Jack Downing?" and that my last letter to you was a "trashy forgery?" and that you would "strip the mask from me?" I feel bad now about writing my last letter to you, for I'm afraid you took it too hard. I beg of you now, my dear friend, to let all drop right where 'tis ; leave Mr. Burke to do the burkin' and the fightin', and you go right out into the country and put yourself under the "cold-water cure" somewhere, and see if your head won't come right again. I "fictitious," and you going to "strip the mask from me!"

Why, my dear friend, if you could only be up here five minutes, and jest lift the mask off of my face one minute, you'd know me jest as easy as the little boy knew his daddy. Your head *couldn't* be so turned but what you'd know me; for you'd see then the very same old friend that stood by you and Gineral Jackson fifteen, sixteen, and eighteen years ago; the same old friend that coaxed up Gineral Jackson, and made him forgive you for calling him such hard names before he was elected. It's very ungrateful for you to forget me now— that is, if you was in your right mind. For I'm the same old friend, the same Jack Downing that was born and brought up in Downingville, away Down East, in the State of Maine, and that drove down to Portland in Jinnerwary, 1830, with a load of ax-handles and bean-poles, and found the Legislater in a dreadful snarl, all tied and tangled, and see-sawin' up and down a whole fortnight, and couldn't choose their officers. I found my ax-handles and bean-poles wouldn't sell, so I took to polytix, and went to writin' letters. The Legislater fout and fout all winter; but I kept writin', and at last I got 'em straitened out. I kept on writin' for a whole year, and got the polytix of Maine pretty well settled. Then I see Gineral Jackson was getting into trouble, and I footed it on to Washington to give him a lift. And you know I always stuck by him afterward as long as he lived. I helped him fight the battles with Biddle's monster bank till we killed it off. I helped him put down *nullification*, and showed exactly how it would work if it got the upper hand, in my letter about carrying the raft of logs across Sebago Pond, when Bill Johnson got mad and swore he'd have his log all to himself, and so he cut the lashings and paddled off on his log alone; and then his log begun to roll, and he couldn't keep it steady, and he got ducked head over heels half a dozen times, and come pesky near being drowned. And that wasn't all I did to keep off nullification and help put it down. I brought on my old company of Downingville militia to Washington, under the command of Cousin Sargent Joel, and kept 'em there, with their guns all loaded, till the danger was over. And I used to go up top of the Congress House every day, and keep watch, and listen off toward South Carolina, so as to be ready, the first moment nullification bust up there, to order Sargent Joel to march and fire. The Gineral always said the spunk I showed was what cowed nullification down so quick, and he always felt very grateful to me for it. Well, I stuck by the Gineral all weathers; and I kept writin' letters from Washington to my old friend, the editor of the Portland Courier, and kept old Hickory's popularity alive among the people, and didn't let nobody meddle with his Administration to hurt it. Well, then, you know, the Gineral, in the summer of 1832, started off on his grand tower Down East, and I went with him. You remember, when we got to Philadelphy, the people swarmed round him so thick they almost smothered him to death; and the Gineral got so tired shakin' hands that he couldn't give another shake, and come pretty near faintin' away; and then I put my hand round under his arm, and shook for him half an hour longer, and so we made out to get through. I sent the whole account of it to my old friend of the Portland Courier. Well, then we jogged along to New York; and there, you remember, we come pesky near getting a ducking when the bridge broke down at Castle Garden. I sent the whole account of it to my old Portland friend. Well, the next day *your* "original" Major Downing published his first original letter in a New York paper, giving an account of the ducking at Castle Garden. Nobody couldn't dispute but this was the true, ginuine, "original" Downing document, although my "vile imitations" of it had been going on and published almost every week for two years. I say nobody couldn't dispute it, because 'twas proved by Scripture and poetry both. For the Bible says, "The first shall be last, and the last first;" and poetry says, " Coming events cast their shadows before." So the shadows, the " vile imitations," had been flying about the country for more than two years before the original event got along. I hope your head will get settled again, so that you can see through these things and understand 'em, and know me jest as you used to. I can't bear the idea of your not knowing me, and thinking I'm "fictitious."

Du try to refresh your mind a little; think how I stood by you and Mr. Polk, and helped you along through the Mexican war; and how I carried out dispatches from Mr. Polk to Mr. Trist, in Mexico, and how I carried a private message from you to Gineral Taylor, to try to coax it out of him which side he was coming out on.

Good-by, my dear friend; I hope next time I hear from you, you will be recovered and in your right mind, so as to know me and see that I an't "fictitious;" for you haven't got a truer friend on Mason and Dixon's side of Salt River than your old friend.

MAJOR JACK DOWNING.

LETTER LV.

MAJOR DOWNING'S FIRST DISPATCHES FROM THE CITY OF MEXICO.

CITY OF MEXICO, UNITED STATES, September 27, 1847.

MR. GALES & SEATON—

MY DEAR OLD FRIEND:—I'm alive yet, though I've been through showers of balls as thick as hailstones. I got your paper containing my letter that I wrote on the road to the war. The letters I wrote afterward, the guerrillas and robbers are so thick, I think it's ten chances to one if you got 'em. Some of Gineral Scott's letters is missing just in the same way. Now we've got the city of Mexico annexed, I think the Postmaster-General ought to have a more regular line of stages running here, so our letters may go safe. I wish you would touch the President and Mr. Johnson up a little about this mail-stage business, so they may keep all the coach makers at work, and see that the farmers raise horses as fast as they can, for I don't think they have any idea how long the roads is this way, nor how fast we are gaining south. If we keep on annexin' as fast as we have done a year or two past, it wouldn't take much more than half a dozen years to get clear down to t'other end of South America, clear to Cape Horn, which would be a very good stopping place; for then, if our Government got into bad sledding in North America, and found themselves in a dilemma that hadn't no horn to suit 'em, they would have a horn in South America that they might hold on to.

I hope there an't no truth in the story that was buzz'd about here in the army, a day or two ago, that Mr. Polk had an idea, when we get through annexin' down this way, of trying his hand at it over in Europe and Africa, and round there. And to prevent any quarreling beforehand about it on this side of the water, he's agoing to agree to run the Missouri Compromise line over there, and cut Europe up into Free States and Africa into Slave States. Now, I think he had better keep still about that till we get this South America business all done, and well tied up. It isn't well for a body to have too much business on his hands at once. There's no knowing what little flurries we may get into yet, and there's always danger, if you have too much sail spread in a squall. However, I haven't time to talk about this now.

You will get the accounts of the battles in Gineral Scott's

letters, so I needn't say a great deal about them. But it's been a hard up-hill work all the way from Vera Cruz here; and I don't think my old friend, Gineral Jackson himself, would have worked through all the difficulties and done the business up better than Gineral Scott has. But the killed and the wounded, the dead and the dying, scattered all along the way for three hundred miles—it's a heart-aching thought. I don't love to think about it. It is too bad that we didn't have more men, so as to march straight through without fighting, instead of having jest enough to encourage the enemy to bring out their largest armies and fight their hardest battles.

One of the hardest brushes we had, after I got here, was the attack on Chapultepec. I had been into the city trying to bring Santa Anna to terms; but, when I found it was no use, I come out and told Gineral Scott there was no way but to fight it out, and, although I was only the President's private embassador, I didn't like to stand and look on when he was so weak-handed, and if he would tell me where to take hold, I would give him a lift. The Gineral said he expected there would be a hard pull to take Chapultepec, and as Gineral Pillow was placed where he would be likely to have the heaviest brunt of it, I might be doing the country a great service if I would jine in with Gineral Pillow, as my experience under Gineral Jackson, and insight into military affairs, would no doubt be very useful to that valiant officer. So I took hold that day as one of Gineral Pillow's aids.

When we come to march up and see how strong the enemy's works was, says I, " Gineral Pillow, it is as much as all our lives is worth to go right straight up and storm that place, in the face and eyes of all their guns; I think we ought to fortify a little. Suppose we dig a ditch round here in front of the enemy's works."

At that the Ginneral's eyes flashed, and he swore right out. Says he: "No, d—n the ditches, I've no opinion of 'em; they are nothing but a bother, and never ought to be used. The best way is to go right into the enemy, pell-mell."

So on we went, and Pillow fit like a tiger till he got wounded, and then the rest of us, that wasn't shot down, had to finish the work up the best way we could.

The long and the short of it is, we fit our way into the city of Mexico and annexed it. Santa Anna cleared out the night afore with what troops he had left, and is scouring about the country to get some more places ready for us to annex. When he gets another place all ready for the ceremony, and gets it well fortified, and has an army of twenty or thirty thousand men in the forts and behind the breastworks, we shall march down upon 'em with five or six thousand men, and go through the flurry. After they have shot down about half of us, the rest of us will climb in, over the mouths of their cannons, and annex that place; and so on, one after another.

It is pretty hard work annexin' in this way; but that is the only way it can be done. It will be necessary for the President to keep hurrying on his men this way to keep our ranks full, for we've got a great deal of ground to go over yet. What we've annexed in Mexico, so far, isn't but a mere circumstance to what we've got to do.

Some think the business isn't profitable; but it's only because they haven't ciphered into it fur enough to understand it. Upon an average, we get at least ten to one for our outlay, any way you can figure it up—I mean in the matter of people. Take, for instance, the City of Mexico. It cost us only two or three thousand men to annex it, after we got into the neighborhood of it; and we get at least one hundred and fifty thousand in that city, and some put it down as high as two hundred thousand. Some find fault with the *quality* of the people we get in this country, jest as if that had anything to do with the merits of the case. They ought to remember that in a Government like ours, where the people is used for voting, and where every nose counts one, it is the *number* that we are to stan' about in annexin', and not the quality, by no means. So that in the matter of people we are doing a grand business. And as to the money, it is no matter what it costs us, for money grows in the ground in Mexico, and can always be had for digging.

There's a thousand things in this country that I should like to tell you about if I had time; but things is so unsettled here yet, that I have rather a confused chance to write. So I must break off here, and write a few lines to the President; but remain your friend in all latitudes, clear down to Cape Horn.

MAJOR JACK DOWNING.

To James K. Polk, President of the United States and all annexed countries.

DEAR SIR :—I've done my best, according to your directions, to get round Santa Anna, but it is all no use. He's as slippery as an eel, and has as many lives as a cat. Trist and I together can't hold him, and Scott and Taylor can't kill him off. We get fast hold of him with our diplomatics, but he slips through our fingers; and Scott and Taylor cuts his head off in every town where they can catch him, but he always comes to life in the next town, and shows as many heads as if he had never lost one. I had a long talk with him in the city, and pinned him right down to the bargain he made with you when you let him into Vera Cruz, and asked him "why he didn't stick to it." He said he "did stick to it as far as circumstances rendered it prudent."

"But," says I, "Gineral Santa Anna, that an't the thing ; a bargain's a bargain, and if a man has any honor he will stick to it. Now," says I, "didn't you agree, if the President would give orders to our Commodore to let you into Vera Cruz, didn't you agree to put your shoulder to the wheel, and help on this annexin' business, so as to make easy work of it? And now I ask you, as a man of honor, have you done it?"

"Circumstances alters cases, Major," says Santa Anna. "When Mr. Polk and I had that understanding, he thought he needed a few more votes than he could muster in his own country to bring him into the Presidency another term. So we agreed, if I would turn over the votes of Mexico to him to bring him in another term, he would afterward turn over his part of the votes in North America to me, so as to bring me in next time. But I soon found it would be throwing our labor away, for Mr. Polk's part of the votes in his country was getting to be so small that they wouldn't do much good to either of us. So I concluded to hold on to what I had got, and stick to the Presidency of Mexico."

"Then," says I, "you an't a going to stick to your bargain are you?"

"No," says he, "circumstances alters cases."

Then I tried to *scare* him out of it. I told him our folks would whip the Mexicans all into shoestrings in a little while. And it made no odds whether he fit for annexin' or against it, we should go on jest the same, and before another year was out, Mr. Polk would be President of every foot of Mexico ; for we should get through annexin' the whole of it.

"Very well," says he, "go on ; the Mexicans like the business ; they can stand it longer than Mr. Polk can ; for Mr. Polk will have all the work to do over again every year, as long as he lives, for there isn't a place in Mexico that will stay annexed any longer than jest while you are holding on to it."

So you see there's no doing anything with **Santa Anna**. What course it is best to take now, seems rather a puzzler. I haven't time to give you my views about it in this dispatch, but will try to soon. Give my love to Mr. Ritchie. I meant **to write** him, too, but I shall have **to wait till next** time.

Your faithful friend and private embassador,

MAJOR JACK DOWNING.

LETTER LVI.

MAJOR DOWNING'S SECOND DISPATCHES FROM THE CITY OF MEXICO.

Head-quarters, **Mexico,** New Addition **to the United States,** October 25, 1847.

Mr. Gales & Seaton—

My Dear Old Friends:—Gineral Scott and **I** find a good deal **of bother about getting** our dispatches through **to Vera Cruz, or else you'd hear** from me oftener. I do think the President is too backward about clearing out this road from **here to** Vera Cruz, and keeping it open, and introducing the improvements into the country that we stand so much in need of here. He and Mr. Ritchie pretends **to have** constitutional scruples about it, and says the Constitution **don't allow of** internal improvements; and Mr. **Ritchie says the resolutions** of '98 is dead agin it, too; and, besides, Mr. Ritchie says these internal improvements is a Federal **doctrine, and he'd always** go agin 'em for that, **if nothin'** else. But 'tis strange **to me** the President hasn't never found out yet that where there's a will there's a way, Constitution or no Constitution. All he's got to do is, to call all these roads round here in Mexico "military roads," and then he'd have the Constitution on his side, for everbody knows the Constitution allows him to make military roads. I know the President is very delicate about fringing on the Constitution, so I don't blame him so much for holding back about the internal improvements here in Mexico, though I don't think there's any other part of the United States where they are needed more. But there's no need of splitting hairs about the roads ; military roads isn't internal improvements, and he's a right to make military roads as much as he pleases. And as them is jest the kind of roads we want here, and shall want for fifty years (for our armies will have to keep marching about the country for fifty years before they'll be able to tame these Mexicans, and turn 'em into Americans), it is confounded strange to me that the President is so behind-hand about this business. What's the use of our going on and annexin' away down South here, if he don't back us up and hold on to the slack? And there's no way to hold on to it but to keep these military roads open so our armies can go back and forth, and bring us in victuals, and powder, and shot, and money.

Here we've been, weeks and weeks since we annexed the city of Mexico, waiting and holding on for the President to send us more men and more money, and tell us what to do next. This backwardness of the President, since we got into the city of Mexico, seems the more strange to me, considering. For, when he was fixin' me off to come out here and see if I could make a settlement with Santa Anna, I tried to persuade him to let the armies hold still while I was making the bargain. I told him he never could bring a man to reason or to trade when he was knocking of him down all the time. But I couldn't make him seem to understand it. He stood to it his way was the best—the sword in one hand and peace in t'other, all the way—a word and a blow, and the blow always first.

"Why, Major Downing," says he, "if you want to reason a man into a peace, that's another thing ; but if you want to *conquer* a peace, my way is the only way. That's the way I begun this war, and that's the way I mean to carry it out."

"How so?" says I; "did you begin the war in that way?"

"Why," says he, "Slidell was the word, and Taylor was the blow; and not only my friends, but even my enemies, admit that the blow come first."

The President said that was the rule he had gone by all the way along, and he meant to stick to it; and not hearing anything from him so long, I'm afraid he's got a notion that peace is conquered. But that would be a bad mistake, if he has got such a notion; for it isn't conquered—it's only scattered. It's a good deal as 'twas with Bill Johnson, when he and I was boys, and he undertook to conquer a hornet's nest, expectin' to get lots of honey. He took a club, and marched bravely up to it, and hit it an awful dig, and knocked it into a thousand flinders.

"There, blast ye," says Bill, "I guess you're done tu now," as he begun to look round for the honey. But he soon found 'twasn't conquered—'twas only scattered. And presently they begun to fly at him, and sting him on all sides. One hit him a dab on his arm, and another on his leg, and another in his face. At last Bill found he should soon be done tu, himself, if he stayed there, so he cut and run.

"Hullo," says I, "Bill, where's your honey?"

"Darn it all," says he, "if I hain't got no honey, I knocked their house to pieces; I've got that to comfort me."

I wish you would try to convince the President that 'tis only scattered here; 'tisn't conquered, and he must give us the means to keep moving, or we shall get badly stung bimeby. If he only backs us up well, I'll pledge myself that we'll carry out the campaign marked out in my last dispatches, which would bring us clear down to Cape Horn in four or five years; and I'm very anxious to get there—it strikes me that would be such a good horn to hold on to in all dilemmas, even if all the rest of the country went by the board. I dreamt t'other night that we had got through annexin' all North and South America ; and then I thought our whole country was turned into a monstrous great ship of war, and Cape Horn was the bowsprit, and Mr. Polk the captain. And the captain was walking the deck with his mouth shet, and everybody

THE MAJOR'S ANNEXATION DREAM.

was looking at him and wondering what he was goin' to do next. At last he sung out, "Put her about ; we'll sail across now and take Europe, and Asha, and Africa in tow—don't stop for bird's-egging round among the West India Islands ; we can pick them up as we come back along—crowd all sail now and let her have it."

Away we went; I never see a ship sail faster. The wind begun to blow harder and harder, and then it come on an awful storm, **and at last it blowed** a perfect harrycane. The sails begun **to go to flitters,** and she rolled as if she was going to upset. Some of the oldest **and best** sailors among the crew told the captain we should all go to destruction, if he didn't take in sail, and furl and clew up, and get things tight, and bring her head round to the wind. Mr. Ritchie was standing by his side, and says he, "Captain Polk, **them is all nothing** but Federal lies, as I've shown hundreds of times, not only in the Union, but years and **years ago in** the Enquirer. Them fellers only want to **give aid and comfort to the enemy**; don't pay any attention to 'em. Here's the chart"—he held up in his **hand the** resolutions of '98—" sail by this, and I'll risk her on any tack, and in all weathers."

On we went, lickity-split; **the harrycane** blowed harder, the timbers begun to creak, **the sails split to** ribbons, some of the spars begun to snap **and go by** the board, and then **all at once** there was a terrible cry, "Breakers ahead!" The captain then jumped as if he was wide awake; and says he, "Call all hands and **put her about."** But when the officers come to **give** orders to the crew, **not one of** them would mind or **pay** any attention. The whole crew was in a mutiny; and the ship was so large, and the crew was such **a mixed up mess** of different **sorts** of folks that there was twenty different mutinies all at once, in different parts of the vessel.

"Well," says Captain Polk, "I wash my hands of this mischief; if the crew won't help, the ship must go ashore."

Then an old sailor spoke up and said: "All the crews in the world couldn't do any good now; the ship was dished, and must be plumped on the rocks; her sails and spars was gone, the timbers sprung, and the hold already half full of water." In a few minutes she struck, and the rocks gored a hole through her side, and the water poured in, and down she sunk lower and lower, till at last she gave one mighty guggle, and plunged all under the water, except a piece of the bowsprit that still stuck out. The storm and the waves swept over her, and the whole crew and everybody aboard was lost, except a few of us who scrabbled up and clung to the bowsprit. Mr. Ritchie went down with the resolutions of '98 in his hand.

The hard spring I had to make, to get on to the bowsprit, waked me up; and, although I an't one that thinks much of dreams, I can't help thinking a good deal of Cape Horn, and naterally feel anxious to get along down that way as fast as we can; so I hope you'll urge the President to be a little more stirring, and let us have men and money a little faster.

I shall have to break off here for to-day, because I've got to write a little dispatch to the President to send by the same post. I send you some letters from Uncle Joshua, and other relations and friends, which you can, if you think best, hitch on to my dispatches, jest as Gineral Scott takes the letters of his under-officers and hitches on to his dispatches.

So I remain your old friend,

MAJOR JACK DOWNING.

HEAD-QUARTERS, CITY OF MEXICO,
ANNEXED UNITED STATES, October 25, 1847.

To James K. Polk, President of the United States and all annexed Countries.

DEAR COLONEL:—Things is getting along here as well as could be expected, considerin' the help we have, but we are all together too weak-handed to work to profit. If you want us to hurry along down South, we need a good deal more help and more money. It wouldn't be no use to give that three millions of dollars to Santa Anna now, for the people have got so out with him that he couldn't make peace if he had six millions. He's skulking about the country, and has as much as he can do to take care of himself. So I think you had better give up the notion about peace altogether, it'll be such a hard thing to get, and send on the three millions here to help us along in our annexin'. It's dangerous standin' still in this annexin' business. It's like the old woman's soap—if it don't go ahead, it goes back. It would be a great help to us in the way of holdin' on to what we get, if you would carry out that plan of giving the Mexican land to settlers from the United States, as fast as we annex it. I've been **very** impatient to see your proclamation offering the land to settlers to come out here. You've no idea how much help it would be to us if we only had a plenty of our folks out here, so that as fast as we killed a Mexican, or drove him off from his farm, we could put an American right on to it. If we could only plant as we go, in this way, we should soon have a crop of settlers here that could hold on to the slack themselves, and leave the army free to go ahead, and keep on annexin'. I thought when I left Washington, you was agoing to put out such a proclamation right away. And I think you are putting it off a good deal too long, for we've got land and farms enough here now for two hundred thousand at least; and, if they would only come on fast enough, I think we could make room for twenty thousand a week for a year to come. But I'm afraid you're too delicate about doing your duty in this business; you are such a stickler for the Constitution. I'm afraid you're waiting for Congress to meet, so as to let them have a finger in the pie. But I wouldn't do it. From all I can hear, it looks as if the Whigs was coming into power; and if they should, it would be a terrible calamity, for they are too narrow-minded and too much behind the age to understand the rights of this annexin' business, and it's ten chances to one if they don't contrive some way to put a stop to it.

I must tell you I went t'other day to see Gineral Cushing, and found him awfully tickled about being nominated for Governor of the old Bay State. At first he **was a good deal** amazed at it; he was as much surprised as you was, Colonel, when you first heard you was nominated for **President**. What amazed him so much was that he'd always been thinking all along that he was a Whig, till the nomination come, and **then** he jumped up and snapped his fingers, and said he believed, after all, the Democrats was the right party. **He's in great** sperits, and says he's no doubt he shall be elected. He goes for annexin' now the hottest of any of us, and says he takes the great Alexander for his model, and goes for annexin' as long as there is any country left to annex. His ancle is quite well, and Gineral Pillow's foot is a good deal better.

I have the honor to be your private embassador and faithful **friend**, from fifty-four forty on one side, down to Cape Horn on t'other.

MAJOR JACK DOWNING.

LETTER LVII.

MAJOR DOWNING'S THIRD DISPATCHES FROM THE CITY OF MEXICO.

CITY OF MEXICO, ANNEXED U. S., Dec. 30, 1847.

PRIVATE.] *To James K.* **Polk,** *President of the United States of America, Mexico, &c.*

DEAR COLONEL :—**I feel** a good deal anxious to hear how you are getting along there **to** home, and I s'pose you are full as anxious to know how we are going it out here. I got your message to Congress, and their first three days' doings, and **that's** the last I've heard. When I found the Whigs had fairly carried the House, I see in a moment there was a bad time ahead for us. Says I, look out for squalls; the old ship will have a hard time of it this winter. I had a good mind to come right home to help stan' by the helm, for I knew you would need me. But then I see at once that wouldn't do, for our officers have got into a dreadful snarl here, and I shouldn't dare to leave till things is **settled,** for fear the annexin' would all go back again, and we should lose our two years' work. So, as I can't come, all I can do is to give my notions about things a little, by way of advice.

I see how 'twill be; the House will be quarreling with you all winter; they'll be asking you all the hard questions they can think of, and all the time prying into your secrets about the war and annexin'. And I don't believe the Senate will be a copper better. 'Tis true there an't so many Whigs there, but there's them there that is full as bad. You never can do anything with Mr. Calhoun; you know he always splits everything in two, even to a hair; and the most he'll ever do for us about this annexin' business will be to split off a little piece of Mexico. If he finds out we are annexin' the whole of it, he'll fight agin us till all is blue. Then there's Colonel Benton I don't think is a whit better than Mr. Calhoun. You know what a fuss he made when we took in Texas, because we sot out to take in a little strip of Mexico with it; only a little reasonable strip, too, jest on our side of the river, so as to make square work of it. Colonel Benton's ebenezer was right up about it: he said it didn't belong to us, and it didn't belong to Texas, and we had no right to it, and shouldn't touch it. Now, if he made such a fuss about that little strip on our side of the river, he'll be likely to raise Ned and turn up Jack, if he finds out we have a notion of annexin' the whole of Mexico. And he's a terrible enemy to have, **I can tell you;** I don't believe there's another man in the country that can look down opposition equal to him. Now, with such men as these in the Senate, besides all the thunder of Webster, and all the persuadin' of Crittenden, how are you going to get along? I think there is no way for us to get along safe but to keep such men in the dark. Keep coaxing the money out of 'em to "conquer a piece," but never let 'em mistrust that we intend to conquer the whole. We must look one way all the time, and row t'other. I know you'll have a hard time of it, for Congress will keep diving into you all the time with this question and that, and pryin' into all the secrets about the war, and want to know what orders you give to us out here in Mexico, and what the armies are going to do, and where all the money goes to, and a thousand things that they've no business with. Now, when they keep coming to you with these ugly questions, I think the only safe way will be for you to shet your mouth right up, and keep a stiff upper lip, and not say a word. And do pray be careful what you tell to good old Mr. Ritchie, for you know he never *could* keep his mouth shet. There's some dogs, you know, that always bark at the wrong time, and frighten away the game. You never can train 'em to keep still when they ought to. You remember, more than two years ago, before the war begun, when you was laying out the work privately and carefully, and getting your ships around to the Pacific, and giving the officers their orders to stan' ready and wait till the train was touched on this side, and the moment they heard the first sound of the war to snap up California and annex it, and hold on to it, so that if we found the people wouldn't let the war go on, we could come to a settlement, and each side hold what they had got, you remember how Mr. Ritchie got so full of the matter that he liked to blowed the whole business up by letting on about the conquest of Mexico. A little more such carelessness at that time would a been likely to upset our whole kittle of fish—we might a lost

California, and Santa Fe, and likely enough even that little strip on our side of the river jining Texas. And as for the whole of Mexico, our jig would a been up at once; we might a whistled for it till doomsday, but 't wouldn't come.

I think you did right to make believe, in your message, that you had no idea of conquering the whole of Mexico. I don't believe it would be safe to take that ground till the work is all done. The people of our country are too skittish yet about conquering other countries; they haint got used to it. And for this reason you will have to be very firm with Congress, and not let 'em cross-question you too close, and get you into a bother. Call upon them boldly for large armies, and all the millions of money the mints can make, and all that Mr. Walker can borrow, and tell 'em you are digging into the vital parts of Mexico to get that five millions she owes us.

If they ask you if Mr. Tyler didn't offer to give up that five millions to Mexico to pay her for our taking Texas without her leave, jest shet your mouth up.

If they ask you if we hadn't ought to give up that five millions to Mexico for that strip on our side of the river that you sent General Taylor to take, jest shet your mouth up.

If they ask you if Mr. Trist didn't offer to give up that five millions to Mexico, and pay her twenty millions more, if she wouldn't try to get back California and New Mexico, that you had taken from her without her leave, jest shet your mouth up.

If they ask you what upon earth you can want of a hundred thousand soldiers in Mexico, and a hundred millions of dollars a year for spending money, jest open your lips carefully a little ways, and tell 'em you are digging into the vital parts of Mexico to get that five millions she owes us.

Then shet your mouth right up again, and keep it shet, and I guess you'll be safe. Don't be afraid of 'em; they can't pry your mouth open if they should try; and I guess that answer will pacify 'em till we get the work all done, and Mexico all annexed. Then you can step up to 'em boldly, and tell 'em you have made the greatest bargain that anybody ever made on this airth; you have got the whole of Mexico, people and all, for five millions of dollars, which is only about fifty cents a head for the people, and the lands and the gold mines thrown in for nothing.

I'm persuaded it will make the greatest man of you that ever lived yet; greater than Washington, or Jackson, or anybody else. The world will then say, " What great things was Washington ? He only defended his country, and built up a Republic; but there was Colonel Polk, he conquered a country and annexed a Republic." I'm so sure it will come to this that I wish you could stop their setting up that great Washington Monument there in the city of Washington, for that mnnument ought to be raised to you yet, and the money should be saved for that purpose. I don't know how you can stop the work goin' on, unless you can make it out that it comes under the head of internal improvements, and then you might stop it constitutionally. At any rate, it's worth trying for. Never mind the prating of them scare-crow folks who make such a fuss, and say it will be the destruction of the United States if you annex Mexico. What if it should ? You would still stand above Washington, and be remembered longer. Our history books tell us that the name of the man who built the first great temple to Diana at Ephesus is lost and forgotten; nobody knows who he was; but the name of the man who sot fire to it and burnt it down is found in all the histories down to this day. So in this grand annexin' business of yourn, if you should set fire to the great temple that Washington built, and burn it down, don't fear but your name will live on the page of history full as long as Washington.

But I've writ so much already that I haven't room to say

but a word or two about matters here. We keep pushing the business here; we've got pretty well through the vital parts of the country, and the army has now commenced spreading out and turning squatters. But we haven't near enough to spread all over the country yet, without leaving them too scattering. I hope you will hurry on the thirty thousand more men that you promised, as fast as possible; that would make us near a hundred thousand strong—enough to spread out squatters into all parts of the country, and the annexin' business would be pretty much over. That is, the annexin' of Mexico; and I take it you'll give us a holiday, and let us rest a few months before we hitch on to the next country down South. And, besides, we shall need that holiday to see about electing you President another term; for you'll have to be elected in the common way once more before you will be strong enough to stand President all the time.

I remain your faithful friend,

MAJOR JACK DOWNING.

LETTER LVIII.

MAJOR DOWNING'S FOURTH DISPATCH FROM THE CITY OF MEXICO.

CITY OF MEXICO, DOUBTFUL TERRITORY, Feb. 14, 1848.

PRIVATE.] *To James K. Polk, President of the United States, and nearly half of Mexico certain, with a pretty tolerable fair chance yet for the whole.*

DEAR COLONEL :—If anybody asks you that impudent question again, "What are we fightin' for?" jest tell him he's a goose, and don't know what he's talking about, for we *an't* fightin' at all; we've got peace now; got an armistice, they call it; so there's no sense at all in their putting that question to you any more. We've got the opposition fairly on the hip upon that question, if no other; fairly gagged 'em; they can't say to you any longer now, "What are we fightin' for?" This is some consolation for the shabby trick Trist has served us. That fellow has made a bargain with the Mexicans to stop the war, in spite of the orders you sent to him to come right home and let things alone. I felt uneasy about it when I see him hanging about here so long after he got his orders to come home, and I said to him, once or twice, "Mr. Trist, what's the reason you don't go off home and mind the President? This unlawful boldness of yourn is shameful."

"Why, Major," says he, "he that does his master's will does *right*, whether he goes according to orders or not. The President sent me out here to make peace, and it's a wonder to me if I don't fix it yet, somehow or other, before I've done with it." And then he put his finger to the side of his nose and give me a sassy look, as much as to say, "Major Downing, you better not try to be looking into diplomatic things that's too deep for you."

Says I, "Mr. Trist, I'm astonished at you; I thought you was a man of more judgment, and looked deeper into things. Don't you see what advantage it gives the President to let things now stand just as they be? He's offered peace to the Mexicans, and they have refused it. Therefore, the opposition at home can't cry out against him any more if he goes ahead with the war. He's shet their mouths up on that score. He's made the war popular, and can go into the Presidential campaign now with a good chance of being elected another term. And now, if you go to dabblin' in the business any more, I'm sure you'll do mischief. As things now stand, peace is the last thing in the world that the President wants. You've done your errand here and got your answer; and it's turned out jest right ; we can go on with our annexin' all Mexico now, without such an everlasting growlin' among the opposition at home, for we've offered the Mexicans peace, and they wouldn't take it. So you've nothin' to do now but to be off home, for the war is jest in the right shape as it **is.**"

Well, now, after all this plain advice—for I felt it my duty to be plain with him—he **still kept hanging about** here, day **after day, and the first I knew we was took** all aback by being told that Mr. Trist had made a treaty, and Gineral Scott was to order an armistice. I couldn't hardly believe my ears at first. I posted right off to Gineral Scott to know what it all meant.

" Gineral," says I, " are you going to order an armistice ? "

" **Yes,** Major Downing," says he, " Mr. Trist and **the** Mexican Commissioners have signed the preliminaries **of** a treaty ; **so, of** course, we shall have an armistice."

" Well, now, Gineral," says I, " I don't think the President will thank you for that."

" **Can't** help that," says he, " I must obey the orders of the Government, thanks or no thanks. And when Mr. Trist was sent **out** here to make a treaty, I was directed, whenever the plan **of a** treaty should be signed on both sides, **to order an armistice, and wait for** the two Governments **to ratify the treaty.** Well, Mr. Trist and the Mexican Commissioners have at last fixed **up some kind of a bargain, and signed it, and,** of course, according to my orders, we have nothing to do but to stand still and wait for the two Governments to clinch the nail."

" But," says I, " Gineral, **you know** Mr. Trist has no right to make a treaty any more than I have, for the President has ordered him to come home ; and if he has made a treaty, **it's** no better than a piece **of** blank paper, and you shouldn't mind it."

"Don't know anything about them matters," says he; "I can't go behind the curtain to inquire what little maneuvers are going on between the President and his Commissioner. Mr. Trist came out here with his regular commission to make a treaty. He has brought me a treaty signed by himself and the Mexican Commissioners, and my orders are to cease hostilities. Of course, we can do nothin' else but halt and stack our arms."

"Well," says I, "Gineral, it an't right; it's bad business;

THE MAJOR REMONSTRATING WITH GENERAL SCOTT.

it'll break up this grand annexin' plan that was jest going on so nice that we might a got through with it in a year or two more; and then it will bother the President most to death about his election for the second term. That treaty must be stopped; it musn't be sent home; and I'll go right and see Mr. Trist about it."

So off I went and hunted up Mr. Trist, and had a talk with him. Says I, "Trist, how's this? They tell me you've been making a treaty with these Mexicans."

"Shouldn't wonder if I had," says he; "that's jest what I come out here for."

"Well, I must say, sir," says I, "I think this is a pretty piece of business. How do you dare to do such a thing? You know the President has ordered you home."

"Yes," says he, "and I mean to go home as soon as I get through the job he sent me to do."

"Well, now," says I, "Trist, I claim to know what the President is about, and what he wants, and I'm his confidential friend and private embassador out here, and I shall take the liberty to interfere in this business. This high-handed doings of yourn must be nipt off in the bud. What sort of a bargain have you made? Jest let me look at the treaty."

"Can't do it," says he, "it's half way to Vera Cruz by this time; I sent it off yesterday."

"Blood and thunder!" says I, "then you have knocked the whole business in the head, sure enough. You've committed an outrageous crime, sir, and a great shame; and don't you know, sir, that great crimes deserve great punishments? I don't know what Colonel Polk will do; but I know what my friend, *Old* Hickory, would do if he was alive; he would hang you right up to the first tree he could come at."

"What! hang me for doing jest what I was sent here to do?" says he. "For I've made jest such a bargain as the President told me to make; only a leetle better one."

"That's nothing here nor there," says I, "you know circumstances alters cases. And you know well enough, or you ought to have sense enough to know, that, as things now stand, the President don't want a treaty. Now," says I, "Mr. Trist, answer me one plain question—Do you think you have any right at all to make a treaty after the President has ordered you home?"

"Well," says he, "I think circumstances alter cases, too;

and when the President ordered me home, I suppose he thought I couldn't get through the job he sent me to do. But I thought I could, and so I kept trying, and I've got through with it at last, and done the business all up according to my first orders; and I don't see why the President shouldn't be well satisfied."

"Well," says I, "what's the items of the bargain? What have you agreed upon?"

"Why," says he, "we have the whole of Texas clear to the Rio Grande; we have all of New Mexico, and all of Upper California. And we pay the Mexicans fifteen millions of dollars, and pay our own citizens five millions that the Mexicans owed them. And we stop firing, draw our charges from the guns that are loaded, and go home."

"Well, now," says I, "Trist, don't you think you are a pretty fellow to make such a bargain as that at this time of day? The President will be mortified to death about it. Here we've been fightin' near about two years to make the Mexicans pay over that five millions of dollars they owed our people, and now you've agreed that we shall put our hands in our pockets and pay it ourselves. The whole plan of the war has been carried on by the President upon the highest principles, to go straight ahead and 'conquer a peace,' man-fashion; and now you've agreed to back out of the scrape, and *buy* a peace, and pay the money for it. You know very well the President has declared, time and again, that the war should go on till we got indemnity for the past, and security for the future—them's his own words—and now you've agreed to settle up without getting one jot of either. For the past we are at least a hundred millions of dollars out of pocket, besides losing ten or fifteen thousand men. As for the men, I s'pose you may say we can offset them against the Mexicans we have killed, and as we have killed more than they have, maybe it foots up a little in our favor, and that's the only advantage you've secured. As for the hundred millions of dollars, we don't get a penny of it back. So all the indemnity you get for the past is a few thousand dead Mexicans, that is, as many as remains after subtracting what they've killed of us from what we've killed of them. But the capsheaf of your bargain is the 'security for the future.' The cities and towns and castles that we have fit so hard to take, and have got our men into, and all so well secured, you now agree to give 'em all right up again to the enemy, and march our men off home with their fingers in their mouths; and that's our security for the future. As for the fifteen millions of dollars you agree to pay for New Mexico and California, you might jest as well a thrown the money into the sea, for they was ours afore; they was already conquered and annexed, and was as much ours as if we had paid the money for 'em."

Here I turned on my heel and left him, for I was so disgusted at the conduct of the feller that I wouldn't have any more talk with him. And now, my dear Colonel, there is nothing for us to do but to look this business right in the face, and make the best we can of it. If there was any way to keep the thing out of sight, it would be best for you to throw the treaty into the fire as soon as you get it, and send word on to Gineral Scott to go ahead again. But that is impossible; it will be spread all over the country, and known to everybody. And I'm convinced it will be the best way for you to turn right about, make believe to be glad about what can't be helped, and accept the treaty. The nominations for President is close at hand, and you must get ready to go into the election for your second term with what you've got, and make the best show you can with it. If you should reject the treaty, the opposition would get the advantage of you again; they would then cry out that the Mexicans has asked for peace, and *you had refused it;* and there would be no end to their growling about this oppressive war of invasion. But if you accept the treaty, it puts an end to their grumbling about the war.

To pacify our friends that are very eager for the whole of Mexico, you must tell 'em to look at it and see how much we have already got; keep telling of 'em that half a loaf is better than no bread; tell 'em to keep quiet till after your next election is over, and maybe you'll contrive some plan to be cutting into t'other half. Keep Mr. Ritchie blowing the organ, all weathers, to the tune of half of Mexico for a song. Tell the whole country, and brazen it out to everybody, that you've made a great bargain, a capital bargain, much better than Jefferson made when he bought Louisiana for fifteen millions of dollars; tell 'em for the same sum of money you have got a great deal more land, and more men on it. I'm satisfied this is the best ground to take; we must go for the treaty, and, bitter pill as it is, we must swallow it as though we loved it. I s'pose it will have to go before the Senate, as the Constitution now stands (the Constitution is very defective on that pint, and ought to be mended, for it's dangerous trusting important matters to the Senate); but you must drive your friends all up to vote for it; don't let it fail on no account; don't let 'em go to fingerin' it over, and putting in amendments that will make the Mexicans so mad that they will kick it all over again. For that would put things into such a hurly-burly that I'm afraid you would lose your election.

Ratify the treaty, and then gather up all the glory that's been made out of this war, twist it into a sort of glory wreath round your head, and march with a bold step and a stiff upper lip right into the Presidential campaign, and I shouldn't wonder if you beat the whole bunch of all your enemies and all your friends. And if you went into your second term on the strenth of half of Mexico, it would be a pretty good sign that you *might go into* a third term **on** the strength of the whole of it.

I remain your faithful friend,

MAJOR JACK DOWNING.

LETTER LIX.

FIFTH DISPATCH OF MAJOR DOWNING FROM THE CITY OF MEXICO.

CITY OF MEXICO, March 22, 1848.

MR. GALES & SEATON—

MY DEAR OLD FRIENDS :—When I have to write about the war, and the treaty, and things of that sort that belongs to diplomatics, of course I send my dispatches to the President or Mr. Ritchie; but when things branch off into the newspaper line, then I send 'em to you. We've had Gineral Scott on trial here five days, for high treason against Gineral Pillow and Gineral Worth. If it goes agin him, I don't know whether they will conclude to hang him or shet him up in some of the mines of Mexico for life. But he fights like a Turk, and an't skeered at nuthin'. The President better send on some more help, for I an't sure that what there is here will be able to handle him. The battle has been pretty hot for five days, and I don't see as they get the upper hand of him at all yet. It would be a great pity if a man that has been guilty of such horrible crimes as he has out here in Mexico, should slip through their fingers at last, and escape punishment. I begin to feel a little afraid how it will come out. For my part, I go for justice, hit who 'twill. If a man will commit crimes, let him be punished for it. I'm afraid the President has missed a figger in leaving it out to such men as he has. It would a been safer and more sure to leave it out to a jury of Mexicans. I've no doubt the least verdict they would give would a been two years in the deepest and darkest mine in Mexico for his taking Vera Cruz and the Castle; two years more for the cutting and slashin' he give 'em at Cerro Gordo; two

GENERAL SCOTT COURT-MARTIALED IN MEXICO.

years more for Chapultepec and Churubusco; and all the rest of his life for his taking the city of Mexico. In that case, you see, his punishment would a been measured out something according to his crimes.

I was thinking last night that I ought to make up a little budget about this trial and send it on to you, as I promised to let you know once in a while how things was getting along out here. And while I was bothering my head to know which end to begin at, a man came in and brought me a little letter. I took it and opened it, and I couldn't hardly believe my eyes at first, to see the name of Gineral Pillow signed to it. He "requested me to call at his quarters in the evening," on very urgent and important business. Thinks I to myself, what in thunder can this mean? Then I thought maybe they had got a hint that the prisoner intended to run away, and they wanted me to help keep guard round Gineral Scott's quarters to see that he didn't escape.

So, jest at dark, I went round to Gineral Pillow's quarters. He seemed to be amazin' glad to see me, and *took me by the arm* and led me into t'other room.

"Major Downing," says he, "I'm very happy to see you. I wish you wouldn't make yourself such a stranger to my quarters; it would give me a great deal of pleasure to see you oftener."

I thanked him, and told him that his rank was a good deal superior to mine, and I always felt kind of delicate about putting myself alongside of them that was so much above me.

"Not at all," says he, "Major, not at all; we have to observe rank, to be sure, when we are on the field; but everywhere else we are all equals, Major, all equals; give us your hand." And here he giv my hand another hearty shake.

"Major," says he, "I understand you write letters to the National Intelligencer sometimes, about matters out here in Mexico."

"Well, yes," says I, "Gineral, I do sometimes, when it don't interfere with my public duties as the President's private embassador."

Then he turned round and put the door to, and begun to speak in a little lower tone.

"Major," says he, "that Intelligencer is a capital paper; it deserves to be encouraged. I take *a warm interest in the prosperity of that paper, and mean to do something for it.* I'll be *the making of it yet,* when I get to the rank and situation I expect to get. I s'pose you'll send some account of this court-martial down by the courier to-morrow, to go to the Intelligencer?

"Well, yes," says I, "I was thinking of sending some little outline of it, so the folks at home in the United States might understand the substance of it as far as it has got along."

Then he took a written paper out of his pocket, and says he, "Major, here is a clear account of the proceedings, as far as they have gone, all carefully drawn up, and putting everything in a true light. I should like to have you take this and send it on to the Intelligencer, and have it inserted as coming from an authentic source; or, if you choose, you can work it in and make it a part of your letter, and then nobody will doubt but what it comes from an authentic source."

After I took it and looked a while over some parts of it, says I, "Gineral, it seems to me it is most too soon to send on such a particular account as this, for fear of making some mistakes. It must take some time to pick the matters all up and put them together in the right shape, so as to give every one his fair share. I thought I would send on now the main points of it, and send on the particulars when we've had a chance to pick 'em all up and put 'em together right."

"But, Major," says he, "I'm *very anxious this account should go off with the first impressions.* You know a great deal depends on first impressions; therefore, no time should be lost in getting this before the public; and the best way to do it is to work it into your report. To be sure, the paper does considerable justice to me, but not more than I think you will be satisfied belongs to me. *I never ask any one to puff me; but I have confidence in you to believe that you will do me justice. I never forget my friends.* There's no knowing but the upshot of this trial may tip Gineral Scott out of the tail-end of the cart yet; and if so, I stand a good chance of being placed at the head of military affairs here; and, between you and me, that would give me a strong chance of succeeding Mr. Polk in the Presidency. And, you know, I never forget my friends."

"Well," says I, "Gineral, seein' you are so arnest about it, I'll take the paper home with me, and look it over, and if I find I can work it into my letter, so it will look ship-shape, I'll do it. And then, I take it, I shall have your word, upon the honor of an officer, that you never will forget me and the National Intelligencer."

"That you shall," says he, giving me another shake of the hand. "But," says he, "you better stop with me to-night, and do it all up here; *I'll give you a comfortable place to write, some place to sleep, and soldier fare.*"

I thanked him very kindly for his hospitality, but I told him I should have to go back to my quarters, where I had left some parts of my dispatch ready fixed up. In bidding me good night, he shook me very warmly by the hand, and urged me again to put the document he had given me into my letter, as he was *very anxious it should go off with the first impressions*. So, here it is; and if I find it necessary, after copying it, to add any notes or interlinings, I can do it:

DOCKYMENT.

GREAT BATTLE IN THE COURT-MARTIAL.

This important investigation, which has been going on for five days, is likely to use General Scott all up to nothing; there won't be so much as a grease spot left of him; while, at the same time, it cannot fail to add to the renown and fair fame of General Pillow, till it raises him above all Greek, above all Roman fame. General Worth, also, has shown a magnanimity in this contest which will crown him with immortal honor. He had a forty-nine pounder, loaded to the muzzle, pointed directly at the head of Scott, which would a blowed his brains clear to the North Pole; but seeing the weakness and imbecility of Scott, who was almost ready to get down upon his knees, and, with tears in his eyes, ask his pardon, Worth, with unparalleled magnanimity, refused to fire, and absolutely withdrew the charge from the gun, saying to the by-standers, "The President has given me all I want; why should I stoop to kill this poor devil of a Scott?" After Worth had thus generously thrown away his powder, Scott, with his usual meanness, put on a bragadocio show of courage, and dared him to the fight; but of course Worth wouldn't take any notice of him.

Scott had bullied Duncan, but when he found Duncan was prepared to defend himself, with the most craven spirit he coaxed him to let the matter drop, and hush it up. He had, also, in the most shameful manner, bullied General Pillow; but when he found he had roused the lion, he did not dare to beard the lion. As soon as the gallant Pillow, the high-souled Pillow, the chivalric and courageous Pillow, appeared on the field of combat, Scott commenced a rapid and ignominious retreat. But General Pillow, actuated by a high sense of public duty, as well as a proper regard for his own honor, would not allow public sentiment to be so outraged with impunity; he, therefore, pursued the cowardly Scott, determined that, poltroon as he was, he should either fight or die. For two or three days Scott was fleeing for his life, and making the most desperate efforts to escape from the field of battle; but the gallant Pillow pursued him and cut him off on every tack, and foiled and floored him at every turn. The talent, tact, prowess and generalship displayed by General Pillow on this occasion has probably never been equaled, except by the same gallant officer on the battle-fields of Mexico, when he killed the Mexican officer in single combat, was struck down upon his knees by the concussion of a cannon-ball upon his head, and led his troops to victory by wading chin-deep through a creek of mud and water. The hot pursuit of Pillow at last drove Scott into a corner, from which it was impossible for him to escape. He then turned and raised his puny arm to fight; but the weakness of his weapons, his little pointless darts, and pop-gun squibs, were almost too ridiculous even to excite a laugh. The heroic Pillow stood in peerless majesty, and shook them off as unconcernedly as the lion shakes the dew-drops from his mane. During this whole contest *Gen. Pillow's well-devised plans of battle, his judicious disposition of his forces, his coolness and daring during the whole of this terrible battle, is the subject of universal congratulation among his friends, and general remark with all.*

LION—ASS.

Erased from the above: "During this great battle, which has lasted now for five days, Pillow was in command of all the forces engaged except Worth's division, which was not engaged." Also erased: "He (Pillow) has completely silenced his enemies."

On the whole, the above docyment seems to give such a clear, candid view of the proceedings of the court-martial during the first five days, that I don't think it is necessary for me to add another word. Give my love to the President and Mr. Ritchie; and I remain your old friend, whether we go on annexin' any more or not,

MAJOR JACK DOWNING.

LETTER LX.

PRIVATE LETTER TO MAJOR **JACK DOWNING.**

Post-Office, Downingville,
State of Maine, June 30, 1848.

Dear Nephew :—Bein' our army is about breakin' up in Mexico and coming home, I thought the best chance to get a letto you would be to get your old friends, Mr. Gales and Seaton, to send it on that way, and maybe it might come across you somewhere on the road, if you are still in the land of the living. Your Aunt Keziah is in a great worriment about you, and is very much frightened for fear somethin' has happened, because we haven't heard nothin' from you since your last letter. I try to pacify her, and tell her the fighting was all over, and nothin' to do but to finish up the court-martial the last time you writ, and that there isn't agoing to be no more annexin' till Mr. Cass comes in President, and you'll soon be along. But all won't pacify her ; she's as uneasy as a fish out of water, and says she lays awake half the night thinking of them garillas, for fear they've got hold of you. So I hope you'll write home as soon as possible, and let us know whether you are dead or alive, and set your Aunt Keziah's heart to rest.

For my part, I hope you will hurry along back as fast as you can. Our politics is very much mixed up and in a bad way about the Presidency. It would puzzle a Philadelphy lawyer to tell how it's comin' out. It was a very unlucky hit when President Polk sent Old Zack Taylor down to Mexico. He wasn't the right man. But, then, I s'pose Mr. Polk had no idea of what sort of a chap he had got hold of. It can't be helped now, but it's like to be the ruin of our party. The

Democratic party haint seen a well day since Taylor first begun his Pally Alto battles ; and now we are all shiverin' as bad as if we had the fever and agay. I don't know, after all, but this annexin' Mexico will turn out to be an unlucky blow to the party ; for what will it profit the Democratic party if they gain the whole world and lose the Presidency? Ye see, the Whigs have put up Taylor for President ; and it has completely knocked us all into a cocked hat. There isn't one-half of us that knows where we stan' or which way we are goin' ; and there isn't a party fence in the country that is high enough to keep our folks from jumping over. They are getting kind of crazy, and seem to feel as if Old Hickory had got back again, and they was all running to vote for him. The Whigs laugh and poke fun at us, and say they have got as good a right to have a Hickory as we Democrats have. We put up Gineral Cass first, and thought we should carry it all hollow ; for he's a strong man, and took a good deal of pains to make the party like him all over the country. And if the Whigs had done as they ought to, and put up Clay, or any one they had a right to put up, we should a carried the day without any trouble. But the conduct of the Whigs has been shameful in this business. Instead of taking a man that fairly belonged to 'em, they have grabbed hold of a man that got all his popularity out of our war, and was under the pay of our Administration, and has been made and built up by our party, and the Whigs had no more business with him than they had with the man in the moon. But, for all that, the Whigs had the impudence to nominate him. Well, that riled our water all up, so we couldn't see bottom nowhere. But we soon found there was a shiftin' and whirlin' of currents, and the wind and the tide was settin' us on to the rocks in spite of us. We soon see that old Rough and Ready, as they call him, was going to be too much for Cass. But, as we was all making up our mind that it was gone goose with us, Mr. John Van Buren, of York State—he's a smart feller, a son of President Van Buren, and a chip of the old block—he sings out: "Don't give up the ship yet; if one hoss an't enough to draw the load, hitch on another. There's father, he'll draw like a two-year-old." Well, the idea seemed to take; and they stirred round and got up another Convention at Utica, in York State, to see who they should put up, and they all pitched upon President Van

RACE FOR THE PRESIDENCY—OLD ZACK AHEAD.

Buren. Mr. Van Buren patted them on the shoulder, and told 'em to have good courage and go ahead, for they was on the right track, but they must hitch on somebody else besides him, for he had made up his mind four years ago not to take hold again. But they stuck to him with tears in their eyes, and told him there wasn't another man in the country that could draw like him alongside of Cass, and if he still had any patriotism for the party left he musn't say no. And they worked upon his feelin's so much that at last he didn't say no. So now we've got two candidates, Cass and Van Buren, and good strong ones, too, both of 'em ; and if we can't whip Taylor, I think it's a pity. I know as well as I want to know that we shall give him a pesky hard tug. Some are afraid we an't hardly strong enough yet, and they've called another convention, to meet in Buffalo the 9th of August, to put up another candidate. But others are faint-hearted about it, and say it's all no kind of use ; we may put up twenty candidates, and Taylor will whip the whole lot ; it's a way he has ; he always did just so in Mexico. If they brought twenty to one agin' him, it made no odds ; he whipt the whole ring, from Pally Alto to Bona Vista.

So you see what sort of a pickle we're in, and how much we need your help jest now. But there's one thing on my mind pretty strong : You know this appointment in the Downingville Post-Office, that you got Gineral Jackson to give me, has always been a great comfort to me, and it would be a sad blow to me to lose it now in my old age. I wish you would make it in your way to call and see Gineral Taylor as you come along home, and try to find out how he feels toward me ; because, if he is to be elected anyhow, I can't see any use there would be in my biting my own nose off for the sake of opposing his election. And I don't think that patriotism to the party requires it ; and I'm sure prudence don't.

When you get to Washington, call and see Mr. Ritchie, and try to comfort him ; I'm told the dear old gentleman is workin' too hard for his strength—out a nights in the rain, with a lantern in his hand, heading the campaign. Try to persuade him to be calm and take good care of himself. And be sure and ask him how the Federals are goin' this election, for we can't find out anything about it down here. I used to know how to keep the run of the Federals, but now there is so many parties—the Democrats, and the Whigs, and Hunkers, and Barnburners, and Abolition folks, and Proviso folks—all criss-crossin' one another, that I have my match to keep the run of 'em. But your Aunt Keziah says the clock has struck, and I must close the mail. So I remain your loving uncle,

JOSHUA DOWNING, P. M.

LETTER LXI.

The Mexican war is over. General **Taylor** has come home to become the people's candidate for the Presidency, and Major Downing has also returned to stump the country for the Democratic party. But finding the tide all against him, and everywhere setting for Old Zack, he mounts a telegraph post and sends a hasty, though rather discouraging, dispatch to President Polk :

PRIVATE REPORT TO JAMES K. POLK, PRESIDENT OF AMERICA, AND HIS PART OF MEXICO.

TELEGRAPH WIRES, October 31, 1848.

DEAR COLONEL :—I've been stumping it round all over the lot for two or three months, tight and tight, for our American friend, Gineral Cass, and as I s'pose you are very anxious and uneasy to know how it's coming out, I thought I would set down and make out a private report, and send it on to you by the telegraph wires, for they say they go like lightening, and give you some of the premonitory symptons, so that when the after-clap comes you may be a little prepared for it, and not feel so bad. As I said afore, I've been all round the lot, sometimes by the steamboats, and sometimes by the railroads, and sometimes by the telegraph, and when there wasn't no other way to go, I footed it. And I'm satisfied the jig is up with us, and it's no use in my trying any longer; and Mr. Buchanan's speech was all throwed away, too. I'm very sure we shall get *some* of the States, but I'll be hanged if I can tell which ones. There an't a single State that I should dare to bet upon alone, but taking 'em all in the lump, I should still stick out strong for half a dozen at least. I see where all the

WRITING BY TELEGRAPH.

difficulty is, as plain as day. You may depend upon it, we should elect Gineral Cass easy enough if it wasn't for Gineral Taylor; but he stands peskily in the way, jest as much as he stood in the way of the Mexicans at Bony Vista. As for Mr. Van Buren, if he stood agin us alone, we should tread him all to atoms; he couldn't make no headway at all, especially after we got the nomination at Baltimore. Jest between you and me, I don't think much of Mr. Van Buren now. I don't believe he ever *was* a Democrat. I think he only made believe all the time; and I'd bet two to one *he's only making believe now*. I wish the Old Gineral, dear Old Hickory, that's dead and gone, could be here now to have the handling of him for a little while; if he didn't bring him into the traces I wouldn't guess agin.

But, as I said afore, Gineral Taylor is peskily in the way all over the country. First, I thought I would figure round in some of the strong Whig districts; for, thinks I, if I can make our friends show a bold front for Cass there, it will be such a wet blanket for the Whigs that they'll give it up. Well, I called a public meeting, without distinction of party; and I put it to 'em strong for Cass, and the Constitution, and Californy forever. They all listened, and every little while they hurra'd and clapped; and thinks I, the tide is turning— I'm going to carry this place all hollar, Whigs and all. But when I got through, an old rusty-faced farmer, away back in one corner, got up and looked round, and says he, "Three cheers for Zachary Taylor." Thunder and cannon! if there wasn't a roar, set me down for a liar. Why, Colonel, I han't heard nothin' like it since the storming of Chepultapec. It took me right off my feet. I see at once the battle was all agin us there, and thought I better make my escape under the smoke of it as fast as possible. At first I felt rather bad about it. And then, agin, I thought I ought to have expected it, for I knew the Whigs had voted that Gineral Taylor was a Whig, and had made up their minds to go for him. So I I streaked it off for a strong Democratic district; for I found our main dependence must be among our own friends. Here I called a mass-meeting, without distinction of party, for I was sure we should get up such a roar for Cass that the

Whigs would be dumbfounded, and be pretty likely to fall in with us. **Well, how** do you think it worked? I made a roarin' speech for Cass; told 'em what a great statesman and great warrior he was; and how he had proved the former by offering to swallow all Mexico, and how he had proved the latter by breakin' his sword in a passion; and more than all **that,** since the nomination at Baltimore, he was the greatest Democrat in the country. "And now," says I, "**my** friends, three cheers for Cass, the Constitution and Californy." Well, they gin three good, loud cheers, and I thought that nail was **well drove and clinched.** Then a blacksmith, with a smutty nose and a leather apron on, gets up and sings out, "Nine cheers for old Rough and Ready!" And, by jingo, it went like a hurricane; full twice as loud, and three times as many, as the cheers for Cass. I had **a good mind to cut and run, and** give it all up. But at last I plucked up courage and faced the storm. I called out to the blacksmith, **and says I, "My friend, when we called** this meeting, **without** distinction of **party, it was all meant for** Gineral Cass, the Democratic candidate, **and it's very** unhandsome for a Whig to come here and interrupt us in **this** way."

"**You take me for a** Whig, do you?" says he.

"To be sure I do," says I; "**you are no** Democrat to act in this way."

At that he reddened up so the smut on his face turned blacker than **it** was before, and, says he, "I'd have **you** know, Sir, I'm as good a Democrat as you are. My father and mother was Democrats before me. I was born and bred a Democrat; and I mean to live and die **a** Democrat, but I go for Old Rough and Ready, **let** who will go agin him." Then he called out agin for nine cheers for Old Rough and Ready; and the way they roared 'em out was a caution. I see it was no use in talking about Whigs and Democrats—I must try some other hook.

So I cruised round on the Free Soil territory, and got up meetings, and preached up the Wilmot Proviso hot and heavy, and told 'em Gineral Cass would go for it with all his might to the day of his death. Then I thought I would get 'em on the hip in a way they couldn't help giving me a rousing hurra, so I called out, "Three cheers for Free Soil and Gineral Cass!" Well, the three cheers come as quick and as true as Paddy's echo, for it was "three cheers for Free Soil and Gineral Taylor?"

I begun to think the only chance was for us to try to carry the South. So I wheeled about, and turned about, and jump'd Jim Crow, in the slave States. I told 'em they must stir round and elect Gineral Cass or the whole slavery business would be upset; but if they would only elect him they might feel safe, for they had his letters to show that he was in favor of upholding slavery all weathers, and of carrying it into every territory we could lay our hands on. They all answered me very cooly, that they had much rather trust a straightforward Southern man, that they knew had no tricks about him, than to trust a Northern man with Southern principles; and they reckoned, on the whole, they should go for Gineral Taylor. As a last chance, I thought I would try to rouse 'em up in old Pennsylvany. So I went to 'em and told 'em their coal and iron was in danger, and the only way for 'em to save it was to elect Gineral Cass, who would protect it to the bat's end, for he was as good a tariff man as Henry Clay. At that, every one of 'em—Quakers and Germans, and Dutchmen, and all—put their finger agin the side of their nose, and said, "Friend, we tried a tariff man last time, but we didn't save our coal and iron by it; so we have made up our minds to try *an honest man* this time—we are going for Zachary Taylor."

By this time I was convinced the game was up, and it was no use to stump it any longer. We've got into the current where we can't help ourselves, and are going down over the falls of Niagara as fast as we can go ; and I hope you and all the rest of our party will be as calm and composed, and considerate, as the Indian was that went down over then awful falls a great many years ago. He tugged and pulled his canoe against the current with all his might till he found there

THE LAST SUP AT TREASURY PAP.

was no chance left, and then he laid down his paddle, and took up his bottle of rum, and sot down quietly in the bottom of the canoe, and tipped the bottle up to his mouth, and sot and drinked, and took the good of it, till he pitched head over heels down the falls, and went out of sight forever.

Now, my last advice to you, dear Colonel, and to all our friends, and especially to dear old Mr. Ritchie, is, to set down quiet and composed in the bottom of the boat, and eat away at the public crib, and drink away at the bottle of the sub-treasury till the 4th of March, when we shall all pitch over the falls together, drinking our last guggle.

I remain your dear friend,

MAJOR JACK DOWNING.

LETTER LXII.

A VERY PRIVATE LETTER FROM MAJOR DOWNING TO **PRESIDENT POLK.**

HEAD OF SALT RIVER,* Dec. 18, 1848.

DEAR COLONEL :—It all come out jest exactly as I told you 'twould in my last dispatch, a few days before the 'lection. The arthquakes and harrycanes was awful. Some of our friends was throwed up sky high, and haint been seen nor heard of since ; some was swallowed up in the ground and buried alive ; and all of us was ship-wrecked and splashed overboard, and left to the marcy of the wind and the tide. I was lucky enough to get a-straddle of a plank, and made out to keep my head above water. I drifted about awhile, kind of confused like, and couldn't hardly tell whether I was on the ocean, or on a lake, or where I was.

---

* EDITORIAL NOTE.—On the election of General Taylor to the Presidency, November, 1848, the Whigs, who had been sojourning for four years in Salt River Territory, came down the river in full force and high spirits, while the Democrats moved quietly up and took possession, and went to work and tried to organize the Territory, in order to get it admitted as a State. Major Downing, in this letter, describes Salt River and the philosophy of its navigation more accurately and satisfactorily than has ever been done by any other author.

At last I floated along into a river, and then I concluded, of course, I was bound down Niagara, and should have to plunge head and ears over the big falls. I seemed to be floating along down the middle of the river, and away off before me and away behind me I could see a good many others going the same way; and, away in close to the shore, on both sides of the river, there seemed to be a good many going the other way—that is, as I thought, going up stream. I was kept along in this way till I come to a narrow place in the river, which I learnt afterward was called the half-way narrows. Here the current grew more rapid, and I floated along very fast; but I was so near the shore I could see folks on both sides, and hear 'em speak.

Presently I met a man on one side of the river, footing it along the shore, and towing a one-masted boat after him, as I thought, up stream. At first, by his stooping walk and bald head, I thought he was too old a man to be doing such hard kind of work; but when he come nearer, I see he had flaxy hair, and a young and almost boyish looking face. He went straight ahead, with a line over his shoulder, drawing the boat after him, and singing a merry kind of a song, which I couldn't make out, only one varse of it, which seemed to be this:

> "Life is real, life is earnest;
> Things are jest what they do seem;
> Down Salt River thou returnest,
> Oh, my Tribune, 'tis no dream."

When I saw who it was I was amazingly puzzled. I'd heard a good many songs that had more truth than poetry in 'em, but this one seemed to have more poetry than truth. Any how, if this was really Salt River, that we had heard so much tell of, I couldn't seem to make out how I should be sailing down stream so fast, and the Tribune-man be tugging

NAVIGATING SALT RIVER.

up stream so hard. This didn't agree with the election returns at all. Something has got twisted **round**; things is *not* jest what they seem. While **I was bothering** my head about it, I looked over on t'other side of the **river, and** there was another man with a line over his shoulder, towing a larger and heavier **boat up stream, as** I thought. **He was** a tall, officer-looking man, **with large** whiskers, and stood up straight, and walked **strong, as** though he didn't care for nobody. He, too, seemed **to be singing a very merry** song. All **I could hear of it was just this varse**:

> "Old Uncle Sam was a jolly old soul,
> And a jolly old soul was he;
> He called for his pipe, and he called for his bowl,
> And he called for Taylor and me."

As he passed by me **I see the** name on the starn of the boat was New York Courier **and Enquirer.** I was in **a** great puzzlement; **these Whig chaps** was all so merry; and yet, if this was **really Salt River, it seemed** to me they was going the wrong **way,** according to the 'lection, and I couldn't tell what to make of it. As I was near enough to hail the Courier man, I thought I would call to him and see if I could get any light on **the subject. So says I—**

"Hullo, **Colonel!"**

He stopped and turned round, and answered, "Hullo."

Says I, "I ask your pardon, Colonel, but I'm **a** stranger in these parts, and a stranger to you, but **I know you by your** boat. Will you be so kind as **to tell me** where I'm bound to? For I'm kind of **lost."**

"Oh," certainly," **says he,** "with the greatest pleasure, my dear sir. **You** are bound straight up to the head of Salt River; you can't miss your way, for there isn't a single path that turns out between here and there."

"Well, now," says I, "Colonel, you or I must be under

some strange mistake. Don't you see I'm floating down on the current? Ain't the river running down this way, and carrying me along with it?"

At that he laughed outright, and says he, "I see you are nothing but a fresh-water sailor, and don't know anything about the navigation of Salt River."

"Well, how should I," says I; "for I never was in these waters before?"

"Well," says he, "*Salt River runs up stream;* jest bear that in your mind, and you'll find it all plain sailing."

"But that can't be possible," says I; "you, nor I, nor nobody else, ever knew a river to run up stream."

"You may depend upon it," says he, "Salt River runs up stream; and I suppose that is the only river in America that does run up stream."

By this time I had floated so far by that I couldn't hear anything more he said. But it wasn't long before I was satisfied the Colonel was right; for, as the current carried me along back into the country, the land kept growing higher and higher, and at last I found myself quite up among the mountains; and, when I come to the head of the river, the current run my plank right plump ashore.

I found a good many of our friends already here before me, and I understand a great many more are on the way. Our annexin' friend, Gineral Cass, hasn't got here yet; but he's expected now every day. This is a pretty good sort of a country up here, after all, and has a good many advantages. But I haven't time to give you much account of it to-day; I'll try to describe it more another time. I've spent considerable time examining and exploring this curious river, and I think I've learnt more about it than anybody that's been up here afore. It's different from all the other rivers that I ever see. It has no springs or streams running into it to feed it, but feeds itself from its own waters. All the center of the river is a strong current, running up stream till it gets to the head of the river ; and then it divides and turns off each way, and works along down in eddies and currents by each bank of the river till it gets to the mouth ; and then it turns round regular into the center current agin, and up it comes.

This shows the reason why anybody that happens to get into the current of Salt River has to go clear to the head of it before he can **stop**. It shows the reason, too, why anybody that sets out to go down with **a boat, or a** raft, or anything, has to lead it along the shore by a line ; **for, if** it happens **to get out a** little too far from shore, and get ketched in the center current, it's gone goose with **it** ; **it has to** go clear back to the head of the river, and take another start. This, of course, makes the navigation **of Salt River**, on the passage out, very hard and difficult.

Now, I'll tell you **what I advise** you by all means to do. **You know Congress is in a great taking** to pass a bill for the improvement of the navigation of lakes and rivers, and they are afraid they can't do it this session because you'll put your veto on it. **Now**, you jest strike a bargain with 'em ; if they'll **put in a million of dollars into the bill to** improve the navigation of Salt River, **and let Gineral Cass have the laying of it out,** you'll sign **the bill**. If we could get that bill through, it would be of immense importance to us and our friends for a **good many** years to come.

We can't, **of** course, look for you up **here till** after the 4th of March ; **but I shall be getting everything ready for you as fast as I can.** I've got **a** notion in **my** head, however, that you might hold on there at Washington some years longer yet ; and be in a situation to do our friends more good, **may** be, than you could up here. I see they are looking round all over the country for men to make up a Cabinet for Gineral Taylor; and they seem to be going upon the rule that them that did the most toward electing him must have the first chance in the Cabinet. Now, going upon that rule, the first chance belongs to you, of course; for there isn't no other man in the country that did a quarter so much toward electing him as you did. In fact, if it hadn't been for you he never would a been elected at all; and if he doesn't give you the first place in his Cabinet, if you'll take it, he'll be the ungratefulest man that ever lived I think it would be best, all things considered, for you to take a place at the head of the Cabinet.

As for dear old Mr. Ritchie, as the weather is warm and pleasant, and comfortable for making the voyage, why not start him right along? He'll find nothing to trouble him, for I've been all round here, and there isn't no bears, nor wolves, nor Federalists, nor anything of that sort. I don't think I ever see a country clearer of Federalists in my life; and every man I've talked with here is in favor of the resolutions of '98.

I remain your friend and pioneer,

MAJOR JACK DOWNING.

LETTER LXIII.

MAJOR DOWNING ADVISES MR. RITCHIE TO KEEP COOL, AND NOT FIGHT SO HARD AGAINST THE WHIG ADMINISTRATION.

MASON AND DIXON'S SIDE OF SALT RIVER, Aug. 11, 1849.

MY DEAR MR. RITCHIE :—You don't know how glad I be to see how you have spunked up since my last letter to you. You are raly giving it to the "corrupt and imbecile Administration" pell-mell. I should think every "dolt," and every "butcher," and every "Nero" among 'em must have a bung'd eye by this time. You do give it to 'em, right and left, about right. Uncle Joshua says you are the *Tom Hyer* of our party, and can whip anybody the Feds can bring into the ring. But now I begin to feel uneasy for fear you'll overdo yourself, and break down, and then **we** shan't have nobody to take care of **us.** Don't you remember the story of the tame elephant that was used to help launch vessels? One time they put him to launch a vessel that was too heavy for him. After he tried once or twice, and couldn't start it, the keeper called out, "Take away this lazy beast, and bring another." At that the poor elephant roused up, and put his head to the vessel again, and pushed and strained himself so hard that he fell down and died. Now, I don't want you to do so. When I writ that letter to you, **two or** three weeks ago, to rouse you up a little, I didn't mean to make you so furious **that** you should run your head agin the Administration **so** hard as to break your neck, or strain yourself so much as to fall down dead. Nor I didn't mean that you should kill off all the Administration, smack smooth, as dead as herrings, in two months. I meant to give you two or three years to do it in. Any time before the next election would do. If you should kill 'em all right off, before we have time to choose anybody to take their places, you would have all the Government on your own shoulders; and I'm afraid it would be too much for **you.** So I think you had better try to cool down a little; it an't prudence to keep so hot all the time. That is, I mean on your own account, for fear you should overdo yourself and break down. **And then,** again, there is such a thing as drawing too long a bow to hit the thing **you** shoot at. Major Longbow used to be quite unlucky in that way. You can make folks believe a middlin'-sized fish **story,** if you tell it well; but if you try to back it up with **a** tarnel great cock-and-bull story, they'll **go** right **back** again and **swear** they don't believe the fish-story. It's dangerous loadin' guns too heavy; **for then there's** no knowing which will get the worst of it—him that stands before the muzzle, or him that stands behind the britch. So I hope you will try to cool down a little; for I'm satisfied, since my last letter, you are firing away your ammunition too fast. And, besides, I don't think it's right for you, at your time of life, to be fightin' so hard. Nor I don't think its necessary nuther; for things is brightenin' up all over the country. Our party is all coming together again, and is going to carry all afore 'em. It's true the flocks and herds of our party has been dreadfully broke up and scattered about. The oxens didn't know their owners, and the sheeps hadn't no shepherds, and the Taylor wolves has been prowlin' about the country, and carried off a great many of 'em. But, from what I hear all over the country now, I am satisfied they are all comin' together again, and on a new platform; and that platform is, *Mason and Dixon's side of Salt River.* Mr. John Van Buren is shoo-shooin' all over the Northern States, and drivin' of 'em and headin' of 'em all as fast as he can toward Mason and Dixon's side of Salt River. Mr. Calhoun, in the Southern States, is whistlin' round his springy rattan, making the hair and skin fly, and headin' 'em all up toward Mason and Dixon's side of Salt River. And Colonel Benton is cracking his long whip all over the great Western country, and headin' 'em all across the prayries toward Mason and Dixon's side of Salt River. And Gineral Cass stands, you know, where he always stood, on Mason and Dixon's side of Salt River, with a handful of salt in one hand and a nub of corn in t'other, and lookin' all round, and calling of 'em to come to him and he'll feed 'em. So, you see, it won't be long before all the scattered flocks and herds of our party will be got together again.

So I remain your faithful friend,

MAJOR JACK DOWNING.

LETTER LXIV.

SHOWING THE FOLLY OF THE UNPROFITABLE QUARRELS OF UNCLE SAM'S SONS, AND THE EFFECT OF A HIGH FENCE ON MASON AND DIXON'S LINE.

Mason and Dixon's Side of Salt River, Oct. 25, 1849.

My Dear Mr. Ritchie :—To-morrow Uncle Joshua, our delegate to Congress from Salt River Territory, starts for Washington. As I haint writ to you for some time, I thought I would send a few lines by him to let you know how matters are getting along up here. We are talking pretty sharp about forming a State Government, and some are for doing it right off, and sending Senators and Representatives to this Congress. But the majority was in favor of only sending a delegate now, and waiting to see what Congress will do with the other Territories that are sprouting up round ; for, as things now look, we couldn't seem to tell whether a State on Mason and Dixon's side of the river would be allowed to come in. So we called a meeting to choose a delegate, and to fix up the instructions for him to follow when he gets there.

After the meeting come to order, and Colonel Jones was appointed cheerman, Uncle Joshua got up and said the common practice of choosing a representative or delegate first, and then tying his hands afterward with instructions, he didn't think was hardly a fair shake. He thought the instructions ought to be agreed upon first ; then if the representative had a mind to tie his own hands he couldn't blame nobody else for it. The meeting seemed to take the idea at once, and agreed to go right to work upon the instructions first.

The cheerman said : " It was evident from the newspapers,

and the way things looked at Washington, and all over the country, that this was agoing to be a hot Congress. There was trouble a brewin' about the Wilmot Proviso, and about admitting California as a State; and then that monster, nullification, that everybody thought that Gineral Jackson had killed, years and years ago, wasn't by no means dead yet. He seemed to be more alive than ever, and showed ten times as many heads now as he did in Old Hickory's time. He was a hard animal to handle then, as my worthy friend there on my right can testify, for he had a hand in it. (Here the cheerman pointed to me, and made everybody look at me).

"I say," says he, "if Old Hickory and Major Downing had their hands full to master nullification, when he was only a young critter, and hadn't but one head, the country may well tremble and ask what is to be done with him now that he has growed up so large and tuff, and shows so many heads."

At that Bill Johnson jumped up, as quick as a flash, and says he, "Ill tell you what, Mr. Cheerman, jest send old Rough and Ready arter him, and I'll resk him if he had twenty heads. If he wouldn't scatter and run as fast as Santa Anna did at Bony Vista, I'll pay the toddy."

"Well," said the cheerman, "that an't the question before the meeting. The question is, what instructions shall we give our delegate about the Wilmot Proviso, and the State of California, and nullification, and such like troublesome consarns. Gentlemen will please to speak their minds on the subject."

When Colonel Jones set down, the whole meeting turned and looked toward Uncle Joshua; for they think he knows more about these matters than anybody else in the Territory; and, besides, he's a considerable speaker when you once get him started. They kept looking and nodding to him, and at last Uncle Joshua got up.

"Mr. Cheerman," says Uncle Joshua, says he, "If you know jest how things work in one case, you can pretty commonly tell pretty near how them same things will work in another case; for I've always observed in my lifetime, that when things worked jest so in one case, them same things would most always work jest so in another case. Now, when I was a boy I knew a case a good deal like this 'ere case **you've** been speakin' about. And if I should tell **you** and this meeting how things worked out in that case, may be you could **judge** better how things will work in this 'ere case, and then you can instruct your delegate accordingly. The case, Mr. Cheerman, was this:

"**Old Mr. Sam West**, a very clever, respectable old gentleman—everybody used to call him Uncle Sam—he was a very stirrin', thrivin' man, and a **good farmer**; he owned a very large farm, and picked up a good deal of property. His oldest son, Jonathan, **lived on the northern half of the farm**; and his other son, John, lived on the southern half; and they both of 'em had large families growing up around 'em before the old gentleman died. One day, sometime before he died, he spoke to his two sons, and said: 'Boys, I can't be with you much longer. I shall leave the farm and all the property to you and your children. The farm is under a good way **now**, and there's a plenty of land for you and your children, and your grandchildren, and great-grandchildren; and I charge you to always **keep** the families together on the farm, and live in peace, and help **each** other along. There's no knowing what sort of **neighbors** you may get round you; therefore, cling together and take care of each other.' The sons promised that they would mind him, and wrote it down in a book, and showed it to the old gentleman, who said he was satisfied, and could die in peace.

"Well, after **the old** gentleman was dead and gone, the

sons continued to thrive, and prosper, and grow rich. Their large families had enough to eat, drink and wear, and a plenty of fat turkeys for Thanksgivin' and Christmas dinners, and everything they wanted. The two brothers carried on the farm, as brothers should do, in peace and harmony, and helped each other along. What one didn't raise, t'other did, and between 'em they always had enough of everything. There was only one thing that they ever had any jarring about, and that was *thistles*. John's half of the farm was covered all over with thistles. And from some cause or other, John had a strange fancy for thistles, and would never allow 'em to be dug up or rooted out of his half of the farm. But Jonathan hated the very idea of a thistle; he couldn't bear 'em no how. There used to be some on his part of the farm when it was new, but he kept mowing of 'em down, and diggin' of 'em up, and rootin' of 'em out, till there wasn't one left. Jonathan used to talk to John, and try to get him to do the same. He told him it was a disgrace to a farm to have thistles on it. But John declared they was the glory of a farm, and no farm could be perfect without thistles. Jonathan said that besides scratching and hurting everybody that come near 'em, they would run the land all out, so that it wouldn't produce nothing; and if John kept all them thistles on his farm, he would die a poor man at last. John said he wasn't afraid of that; his land was rich enough to produce all he wanted with the thistles on it; and he was sure they gave a higher character and dignity to his family, for they was a sign to everybody that passed along the road that the family lived on a good rich farm, that supported 'em without their having to work for it. Things went along in this way for some time. John's children all grew up to be very fond of thistles, and Jonathan's all hated thistles; and if the cousins ever had any sparring or quarreling, it was most always about thistles.

"At last a squabble broke out between some of John's family and the family of the Silverbuckles. The Silverbuckle family lived on a very large, rich old farm, lying south-west of John's. But as the land where they jined hadn't been cleared up, and the line hadn't been fairly run out, and no marks set up, the boys on each side got into a dispute about the line. The Silverbuckles said the Sams were getting on to their land. (They called 'em all Sams, because they were the descendents of old Uncle Sam.) So a whole gang of the Silverbuckles went down and ordered the Sams off, and told 'em to keep on their own land. The Sams said they was on their own land, and they wouldn't stir an inch back. The quarrel grew so hot that they soon come to blows. John heard the rumpus, and seeing that his boys were in great danger of getting an awful lickin', he called to Jonathan to send over his boys to help lick the Silverbuckles.

"'Well, now, brother,' said Jonathan, 'I think your boys have been very foolish to get into this scrape, and I guess they've been more to blame than the Silverbuckles. But still, as you've got into the difficulty, we'll take hold and help you out of it.'

"So Jonathan called his boys out, and they went over to help John's; and all the Sams went at the Silverbuckles and licked 'em like a sack. They drove 'em back and followed 'em half way over the Silverbuckle farm, thrashing of 'em from house to house, and from field to field, wherever they met them. At last the Silverbuckles give up, and owned themselves licked, and begged the Sams to quit and go home.

"Well, the Sams said they was ready enough to do that, but they warn't agoing to have all this trouble for nothin'; and they should demand the gold-apple field to pay them for their trouble. This was a very valuable field on the north-west end of the Silverbuckle farm, and took its name from an orchard on it that bore very rich gold-colored apples. Them Siverbuckles sot very high by this field, and declared they couldn't part with it no how. But the Sams said they must have it, and they wouldn't stir an inch home till they had a deed of it. The Silverbuckles said they wouldn't give a deed. They acknowledged the Sams was the strongest, and could take it by force, if they'd a mind to.

" 'Oh,' the Sams said, ' we an't no robbers, to take a thing by force. We calculate to make a fair bargain of it.'

" The Silverbuckles said no, they wouldn't give a deed.

" 'Well, then,' said the Sams, ' you may take your choice—give the deed or take another lickin' all round.'

" The Silverbuckles, with bung'd eyes and bloody noses, felt as if they couldn't stand another lickin' no how, so they give up and signed the deed voluntarily.

" So the hot quarrel between the Sams and the Silverbuckles was ended ; gold apple-field became the lawful property of the Sams, who pocketed the deeds, shook hands with the Silverbuckles, agreed to be good friends, and bid them good-by. The poor Silverbuckles, glad to get rid of the Sams, went to work to heal up their wounds and bruises, and repair the damages done to their farm.

" The Sams went home in high glee about their gold-apple field, and sot down and talked the matter over ; what a fine addition it was to the old farm, and what pleasant garden spots it would make for their children and children's children to live on. And some of Jonathan's boys, who were always wide awake, started right off over to the field, and went to diggin' on it. And when they come home, they brought bags full of rich gold-colored apples. And when some of John's boys begun to stir round, and talk about going over to dig and build on the apple field, Jonathan said to John—

" ' Now, brother, I'm entirely willing your boys should go

over on to the apple field, and dig as much as they are a mind to, and build, and plant, and sow, and reap; but before they go, there is one thing that we must have a fair understanding about—and that is, they can't never have no thistles there, for I've made up my mind that there shan't never be no thistles allowed to grow on gold-apple field.'

"At that, John flared right up, and said he never would stand that; for gold-apple field belonged to him as much as it did to Jonathan, and his boys had as good a right to dig there, and build there, as Jonathan's boys had; and if his boys chose to have thistles there, they had a right to have thistles there, and they should have thistles there. Jonathan declared again he had made up his mind 'that there shan't never be no thistles allowed to grow on gold-apple field.'

"While they were disputing about it, one of Jonathan's boys, that had been over on the field a good deal, and knew all about it, come along, and, hearing the dispute, said:

"'Father, there needn't be no trouble about that, for thistles can't never grow there; it an't the right kind of land for thistles, and you couldn't never make a thistle grow there.'

"'So much the better,' said Jonathan, 'and I'm determined the whole world shall know there an't no thistles there, and shan't never be any there; and I'll write it in large letters on a board, and set it up on a post by the side of the road where everybody goes along; and the writing shall be, *There shan't never be no thistles allowed to grow on gold-apple field.'*

"'Well, then,' says John, 'I'll tell you what 'tis, brother, if it is the last words I have to speak, if you do that thing I'll split the farm right in tu, and build up a high fence between us, and I'll never have anything more to do with you.'

"'I can't help that,' said Jonathan; my mind is made up, and the world shall know that there shan't never be no thistles allowed to grow on gold-apple field.'

"And while their blood was up, Jonathan went to work and put up his sign-board, all writ out in large letters. At that, John turned as red as fire, and called his boys and went to work and run a great high fence across the farm, between

"GOOD-BY, JONATHAN, I'VE DONE WITH YOU FOREVER."

him and Jonathan, so that they had to get up on a ladder to look over it. And when 'twas done, John went up on the ladder and looked over, and called out as loud as he could call, 'Good-by, Jonathan, I've done with you forever.'

"'I can't help that,' said Jonathan, 'there shan't never be no thistles allowed to grow on gold-apple field.'

"After this the families lived entirely separate, and got along the best way they could, but with much less comfort than they used to have. Some things that Jonathan raised he had as much agin as he knew what to do with, and it rotted on the ground. And some other things that he didn't raise, and wanted very much, was rotting on John's ground. And jest so 'twas with John on t'other side of the fence. Things went on in this way a few years, and they didn't know much about how each other got along. At last one day Jonathan heard John up top of the ladder, calling out most bitterly, 'Brother Jonathan, brother Jonathan, do come; the Silverbuckles are here, lickin' my boys half to death, thrashin' of 'em with thistles, and scratchin' their eyes out. Do come, and bring your boys over, and help drive 'em away.'

"'But you've done with us forever,' said Jonathan; 'and besides, it's too much of a job to get over that fence. I don't see but you'll have to fight your battles out the best way you can. Remember, I always told you that you better weed out them thistles. If you had followed my advice they wouldn't now be scratchin' your boys' eyes out; but, instead of that, your boys might now be over along with my boys diggin' in gold-apple field.'

"'Gold-apple field be hanged!' said John. 'I wish I never had heard of it, and then this fence wouldn't a been here to prevent your coming over to help us.'

"The upshot of the matter was, that John's boys all got a dreadful lickin', which they didn't get over for a long time, and the Silverbuckles carried off as much plunder as they had a mind to, and made John give 'em a deed of a strip of his land.

"Some time after this, while Jonathan's boys were busy diggin' on gold apple-field, the Silverbuckles, who had always been wrathy about that field, agreed with the Goldthread family, who lived south of 'em, and with the families of the Boheas and the Shushons, who lived over t'other side of the pond, to go together and give Jonathan's boys a lickin' and rob the orchards. So down they went, in whole flocks and swarms, and the first thing Jonathan's boys knew they were having it, rough and tumble, and were getting the worst of it. Jonathan heard the outcry, and run puffing and sweating down to the high fence, and looked through a crack, and called out to John, 'Brother John, brother John, the Silverbuckles, and the Goldthreads, and the Boheas, and the Shushons are swarming over on gold-apple field, and fell afoul of my boys, and I'm afraid they'll half kill 'em. Do jest send your boys over to help drive 'em away.'

"John put his finger up to the side of his nose, and says he :

"'Brother Jonathan, I'll tell you what 'tis, my boys are out of the scrape now, and I reckon they better keep out of it. And, besides, they've had one all-fired thrashin' lately, and I reckon that's their part.'

"The upshot of the matter this time was, that Jonathan's boys got an awful drubbin', and had their orchards all robbed, and the Silverbuckles, and the Goldthreads, and the Boheas, and the Shushons went off with the plunder.

"Not long after this, Jonathan was walking one day along by the high fence, thinkin' and ruminatin', and he thought he would look through the crack and speak to John. And, as he put his face to the crack, John was that minute putting his face to it to speak to Jonathan, and their noses almost hit each other.

"'Hullo,' said John, 'is that you, brother Jonathan? How do you all do to-day? I should like to shake hands with you, but I can't get my hand through this crack, so you must take the will for the deed.'

"'Well, it seems to be a pity,' said Jonathan, 'that this fence should stop our shaking hands. Don't you think it

PEEPING THROUGH THE FENCE ON MASON AND DIXON'S LINE.

would be as well if it was out of the way, and we should agree to be friends again, and help each other along as we used to?'

"'That's jest what I've been thinkin' of,' said John.

"'I guess we should be better off,' said Jonathan.

"'I reckon we should,' **said John.**

"The upshot of the matter was, the next day the boys on both sides were at work tearing down the high fence.

"And now, Mr. Cheerman," said Uncle Joshua, lowering his voice, "seeing how things did work in one case, and, judging from that, how they would work in another case, I move that our delegate to Congress shall be instructed—

"*Firstly*, to vote against Jonathan's putting up the sign-board. But, if it is put up,

"*Secondly*, to vote against John's putting up the high fence. But, if the fence is put up,

"*Thirdly*, to vote for pulling it down again as quick as possible, without waiting for both sides to get a lickin' first."

Here Bill Johnson jumped up, and slapped his hand down on the bench so hard that it made the house ring again, and says he: "I second that motion, Mr. Cheerman; and I move that Uncle Joshua Downing shall be our delegate to Congress."

No sooner said than done; the instructions and the delegate was all carried to once by a unanimous vote.

So I remain your old friend,

MAJOR JACK DOWNING.

LETTER LXV.

THE MAJOR'S PLAN FOR CONSOLIDATING TWENTY PARTIES INTO **TWO.**

DOWNINGVILLE, State of Maine, Nov. 10, 1851.

MR. GALES AND SEATON—

MY DEAR OLD FRIENDS:—If you are yet in the land of the livin', I long to have a little talk with you about the affairs of the nation. And if you an't in the land of the livin', but have dropped off since I've been away in the gold diggings of Californy, if you'll contrive to let me know it I'll go to one of the "sperrit rappers" (Cousin Nabby knows one of 'em), and try to have a chat with you that way. And my old friend Mr. Ritchie, too, I want to have a chat along with him. But I don't know where to find him, for Uncle Joshua tells me he isn't in the Washington Union paper now, and they've "carried him back to old Virginny." Now, that's very bad; it's treason agin the Government. How can the country get along through a Presidential campaign without Mr. Ritchie? They never have done it, and it can't be done; it's impossible. I don't know who they've got in his place in the Union, nor I don't care; but I know they never will find one that can fight agin the Federalists like Mr. Ritchie. How many times he saved the country from bein' eat up by the Federalists; and, what's very remarkable, he could fight agin 'em for years and years after they was all dead jest as well as he could when they was alive. There's to be a great battle for the next President, and we can't get along without Mr. Ritchie. He ought not to a gone off so; he owed his services to the country, and he ought to be ketched and brought back to Washington under the "Fugitive Slave Law." That law is carried out everywhere to the North, and they expect it to be carried out to the South. What is sass for the goose is sass for the gander. If the South wants to keep the North in the Union, she must give some good strong proof that she is willing to fulfill and carry out the Fugitive Slave Law. And she couldn't do it any better than to ketch Mr. Ritchie and carry him back to Washington, and shet him up in the Union paper office, and tie him down to the editorial chair, and put a ream of paper before him, and a pen in his hand, and set him to writing about the next Presidency. Then the dark fog which hangs over the whole country would begin to be blowed away, and parties could begin to see where they are again; and the knots and the snarls of politics would begin to be unraveled, so that we could all tell where to take hold and pull with a fair chance of doing some good. Then we might stand a good chance to get a President next year. But as things now go, the chance looks slim enough.

Times isn't now as they used to be, when we hadn't only two parties, and everybody could tell who he was fightin' aginst. Then a single blast from Major Ben Russel, in the old Boston Centinel, would call out all the Federalists in the the country, and make 'em draw up in a straight line; and then another blast from Mr. Ritchie, in the Richmond Enquirer, would call out all the Republicans into another line; and when these two parties were called out, there wasn't nobody left but women and children, and then the two parties had a clear field before 'em, and marched up face to face and had a fair fight, and they always knew which got whipped. But things isn't so now-a-days. There's more parties now than you can shake a stick at. And they face in all manner of ways, so that when you are fightin' for one party, it would puzzle a Philadelphy lawyer to tell what party you are fightin' aginst, or to tell who is whipped when the battle's over. I didn't know things was in quite so bad a snarl till I got home 'tother day from Californy, and sot down and had a long talk with Uncle Joshua, who told me all about it. Uncle Joshua is getting old, but he holds his age remarkably well—I think full equal to Mr. Ritchie, and I don't see but he keeps the run of politics as well as he used to.

Says I: "Uncle Joshua, what's the prospect about the Presidency?"

"Well," says he, "Major"—he always calls me Major—says he, "Major, there an't no prospect at all."

"How so," says I; "how can you make that out?"

"Well," says he, "there's so many parties now, and they are all so mixed up, higgledy-piggledy, that you can't see through 'em with the longest spy-glass that ever was made."

"Well, now, Uncle Joshua," says I, "jest name over all these parties, so I can begin to have some idea of them."

"Well," says he, "We'll begin first south side of Mason and Dickson's line. There's the old Whig party, and the old Democratic party, and the party of Union Whigs, and the party of Secession Whigs, and the party of Union Democrats, and the party of Secession Democrats, and the party of absolute, unqualified Secessionists, and the party of Co-operation Secessionists. And then, if we come to the north side of Mason and Dixon's line, we find the regular Whig party, and the regular Democratic party, and the Union Whigs, and the Abolition Whigs, and the Union Democrats, and the Abolition Democrats, and the Silver Gray Whigs, and the Woolyhead Whigs, and the Hunker Democrats, and the Barnburner Democrats, and the Seward party, and the Union Safety Committee party, and the regular Free-Soil party, and the regular Vote-Yourself-a-Farm party."

Here Uncle Joshua paused a little, and Aunt Keziah laid down her nittin'-work, and looked over her spectacles; and says she to me, "Your Uncle Joshua must have a wonderful memory to keep all them hard names in his head; for my part, I don't see how he does it"

Then Cousin Nabby she clapped her hands and laughed, and says she, "Now, Jack, which party do you belong to?"

Says I, "I'll be hanged if I know. If the old Gineral was alive—I mean Old Hickory—I'd go with his party, let it be which 'twould; for then I should know I was going for the country. The old Gineral was always ready to fight for the country against bank monsters, and nullification monsters, and all sorts of monsters."

"Well, now," says Uncle Joshua, "how do you suppose we are going to work to make a President, with all these parties in the field, fightin' cross-handed, and every which way?"

"I'm sure I can't see," says I, "unless we can get up a party that will surround the whole of 'em, as the Irish corporal surrounded the half a dozen prisoners."

"What do you think of Mr. Calhoun's plan," said Uncle

AUNT KEZIAH ASTONISHED AT UNCLE JOSHUA'S MEMORY.

Joshua, "that's laid down in his works, just published?"

"What's that?" says I; "I don't think I've heard of it."

"Well," says he, "he recommends to choose *two* Presidents, one for the North and one for the South—each side of Mason and Dixon's line; and no law of Congress to become a law till it is signed by both Presidents. How think you it will work?"

"Well, I guess," says I, "if the country depended upon laws to live on, it would starve to death as sure as the ass between the two bundles of hay."

At that, Cousin Nabby spoke up, and says she, "More like, the country would be like a bundle of hay between two asses, and would get eat up pretty quick."

Uncle Joshua couldn't help smiling, but he looked as sober as he could, and says he, "Come, come, **Nabby, you hush up**; what do you know about politics?"

"Well, now," says I, "let us **look at this plan of Mr. Calhoun's** a little, and see what it amounts to. His notion was, that two parties, one north and one south of Mason and Dixon's line, under one President, could never agree, **but** would always be quarrelin', and fightin', and crowdin'; but **if each party** would choose a President, then they would get along smooth and quiet, and live as peaceable as lambs. Now, if the doctrine is good for two parties, it is good for twenty. So, if Mr. Calhoun was right, the best way would be to let the twenty parties that are now quarreling like cats and dogs, go to work, and each choose a President for itself. Then what a happy, peaceable time we should have of it."

"Well, you've fairly run it into the ground now," says Uncle Joshua, "and I guess we may as well let it stick there. I'm more troubled about electing one President than I am two, or twenty; and I should like to get your idea how it can be done. I know General Jackson used to think a great deal of your opinion, and may be you can contrive some plan to get us out of this hurly-burly that we are in, so that we can make a President next year, when the time comes round."

"Well," says I, "Uncle Joshua, according to what you say about the parties now-a-days, all split up into flinders, and cross-grained every way, I don't think there's much chance for any of 'em to elect a President, especially if Mr. Ritchie don't help. But for all that, I think the thing can be done, and I think there's two ways of doing it. One way is, to get a new party that shall surround all the other parties—I mean a real constitutional party, an out and out national party, a party that will stand up to the rack, fodder or no fodder—and go for the Union, the whole Union, and nothing but the Union, live or die. This party would have to be made up out of the twenty parties you have named, so I guess we might as well call it the party of '*National Come-outers.*' T'other way would be, to get up a sort of revolution-annexation manifest-destiny-glory party, and have a great banner painted, with Cuba on one end, and Canada on t'other, and what there is left of Mexico in the middle; and get up a great torch-light procession from one end of the country to t'other, and hire Kossuth to make stump speeches for our candidate through all the States. If we didn't elect him, I'd go into retiracy, and settle on the banks of Salt River for life."

"Well, Major," says Uncle Joshua, "I think a good deal of your notions, and I wish you would draw up some plan for us to go by, for it's high time we was doing something."

So, Mr. Gales & Seaton, I remain your old friend,

MAJOR JACK DOWNING.

LETTER LXVI.

THE MAJOR AND UNCLE JOSHUA AGREE ON A NEW POLITICAL PLATFORM.

Downingville, State of Maine, Nov. 24, 1851.

Mr. Gales & Seaton:—Since my letter to you, two or three weeks ago, I've had another long talk with Uncle Joshua about the rickety consarn of our politics all over the country, and about contrivin' a new platform to stand on. Uncle Joshua takes hold of the business like an old apostle of liberty. He says something must be done, or we are a gone-goose people ; we can't never get along in this way, split up into twenty parties, and every one fightin' agin all the rest. When we didn't use to have but two parties, he says, one or t'other most always stood a chance to beat, and they that wasn't beat could take command of the ship, and trim the sails as they thought best, and man the helm, and keep her movin' on the voyage. But now it's one agin nineteen everywhere, all over the country ; and if the good old ship don't get ashore in the squabble, or run on the rocks somewhere, it must be a miracle that'll save her "

"Ye see, Major," says Uncle Joshua, " we must 'malgamate these twenty parties into two parties agin, somehow or other. I can't exactly see yet how to do it ; but the thing must be done, or I say it's gone goose with us. All parties always run out after awhile, and have to begin anew. It can't be helped—it's the nater of the thing. All crops will run out if you keep 'em too long in the same field ; and when you find the land don't bear hardly nothin' but weeds, it's the best way to change the crop at once. It was so with the first two old parties—the Federalists and Republicans ; they had something to fight about and keep 'em alive for some years. One was afraid the Federal Government wasn't strong enough to get along well, and t'other was afraid it was too strong. And so they fit that battle out, year after year, till at last they got used to the working of the Government, and found it didn't want any tinkerin' either way. And so they left off fightin', except a little once in a while, for the fun of it ; and the two parties begun to be social like, and to talk together across from one rank to t'other, and wasn't afraid to come up so near as to reach a chaw of tobacco across to one another at the pint of the baganut. At last, they got kind of mixed up like, and some went one side, and some t'other, and forgot which side they belonged to. And so when Mr. Monroe come and looked round to see how his ranks stood, his first words was, ' *Why, fact,* what Jefferson once said—*we are all Federalists, we are all Republicans*—has come to pass.' And here the first two old parties died out, and new ones sprouted up and took their places."

Here Uncle Joshua got up and went to the fire, and knocked the ashes out of his pipe, and put in a little more tobacco, and sot down agin.

"Well, now, Major," says he, "it's been jest so with the last two great parties, the Whigs and Democrats. As long as they had anything to fight about, they could keep their ranks straight, and tell who was who; and they did do it for a good many years. One wanted a great national bank, and t'other didn't; one wanted a very high tariff, and t'other didn't; one wanted to drive ahead, like all possessed, with making roads and canals, and the like, and t'other didn't want to go a step that way. And so they drew the lines, and fit it out. How long and how hard they fit I needn't tell you, Major; for you and Gineral Jackson had a hand in it, and know all about it. Well, arter awhile, both parties found out they could do as well without a great national bank as they could with one. So they dropped that quarrel. Then some of them that wanted a very high tariff begun to think they had pitched it rather too high, and were willing to take one considerable lower. And some of them that wanted a very low tariff begun to think, and to *feel,* too, that they had pitched it too low, and begged for one considerable higher. So the jig was up about any more figtin' on that score. Well, as for roads and canals, everybody found at last that them sort of things would go ahead anyhow, party or no party, and it was no sort of use to fight agin 'em. So here was the end on't. The old parties have had their day; and I tell you,

Major, they are both as dead as herrins—they've died a natural death."

"Why, Uncle Joshua," says I, "it seems to me you are getting wild. Do you say the old parties are dead? Why, an't Whigs and Democrats in everybody's mouth from morning till night? Haven't we got Whig papers and Democrat papers from one end of the country to t'other? Don't we every day hear of Whig meetings and Democrat meetings in all the States? Haven't Mr. Donaldson and Green got all things cut and dried for a Democrat Baltimore Convention, to nominate a President? And an't the Whig papers all the time talking about a National Convention, to nominate a President on their side? Then how can you say the Whig and Democrat parties are dead?"

Here Uncle Joshua laid his pipe down, and I see he was in arnest; and Aunt Keziah laid her nittin'-work down, for she see he was in arnest, too. And Uncle Joshua turned round to me, and says he, "I tell you the old Whig and Democrat parties are as dead as two old stumps. Their names may be alive yet, and some folks may think for a good while to come that they are fightin' agin the Whig party, or agin the Democrat party, jest as Mr. Ritchie thought he was fightin' agin the old Federal party for more than twenty years after they was all dead. But what signifies the names when the life is gone? The two parties can't never be straitened out into a line agin, and fight each other as they used to. Folks may keep mumbling the names over, but the Whig and Democrat parties are dead and gone, and dried up, and about twenty parties have sprouted up to take their places. This is the reason why some Whig States, now-a-days, choose Democrats for Governors, and some Democrats choose Whigs for Governors, and why some Whig papers take sides with Democrats, and some Democrat papers take sides with Whigs. It's all nothin' else but jest the crowdin' of these twenty young sproutin' parties to see which shall get the most ashes out of the two old stumps, to spread round their own roots to make 'em grow and overtop the rest.

"Now, suppose some folks," says he, "thinkin' the Whigs and Democrat parties was alive yet, should go ahead and call the national conventions as they used to, and should let nobody in but jest the two old parties, and nominate their Presidents. Each party would then have jest about nineteen parties fightin' agin 'em, and nobody would stand any chance to choose a President. There would be the Union Whigs, and the Abolition Whigs, and the Union Democrats, and the Abolition Democrats, and the Silver Gray Whigs, and the Woolyhead Whigs, and the Hunker Democrats, and the Barnburner Democrats, and the Seward party, and the Union Safety Committee party, and the old Abolition party, and the regular Free-Sile party, and the regular Vote-Yourself-a-Farm party, and the old Secession party, and the Co-operation Secessionists, and the Out-and-out unqualified Go-alone Secessionists, all in the field, and every one fightin' on their own hook. If anybody can tell where a ship is likely to go to when the crew is in mutiny and nobody at the helm, they can guess where we shall be likely to go to if things go on in this way."

"Well," says I, "Uncle Joshua, accordin' to your account, I think we are in a pickle."

"That's what we be," says he; "and there's nothing will get us out of it but to go back to the old fashion of two parties again. These twenty parties must be 'malgamated down into two parties, and we must begin anew, get on to a new platform, and go ahead. But how it's to be done, puzzles me and worries me a good deal. I wish, Major, you would set your wits to work, and see if you can't contrive some plan."

"Well, Uncle Joshua," says I, "I never got so fur into the woods yet but what I found the way out again; and I don't see any difficulty here. It seems to me the road out is jest as plain as the road to mill."

At that, Uncle Joshua gin me a slap on the shoulder that e'n a'most fetched me over, and says he, "Major, that makes me feel as if a flash of lightning went through me. If anybody else had said it, I should say 'twas all humbug; but if you say it, I believe it. Now, in the name of Old Hickory, du go to work and show us the way out of the woods."

"Well," says I, "Uncle, I don't think we can *'malgamate* the twenty parties down into two, but I think we can *sift 'em out* into two parties, and make clean, square work of it. In the first place, we must get a *principle* to fight about, for you've jest proved that that's the whole life of parties, and the greater the principle is, the straighter will the parties draw the lines, and the harder they'll fight. Now, let us go right to work and hew out a new platform, that shall reach clear from Maine to t'other end of Texas, and from New York to Californy, and run up our flag on it, with letters large enough for all to read—

'THE UNION AND THE CONSTITUTION, NOW AND FOREVER.'

"Then we'll call out to the twenty parties and say: 'Here, look up there; that's our flag, and them's our sentiments. Now, all of ye that an't got tired of them things, and don't want to see 'em all upset and smashed to pieces, and sunk to the bottom of the sea, jest *come out* of your twenty quarreling parties, and get up onto this platform and fight for the Union and the Constitution.'

"I tell you what 'tis, Uncle Joshua, there's always a majority in every ship that had rather get safe through the voyage than to be upset and go to the bottom. And I an't a bit afraid but what there would soon be a party of Come-outers on that platform that would be big enough to take care of the ship.

"It might not be big enough to go over to Europe and whip all Russia, but I'll wager my head it would be big enough to keep Russia from coming over here and whipping us. Now, what do you think of my plan, Uncle Joshua! Don't you think it'll work?"

THE DOWNINGVILLE POLITICAL PLATFORM.

'Well, I don't doubt but that would be a good way to get up *one* party," says Uncle Joshua; "but I don't see how that would get us out of the difficulty after all; for there would still be as many parties left as there is now. It would still have to be one agin nineteen; and I'm afraid your Come-outer party would have hard work to get a President if they had to fight agin the nineteen or twenty quarreling parties. I can't see much chance to do anything unless **we can** come down to two parties as we used to."

"Well, that is jest what I've done," says I ; "I *have* come down to two parties."

"How do you make that out ?" says Uncle Joshua, opening his eyes about half an inch wider. "When you had got some out of all the twenty parties to make up your Come-outer party, wouldn't there still be twenty parties left ?"

"No," says I, "Uncle Joshua, there wouldn't be but one party left."

"How do you make that out ?" says he ; "I've cyphered as fur as the rule of three, but that sum beats me. You say, substract one from twenty and *one remains*. Now, the way I always used to do the sum was, one from twenty *leaves nineteen*."

"No," says I, "Uncle Joshua, that an't right. One from twenty leaves *one*. There wouldn't be but one party left."

"Well, what party would that be ?" says Uncle Joshua, with his eyes and mouth both pretty well open.

"Well," says I, "Uncle Joshua, it would be the *regular* **Fillibuster party**; for, when all that are willing to stand up for the Union and the Constitution had come out from the twenty parties, you may depend on't that all that was left would be *fillibusters*. Then it would be the 'National Come-outers' on one side, and the 'Fillibusters' on t'other ; and if one or t'other wouldn't get licked I'm mistaken."

At that Uncle Joshua hopped up like a boy and ketched hold of my hand, and says he, "Major, you've hit it ; that's the road ; go ahead. I see now there's a good chance to have two parties agin, and a fair scratch for President ; and, old as I be, I'm in for another campaign."

Here Sargent Joel, who had been setting in the room all

the time, and hadn't said a word, straightened himself up, and smit his fists together, and says he, "Hoorah for Gineral Jackson!"

"Well, now," says Uncle Joshua, "set right down, Major, and write to Mr. Gales and Seaton, and to Mr. Ritchie tu, and ask them what they think of it. If they'll set it agoing down South we'll set it agoing away down East, and have the platform right up."

So, hoping to hear from you soon, I remain your old friend,

MAJOR JACK DOWNING.

LETTER LXVII.

MAJOR DOWNING'S LETTER OF FRIENDSHIP AND ENCOURAGEMENT TO GOVERNOR KOSSUTH, OF HUNGARY, SOON AFTER HIS ARRIVAL IN NEW YORK.

DOWNINGVILLE, Away Down East,
In the State of Maine, December 22, 1851.

DEAR GOVERNOR:—I hope you won't feel slighted because I haint writ to you afore. The truth is, I haven't had no time. I've been so busy for about a 'month past, I couldn't get time to write no how. Uncle Joshua and I have been hard to work all the time, day and night, reading your speeches and the duins of the meetins in New York and England. We begun a week or two before you got to York, and have been at it ever since. We commonly get up and go at it before breakfast, and take turns reading, and keep it up till bed time— that is, till nine o'clock in the evenin'; for that's the time we Downingville folks go to bed. So I hope you won't feel slighted because I haven't found time to write to you afore now, and I hope you haven't felt lonesome since you've been in York. I see you are on the way to Philadelphy, and Baltimore, and

Washington ; and if you should feel lonesome in them places, jest turn about and come down here to Downingville, and we'll try to cheer you up and make you feel at home. I say this because I have took a great liking to you, and I always mean what I say. I've took a greater liking to you than anybody else since I lost my dear old friend, Gineral Jackson. May be it is because you are so much like him. Fact, in some things it seems **to me you are jest** like him. Old Hickory was the man what "took the responsibility" when he wanted to do anything, and I see you are jest so—you an't afraid to take the responsibility ; **and,** what's better still, you are trying to encourage other folks to take the responsibility tu. Old Hickory was a great hand to make principles, and **then** fight 'em through. And there, agin, I think you are a good deal like him. And, **by the way, I** begin to feel quite a liking for President Bonaparte, of France ; for I see he's took the responsibility at last, and been makin' principles, and fightin' of 'em through. There's some smart folks in **the** world yet ; and it's well there is, for it's pretty likely there'll be a use for 'em before another year is out. And then another thing which makes me think you are so much like Old Hickory is the *hoorahs*. Why, it seems to me I can hear 'em all the way from York to Downingville ; and it carries me right back to old times, when the whole country was ringing with "Hoorah for Jackson."

I think, dear Governor, you better stop here till next summer, and not go back to Hungary. We shall have to make a new President next summer, and you might get in to **be** President jest as easy as a cat could lick her ear ; and a President, you know, is higher than Governor. Hadn't you better take it ? I know you can get it if you'll only say the word. Our parties in this country have been so broke to pieces, and mixed up lately, that nobody could tell who to pitch upon for President; and we've been a good deal worried for fear we shouldn't make out to choose any President at all next summer. And I an't sure but what you've got here just in the nick of time to get us out of this scrape; for, if you'll only stand as a candidate, you'll go in all holler. I never knew it to fail, when the hurrahs got up **so** strong as they have been since you got to York. We've got about twenty parties in this country now; there's the old Whig party, and the old Democrat party, and the Woolyhead Whigs, and the Silver Gray Whigs, and the Hunker Democrats, and the Barnburner Democrats, and the Seward party, and the Union Safety Committee party, and the Liberty party, and the regular Free-Soil party, and the regular Vote-Yourself-a-Farm party, and the old Abolition party, and the old Secession party (which sprouted up out of the old Nullification party that I and Old Hickory killed off), and the Co-operation Secessionists, and the Out-and-out Go-alone Secessionists; **and** now there's two new parties added that an't hardly three weeks old yet—the Intervention party, and the Non-Intervention party; and I believe these are divided again into the party for Intervention, *without war*, and the party for Intervention, *war or no war*.

It was lucky you took a stand and put your foot down, **when** you first got to New York, that you wouldn't be mixed **up** with any of our parties in this country; for if you had once fairly got mixed in with 'em, you would a found yourself **in such a** snarl that I am afraid you would wish yourself back to Turkey again before you would ever get out of it. And it's lucky, on another account, that you haven't mixed up with any of our twenty parties; for now you are the only man in the country that can get their votes. As you haven't said nothin' agin none of 'em, they can all turn round and vote for you and if you'll only say the word they'll do it,

and be glad of the chance ; for that seems to be the only way
they can get handsomely out of the everlasting snarl they've
got into all over the country. You needn't be afraid there's
anything in the way agin your being President. To be sure,
there is some little rules laid down about it in our Constitution, but that can all be managed well enough ; it only wants
somebody to take the responsibility. Folks can't always go
according to the Constitution when they get into a bad snarl ;
they have to make new principles to go by. See how President Bonaparte has jest got out of his snarl ; the Constitution
didn't stand in his way a bit ; he's jest sot up a new principle, and fit it out. And you see he's come out all straight,
and now can wind his yarn anywhere to suit himself.

I don't see nothin' in the way to prevent your getting **in to**
be President, if you've a mind to. You haven't mixed up
with no party, so you wouldn't have to fight agin no party,
and it's pretty **likely no party** wouldn't fight agin you. But
there's another thing makes it more sure than all that : You
know this is a free country, and all the offices belongs to
everybody ; and them that can make the best and the most
stump speeches commonly gets in. Now, I know we haven't
got anybody in this country, from Maine to Texas, nor from
Dan to Beer Sheba, that can hold a candle to you in that kind
of business. Of course, when I say this, I mean the old Bible
Dan and Beer Sheba ; there is *another Dan* in this country,
that if you should happen to run afoul of, I don't **know but
the case** might be different.

Now, it seems to me, you better go in for the Presidency,
instead of going back to Hungary ; a bird in the hand is
worth two in the bush anyhow ; and the country is fairly
under your thumb now, but Hungary is still under the paw of
the Russian bear. So that although you are the *Governor* of
Hungary, it's likely enough there would be a pesky hard

scratch before you could govern it, if you went back. But I see some of the papers say that you *an't* Governor of Hungary now, although they don't deny but you was once. I wish them papers had better manners; they might jest as well say that I an't a Major now, because I an't all the time riding a hoss-back at the head of a regiment of sogers. No, no; that **won't** do—its nonsense and impudence tu. The rule in this country is, once a Major always a Major, and once a Governor always a Governor. A man's title belongs to him as much as his name does. My Major belongs to me, and your Governor belongs to you, and nobody hasn't any right to take it away from us any more than he would have to upset a nation. Because it's a principle, and founded in everlasting justice; therefore, it is not only the law of this country, but it is the true and just law of nations; and our Government and our country not only ought to respect it themselves, but to *make others respect it*.

"Well, **now**, dear Governor, if you shouldn't think it best to accept my offer about the Presidency, and should rather go back and run your chance in Hungary, the next question is **to see** what can be done for you on that score. You say, you **want that** we—that is, all America and the universal Yankee nation—should say you have a fair right to be called Governor of Hungary. Agreed; I've already proved that you have **that** right, and shall have it as long as you live. There won't be no more trouble on that score. That question is disposed of forever, I hope.

In the next place, you want us to say that Hungary got her independence of Austria fairly, and ought to have it. Agreed to that, too. We say it, and will stand to it, all weathers. Hungary fit it out like a man, and ought to be free forever, **and** a thousand years afterward. And the traitor Gorgey ought to have his neck stretched, and the Russian bear ought to have his toe nails cut off and his nose muzzled, so that he couldn't bite and scratch anybody agin, nor interfere in other folks' domestic affairs.

In the next place, you say you want "something else," which, as near as I can find out by the papers, means money matters, and food, and raiment, and clothes, and a few guns, and the like of that, because you are going back to have another tussle with Austria and Russia. Agreed to that, too. You shall have all you want. Jest hold your basket and we'll fill it, if it is a dozen times a day. I see money is beginning to pour in upon you in a thousand little streams, and some pretty large rivers; and it won't be long before you'll have a whole mint of it, besides guns, and knapsacks, and cartridge-boxes. When I read some of your speeches to our folks about your poor, down-trodden country, it made the tears come, I tell ye. Cousin Nabby said she would knit stockins all winter, and send 'em over for your sogers, so they shouldn't have to go barefoot, as ours did in the Revolution. Aunt Keziah said, them two great cheeses that she was going to buy a silk gown with, she would sell for money and send it to the Kossuth fund in New York. Uncle Joshua said he would sell his three-year old steers, for he could do his plowing next summer with the old oxen, and send the money to you. Cousin Sargent Joel sot in a deep study; at last says he, "I don't know as I've got anything to send but that little piece of re-monstrance," and he pointed to his old rifle that hung up against the wall; says he, "I'll send that over to Hungary to shoot the old Russian Bear if he comes growling round agin." And then he sot thinking a minute longer, and he jumped up and smit his fists together, and says he, "No, I won't send it; *I'll go and carry it myself.*" So you see, dear Governor, there isn't much danger but what you'll get "something else."

In the next place, when you come to the scratch, you want

our Government and this whole nation to hold the Russian Bear back and not let him meddle, while Hungary and Austria has a fair tussle. And you want we should give him fair warning before-hand, and tell him he shan't meddle, no how; and, if we do, you think he'll mind us. Maybe he would, and maybe he wouldn't; and if he wouldn't, what then? Then

AID AND COMFORT TO GOVERNOR KOSSUTH.

you want us to go right at him, and fight him down, and *make* him mind, because it's right and just; and now we've got to be a great and powerful nation, it is our duty to look round and take care of the world, and make all the folks do right.

. Well, now, dear Governor, as to that, I don't know but we aught to stop and think about it a little. In the first place, we have a rule here that "all just government derives its powers from the consent of the governed." So, if we've got to look round and govern the world, hadn't we aught to get the world's consent first? And, as you want to take hold of Russia first, I s'pose she is the first one we aught to ask consent of. And if the Russian will consent that we shall hold him back, we'll hold him back and run the risk of it.

And in the next place, dear Governor, it might be very well for us to take care of the world, and carry out the laws of nations, and make everybody do right everywhere, if there wasn't no danger of our getting more than our hands full. But only look at it. Suppose, when Hungary begins her tussle, the Russian should show his teeth and grab hold of her. Then we should have to send over an army and ships to help drive him back. Then suppose Poland should start up and want to be free—and she has as bloody a right to be free as any nation in the world—then we must send an army to take care of Poland, for the Russians would fight most awfully there. And there's France, too. You say "the Government of France is on the side of the oppressors, and the nation of France is one of the oppressed nations." Then, of course, it will be our next duty to send an army and put down the Government of France, and let the nation go free. And then, besides the East Indies, and China, and Circassia, and lots of other places that the geography tells about, there's a good many things that we should have to look after nearer home. When fillibusters go to upset Cuba, we must send our ships and armies to take care of that. And, then, in Mexico and South America there's troubles all the time to look after.

Now, don't you think, dear Governor, there might be a leetle danger of our getting our hands full? But, come what may, dear Governor, I shall remain your friend forever,

MAJOR JACK DOWNING.

LETTER LXVIII.

PROCEEDINGS OF THE DOWNINGVILLE CONVENTION TO CHOOSE A DELE-
GATE TO BALTIMORE, AND DECIDE ON THE PRESIDENCY.

DOWNINGVILLE, State of Maine, Feb. 9, 1852.

The following notice was posted up, bright and early, yesterday morning, on the meetin'-house, and on the center school-house, and on Bill Johnston's store :

NOTICE—DEMOCRATS AROUSE!

"The Democrats of Downingville, *without distinction of party*, are requested to meet at the center school-house to-morrow evening, February 9, at seven o'clock, to settle the question about the next Presidency, and choose a Delegate to the Baltimore Convention. The country expects every Democrat to do his duty, **and** the whole Democracy of all parties is especially requested to attend. The interest of the country and the Democratic party is at stake. **Therefore, come one, come all.** And it is expected that every true Democrat will leave all party prejudices at home.

" By order of the Democratic Town Committee."

Pursuant to the above notice, the largest **and most respectable** Democratic meeting ever held in Downingville assembled at seven o'clock, and filled the school-house chock full.

Joshua Downing, Esq., Postmaster (Uncle Joshua), was unanimously appointed Chairman, and Mr. Seth Stiles (schoolmaster), was chosen Secretary. Uncle Joshua took the chair, amid the cheers of the **meetin'**. He's always been Chairman **of the Democracy** this last **thirty years**. So he knew **what** he had **to depend upon, and come prepared for it. Aunt** Keziah had combed his hair all down smooth, and he wore his fur hat and go-to-meetin' coat. The chairman put on **his** spectacles, and read the notice calling the meetin', and says he, " Gentlemen and fellow-Democrats, the important business we have before us seems to be to settle the question about the next Presidency, and choose a delegate to Baltimore. As there is two branches to the business, which shall we **take** hold of first ?"

Doctor Briggs. **I move that** we take the question of the Presidency first, as that comes first in the notice, and I take it that is the main question.

Chairman. If that is your minds, gentlemen, you will please—

Bill Johnson, (in a sharp, loud voice.) Hold on there, Squire, or Mr. Chairman, I should say ; don't put that ere question yet, for I've got something to say first. I don't think that would be the best way to go to work. I've no notion of taking hold of the poker at the hot end. Let us go to work and choose a Delegate first, while we are cool, and go into the Presidency arterwards. We are all quiet and unanimous now, and it is the largest meeting of the Democracy that we've ever had since Old Hickory's second term. It looks as if the good Old Hickory times was coming back again, and the Democracy of the country will once more be on its legs. Now, I say, seeing we've got into a little clear, smooth water, don't let us rile it. The next Presidency is a ticklish question, and if we begin to stir it, may be it'll be hard work to see bottom. Therefore, Squire, I move that we begin our business t'other eend foremost; and I move that we choose Major Jack Downing for our Delegate to Baltimore.

Chairman. If that is your minds, gentlemen, you will please to—

Solomon Jones, (trader at the upper corner, and nateral enemy to Bill Johnson, trader at the lower corner.) Mr. Chairman, I hope that motion won't pass. I didn't come here to be ketched in an Abolition trap, and I won't be if I can help it. I don't want no underhand work, and I shan't take a step on the road till I can read on the guide-board where it's going to. Before we choose a delegate, I want to know what he is going to do. Let the work be chalked out beforehand, and then choose the best man to do it. I'm a Democrat of the Jackson stamp, but I aint no Abolitionist. I always went for Jackson, and will always go for his successors, as long as they follow in his footsteps. I always went for Van Buren as long as he followed in Jackson's footsteps; but when he turned Abolition I don't go for him no more, nor his son John neither.

Bill Johnson. Squire, I wish you to put my question, to choose Major Jack Downing to Baltimore. If we can't trust him as a good Jackson Democrat, there isn't a man in the United States that we can trust. He was always the old Gineral's right hand man. And as for Abolition traps, I wish

Mr. Jones's store was as free from rum-traps and gin-traps as I am from Abolition traps—

Solomon Jones. Mr. Chairman, I call the gentleman to order. I **want to** know, before he goes any further, whether this is a temperance meeting or a Democratic **meeting** ?

Bill Johnson. It is as much of a temperance meeting as it **is an** Abolition **meeting.** If **Mr.** Jones brings in Abolition, I've jest as good a right to bring in temperance. And as for **traps, sir,** if the gentleman undertakes to talk about Abolition traps, I'll jest let him know the war can be carried into Africa. Yes, sir, the boot is decidedly on t'other leg. The trap is all on t'other side, sir ; all on the slavery side. I'm a good Jackson Democrat ; but I've no notion of being ketched in a slavery **trap.** And **that's why I want to send** a delegate to Baltimore that we can depend upon, such as Major Downing ; **one that'll keep** us out of the slavery trap. For, I tell you, **sir, the South** has got the slavery trap set all over the country, **and** covered with a good many pieces of sly tempting bait. There's a bit of nice-flavored Buchanan bait here, and a strong Cass bait there, and a little Douglas bait further along, and **a fat** Houston bait out yonder, and on the middle of the pan there's a mysterious bit of Butler bait, nicely rolled in meal— **yes, sir,** all rolled in meal, and what's more, to make it easy **to** swallow, it's rubbed over with a little Van Buren oil. Now, **sir, I** don't swallow none of them baits, and no man don't get **my** vote for President without he comes right up to the chalk **first, and** declares, up and down, that he isn't no slavery man.

Doctor Briggs. Mr. Chairman, it seems to me neighbor Johnson **has got hold of** the *hot end of the poker* after all, and has fairly got to stirring the Presidency with it, whether we will or no. So that my motion to go into the question of the Presidency first seems to be carried without being put to vote. **Now,** sir, I am glad to see that Mr. Jones and Mr. Johnson agree exactly in one thing, that is, that they wont neither of 'em move a step in the dark, nor stir an inch till they know where they are going to. Mr. Jones wont vote for a delegate till he knows his man, and knows exactly what that delegate is going to **do**. And Mr. Jonnson wont vote for a President till he knows his man, and knows he's **all right, and isn't no** slavery man.

Solomon Jones. Nor I wont vote for no President **till I know** he's all right, and isn't no Abolitionist.

John Robinson. Mr. Chairman, nor I wont vote for **no President** that isn't a friend to Cuba. If a lot of fellers is **a mind to go and help** Cuba get her independence, **I say I don't want a** President that'll be dogging after 'em and stopping of 'em.

Sargent Joel Downing. For my part, Mr. Chairman, I've made up my mind not to vote for any man for President that won't go for Kossuth, clear up to the hub, and stand ready to fight the Russian Bear, if he meddles with Hungary. I say freedom is the right of everybody, and I go for it; and I want a President that'll go for it, too, up to fifty-four forty and fight, if it can't be got without. I call that good Jackson doctrine. Old Hickory would go for it if he was alive, and the Democracy must see that he has a successor that'll go for it **now**. That's the foundation of the Democratic principle—freedom for everybody.

Solomon Jones. Freedom for everybody, is it? I want to know if the gentleman means freedom for the niggers south of Mason and Dixon's line? If he does, I pronounce **him a** bloody Abolitionist, and no Democrat.

Sargent Joel. I said freedom for everybody, and I'll stick to it. You can't split a hair; nobody can't split hairs now Mr. Calhoun's dead. And you can't split a principle; and I say the foundation of the Democratic principle is freedom for everybody, and I'll stick to it. And I want a President that will carry that principle out straight on all sides, in Hungary and everywhere else. **And when we choose our** delegate to Baltimore, I shall move to give him instructions to vote for a Kossuth candidate for the Presidency.

Solomon Jones. Then, sir, you are an Abolitionist, and your candidate will be an Abolitionist, and the whole South will be agin you; and you'll find, if you can't split hairs, you can split the country, **and the whole** Democracy will be torn to flinders, and we shall loose all the offices.

Sargent Joel. I don't fight for offices, I fight for liberty; freedom for everybody; that's my motto.

Deacon Snow. I feel it my duty, Mr. Chairman, to caution our Democratic brethren not to be too **rash.** I think we aught to have a President that will be prudent, and not get us into any tangling alliances with other nations, and will carry out the safe neutrality doctrines laid down by Washington.

Doctor Briggs. Mr. Chairman, we seem to be going all round Robin Hood's barn, but I don't see as we are anywhere near coming to the point. Now, sir, it seems to me the way we should go is as plain as the road to mill. Is this a Democratic meeting? and are we all Democrats? That's the question. If we are all Democrats, then of course we all want a Democratic President; and we aught to fix ourselves on that point, and not be looking round for any other nails to hang our hats on. Therefore, I move that we instruct our delegate to Baltimore to vote for a candidate for President that is a stanch Democrat, and in favor of *all sound Democratic principles.*

Chairman. Are you ready for that question? If that is your minds, gentlemen, please—

Solomon Jones. Mr. Cheerman, I oppose that motion, and before it's put I want to know what *is* sound Democratic principles. I want to know if Abolition is one of 'em?

Bill Johnson. And I want to know if slavery is one of 'em?

Sargent Joel. And I want to know if Russia's tramplin' down Hungary is one of 'em?

John Robinson. And I want to know if Cuba is one of 'em?

Deacon Snow. Mr. Chairman, as there seems to be some confusion and misunderstanding about Democratic principles, and there don't seem to be much chance of doing anything till these matters are settled, I move that Squire Downing, our venerable Chairman, shall make a plain, full statement to this meeting of all the sound Democratic principles; and then we shall have something to go by.

[This was seconded all round, and Uncle Joshua, coloring a little, laid his specs on the desk, and got up out of his chair.]

Chairman. Gentlemen and Democrats, as for the Dimocratic principle, I view it is very important we should have a fair understanding of it, for it is the vital principle of the party, and without it we can't hold together. In the old Gineral's time, if my memory sarves me right, we had three principles to go by—one was the Bank, and one was the Tariff, and t'other was the Internal Improvements. That is to say, them was the principles we had to fight agin. Them was the Whig principles; and the Democratic principle was to fight agin the three Whig principles. And as long as we stuck to that we beat, and got the offices. But the science of politics has advanced a good deal in these latter years, since the Gineral's time, and so many new principles are crowded in, helter skelter, that we get kind of confused and mixed up. I don't think they do any good. Some of these new principles, instead of holding us together, seem to be pretty likely to blow us apart like gun-powder. But the good old Jackson principles work t'other way; they hold us together like wax, and give us the offices. Therefore, I think we may safely say we go agin the Bank, we go agin the

Tariff, and we go agin Internal Improvements. And I think our delegate to Baltimore should be instructed to stand on that platform.

Bill Johnson. I move that we amend that platform by adding that we go agin slavery.

Solomon Johnson. I move, Mr. Cheerman, that we amend it by adding that we go agin Abolition.

Sargent Joel. I move that we amend it by adding that we go agin Russia.

Chairman. Shall we put the question on the platform, with the three amendments added to it?

Deacon Snow. Mr. Chairman, if these amendments are added, I think there's a number of other amendments that aught to be added besides, particularly the neutrality doctrines of Washington. Therefore, I move that we adjourn this meeting for one week, and that the whole subject be referred to a committee, to be appointed by the Chairman, and that they report to the next meeting a Democratic platform containing all the sound simon-pure Democratic principles.

[Deacon Snow's motion was put and carried, and the Convention adjourned.]

NOTE FROM MAJOR JACK DOWNING TO MR. GALES & SEATON.

MY DEAR OLD FRIENDS :—I've correctified the minutes of Secretary Stiles, and send it to you to publish, to let our Democratic brethren, all over the country, know that we've made a rally here to try to save the party (which you know we thought awhile ago was dead), and so fur we've met with very encouraging success.

MAJOR JACK DOWNING.

LETTER LXIX.

PROCEEDINGS AT THE ADJOURNED MEETING OF THE DEMOCRATIC CONVENTION IN DOWNINGVILLE, TO CHOOSE A DELEGATE TO BALTIMORE, AND DECIDE ON THE PRESIDENCY.

DOWNINGVILLE, State of Maine, March 10, 1852.

According to a call from *Uncle Joshua*, the Chairman, posted up in the usual places—that is, on the meetin'-house, and on the center school-house, and on Bill Johnson's store—the adjourned meeting from February 9 was held this evening in the center school-house. Democrats all on hand, *without distinction of party*, and the school-house chock full before seven o'clock. On taking the chair, *Uncle Joshua* called the meetin' to order, and addressed them as follers :

"Gentlemen and feller-Democrats, before we take up the business of the evening, I feel it my duty to say a few words about the present state of our party, and to lift up my warning voice against *divisions*. If we can't come together like brothers, and all pull at one end of the rope, we're gone. If part pulls at one end of the rope, and part pulls at t'other end, the rope snaps, and we all tumble head over heels and come to the ground. So I hope, feller-Democrats, the divisions and disputes that broke out in our last meetin', February 9, won't be seen to-night. I say, feller-Democrats, if we mean to beat, we must harmonize, as Mr. Ritchie used to say ; we must *harmonize*. It's true there's some pretty hard difficulties in our way, but we must get round 'em. When I'm ploughing in the field with a smart team, and see a hard stump right in the way, I know better than to go straight ahead, and keep the plough in, and stick the plough-share right among the roots, and tear the plough to pieces. But what do I do ? I jest run the plough out of the ground, and slip round the stump, and then set in again, and go along as smooth as ever. And so when I'm mowing in haying time, and see a hornet's nest in the side of a stump, or in a heap of stones, I had a good deal rather leave a little grass standing round 'em than to mow up so close as to stir 'em up, and bring the whole swarm out round my ears. Now, I say, feller-Democrats, if

RUNNING THE PLOUGH INTO AN ABOLITION STUMP.

the Democratic party would only jest keep out of the way of stumps and hornets' nests, we could get along smooth enough, and carry the day any time. But if we are agoing to run our plough-share into every Abolition stump that stands in the way, and stick our scythe into every slavery hornets' nest that we come across, the jig is up with us, and we may as well give up the farm at once, and go off to the Grand Banks and ketch codfish, for it would be no use for us to fish for offices any longer, unless we can harmonize.

"Gentlemen, that distinguished old Democrat of Pennsylvania, Mr. Buchanan, lately wrote a letter to the Democrats of Baltimore; it was dated the 23d of February; it was a great letter; and Mr. Buchanan is a great man. In that letter he says: 'There has seldom been a period when the Democratic party of the country was in greater danger of suffering a defeat than at the present moment.' And, gentlemen, a Democratic member of Congress, from Ohio, Mr. Olds, made a speech in the House the fifth of this month, in which he says: 'Mr. Chairman, I am free to acknowledge, as a National Democrat, that I am humiliated at the bickerings exhibited by prominent Democrats upon this floor.' Gentlemen, these handwritings on the wall show us what we are coming to if we don't harmonize. Therefore, I hope we shall set an example of harmony here to-night that will send a thrill through the whole country, from Maine to Texas, and from the Atlantic to Californy."

Uncle Joshua sot down, and the meetin' give three cheers *for the harmony of the Democratic party.*

Bill Johnson. Mr. Chairman, I rise to renew the motion that I made at the last meeting, that we choose Major Jack Downing for our delegate to the Baltimore Convention.

Doctor Briggs. My motion was before that, Mr. Chairman, which was, that we take up the question of the Presidency first. And I still think we aught to discuss that matter, and have a fair understanding about it, before we choose our delegate to Baltimore. However, in these times I go for harmony, and for the sake of harmony I withdraw the motion, and am ready to vote on the delegate.

[The motion was then put by the chairman, and Major Downing was elected delegate to Baltimore by the *unanimous vote* of the Convention, followed by three cheers.]

Chairman. There, feller Democrats, is an example of harmony. That shows us what we can do when **we all pull together**. If we can only make the Democrats all over the country pull together, we shall choose our President jest as easy as we have our delegate.

Doctor Briggs. In order to do that, Mr. Chairman, we must fix on the right candidate. And I hope we shall now have a full and free discussion, lay down our platform of Democratic principles, and then examine the candidates and see who is the best man to stand on our platform.

Chairman. Well, yes, Doctor, you are about right in theory, but sometimes practice, in order to get along, has to be different from theory. I am an old Democrat, as you all know, and I've seen how things has worked this forty years. Now, my own opinion is, that the first and the main thing is to pick out the man *that we can elect*, and not bother much about principles. It isn't principles that gives us the offices, but the man ; and we must elect our man, or get no offices. The Dimocratic principles can be regulated after we agree on our man, for they are all very simple and plain ; and the fewer the better. In Gineral Jackson's time we didn't have but three. One was the Bank, and one was the Tariff, and one was Internal Improvements. Them you know was the Whig principles, and them was the ones we had to fight agin. And I don't think we can do any better than to stand on the same ground now. I've thought for some years past that all Dimocratic principles might be reduced down to one plain simple principle, and that is, *to fight agin the Whigs*. That is the safest and most important principle in the whole Dimocratic creed. And it is one that is easy to be understood, and easy to rally the party upon. The Whigs may bother about as many principles as they are a mind to; we no need to have but one. We may bring 'em all under one rule, and that is, to fight agin the Whigs. We are agin the Bank, and agin the Tariff, and agin Internal Improvements, because them are Whig doctrines. Now, let us follow out the same rule, and wherever the Whigs go for Abolition we must fight agin Abolition, **wherever** the **Whigs go for slavery we** must fight agin slavery. If **we stick** to this rule through thick and thin, and only *stick together*, there's no danger; we shall carry everything all afore us.

Doctor Briggs. Well, Mr Chairman, I think there's a good deal of meaning in what you say. And I go for harmony; **so I move we** go according to your plan, and pick out a candidate we can elect, and fix up the principles afterward; for, jest as you say, what good will the principles do us if we don't elect our candidate? Now, Mr. Chairman, as you are Postmaster, and have all the papers at your office, and know **how** things get along, I move that you name over the candidates for the Presidency, and tell us how they stand, so we may see which is the strongest, and go in for him.

Chairman. Well, as to that, all the States hasn't put up their candidates yet, but a good many of 'em has, and some of 'em I can name over. There's New York, she puts up Governor Marcy; and Pennsylvany puts up Mr. Buchanan; and Michigan puts up Gineral Cass; and Kentucky puts up Gineral Butler; and Illinois puts up Judge Douglas; and Indiana **puts up Gineral Lane**; and Texas puts up Gineral Houston. And I 'spose there may be more that I don't think of now, but these is some of the foremost ones. The Dimocratic Review, printed in New York, that is thought to take the lead in these matters, divides these candidates into two classes, the old class and the young class; or, as some of the papers calls 'em, Old Fogies and Young America. The Old Fogy class is

16

Governor Marcy, and Gineral Cass, and Mr. Buchanan, and Gineral Butler, and Gineral Houston. And the Young America class is Judge Douglas. And the Dimocratic Review goes in decidedly for this last class.

Deacon Snow. I should like to have the opinion of our venerable chairman about Judge Douglas, as to whether he's the **right** man for us, and whether we better **go in** for him along with the Dimocratic Review.

Chairman. As to that, I can only say Judge Douglas is **a mere** boy yet, only about forty years old, and some folks thinks he better tarry at Jericho till his beard is grown. There is good mettle in him; but let him wait twenty years longer, then maybe it will do to begin to **talk** about **him**.

Deacon Snow. That's correct. **I move we** pass over the Young America class, and take up the Old Fogies.

Chairman. Well, what say to Governor Marcy? Our Democratic brethren will please to express their minds freely. In order to harmonize, we must know each other's opinions.

Sargent Joel Downing. I've no doubt, Mr. Chairman, but what Governor Marcy is a good sound sort of a Dimocrat, and has **done** good **service in** the party, but I think that patch on his trouses has **done** the job for him so he'll never get over **it**. If we undertake to run him, we shall get lick'd, that's all.

Chairman. **Well,** how will Mr. Buchanan do? He's a strong candidate, and lately got a majority in the Dimocratic **Convention** of Pennsylvany, in spite of Gineral Cass, who didn't get half so many votes as he did.

Deacon Snow. The greatest thing I know agin **Mr. Buchanan** is, that I've heard he was once an old Federalist. **If** that's the case, I shouldn't like to vote for him; and, moreover, if there's the least taint of Federalism about him, Mr. Ritchie will be sure to fight agin him, tooth and nail. So there wouldn't be no chance to elect him.

Chairman. Well, there's Gineral Cass, how does he stand? Is there any reason why he wouldn't run well?

Sargent Joel Downing. Mr. Chairman, I don't want to be too particular, and I aint hard to please; but Gineral Cass, I don't think, would run better than some one of the others. And, besides, he's got off the true Dimocratic platform, and wouldn't come under your rule, *to fight agin the Whigs.* For a year or two ago he and Gineral Foote and some others went off upon a slant and jined Webster and Clay, and got up the Compromise. We can't call that fightin' the Whigs. The Dimocrats have been a good deal wrathy about it; and it isn't but a little while ago I see a Dimocratic paper in Richmond, Virginia, calls 'em " the miserable set of ragamuffins who got up the Union party." It wouldn't do to have a candidate that the Dimocratic papers can talk so about. It wouldn't produce the right sort of harmony in the ranks of the Dimocracy. I think, Mr. Chairman, we better go further, if we fare worse.

Chairman. Well, gentlemen, then there's Gineral Butler, of Kentucky. He's said to be a very safe, careful, sound Dimocrat; one that it will be hard to pick any flaws in. What say to him?

Bill Johnson [Mounting on a bench with two or three papers in his hand]. Mr. Chairman, General Butler is the worst candidate of the whole lot. Ginerally speaking, he isn't nowhere; and when you do happen to find him, he isn't never in the right place. You remember, sir, at our last meeting, I described in my speech, the Butler bait as being all nicely rolled in meal and rubbed over with a little Van Buren oil. Well, sir, since then the meal has been shook off; the Van Buren oil couldn't make it stick. It's all shook off, and shows nothing but a black slavery cat. A few weeks ago Mr. Cabell, of Florida, in Congress called Gineral Butler a " *mum* candidate." That straitened him out, and showed his color, and one of his friends in the House read a letter from him that showed he went the whole hog in favor of the "ragamuffins' compromise." Sir, I hold that letter in my hand, and in it Gineral Butler preaches about the compromise like a Methodist minister. He says: "It is as though a great

BILL JOHNSON ADDRESSING THE CONVENTION.

national altar had been erected in our midst, on which every lover of our common country is invited to lay his offering of peace, and to offer up his prayers for the perpetuity of the Union and the continuance of the inestimable blessings which we enjoy under its protection." Sir, that language shows that he isn't fit for President; it's enough to turn the whole Dimocracy agin him. The great Dimocratic paper in New York, the Evening Post, that was in favor of him awhile ago, now says: "We cannot congratulate him on the skill with which he is playing his game for the Presidency."

And sir, I have in my hand the Dimocratic Review, the great organ of our party, and that shows Gineral Butler up in his true colors. It says he isn't nothing nor nobody; nothing but "a mere beaten horse." It says the country might be lost "before Gineral Butler could get an idea into his head, or a word out of it." The Review says: "From his almost total lifelessness in public affairs, it was denied, at the last Presidential election, even in his own neighborhood, that he was a Democrat at all. * * * * And General Butler went to the polls in 1848 and voted for himself, to prove his own Democracy." On the whole, the Review says.: "We declare him made up of feeble negatives." Mr. Chairman, I move we skip Gineral Butler, and take up the next.

Deacon Snow. I won't pretend to say we can do anything with Gineral Butler; may be he is out of the question. But there is some reason to think it is possible the Dimocratic Review hasn't exactly done him justice. I like to see fair play all round. Mr. Breckenridge, a representative in Congress from Kentucky, made a speech on the Presidency a few days ago—the fourth of this month, if I mistake not—and he declares the Dimocratic Review is "full of gross misrepresentation." I will read, with your leave, Mr. Chairman, one extract from his speech: "There was a gentleman, full of talent, full of activity, a particular partisan and friend—as he had a right to be—of a particular gentleman mentioned in connection with the Presidency. That gentleman went to the State of Kentucky upon a political pilgrimage last fall, the object of which was, I suppose, to drive General Butler from his own soil, to dishonor him at home, by fastening upon him a corrupt political intrigue. But he failed in his object; and came back and bought up the Democratic Review for a political partisan paper for the campaign; and, with no names at the mast-head, that Review is now pursuing a course as fatal to the Democratic party as it is false and unfair." And, Mr. Chairman, the Washington Union, our great Dimocratic organ at the seat of Government, comes out agin the Democratic Review about as hard as Mr. Breckenridge. Jest hear what it says: "And last, but not least, among the numerous organs which create dissention and promote discord, is the Democratic Review. This periodical, once so elevated in its objects, descends to the level of mere faction, and opens its batteries upon all the prominent members of the Democratic party who happen not to suit the taste of the editor." The Union paper goes on to give the Democratic Review a good drubbing. But as Gineral Butler is such a disputed candidate, perhaps we better pass along to the next.

Chairman. Well, there's the old hero of San Jacinto left, Gineral Houston, of Texas; what say you to him? He's said to be a great favorite with the Dimocracy, and has a good deal of the grain of Old Hickory about him. What's the reason we can't all harmonize upon him?

Solomon Jones (Trader at the upper corner). Mr. Chairman, old Sam Houston's hoss can be curried in short order, I can tell ye. The fact is, he's been all over the country, giving temperance lectures and making temperance speeches, and I solemnly swear he never shall have my vote as long as there's any strength in brandy. [Great sensation. Deacon Snow called the speaker to order.]

Chairman. Well, gentlemen, we've been through all the foremost candidates, and there seems to be difficulties all round. I would call upon our respected delegate to Baltimore,

Major Downing, who has had a good deal of experience in political matters, to give us his views. Now, he has seen the proceedings this evening, and heard the Dimocracy of Downingville express their sentiments. I would ask him what course he will feel it his duty to take when he gets into the Baltimore Convention?

Major Jack Downing. Mr. Chairman and fellow-Democrats, after returning you my sincere thanks for the honor you have conferred upon me this evening, I beg leave to state, that from the instructions which I seem to get from this meeting to-night, and the light I now have on the subject, I should feel bound to propose to the Convention to take a gineral vote whether they will have a candidate from the Old Fogy class or the Young America class. If they decide in favor of the Old Fogies, I should move that Governor Marcy, and Mr. Buchanan, and Gineral Cass, and Gineral Butler, and Gineral Houston, be put into a hat and shook up, and then the President of the Convention draw one of 'em out; and whichever come out first, the Convention should unanimously agree to run him, and ask no questions. But if they should decide in favor of the Young America class, I should move to put Judge Douglas into the hat, and shake him up, and draw him out, and agree to run him at all hazards. [Here three cheers were given for Major Downing.]

Chairman. Gentlemen and feller-Dimocrats, if it be your minds that our delegate, Major Downing, be instructed to follow his own instructions, please to say *aye.*

[The question was carried by a unanimous and very loud vote. And after three more cheers for the harmony of the Democracy, the meeting adjourned.]

Copy of the Secretary's minutes, examined and approved for the press by

MAJOR JACK DOWNING.

LETTER LXX.

THE MAJOR GIVES UNCLE JOSHUA **A FULL** ACCOUNT OF THE SEVERE TUG THEY HAD AT BALTIMORE TO NOMINATE A CANDIDATE FOR PRESIDENT.

BALTIMORE, Saturday night, June 5, 1852.

To Joshua Downing, Esq., Postmaster, Downingville, State of Maine.

DEAR UNCLE JOSHUA :—The job is done, and it's been about the toughest week's work that ever I did. I've sweat like a tiger all the week, and I'm as hungry as a bear; not but what there's been vittles enough, plenty of it, and good too, and a plenty of liquor too, more than the Maine liquor law could upset and spill in six months; but the trouble is, we had so much to do we couldn't get time to eat. I guess I've made out to ketch a lunch of a few mouthfuls about twice a day, and got a chance to sleep, upon an average, about two hours a night. After I've writ this letter to you, I mean to turn in and sleep over till Monday, and then streak it home and help get up the mass-meeting to ratify the nomination. The ratification of Downingville must be a roarer—you better be getting things ready for it till I come. I wish I could give you some idea of the week's work we have had here. I've worked in the logging swamp, and know what 'tis to handle logs, and pile 'em on the bank, and roll 'em into the river; and I've worked on burnt fields in clearing up, and know what 'tis to chop and pile from Monday morning till Saturday night; but, I declare to man, this has been the toughest week of log-rolling I ever see. But I don't begrudge the work a bit, we've made such a nice job of it, and saved the country. We've put life into the Democratic party again, that we thought last fall was dead as a door-nail. **We've killed off Abolition ; we've** choked to death Secession, and **gin Freesoil the fits ; and I** expect we've thunderstruck Whiggery **so that** it'll never get **over it.** We've got the Democratic party fairly on its legs again, standing on the good old platform that Giueral Jackson left it on ; that is, **agin the Bank, agin the** Tariff, and agin Internal **Improvements ; and now** we've nothing to do but go ahead.

But I must tell you something about the duins. **I couldn't get in as one of** the regular **delegates** from Maine, because the President said my name wasn't on the list. But as soon as I had told him **I was** the delegate from Downingville, he took me by the hand, and says he, " All right, Major Downing, I'm very glad to see you here ; you can come in as supernumerary, and you can do a great deal more good than if you was a regular delegate, for you can go round quietly among all the delegates, and help to make 'em *harmonize*. There's a **great** deal of that work to be done before we can get along, and I don't know of anybody who can do more in that line than you. In fact, Major, if you hadn't been sent as a delegate from Downingville, you would readily be admitted to take part in the proceedings of the Convention, out of respect for the great services that you rendered Giueral Jackson in the times that tried the souls of Democrats." So I went right in and took hold, and went to work. There was an awful **jam ;** it seemed almost impossible to do anything. But I off coat, and elbowed my way right through 'em, from one end of the hall to t'other ; and I pretty soon got the swing of it, so I could tell where to pull and where to push, and where to put under the hand-spikes and lift. And when the members got up to make speeches, and got to talking too much, or talking the wrong way, I knew jest when to take hold of their coat-tails, and pull 'em down on to their seats. And

16*

sometimes I had to go into the gallery, too, to keep the people straight up there ; and in spite of all I could do, they would sometimes hoorah and hiss in the wrong place. So you may judge I've had my hands full all the week. But I was determined to have a nomination, if I worked my hands off up to my elbows. It was very hard to get a nomination this time, and if I hadn't been here, though I say it myself, I don't believe they would a got one at all.

The first real hard piece of sledding we come across was the platform business—that is to say, the question whether we should go to work and make a platform first, or take right hold and nominate first. It was a knotty question, and seemed to bother some of the members a good deal. Mr. Nabers, and Mr. Wise, and some others, insisted upon it that we should begin at the foundation, and make a platform first for the Democratic party to stand on, and then make a candidate to fit to it. No work would ever stand well unless you begin at the bottom and lay a good foundation first. Here's a dozen parties here, every one fighting for their particular candidate, and each one hoping to get the nomination. As long as that hope lasts it will hold 'em all together, and we can make 'em all work to help build up a platform. But the moment one gets the nomination, the rest will fly off in a tangent ; there will be no more working on a platform, and your candidate will be left standing on nothing. But Mr. Soule, of Louisiana, and Governor Floyd, of Virginny, rowed as hard t'other way. They declared we never could make a platform first. If we undertook to go to work upon it now, every one of the dozen parties would be pulling and hauling agin each other, and each one hewing and cutting and carving to make the platform to suit his own candidate. In that way we never could make a platform if we should work from the first of June to the end of time. The fact is, the platform must be made for the country; that is, for the Democratic party, and not for a candidate. As soon as the candidate is ketched and haltered, and tied to a stump, we can all set down calmly and work together, and make a platform to suit the whole Democracy. The dispute went on pretty high nearly all day, and was got over at last by a sort of compromise to have the platform and the nomination both going on together. So a committee of one from each State was appointed to go to work building the platform while the Convention went on to nominate; then, as soon as the candidate was nominated, the platform could be all ready to set him right on to it.

Then come the nominating, and that was all an up-hill business for about three days and two or three nights. It was found on the first pull that the Old Fogies was a good deal too strong for Young America, and if there hadn't been so many Old Fogies in the field we should a got a candidate the first haul. Gineral Cass and Mr. Buchanan each started with a very smart team. Mr. Cass was a little ahead, and he kept the lead for about twenty pulls, and we thought by sticking to him like wax we might be able to get him over the hill. But his team begun to lag after ten or a dozen pulls, and now, at the twentieth pull, it seemed to be slowly backing down hill, and the Buchanan team struggled up and got ahead. Then we thought we better hitch on to Buchanan, and may be we might fetch him over the hill. We spurred up for a few pulls pretty well, but didn't get near to the top before the Buchanan team got stuck, and then begun to back down hill, and all we could do we couldn't start it ahead again. But the Cass team, which had backed almost down to the bottom of the hill, after resting and breathing a little, now took a fresh start to come up. At that we hitched on again and determined if possible to shove him over this time. We whipped, and spurred, and pulled, and pushed, and hollered,

THE GREAT TUG AT THE NOMINATION OF GENERAL PIERCE.

and screamed, and the team hauled well. The old ox bows creaked, and we begun to think we should reach the top. But when we got about two-thirds the way up, the team got stuck agin ; and though it took eight or ten smart pulls after this, it didn't get any higher, but every time backed down a little.

It was pretty clear after this that it was gone goose with the Old Fogies. We hadn't no hopes of 'em any longer. If the Cass and the Buchanan teams could a been hitched together, they would a walked over the hill as easy as a cat could lick her ear. But there was so much quarreling among the drivers that this couldn't be done. Every driver was proud of his own team, and would stick to it and have nothing to do with t'other. The Virginny delegation went out a good many times to consider of it and make up their minds, and every time they come in they marched right up and took their stand by the Buchanan team. They stuck to that team without flinching for thirty-three steady pulls ; and for the last ten or fifteen pulls I couldn't think of nothing else but "old Virginny never tire." But there was a good many others stuck it out full as long, and some a good deal longer than old Virginny, before they gin up. We tried a few pulls with the Marcy team and a few with the Butler team, but it was no go. We became satisfied there wasn't an Old Fogy in the field who could ever reach the top of the hill. We begun to look round now to see how Young America was getting along.

The Douglas team was made up mostly of young steers ; and it was a pretty smart team, well trained, and pulled well. But it wasn't equal to the Old Fogies for a heavy pull ; it hadn't so much bone, and sinew, and wind, and bottom. Howsomever, it made a pretty good scratch of it, and kept gaining gradually up the hill ; so we thought we would take hold and give Young America a boost, and see if we couldn't get a

candidate that way. To tell the truth, we bugun to feel
rather streaked for **fear we shouldn't** get a candidate at all,
and felt willing to hitch on to most anything. But the best
we could do with Young America, we couldn't get only about
half way up the hill before the steers begun to back down
agin, and we **see 'twas no use, they couldn't come it.** Well,
there we was, all in a fix. We couldn't see no other chance ;
we'd got to go without a President because we couldn't nominate **a candidate.** **One** of the members actually fainted away
here, and all of us felt a good deal womblecropt and down in
the mouth. But " old Virginny never tire," and when we was
all hitchin on round for the thirty-fifth pull, old Virginny
marched into the field with a bran new team. Everybody
stared, and cried out, " What team is that ? What team is
that ?" And when they heard the answer, "The Franklin
Pierce team, of New Hampshire," they wouldn't **believe their**
own ears. But it was a fact, and Virginny drove that new team
one pull all alone. Then one or two others hitched on with
her and tried eight or ten steady pulls. All of us looked on
and watched the working of that **new team.** At last folks
begun to make up their minds that that was the team to pull
and straighten out the Democratic traces, and with proper
help it might be got over the hill. Old **North Caroliner** hitched
on, and Georgia hitched on, and Tennessee hitched on, and
by-and-by there **was a geneal race** all over the field to see who
should hitch on first. It didn't make no odds who, Old Hunkers and Barnburners, and Free Silers and Abolition, and Union
and Secession, and State-Rights, **and Old Fogies** and Young
America, all run helter skelter and hithed on to the Pierce
team. That team, I tell ye, went up the hill like smoke.
Some of the States run till they was almost out of breath for
fear they shouldn't hitch on before the team got to the top of
the hill. But they all made out to hook on, and every State

was "in at the death," and ready to jine in the general hoorah.

After this, we hadn't no more difficulty; everything went as regular as clock-work. The master told us we had read and spelt well, and we might all go out till four o'clock. So **we went** out and took a little bit of a spree, and then **come** in and took hold and worked jest like brothers, and **hauled** Mr. King right up to the top of the hill in two pulls, and made him Vice-President.

Then the committee brought in the new platform, and we all danced on it. In the crowd and confusion we couldn't see what it was made of; but we was told it went agin the Bank, and agin the Tariff, and agin Internal Improvements, and was a first-rate platform; so we all jumped on, and said it couldn't be no better.

P. S.—I've telegraphed to Gineral Pierce to save the Downingville Post-Office for you; so you may feel easy on that **score.**

I remain your loving nephew,

MAJOR JACK DOWNING.

LETTER LXXI.

SHOWING HOW THE MAJOR PERSUADED UNCLE JOSHUA TO TAKE HOLD AND HELP ELECT GENERAL PIERCE TO THE PRESIDENCY, AND HOW DOWNINGVILLE RATIFIED THE NOMINATION.

Downingville, Away Down East,
In the State of Maine, July 20, 1852.

Mr. Gales and Seaton—

My Dear Old Friends:—We've made out to ratify at last; but it was about as hard a job as it was for the Baltimore Convention to nominate. And I'm afraid the worst on't ain't over yet; for Uncle Joshua shakes his head and says to me, in a low tone, so the rest shan't hear, "Between you and me, Major, the 'lection will be a harder job still." I put great faith in Uncle Joshua's feelins. He's a regular political weather-glass, and can always tell whether we are going to have it fair or foul a good ways ahead. So when he shakes his head, I naterally look out for a tough spell of weather. When I got home from Baltimore, says I, "Well, Uncle Joshua, you got my letter in the Intelligencer, didn't you?" And says he, "Yes."

"Well, didn't we do that business up well?" says I.

"I don't know about that," said Uncle Joshua; "I have my doubts about it."

"Why, don't you think," says I, "the nomination of Gineral Pierce will put the Democratic party on its legs again, and give it a fine start?"

Uncle Joshua looked up to me kind of quizical, and says he, "It *has* gin the party a pretty considerable of a start already, it come so unexpected." And then he sot as much as two minutes drumming his finger on the table, and didn't say nothin'.

And then he looked up again, and says he, "Major, *who is General Pierce?* It ain't a *fictious* name, is it?"

"Why, Uncle Joshua," says I, "how you talk! It is Gineral Franklin Pierce, of New Hampshire."

"Gineral Franklin Pierce, of New Hampshire, is it?" says he. "Well, now, Major, are you sure there *is* such a person, or did somebody play a hoax on the Baltimore Convention?"

"Yes," says I, "Uncle, I'm as sure of it as I am that there is such a person as Uncle Joshua Downing. To make all sure of it and no mistake, I come through New Hampshire, and went to Concord, where they said he lived, and inquired all about it. The neighbors there all knew him perfectly well, and showed me the house he lives in. He wasn't at home, or I should a seen him myself, and should got his promise to keep the Downingville Post-Office for you. But you needn't be afraid but what you'll have it, for I sent a telegraph to him from Baltimore, as soon as he was **nominated, to** keep it for you."

Here I see by the looks of Uncle Joshua's eyes that he begun **to get hold** of some new ideas. Says he, "Well, Major, it is a fact, then, is it, that **he** was nominated in real earnest, and 'twasn't no **joke?"**

"Upon my word and honor," says I, "there isn't a particle of joke about it—it was all done in real arnest."

"**Well, then, if you've really** got a candidate," says Uncle Joshua, "I should like to know something about him. Does he belong to the Old Fogy class or Young America class?"

"**I guess about half** and half," says I, "and he'll be all the stronger for that, because he can draw votes on both sides."

"**After all,**" says he, "I'm afraid it's a bad nomination. Them old pillars of the Democratic party, Gineral Cass, and **Mr.** Buchanan, and Governor Marcy, and Gineral Houston, **and the rest, will feel so insulted and mortified** at being pushed aside for strangers to take the lead, that they'll all **be agin** the nomination, and their friends, too, and that'll up**set** the whole kettle of fish."

"Don't you never fear that, Uncle Joshua," says I; "them old pillars that you speak of are all very much tickled with the nomination. Ye see, it broke the nose of Young America, and they was delighted with it. As soon as the nomination was out of the mould, before it had time to cool, they all telegraphed right to Baltimore that nothin' in the world could have happened to suit 'em better; it was a most excellent nomination, and they felt under everlasting obligations to the Baltimore Convention. You needn't have no fears that they'll feel any coldness towards the nomination. They'll turn to and work for it like beavers."

"Well, how is it," said Uncle Joshua, "about that boy candidate for the Presidency that they call Young America? If his nose is knocked out of joint he'll of course oppose the nomination, tooth and nail."

"There's where you are mistaken again, Uncle Joshua," says I. "On the contrary, he goes for it hotter than any of 'em; and he telegraphed back to Baltimore, as quick as lightning could carry it, that the nomination was jest the thing; it couldn't be no better. Ye see, he looks upon it in the light that it chokes off all the Old Fogies, and leaves the field clear for him next time. He thinks so highly of the nomination, and feels so patriotic about it, they say he is going to stump it through all the States, and make speeches in favor of Gineral Pierce's election. You may depend upon it, Uncle Joshua, we've got a very strong nomination—one that'll carry all afore it—and everybody is delighted with it, and everybody's going to go for it. I didn't expect you to hold back a moment. I thought you would have things all cut and dried for a rousin' ratification meeting by the time I got home."

"Well, you know, Major," said Uncle Joshua, "I always follow Colonel Crockett's rule, and never go ahead till I know I'm right. How foolish we should look to call a ratification meeting here in Downingville, and be voted right plump down. You know the Free-Soilers are very strong among us; they are strong in all the Northern States. And you know the Baltimore Convention fixed up a platform to stand on, that's all in favor of the Compromise and the Fugitive law, and is dead set agin the Free-Soilers. Now, Major, you must have more understanding than to think the Free-Soilers will ever swallow that platform; and if they don't, we are dished."

"You are wrong again, Uncle Joshua," says I, "for the **biggest Free-Soiler** in all America swallowed it right down, and didn't make a wry face about it."

"Who do you mean?" says he.

"I mean Mr. John Van Buren," **says I.**

"But you don't mean," **says** Uncle Joshua, "that Mr. John Van Buren accepts this platform, and is willing to stand on it."

"Yes I **do, exactly so,**" says I, "for he got right up in **Tammany** Hall and made a speech about it; and he said he would go the nomination, and he'd stand the platform; at all events, he'd stand the platform for *this election*, anyhow. You needn't be at all afraid of the Free-Soilers, Uncle; they ain't so stiff as you think for, and they are as anxious to get the offices as anybody, and will work as hard for 'em. Now let us go to work and get up our ratification, and blow it out straight. The Democracy of the country expects Downingville to do its duty."

"Well, Major," **says** Uncle Joshua, "you've made out a better case than I thought you could. I'm willing to take hold and see what we can do. But I declare I can't help laughing when I think it's **Gineral** Franklin **Pierce, of** New Hampshire, that we've got to ratify. I wish we knew something about him; something that we could make a little flusteration about, and wake up the Democracy."

"Good gracious, Uncle Joshua," says I, "have you been Postmaster of Downingville this twenty years, and always reading the papers, and don't know that Gineral Pierce was **one** of the **heroes of the** Mexican war?"

At that, Uncle Joshua hopped out of his chair like a boy, and says he, "Major, is that a fact?"

"Yes," says I, "'tis a fact. You know Mr. Polk sent me out there as a private ambassador to look after Gineral Scott and Mr. Trist. And Gineral Pierce *was* out there ; I knew all about it, and about his getting wounded."

"Good !" says Uncle Joshua, snapping his fingers ; "that's lucky, then we've got something to go upon ; something that the boys can hoorah about. And if we don't have too strong a team agin us we may carry the day yet. Who do you think the other party will put up ?"

"Well," says I, "it's pretty likely to be Mr. Webster or Mr. Fillmore, and they can't either of 'em hold a candle to Gineral Pierce."

"Of course not," says Uncle Joshua, "if he was the hero of the Mexican war. I s'pose it was Gineral Scott's part of the war that he was in, because that's where you was. Which of the battles did he fight the bravest in, and mow down most of the Mexicans ? Did he help storm that Gibralta castle at Vera Cruz ?"

"No," says I, "that little matter was all over before Gineral Pierce got to Mexico."

"Well, the great battle of Cerro Gordo come next," said Uncle Joshua ; "I dare say Gineral Pierce was foremost in marching up that bloody Bunker Hill and driving off Santa Anna and his fifteen thousand troops."

"I'm sure he would a been foremost, if he'd been there," says I, "but he hadn't got into the country yet, and Gineral Scott wouldn't wait for him. It seems as if Gineral Scott is always in a hurry when there is any fightin' to do, and won't wait for nobody."

"Well, the next great battle, if I remember the newspapers right," said Uncle Joshua, "was Contreras ; and after that came the bloody and hot times of Cherubusco, and the King's Mill, and Chepultepec, and marching into the City of Mexico. These was the battles, I s'pose, where Gineral Pierce fit like a lion, and became the hero of the Mexican war. But which battle did he shine the brightest in, and cut down most of the enemy?"

"The truth is," says I, "he got wounded at Contreras, and so wasn't able to take a part in them bloody affairs of Cherubusco, King's Mill, and Chepultepec."

"Then he *was* in the battle of Contreras," said Uncle Joshua, "and that can't be disputed?"

"O yes," says I, "he certainly was in the first part of it, when they was getting the battle ready, for there's where he got wounded."

"Good," said Uncle Joshua, "he was in one battle, and got wounded; that's enough to mak a handle of, anyhow. Whereabouts was his wound?"

"Well, he had several hurts," said I; "I believe in his foot and ancle, and other parts."

"Rifle balls?" said Uncle Joshua, very earnest.

"O no, nothing of that kind," says I.

"What then; sword cuts? Or did the Mexicans stick their bayonets into him?"

"No, no; nothin' of that kind, nother," says I.

"Then it must be grape or bombshells," said Uncle Joshua, "how was it?"

"No, no, 'twasn't none of them things," says I. "The fact was, when they was skirmishing round, getting ready for the battle, his horse fell down with him and lamed him very bad."

Uncle Joshua colored a little, and sot and thought. At last he put on one of his knowing looks, and says he, "Well, Major, a wound is a wound, and we can make a handle of it without being such fools as to go into all the particulars of how he came by it. I say let's go ahead and ratify Gineral Pierce, and who knows but what we can make something out of this Mexican business?"

Well, Mr. Gales and Seaton, the thing was done. We ratified on the 21st of June, in the evening, and it was a tall piece of business. When I begun, I meant to give you a full account of it, with some of the speeches and resolutions; but I've made my preamble so long that I can't do it in this

THE DOWNINGVILLE TORCH-LIGHT PROCESSION.

letter. *We had a torch-light procession.* Cousin Ephraim took his cart and oxen, and went into the woods and got a whole load of birch-bark and pitch-pine knots, and all the boys in Downingville turned out and carried torches. The school-house was illuminated with fifty candles. Uncle Joshua presided, as usual. Banners were hung round the room, with large letters, giving the names of all the great battles in Mexico; and the enthusiasm was immense. When we'd got about through, and was just winding up with three tremendous cheers for the "Hero of Mexico," a message came up to Uncle Joshua from the Post-Office, stating that the telegraph had just brought news that the Whig Convention at Baltimore had nominated Gineral Scott for President. It gin the whole Convention the cold shuggers in a minute. Uncle Joshua looked very serious, and says he, "Feller-Democrats, to prevent any mistakes, I think you had better give them three last cheers over again, and put in the name of Gineral Pierce." So we did, and gin three rousin cheers for *Gineral Franklin Pierce, of New Hampshire, the Hero of Mexico*.

Downingville is wide awake, and will do her duty in November.

So I remain your old friend,

MAJOR JACK DOWNING.

LETTER LXXII.

SHOWING HOW UNCLE JOSHUA AND THE MAJOR STUCK TO GENERAL PIERCE, AND HOW SARGENT JOEL'S HURRAHS FOR GENERAL SCOTT CAME NEAR LOSING THE ELECTION.

DOWNINGVILLE, State of Maine, Sept. 18, 1852.

MR. GALES & SEATON—

MY DEAR OLD FRIENDS:—I wish I had better news to write to you. I'm pesky afraid Gineral Scott is coming in. And, arter all, I don't know why I should feel so much afraid of it, especially on my own account, for I don't s'pose he's a very bad man. But I feel bad for Uncle Joshua. His whole heart is bound up in the Post-Office, and if he should lose it, I'm afraid it would almost be the death of him. He's had it now more than twenty years, and he's more fond of it because it was give to him by dear old Gineral Jackson. He loves it now like one of his own family; and I think it would be about the hardest one of the family for him to part with, unless 'tis Aunt Keziah. If he should lose ary one of 'em, that is, Aunt Keziah or the Post-Office, I know it would break his heart. And that's what makes me feel so bad at the turn things has took down this way in favor of Gineral Scott. If any way could be contrived to keep Uncle Joshua in the Post-Office, I wouldn't care a snap if Gineral Scott did come in. And I guess there's a good deal of the same sort of feelin' amongst a good many of the Democracy. I'll just give you a sample of it:

There's Cousin Sargent Joel, he can't live without hurrahing for somebody as much as two or three times a day. He got in a habit of it in Old Hickory's time, and he couldn't leave it off since. Two or three weeks ago Uncle Joshua and I was in the barn, planning a little about getting out the voters to the election, when all at once we heard somebody back of the barn holler, with all his might, "Hurrah for Gineral Scott." We both started and run round the corner of the barn as fast as we could, and who should we see there but Cousin Sargent Joel, standing on a stump, swinging his hat all alone, and hollering, at the very top of his voice, "Hurrah for Gineral Scott." Uncle Joshua looked as cross as thunder, and Cousin Joel colored a little as soon as he see us, but he swung his hat again, and sung out, once more, "Hurrah for Gineral Scott, and I don't care who hears it."

"What's that you say?" said Uncle Joshua.

"I say, hurrah for Gineral Scott, and I don't care who hears it," says Cousin Joel, putting on his hat, and jumping off the stump.

"Well, this is a pretty piece of business," said Uncle Joshua, "setting such examples as this to the neighbors.

SARGENT JOEL HURRAHS FOR GENERAL SCOTT.

There's many a word spoke in jest that's turned into arnest before it's done with; and you ought to be careful how you set such hurrahs agoin. If you once get 'em started there's no knowing what'll be the end on't."

"I don't much care what'll be the end on't," said Cousin Joel.

"Why, Joel, what do you mean?" said Uncle Joshua; "if you are going to turn Whig, say so, and let us put you out of the synagogue at once, and be done with it. I want a plain, right up and down answer, are you going for Gineral Pierce or not?"

"I s'pose I shall," said Cousin Joel.

"Then, why in the name of common sense don't you hurrah for him?" said Uncle Joshua, "and try and get up some enthusiasm. You ought to be ashamed to throw your hurrahs away on t'other side."

"Now, Uncle Joshua, I'll tell you what 'tis," said Sargent Joel, straightening himself up jest as he used to at the head of the company in Nullification times, says he, "I'll tell you what 'tis, Uncle Joshua, I'm willing to vote for Gineral Pierce to help you to keep the Post-Office, and I mean to; but you needn't ask me to hurrah for him, for I can't stand no such tom-foolery as that. I've tried it, and it won't go, no how. It makes me feel so much like digging small potatoes and few in a hill. But when I get right hungry for a hurrah, I give it to Gineral Scott, and I find there's refreshment and nourishment in that, something like real meat; it makes me feel as it used to when we gin the loudest hurrahs for Gineral Jackson."

Uncle Joshua turned away, looking rather down in the mouth, and saying, "he didn't know what the world was coming to."

As near as I can find out, there's a great many Dimocrats in this State, and other places too, that's in the same fix as Cousin Sargent Joel Downing; they've tried to hurrah for Gineral Pierce, and can't. Over to the raisin of Squire Jones' barn, 'tother day, arter they all got through, Squire Jones, who is a great Democrat, called out, "Now let us give three cheers for Gineral Pierce." As quick as a look, they all swung their hats, and about three-quarters of 'em sung as loud as they could holler, "Hurrah for Gineral Cass." At that, Squire Jones flew in a rage, and told 'em they was traitors to the party, and no true Democrat would hurrah for anybody but Gineral Pierce. That touched the dander of the rest of 'em, and about twenty swung their hats and cried out lustily, "Hurrah for Gineral Scott," and asked Squire Jones if he liked that any better.

These things has kept Uncle Joshua very uneasy along back, and before our State election, which came along last Monday, he got quite narvous; and he aint no better yet. We've been in quite a state of conboberation all the week, trying to find out how the election's gone, but it's a hard sum to work out. I went over this morning to help Uncle Joshua figure up. He was setting to the table with his spectacles on, and the papers spread all round him, and a pen in his hand, and a dark scowl on his brow. He was thinking so hard he didn't seem to know when I come in. Says Aunt Keziah, says she, "I'm dreadful glad you've come in, Major; your uncle will make himself sick working over them figures."

Says I, "Well, Uncle Joshua, how are we coming out?"

"I'm afraid we are coming out at the little end of the horn, Major," said Uncle Joshua, and he looked up over his spectacles so pale and melancholy it made me feel bad. Says he, "I don't like the looks of it a bit; the State is on the back track again towards Whiggery, jest as 'twas when Harrison came in."

"Oh, I guess not," says I, for I wanted to cheer him up as much as I could. "The liquor law has played the mischief this election all round, and got things badly mixed up; but if we sift 'em out carefully we shall find the Democrats as strong as ever." Uncle Joshua shook his head. Says I,

"Let us see the figures. Here's the returns from three hundred towns, all the State except some of the outskirts. Mr. Hubbard and Mr. Chandler, the two Democratic candidats for Governor, has together more than fifty-eight thousand votes, and Mr. Crosby, the Whig candidate, has a little more than twenty-seven thousand. The Democratic vote is more than double the Whig vote. This don't look as though the State was going back to Whiggery."

"That don't amount to nothin' at all," said Uncle Joshua; "a good many thousand of temperance Whigs voted for Hubbard, and a good many rum Whigs voted for Chandler; and when the Legislature comes to meet Crosby will stand jest as good a chance to be chose Governor as any one of 'em, and better too if the State goes over the dam, the 2d of November, and you may depend it's drifting that way, or else I've forgot how to cipher. Jest look at the Legislature. Last year in the Senate there was about five Democrats to one Whig, and now the Whigs have elected *fourteen* Senators and the Democrats only *seven*, leaving nine or ten no choice, or doubtful. And then the House aint much better. Last year we had a clear majority of more than thirty, and now it don't look as though we should have more than ten majority. And if the State goes for Scott, I believe the Legislature will go that way too, Governor and all."

"But, may be, Uncle Joshua," says I, "the Whigs havn't gained so much as you think for, after all. It looks bad in the Legislature, I see, but it may be all owing to the rum business, as you say about the Governor."

"No, no, it isn't that," said Uncle Joshua, with a heavy sigh; "you may depend upon it the State has got a Whig drift. The Congressmen tells the story, and there the rum business has nothing to do with it. In the last Congress we had five Democratic Representatives and the Whigs two.

Well, now how is it? In the next Congress this State has six Representatives, and the Democrats have made out to elect three and the Whigs three. It's jest an even balance, and a few more of them foolish hurrahs for Gineral Scott will tip the State agin us."

"Well, we must stir round," says I, "and try to stop this hurrah business, and may be we can save the State yet. If I ketch Sargent Joel at it again, I'll cashier him. If Democrats can't hurrah for Pierce they musn't be allowed to hurrah for nobody. But, after all, Uncle, suppose we should lose this State, the nation is safe for the Democracy. You must remember we have a large majority of the States, and nigh two-thirds of the members of the last Congress."

"Well," says he, "that don't prove whether we shall have two-thirds or one-third in the next Congress. If the States go on as they have begun, it will be pretty likely to be one-third. There's only three States that has elected their Represnatives to the next Congress yet, and that is Maine, and Missouri, and Iowa. And only jest look at 'em. Three years ago they stood twelve Democrats and two Whigs, and now they stand seven Democrats and six Whigs. How long will it take at that rate, to turn our two-thirds into one-third? I'm afraid there's a Whigh drift going over the country that'll swamp us. Sailors tell about the big tenth wave that rolls up and carries everything afore it, and I'm thinking it seems to be a good deal so in politics. There was a big tenth wave in 1840, and you remember what work it made. It looks a good deal as if there is another big tenth wave rolling up now, to swamp the Democracy and upset Congress. We've got to have trying times, Major. I don't know what'll become of the country if the Whigs get the upper hand." He said this with such a mournful expression that I see the tears come into Aunt Keziah's eyes. She's a good christian woman, and she laid her hand upon his shoulder, and says she, "Oh, Mr. Downing, pray don't be so worried, but trust in Providence."

And now, Mr. Gales and Seaton, if you can say anything to encourage us, or to relieve Uncle Joshua's anxious mind, you would do a great kindness to your old friend,

MAJOR JACK DOWNING.

LETTER LXXIII.

Downingville, State of Maine, Nov. 15, 1852.

Mr. Gales & Seaton—

My Dear Old Friends:—I am as happy as happy can be, and Uncle Joshua is a great deal happier. And as for Aunt Keziah, about the second day arter the election, when New York, Pennsylvania, and Ohio, came rolling on for Pierce and King, she was so completely overflowed with oceans of happiness, that she fell into conniption fits, and has had 'em, more or less, every day since. And as for Cousin Sargent Joel Downing, he don't hurrah for Gineral Scott no more; but ever since the election he hurrahs for Gineral Pierce, day and night, till he's got so hoarse he can't speak above a whisper. You remember I told you in my last letter how Uncle Joshua and I found Sargent Joel, some time before the election, out behind the barn, standing on a stump, and swinging his hat and hollerin', "Hurrah for Gineral Scott," with all his might. Arter that he did it openly, and said he didn't care who heard it. And he kept it up till the day arter the election, when the telegraph wires brought in the thunder and lightnin' news that all creation had gone for Gineral Pierce, and then Cousin Joel chopt round quicker than you ever see a nor-wester set in arter a south-east storm. Cousin Joel is a cunning dog; he knows on which side his bread is buttered, and you may depend he will be on hand in Washington next winter; and if Pennsylvania Avenue don't ring from one end to t'other with his hurrahs for Gineral Pierce, I won't guess agin. I don't know what Gineral Pierce will do for Cousin Joel when the time comes, but he will be bound to do something pretty handsome for him, for no man has hurrah'd louder and heartier for him than Cousin Joel has, especially since the election.

And as for Uncle Joshua, he seems to be in kingdom-come. It does my heart good to look at him, he seems to be so satisfied. He says the good old Jackson times is coming back agin, and the Bank, and the Tariff, and Internal Improvements has got to stand from under, or else be swamped.

"But," says I, "Uncle Joshua, we haint got no Bank now, so it can't stand from under, nor be swamped nother."

"Well, that ain't nothing at all to the argument," says he. "Supposin' we had a Bank, it *would* have to stand from under, wouldn't it?"

"Well, Uncle Joshua," says I, "you ask me as puzzlin' a question as Bill Johnson did t'other day."

"What was that?" says he.

"Well," says I, "you know Bill is always bantering every one he meets to swap watches. So he comes up to me t'other day, and says he, 'Major, how'll ye swap watches?' Says I, 'Mr. Johnson, I haint got no watch.' Says he, 'No matter for that; supposin' you had one, how would you swap?' Now, Uncle, if I had only had a watch, I could a told Bill how I would swap. And so if we only had a Bank, may be I could answer your question, too. For if it was a Whig Bank, I should say, pretty decidedly, it would have to stand from under, or be upset. But Gineral Jackson killed the Bank, and now Gineral Pierce has killed the Whig party. It has always been your doctrine, that the Democratic principle is to fight agin the Whigs. But now there ain't no Whig party, nor no

Bank, I don't know, for my part, what Gineral Pierce is going to do; for of all the hard things in this world there ain't nothin' harder than to kick agin nothin'. And, Uncle, I shouldn't be at all surprised if Gineral Pierce should go to work now and build up a new Bank; and I don't know but I almost wish he would."

Uncle Joshua rolled up his eyes, and says he, "Major, you aught to be the last man to say that arter working as hard as you did to help Gineral Jackson kill the old Bank monster."

"I know that," says I, "but circumstances alters cases. It is being a *Whig* Bank that makes a Bank bad, and does all the mischief. A Democratic Bank might be a very good thing, and I hope Gineral Pierce will try the experiment. The Bank of England has worked well for more than a hundred years, and why shouldn't the Bank of America, if there wasn't no Whiggery mixed up with it? I hope Gineral Pierce will go in for a true Democratic National Bank."

"Well, Major," said Uncle Joshua, "I s'pose you see deeper into statesmanship than I do, and I don't know but you're about right. I think Gineral Pierce aught to take you for one of his Cabinet, if he wants to get along safe; and I think if you would sit down and write a letter to the Gineral, giving him some of your notions about things, it might be a help to him; and I think, Major, it's your duty to do it."

I couldn't help thinking about this last remark of Uncle Joshua all day, and finally I begun to feel as though *'twas* my duty to write to the Gineral. But I see something in the papers about his going to Virginia, or somewhere off South, and I don't know where my letter would find him. But I s'pose, Mr. Gales & Seaton, you keep the run of him, so I will inclose the letter to you, and get you to send it on. By so doing you will much oblige your old friend,

MAJOR JACK DOWNING.

LETTER LXXIV

PRIVATE LETTER TO GENERAL PIERCE.

Downingville, State of Maine, Nov. 16, 1852.

Dear Gineral :—I guess you little thought when we was having that scratch in Mexico, that it was going to make a President of you. But time and chance happens to all men, and why shouldn't luck come to you as well as anybody else? I didn't expect, when I lost dear old Gineral Jackson, that I should ever have a chance to write to another Gineral in the President's chair. President Polk was only a Colonel, and somehow it didn't seem half so natural for me to say "dear Colonel," as it did to say "dear Gineral," I had been so used to it in Old Hickory's time. And I can't help thinking that nobody lower than Gineral ever aught to be President. But that's neither here nor there; you are President, and have got to go ahead and make the best of it. And as I had a good deal of experience in Gineral Jackson's time, and you are kind of young in Government matters, I felt it my duty to write to you and try to encourage you along, for I don't expect you know what very darksome and trying times there is in going through the Presidency. The first thing that is necessary is to keep a stiff upper lip. It was keepin' a stiff upper lip that carried Gineral Jackson through a great many hard trials. There was so many hands to the bellows that blowed you into the Presidency that I'm afraid when they come to settle up accounts there'll be a squabble that will make more trouble for you than ever old Hickory had. When the old line Dimocrats, North and South, and the Hunkers, and the Barnburners, and the Free-Soilers, and the States

Rights Dimocrats, and the Union Whigs, and the Secessionists, and the Carolina Nullifiers, and the Old Fogies, and Young America, all get you by the throat, and every one crying out "pay me that thou owest," I almost tremble to think what will become of you, unless you have a good deal of the true old Hickory grit. You must put on the stiffest kind of upper lip and take the responsibility, or it'll be gone goose with you. You had better shake them all off, and advertise that you won't pay no debts of their contracting.

You must remember that the Whig party is dead and buried, and you haven't got to fight agin that no more. And you must remember, too, that the Whig party has left considerable valuable property, and that the Dimocratic party is the natural heir to it. So you can take up the Bank, and the Tariff, and Internal Improvements, and such kind of notions, and use 'em quietly for the benefit of the great Dimocratic party, and say nothin' about it. Only you must take care to fix 'em over into Dimocratic Bank, and Dimocratic Tariff, and Dimocratic Internal Improvements, and then nobody won't say a word agin 'em.

Well, now, about the Cabinet. That is a ticklish kind of business, and I feel uneasy to know how you'll get along with it. Uncle Joshua thinks you'd better take one out of each party that went for you, and give 'em all a fair chance. But you can't have but seven members in the Cabinet, unless you conclude to have a Kitchen Cabinet too, and I don't suppose you'll do that, for they ain't apt to work very well. Old Hickory himself got rather tired of his before 'twas over. So if you haven't but seven members, there won't be enough to give one to each party, and them that's left to suck their fingers will always be biting their thumbs at you. And then you know the rule is, that the Cabinet should always be a unit. But I'm afraid if you get one in from each party it will be a very quarrelsome kind of unit, and you will have no comfort of your life. And then, if you was to give the whole to one or two parties, you **would** of course have **about a** dozen parties up in arms agin you, and squalls **and** harrycanes blowing from all quarters. Jest **see how it** would work. If you **should** pick out a sound, wise **Old Fogy to** take hold with you to help cook matters up, the **Dimocratic Review** would be down upon you like a thousand of brick, **and blackguard** you like a pick-pocket for trying to hobble along **on** the "mere beaten horse." And **then, if** you was to look t'other way **and set** Young America to the **helm, the** Old **Fogies** would be afraid some of the mad-caps would **run us on** to the breakers and send us all to the **bottom. In** that case, pretty likely there'd be a greater unit out **of** the Cabinet than there was in it, and there would be danger of mutiny all round. So there you are. You seem to be in a snarl, any way you can **fix it.**

Now, if **you** will take my advice, Gineral, you will shet **your eyes,** and stop your ears, and take the responsibility, **and when** they come **pulling and** hauling round you, jest **say** to the Dimocrats, and the Old Fogies, and Young **America,** and the Hunkers, and the Barnburners, and the Abolitionists, and the Secessionists, and the Nullifiers, that you don't know none of 'em, and that you ain't their President, but you are the President of these thirty-one United States, and you mean **" to go for** the whole or none." That is, I mean the whole of the United States that **is fairly ours,** and not the whole of creation, **for this last business is one that** needs to be looked at and thought **on** considerable before **going** into **it.** I know some folks **say** there is **to be a great** deal annexin' done during your administration. Now I don't know what your notions **is** on this subject, but if annexin' is to be the main business of your term, the next question is, what is the best way to do it? Uncle Joshua always says, in nine cases out of ten it costs more to rob an orchard than it would to buy the apples. If that's true, maybe that fillisbusterin' wouldn't be the cheapest way to annex. But some folks have a great fancy for fillibusterin', let it cost what 'twill. If you should think of branching out strong that way, I don't s'pose you could do better than to take Kossuth for Secretary of State, for he is Governor of Hungary, you know, and could hitch that fine country right on to our team, without the trouble of any fillibusterin' about it. It could be done so quick the Russian Bear wouldn't hardly have time to growl. And then a small fillibusterin' army could bring in Cuba and Canada, and Mexico, and the rest as fast as we should know what to do with 'em.

Good by, Gineral; go ahead, and keep a stiff upper lip, and anything I can do for you jest let me know.

So I remain your true friend,

MAJOR JACK DOWNING.

LETTER LXXV.

PRIVATE DISPATCH, TO GO THROUGH THE ORGAN TO GENERAL PIERCE.

DOWNINGVILLE, State of Maine, July 22, 1853.

MR. GALES & SEATON—

MY DEAR OLD FRIENDS:—When I am in a dilemma I always feel sure I shall be safe if I throw myself into your hands. And I am in a dilemma now, 'cause I've got to send a little private official dispatch to Gineral Pierce, and I can't find out what paper is the organ to send it through. I've been hunting and hunting over the papers, from all parts of the country, that come to Uncle Joshua's Post-Office, to try to find out what paper is Gineral Pierce's organ ; but the more I hunt the worse I am off, **and the** darker and more puzzlin' the question grows. Some of the papers says the Washington Union is the organ, and some says 'tisn't.

Sometimes **the** Union comes out with **a fust-rate** Dimocratic leader, loaded down with true, solid Dimocratic principles, that goes into the ground clear **up to the hub.** Wal, then the papers says, "that's by authority ; **the Union is the organ of** the Administration, and no mistake ; **it's jest as** clear as preachin'." Then the next thing, **may be, it** comes out with another Dimocratic leader, puffing the Dimocratic **Government** of Russia sky-high. Wal, then the **papers** goes into a flutteration about it, and says **the** Union isn't **the organ of** the Government, any **more than a** toad wants a tail, every bit and grain.

But the Union says *'tis* the organ, and the New York Evenin' Post, and some of the rest of 'em, eenamost swears, up hill and down, that *'tisn't* the organ. So there they have it ; **and how are we, away** down East here, **to** tell which is what ? And then some of the papers **said** the Republic **was** to be the organ, and **was** cut down near about one-half in size to suit the times ; and **some** said **a true**-blue Dimocratic organ was going to be moved up from New Hampshire ; and some said a bran new organ was going to be made right up **out** of whole cloth, and an editor was going to be brought up from New Hampshire to edit it. So what the upshot of the **business** is I can't find out.

I'm most afraid the Gineral hasn't appointed any organ yet ; and **if he hasn't,** that's very bad ; for the organ aught to be the very first appointment made. But I know the Gineral has had a very **hard** time about some of his appointments, so I can't so much blame him. So here you see was my bother that I was in ; I had to send to the Gineral something that aught to go through the organ, and I can't find the organ. Finally, arter consulting Uncle Joshua about it, he said I'd better write to you, for you would know as much about it as anybody, and if there was an organ you could send my dispatch to it, and if there wasn't, you could put it in the Intelligencer—and for his part, he always thought the Intelligencer was about as good as an organ to put anything into.

So now, Mr. Gales & Seaton, if there isn't no organ in Washington nor nowhere else in America, I shall have to depend on you to get my dispatch along to the Government the best way you can, and I'll try and do as much for you any time.

To Gineral Pierce, President of America, and agoing to be (that is, if Gineral Cushing isn't mistaken) the founder of "Modern Rome."

DEAR GINERAL :—I'm afraid you've thought strange of it that I haint writ to you afore now, for so long time past ; but I couldn't, I've been so busy cruising round among the fishermen down to New Brunswick, and Nova Scotia, and the Gulf of St. Lawrence, that I couldn't get no time to write, nor couldn't find no Post-Office to send it. Ye see, Gineral, I didn't accept your invitation to take a seat in your Cabinet, 'cause I'm one of them sort that can't bear setting a great deal. I can't stan' it without I'm up and knocking about pretty much every day ; and I understood the Cabinet had to set nigh about half the time, so I told you I should a good deal rather have some foreign appointment, where I could stir myself. And you told me the foreign appointments was pretty much all spoken for, twenty times over, but you would give me a commission as Minister-Gineral, and I might go round and ook after the interests of the country wherever I thought

MAJOR DOWNING'S VISIT TO THE FISHING SMACKS.

(See next page.)

best. Now that was jest what I liked ; you couldn't a gin me no appointment that would suit me better.

Wal, my first cruise, Gineral, has been away Down East, and a little beyond ; for I thought 'twas high time them fishermen of ourn down there was looked arter ; I heard they was getting wrathy, and the Britishers was flockin' in there with their armed vessels agin, and there was pretty likely to be a muss if 'twan't seen to ; and I knew it would be a good cool place in this hot summer weather, so I sculled off. I went all along the coast, and boarded the fishermen, and talked with the skippers, and give 'em good advice. I'm sorry to say their backs is up pretty round. They swear they'll never stan' that straight line "from headland to headland," no way you can fix it. They say the codfish and the mackerel are a good deal thicker inside the line than they are out, and they are bound to go where there's the best fishin', let who will stan' in the way. Wal, Gineral, since most all our politicians and office-seekers is doing the same thing, and setting of 'em the same example, I couldn't find it in my heart to blame 'em much, for who is there among 'em all, politicians and office-seekers, that stans much about any straight line from headland to headland when they think there is any better fishing t'other side of it?

Howsever, I guess you may calculate the fishermen will remain quiet this summer, if they are allowed to fish where they are a mind to, and the British vessels don't crowd 'em too hard. But if they do, you must look out for a regular row, that'll stir the whole camp of Young America. I got home last week, and have been overhauling the newspapers, and having talks with Uncle Joshua, and larning how things is gitting on. I see that you and some of the Cabinet have been on to New York to see the openin' of the Crystil Palace, and had a good time. I'm glad to find your Administration is getting on so swiminly, and that you've got such a fust-rate Cabinet round you. I like Mr. Marcy better and better; he's such a prudent man and a fust-rate Dimocrat. I always heard he was prudent and savin', and wasn't ashamed to have his clothes mended as long as they was decent, before he would go into any extravagance to get new ones. And I'm right glad he's agoing to set sich a good example to the country by making our foreign Ministers and Consuls follow his prudent ways. His circular of the first of June has been worth a hundred dollars to me right off, to begin with. When I got home I says to Uncle Joshua, says I, "Uncle, I want you to lend me a hundred dollars, and I'll give you an order on the President for it, to take it out of my salary; for I'm agoing to take a tower to Europe with my commission of Minister-Gineral, to see that England and France puts a stop to that Russian war, and I've got to get a bran new rig for a court dress."

Uncle Joshua laughed, and says he, "Major, you can save yourself all that trouble and expense. I guess you hain't seen Mr. Marcy's circular. Our foreign Ministers and Consuls now have all got to wear the plainest home-spun clothes, jest as Dr. Franklin did when he was a Minister in the beginning of the government. The circular says, 'It is to be regretted that there was ever any departure in this respect from the example of Dr. Franklin.' And it goes on and lays down the rules about plain clothes in a most thorough Dimocratic manner. And the Union newspaper—I don't know whether it's an organ or not, but it puts on airs and speaks as though it was talking by authority—and it says the Administration is determined to 'exhibit the same progressive American spirit' in the clothing business that it does in its other foreign relations; and that 'it is time to restore the strongly-marked republicanism' of Dr. Franklin's clothes. So, Major, your clothes is all good enough now, and jest the right sort. Only may be you better take with you my long drab surtout and my broad-brim hat, for perhaps they'd look a little more like Dr. Franklin than yourn does." And then Cousin Nabby spoke up, and says she, "Yes, Cousin Jack, and I've

DEMOCRATIC COSTUME CARRIED TO THE EXTREME.

got half a dozen pair of blue woolen stockins already knit for you; so you'll be all fixed up nice and warm."

Wal, now, Gineral, I feel a great deal relieved about this

dress business; it will save so much expense, and, besides, I shan't feel afraid now to go to any royal Court in Europe, and face the finest on 'em. The fact is, Gineral, since Mr. Marcy's circular has sot me to thinkin' on this matter of dressin' for our Ministers, I don't know but it would be more Dimocratic and American to go a step beyond Dr. Franklin, and take the real aborigin style. There aint, to my mind, nothin' more becomin than a buffalo-robe or a handsome blanket, with the fine worked Indian leggins and moccasins; and then an American Minister would be knowed everywhere as soon as he was seed. They might paint or not, as they pleased, but it would be real American, and beat the Turks in picturesness, and besides look Roman like too. Give my respects to Mr. Marcy, and hint this Indian notion to him. I am sure it would take like wild-fire.

And, Gineral, you've got another real whaler in your Cabinet, and that is Gineral Cushing. It seems to me, if that man lives, he's agoing to outstrip Gineral Jackson. I had no idea there was so much grit in him till he made that speech t'other day at Newark, in the Jersies. Since I've read that speech I feel all over like an old Roman. It seems as if I can see our country marching right up to the very tip-top of the world's mountain and kicking all the rest of the nations down to the bottom of the heep. That old Greke, that folks tell so much about, never poured out sich a grist of oratory in all his born days. I can't help copying a little piece of it out of the newspapers into my dispatch. Here 'tis:

"There is a destiny to a Republic. There is a law of its existence as clearly and undeniably as there is a law of the existence of a human being, that he shall begin in youth, that he shall grow in juvenescence, that he shall harden into manhood, that in the plenitude of his manful strength he shall overtop the nations around him. [Applause.] We are now the men of the modern Rome. How was it with the old Rome. She conquered. She went on annexin' according to the law of her existence [applase], and so long as she proceeded in the application of that law of her existence, no earthly power could withstand her progress. [Applause.] I say that was the destiny of ancient Rome, and it is the destiny of modern Rome. There can be no pause in our progress, except the pause of decay; when we cease to grow we shall begin to perish. [Applause.] I say, when we cease to grow we shall begin to perish; for upon us as a republic is impressed, not a curse, (though it was a curse to him who thrust from his door the thirsting Saviour on his way to Calvary;) it was his curse that vengeance of God should pronounce over him as the perpetual sentence of his sin— march, march, march; for him there was no pause. I say, as on him was pronounced the curse, on us has been poured down the benediction, [applause;] for us that same Divine voice has said, March, march, march—onward, upward, so long as there remains a celestial hight in the infinite regions of greatness which it is possible for human power to scale."

That speech came over Cousin Sargent Joel like a steak of lightning. He went right to work and scoured up his old fire-lock as bright as a pewter-platter. And now, from mornin' till night, with his fire-lock on his shoulder, he marches about the house and round the barn in a military step, sayin' to himself as he goes, "March, march, march; we are the men of modern Rome! March, march, march; annexin' day is close at hand! March, march, march!"

But, Gineral, I must be in a hurry, and be off on my tower before the countries is all annexed. So I subscribe myself in haste, your faithful friend and well wisher,

MAJOR JACK DOWNING.

LETTER LXXVI.

PRIVATE DISPATCH TO GINERAL PIERCE, TO GO THROUGH ONE OF THE ORGANS—THE UNION OR THE SENTINEL, OR THE STAR, OR ONE OF THE OTHER ORGANS—IF THEY'VE GOT AGOING YET.

DOWNINGVILLE, State of Maine, Nov. 8, 1853.

DEAR GINERAL :—I got back from my tower in Europe yesterday, and found Uncle Joshua and Aunt Keziah, and Cousin Nabby, and Cousin Sargent Joel, all well ; and I hope these few lines will find you enjoying the same blessing. I'm glad of one thing, and that is, that you ain't troubled so much about organs as you was when I went away. There wasn't any organ then, only the *Union*, and that was a disputed one, so I had to send my last dispatch to my old friends, Mr. Gales and Seaton, and get them to forward it to you the best way they could. But I understand now that organs is getting to be as plenty as blackberries, and that seems to be lucky about this time ; for, if what Uncle Joshua tells me is all true, it will need a good many of 'em to play tunes to suit all parties. If you could manage to have an organ for each member of the Cabinet, it would be a great help ; for then each one could play his own tune and no jarring, and harmony is what we need all round. Mr. Marcy needs an organ all to himself, to fire off his forty-four pounders at Austria and the rest of Europe, to keep matters straight over there. And Mr. Guthrie, I'm sure, needs an organ all to himself to manage his New York correspondence. And there's Gineral Cushing, he aught to have a nice organ all to himself, that would play military tunes, so that everybody, as soon as they heard it, would feel as if they wanted to *march*. And Gineral Davis aught to have a military organ, too; but some say he and Gineral Cushing might get along very well with one organ between 'em, and that Gineral Davis could play his variations on Mr. Guthrie's organ.

And then the different "sections" of the party needs different organs, too. I never believed that the same tune would satisfy the "Hards" and the "Softs" of New York; and from what Uncle Joshua tells me, it's jest so. He says the organ has been pouring out delightful strains of harmony all summer; but the more it poured 'em out, the greater was the discord between the Hards and the Softs, till finally it worked them to a pitch of phrenzy, and he says they are now fighting and pullin' caps like mad. That shows clearly to my mind that the different "sections" ought to all have their own organs, and I don't think there'll be any peace till they have.

But about my tower in Europe I've a good deal to say, more than I can get into this dispatch, and some of it, I think, would work well into your message to Congress next month, if I can get time to bring it, or send it on to you in time. Ye see, as I had your commission of Minister-Gineral to go on my own hook wherever I pleased, and look after matters jest as I thought best, it gin me a capital chance to work to advantage. And Mr. Marcy's rules, too, about dress worked first-rate; for when I thought it best to go it a little on the sly, I could jest put on my drab surtout and broad-brim hat, and sagaciate round among the whole biling of 'em, and they wouldn't mistrust who I was. So when I found which way the cat was going to jump, and thought it was best to head 'em and bring 'em to a pint, I had nothing to do but to pull my commission out of my pocket, and show it to 'em, and that did the business. The fact is, Europe's afraid of us. I think we are fast getting the upper hand. There ain't another nation in all creation, without 'tis Russia, that hardly dares to say her soul's her own, for fear we shall be down upon her, and take her soul away from her. And even Russia feels a little ticklish, for fear that, when she gets into her highfalutin with Turkey, and the rest of Europe goes to take sides, we shall turn tu and lick the whole scrape, and annex 'em to our modern Rome. I see somebody has put out

THE MAJOR IN COURT DRESS.

a book that proves, as clear as preachin', that the United States is a modern Rome; so when Gineral Cushing said in his speech we must march, march, march, and do as old Rome did, he was talking by the book.

About this war business in Europe, if there's anything to be larnt in diplomatic circles, and I've sifted the whole of 'em, there's to be a tight scratch all round before it is over. The truth is, Russia is in real arnest after Turkey as ever a bear was to get into a corn-field. She clambered over into the field, like a great bear as she is, jest for the purpose of eating her way through from one end to t'other. But she intended to do it all in a peaceable, friendly way, marching cooly and slowly along, step by step, till she got down to the lower end of the field, and then she would swallow Constantinople just as quick as a cat could lick her ear, and poor Turkey never would know what become of her. The Czar intended to do all this in a very friendly, quiet way, nibbling along at his leisure, and not have any fuss at all about it. But the foolish Sultan got frightened, and worked himself into a tantrum, and declared war, and told Mr. Bear to clear out of his corn-field in fifteen days, or he'd set the dogs arter him. Well, that made the Czar mad; and now he says clear the track, for he's agoing down to Constantinople, whether or no, let who will stand in the way, and there shan't be a Turk's head left anywhere, clear from Dan to Beersheba—that is, if the other nations will jest form a ring and see fair play, and not interfere. But the Czar is a good deal afraid that England and France will be for having a finger in the pie; so he has agreed with Austria and Prussia, who are on his side, to keep quiet and declare themselves neutral, and not stir an inch as long as England and France will keep quiet. But if they begin to meddle, then all hands to fall to, and have a regular scratch, and pulling caps all round.

Well, now, England and France don't mean to keep quiet. They are watching Russia jest as narrow as ever a cat watched a mouse, and before Russia gets half way down to Constantinople, there'll be a terrible fuss. The French rooster will crow, and the British lion will growl and shake his mane; and if the Russian bear don't get licked or scared, and turn tail to and run, but holds on and eats up one end of Turkey, then England and France will clap their heads together and eat up t'other end, just to keep it from spiling.

Now, when all this rumpus gets to its highest pitch in Europe, and all the nations get at it pell-mell, it'll be jest the time for us to strike, and go to annexin', and carry out our manifest destiny in a handsome manner. What's the use of our nibbling about among small fry near home, and annexin' little patches here and there, such as Cuba, and little slices off of Mexico, when we might jest as well branch out and do somethin' splendid—somethin' that old Rome couldn't hold a candle to; somethin' that Gineral Cushing himself could say was quite "up to the occasion?" Who wants to wait for our manifest destiny till one-half the present generation has died off? I say no; now's the time; we must strike when the iron's hot. So, when the Czar and all his troops are away down South, peppering Turkey, let us whip round into the Baltic and annex St. Petersburg, and put a navy and an army there that will command all Northern Europe. By that time England and France will get to quarreling with each other to see which will have Constantinople, and that will be the time for us to be down upon them like a thousand of brick. Take London, and then we shall have John Bull by the horns; take Paris, and that'll give us all the jining countries. Then sail up the Mediterranean, drive the English and French fleets all afore us, force our way through the Darnin-needles, and get possession of that "golden horn" they tell about. Then, if I understand geography right, we shall have full sweep all over creation.

What's to be done on t'other side, over the Pacific way, ain't much Commodore Perry has fairly got his wedge into the oyster-shell of Japan, and that's half the battle. Just send word to him to annex China on his way round, and on his route home pick up the islands along on the Pacific, which will be jest as easy as to pick up so many bird's eggs. And after we get through our manifest destiny, I don't see what there need to be to hinder our enjoying peace and qu'etness at home, and having a good time of it. We shall certainly then have enough for **all hands**, and no mistake ; offices enough for all them that wants offices, and spoils enough for **all them that's hungry for spoils.** And then let every man of us " set his face like a flint as well against right-handed back-slidings as against left-handed defections, which may prejudice or embarrass the onward progress of the Republic." Then there needn't be no more quarreling between the Hards and the Softs about which gets the most, for there'll be enough for the whole biling lot of 'em.

We aught to be going ahead with this business as fast as possible, for Uncle Joshua says the party has got into a terrible snarl, and nothing but a grand *coop-da-tat* can get 'em **out of it. He says Collector** Bronson, of New York, has lost his head, owing to a little misunderstanding between him and Mr. Guthrie. They both tried **to see** which **could** stand up **the straightest on the** Baltimore **platform, and** they both **agreed that the platform was the** rule, and everything aught **to be squared up** to it. Mr. Bronson **was quite** impartial, and Mr. **Guthrie was a** good deal more so. When Mr. Bronson took his seat **at the head of the Custom-House** table, and all " sections" **of the party come crowding** and shuffling round to get **the** best places **at the table and** alongside the best dishes, he tried to give 'em all a fair chance ; but somehow **he** thought it was no more than **right to help round first them** that had always stood fair and square on the platform ; and if some of them that used to *spit* on it had to wait a little, it might do 'em good. But the spitters made a terrible fuss about it, and kept up such a din in Mr. Guthrie's ears that he turned round and told Mr. Bronson, right up and down, that he musn't show *no partiality*. If a spitter wasn't catched spitting on the platform *now*, give him his regular meal. This touched Mr. Bronson a little, and he said he was able to do the honors of his own table, and he would attend to the duties of his office if Mr. Guthrie would his. Mr. Guthrie said that was *rebellion*, so he brought him to the block, and chopped his head off.

Uncle Joshua says it is a very misfortunate business, and has thrown the whole party into a high fever. The fever rages the hardest in the "section" of the New York Hards, and looks as though it might prove fatal. But Gineral Cushing, who is very skillful in such matters, has put a blister plaster to the Massachusetts Softs, in hopes of drawing out the inflammation from the New York Hards. But Uncle Joshua says he don't think the party is out of danger yet. But as long as there's life there's hope; so let us all keep a stiff upper lip and go ahead.

Your faithful friend and Minister-Gineral,
MAJOR JACK DOWNING.

LETTER LXXVII.

THE OSTEND CONGRESS—THE THREE S'S, SOULE, SICKLES, AND SAUNDERS—PEABODY'S **FOURTH OF** JULY DINNER IN LONDON—DEMOCRACY IN ENGLAND, **FRANCE, AND** SPAIN.

Letter of Instructions to President Pierce and Cabinet.

OSTEND, October 28, 1854.

DEAR GINERAL :—We are all prowlin' round here, and duing the best we can, though we haint made out to fetch matters to a head yet; but I guess we are in a pretty fair way for it.

Our team's got grit enough, and, **by** jingo, they'll haul the load they hitch on to, or else somethin's got to give way. **Mr.** Buchanan and Mr. Mason isn't quite spry enough ; they are **a little on the** old fogy fashion, and **not** always ready to come **up to** the scratch ; but with Mr. Sickles spurrin' **up on one side, and** Mr. Sanders spurrin' on t'other ride, and Mr. Souley lrivin' **up** behind, we make out to get a pretty good pull out of them sometimes. We've got things so far ahead **here that** Mr. Sickles **and Mr.** Sanders thinks I better write a dispatch **to you and** the Cabinet to home and give you some instructions how to go on.

I'll tell you what 'tis, Gineral, (when I call you Gineral, I sometimes eenamost feel as if I was writin' to Gineral Jackson **again ;) I say,** Gineral, I'll tell you what 'tis, them three S's (Sickles, Sanders, **and** Souley) are **the** three smartest chaps that ever growed in North America. They make Europe stan' round, and no mistake. Mr. Souley holds old Spain between **his thumb and** finger, and whisks her about jest as he's a mind to, Queen and all ; Mr. Sanders lays down the Democratic law to France, and stans a pretty fair chance to be chose President of the new French Republic after Napoleon goes out ; and as for old John Bull, **I'll be licked if I think the critter dares to stir an inch while** Sickles holds him by the horns.

I suppose you've seen them letters—how Mr. Sickles snubbed Peabody, the great merchant banker, about the 4th of July dinner. Capital, wasn't it ? Ye see, Mr. Peabody gin a 4th of July dinner. He's always doing sich things or giving money away for somethin or other ; for they say he's got money enough to buy a kingdom. **Wall,** he invited Mr. Sickles to come and jine the rest of us and have a good set down. But, ye see, Mr. Peabody didn't know how much patriotism and real Democratic grit there was stowed away in Mr. Sickles' breast; he had no idea o'nt; and that was the rock he split on. You'll hardly believe me, Gineral, when I say it, but it's a fact, Mr. Peabody had Englishmen there to help eat that dinner! **It's** a melancholy fact, **but it's true.** If he had had half a table full of cannibals **we could** all a stood **it, and fit our** way through; but Mr. Sickles couldn't stand Englishmen. He had too much Democratic blood in him for that. To mix up Democrats and Englishmen at the **same** table was awful. But that wasn't the worst of it. When Mr. **Sickles got there** he couldn't hardly **believe his own eyes; for** there was a portrait of the Queen hung right up in the same room with Gineral **Washington!** Wasn't that a stumper? No wonder Mr. Sickles' **Democratic** blood biled over. But that wasn't the worst of it. When **they come** to give the toasts, they toasted the Queen! The rest of the folks stood up to drink the toast, but Mr. Sickles grit his teeth and sot down as hard as a thousand of brick; and he felt so disgusted he couldn't eat another mouthful. And when the music, to increase the insult, struck up "God save the Queen," Mr. Sickles took his hat and marched out. *There* was spunk that Young America aught to be proud of! That Mr. Buchanan didn't take his hat and march out too only shows that he's an Old Fogy.

We've held our Congress, **and got things in a** middling good train, though, as I said before, we haint **brought matters quite to a head yet.** We managed better than your Congress does. We didn't stop to make so many long-winded speeches, but talked right to the pint, and got through in a few days. The members chose me President of the Congress the first thing; for they said I was nearest akin to Gineral Jackson of any of 'em, and the honor belonged to me; so I had to take the cheer. I returned thanks for the honor, of course, and then proceeded to business. I beginned by callin for the reports of the committees that had the business in hand afore we met.

I called for the report on England first, out of respect to her being our venerable old mother. Mr. Sickles, who was the head of that committee, reported that John Bull was an obstinate Old Fogy, and he had found it very hard to make any impression upon him. The people all seemed to be tied to the Queen's apron strings, and didn't appear to care no

MR. SICKLES WHIPPING DEMOCRACY INTO JOHN BULL.

more about Democracy than a horse does about his grandfather. Still he had faith to believe that they could be made to take it, and when the time comes he was ready to off coat and roll up his sleeves and whip it into 'em. [Cheers.]

Upon the question of accepting Mr. Sickles' report, Mr. Buchanan rose and said he objected to the term Old Fogy; he never did like the term, and he thought it would do more hurt than good in the report, and he moved that it be struck out. Mr. Sanders said no ; tnat was the very cream of the report, and he objected to its being struck out. It was then put to vote, and Mr. Buchanan and Mr. Mason voted unanimously to strike it out, and the rest of us all voted to keep it in ; so " Old Fogy" stands in the report by a strong majority.

I then called for the report on France.

Mr. Sanders made a long report ; but the substance was, that the Democratic crop in France wasn't quite ripe enough to harvest. Napoleon had filled the people's heads so full of the Eastern war and glory that they couldn't think of nothin' else but raising troops to go to the Black Sea, and give the Russians an all-fired thrashin', and storm the Malakoff, and blow all Sebastapol down about their ears. So it was no use, jest now, to try to light the fires of Democracy in France. "But," said Mr. Sanders, "there's a good time comin', boys—wait a little longer." [Cheers.]

Mr. Sanders' report was unanimously accepted, with a proviso that, while we had to wait a little longer, we shouldn't stop working, but keep stirrin' round and trying to get up a muss somehow as soon as possible.

I then called for the report on Spain. And here we all felt quite sure we should get something pretty nice.

Mr. Souley rose, with fire in his eye and honey and thunder on his tongue. He reported that if there was any sich thing as getting sunbeams out of a cowcumber he could do it ; and he had come pesky near kindlin' the flame of Democracy from one end of Spain to t'other. He had churned the cream of Spanish Democracy, and churned it well, and the butter began to come and swim on the top of the buttermilk, and he thought for awhile the bisness was done ; but when he looked into the churn again, to his amazement, the witchcraft of despotism had got the upper hand, and the butter was all meltin' back again into the buttermilk. "But," says he, "as true as Jackson flogged the British at New Orleans, I'll have a red-hot horse-shoe before long to put into that churn, and then butter *must* come." [Cheers.]

MR. SOULE CHURNING THE DEMOCRACY OF OLD SPAIN.

So you see, Gineral, how things is over here. We can't do much jest yet, but you may depend on it there is great times ahead. You and Mr. Marcy, and the rest, must hold on and try to keep things snug and tight at home, till we get our Government under way over here, and we'll cut out some work for you to do before long; and them matters and things that we don't send over any particular directions about, you and the Cabinet must try to get along with and manage accordin' to your best discretion. But you better be gettin' your forces ready as fast as possible, for we may call for 'em at any moment. You better enlist the old Downingville company, and get Cousin Sargent Joel to take command of it. Get Mr. Marcy to plan out the right sort of uniform, and get my friend Cushing to address 'em and fill 'em full of grit and ginger, so they can't be held back, but will be ready, at a moment's warning, to "march," and carry Democracy all over Eurup, and Asha, and Afraky, and America.

Postscript.—I don't know but the muss is begun, and we may have to send over by the next steamer for Sargent Joel and his company to come on. The French Emperor has got frightened or mad about matters, I don't know which, and has snubbed Mr. Souley, and forbid his settin' a foot on his land. He turned him right out of the doors of France, and told him to go about his business somewhere else. This was when Mr. Souley was on his way home to Spain from our Congress, which we held at Ostend; for we was very careful not to hold it in France, nor Spain, nor England, so as not to stir up a muss with the Governments before it was time. But Napoleon has been foolish enough to put his foot in it, and now we've all agreed that he has got to knock under and back out, or smell thunder.

In haste and some agitation, I remain your old friend and Minister-Gineral at large,

MAJOR JACK DOWNING.

LETTER LXXVIII.

PRIVATE DISPATCHES TO GINERAL PIERCE—NOT TO BE GIVE UP TO CONGRESS IF THEY CALL FOR IT.

Aboard the Fillibuster Schooner Two Pollies,
 Off the "Hole in the Wall," near the middle of
  March, I forget the day of the Month, 1855.

Dear Gineral :—We are skuddin' round here, and holding on to the slack, waitin' for more help to come up, and you may depend on't Cuba's got to take it. We don't never give up the ship. A fast little clipper jest come along, going to Baltimore, and the skipper said he'd take my dispatches to you in three days. And you can send to me by the skipper, your notions about things ; for he's only going to stop long enough to wood up, and then he's coming right strait back to jine us. He made me promise to hold on and not take Cuba till he comes, for he was very earnest to be in at the death.

That Cuba's a fine country. We've been having a glimpse at it once in awhile with our spy-glasses, through the "Hole in the Wall," and round the corners, and it's raly a fine country ; 'twould do your heart good to look at it. And you shall have a chance before long, for it's got to come down ; it's got to 'nuckle, and no mistake. I've got my commission to go ahead from Mr. Buchanan, and Mr. Mason, and Mr. Souley. And the nub of the whole thing is, we've got to take Cuba, "if we have the power ;".and I know we have, as Sally Giles said to her sweetheart. Says Sally, says she, "you shan't kiss me unless you are stronger than I am, and I know you be."

THE SCHOONER "TWO POLLIES" SCUDDING ROUND CUBA.

Just before we come out, I see by the papers that Louis Napoleon was a notion of goin' to the Crimea to see Sevastopol fall, and so I thought maybe you might like to come out here and **see** us take Cuba. Now, if you du, jest say the word, and tell me in **your letter what day** you will be down on the pint of Florida, and I'll bear up with the *Two Pollies* and take you off.

You mustn't feel hurt because I didn't come to Washington to see you before starting on this cruise; but the fact was, I hadn't time. Our country was in so much danger it wouldn't do to wait. Our Congress in Ostend went over the whole ground, and examined it carefully, and come to the conclusion that it was neck or nothing with us. We must **have Cuba or** our whole country would go to rack and ruin, and we agreed that "the Union can never enjoy respose nor possess reliable security as long as **Cuba is not** embraced within **its boundaries."**

I sent you a dispatch last fall about the duins of our Congress at Ostend, where we took up the affairs of England, and France, and Spain; but finally concluded we couldn't make anything out of that business yet, and should have to wait a **little longer.** Well, then them three S's—Souley, Sickles, and Sanders—said there was one thing we *could* du; we could take hold of that Cuba business and finish it up brown. And, for fear that Louis Napoleon might have spies round us there at Ostend, we concluded it was best to hitch a little **further off.** So we went over to **Ax-le-Shapple** and finished up the business.

The upshot **was, we** concluded we would have Cuba by hook or by crook; and that Mr. Souley should go right back **to old** Spain and tell the Queen so. If she'd a mind to give it up quietly and make no fuss about it, he might promise to give her somethin' pretty handsome in the way of money; we didn't care nothin' about that, as we've got plenty of money to home. If she refused, and told Mr. Souley to mind his own business, and we shouldn't have Cuba no how, then we told him he mustn't be mealy-mouthed, **nor** mince matters, but pick a quarrel the best way he could and clear **out.**

Well, Mr. Souley went back to Madrid with a stiff upper **lip,** and begun to try to **dicker with the Queen's** spokesman for a bargain, somethin' in this way :

Souley. " Oh, now I think of it, there's the little Island of Cuba over there near our coast ; we'd like to have that little island, if it's all the same to you. I s'pose you've no objections ; it isn't the least use in the world to you, and it might be some little account to us. So, if you say so, we'll jest mark Cuba down on the map of the United States."

Spokesman. "Not by a jug full, Mr. Souley ; Cuba is the most valuable patch of ground we've got. Can't spare it no how."

Souley. " Oh, nonsense ; it's no income at all to you, and nothin' but a bill of expense. It's so near to us we might look after it, and maybe make somethin' out of it ; but it's no more use to you than the fifth wheel to a coach. I guess we'll consider it ours."

Spokesman. " I guess you won't. I tell you we can't spare Cuba no how. It's the pride of the Spanish kingdom, and the gem of the Queen's crown."

Souley. " Well, but, my dear sir, we wouldn't mind paying **you quite a** handsome **sum for it ; a** hundred millions, if you **say so. We won't scrimp about the price."**

Spokesman. " There is no price to it. Carry your hundred millions to some other market if you want to buy honor with it. I tell you the honor of old Spain has no price."

Souley. " But, my dear sir, you don't consider what a wonderful deal of help a million would be to you. You must remember you are getting a good deal behind hand. You've no income hardly, and you are a good deal in debt. Only look at it; a hundred millions will enable you to pay off your debts, and make internal improvements, and build railroads and telegraphs all over your country, so that you can spruce up and live comfortable, and get ahead in the world. Say the word, and the hundred millions is yours."

Spokesman. "Offer your hundred millions to some beggar who wants it. The ancient and proud kingdom of Spain is no beggar, sir. I'll thank you, sir, not to insult me."

Souley. "I don't intend any insult, sir; but I'll be frank and plain with you. The fact is, we must have that island. It is absolutely necessary for the safety and welfare of the United States. Our country can't get along without it."

Spokesman. "That's your look out, not mine."

Souley. "Well, now, Mr. Spokesman, you know your people out there in Cuba have for a long time been insulting our folks, searching their vessels, and firing into their steamers, and sometimes ketching our people and shooting 'em, or putting 'em in dungeons. There's a long account of these things that you must settle right up, pint plank, or suffer the consequences. There's three hundred thousand dollars you've got to pay for stopping the steamer *Black Warrior*, and a great many other things as bad as that. These matters have got to be settled right up, or Cuba's got to stand in the gap."

Spokesman. "Can't help that. If you've got any accounts to settle, we'll leave it out to a third party to say how we shall settle. We don't owe you a cent for the *Black Warrior*. She broke our laws, and we fined her six thousand dollars; and then we give back the fine after all, when we might a kept the vessel. And you are so ungrateful as not to thank us for it."

Souley. "I won't stan' this foolery no longer. Leave it

out! No, we know how to settle our own business best. Now, sir, you've got to settle all our accounts right up, and fix things about Cuba, so we shan't never have any more trouble, or else give us up the island to manage in our own way. Now, I'm agoin' to give you jest two weeks to think of this business, and give me your answer; and if it isn't settled by that time, I shall clear out and go home, and *then you'll hear thunder!* Good-by, sir."

That Souley's a smart feller, Gineral. He talked right up to 'em, and wasn't afeared. Well, he waited till the two weeks was out, and no answer didn't come; and then he slat round and picked up his clothes, and locked up his trunks, and cleared out. Then he come over where we had been waiting for him, and told us how the business stood. He said old Spain refused to give up Cuba, and refused to settle, and he had got the quarrel in such a shape now, that we would carry it on any way to suit ourselves. "And now," said Mr. Souley, "what's to be done next?"

Wal, says I, Mr Souley, you've only jest got to look at the instructions drawn up by our Congress, at Ax-le-Shapple, and signed by you, and Mr. Buchanan, and Mr. Mason, and you'll see the course is marked out as plain as A, B, C. Jest open the dockyment and read. It says:

"Cuba is as necessary to the North American Republic as any of its present members."

"The Union can never enjoy repose, nor possess reliable security as long as Cuba is not embraced within its boundaries."

"But if Spain, deaf to the voice of her own interest, and actuated by stubborn pride and a false sense of honor, should refuse to sell Cuba to the United States"—what then?

"Self preservation is the first law of nature with States as well as with individuals."

Matters and things being thus and so, "then, by every

law, human and divine, we shall be justified in wresting Cuba from Spain, if we possess the power."

There, says I, there's your chart, **as** plain as the nose on a man's face; and all we've got to do is to go ahead. So we all put our heads together to draw up a plan of the campaign, and we wasn't long about it. It was finally concluded that Sanders should go **and stir up the** Southern division, head-quarters at New Orleans; Sickles should take charge of the center wing, head-quarters at Washington, and a branch at New York; and I should go as fast as possible " Down East," head-quarters at Downingville, and fit out a naval force that would put Cuba through. And here I am, Gineral, **and** you may depend on't the work's got to be done.

But now I must ask you, Gineral, what in **thunder Mr.** Marcy means by backin' **and** fillin' so. I have jest got some of the latest New York papers by an outer-bound vessel, and one of the first things I see is Mr. Marcy's letter to Mr. Souley, dated 13th **of November, aud it is so full of** milk and water it makes me fairly sick. I was always a little afraid Marcy was an Old Fogy, but I did think he had a little more back-bone than he shows in this letter. He's no Christian, and he's violated **the** Scripter, for he has put his hand to the plough and looked back. He seems now to be for smoothing over matters; thinks maybe our **country** *could* manage some how or other **to** get along without Cuba; don't know but what old Spain means to do the thing that's about right after all; better dicker with her a little longer in a friendly kind of a way; better not do anything to afront her; keep things quiet till Spain gets in the right mood, and then, if **she won't sell us** Cuba, perhaps she'll settle and pay up.

Now, I tell you what 'tis, Gineral, our Eurup Cabinet don't swallow no sich milk and water stuff as that. What's got into Mr. Marcy? Last year he told Mr. Souley to demand three hundred thousand dollars for the Black Warrior, right down on the nail, and not stop to parley about it. But now he quivers and shakes one way and t'other, like a leaf in the wind. I'm afraid Mr. Marcy is getting old. And there's poor old Uncle Joshua, Postmaster of Downingville, I find he's getting old and timersum too. When I got home to Downingville and told the family I was going to fit out the Two Pollies, and be off the next day to take Cuba, Uuncle Joshua was struck all of a heap.

Says he, "Major, I beg of you not to go into any of that fillibustering business; it's next akin to piracy; and there's the neutrality laws dead agin you, too."

"Oh, no," says I, "Uncle Joshua, I aint going to undertake any of your low fillibusterin'; I'm only jest going out to take Cuba man-fashion, because our country can't get along without it, and self-preservation, you know, is the first law of nater, and because old Spain keeps insulting of us and won't pay up."

"But don't you see, Major," says Uncle Joshua, "if you go to take Cuba, you are making war upon Spain; and you can't do that according to the Constitution. Nobody in this country has any power to make war but Congress."

"But you're mistaken there, Uncle Joshua," says I. "Didn't Mr. Polk make war upon Mexico?"

"No, by no means," said Uncle Joshua. "If you look back and read the dockyments of them days, you will find it reads, 'Whereas war *exists* between this country and Mexico.' You see that war come itself. But you have no right to make war upon Spain or Cuba unless you get your authority from Congress. That is according to the Constitution."

"Wal, uncle, I *have* got my authority from Congress," says I; "what more do you want?"

"Oh, no," says he; "Congress haint declared war, because it would be in the papers, and I should a seen it."

"But I don't mean your lazy Old Fogy Congress to Washington," says I; "I mean our Eurup Congress."

And then I took the dockyment out of my pocket and showed it to him, signed by Mr. Buchanan, and Mr. Mason, and Mr. Souley. At first he was thunder-struck, and couldn't say nothin'. Then he fell back on the Constitution agin, jest as he always does, and said he didn't believe our Congress over there in Eurup was constitutional. Then he reached up to the shelf and took down the old Constitution, covered with morocco leather, that Gineral Jackson sent him more than twenty years ago, and he put on his spectacles and looked it all over from beginning to end, and said he couldn't find nothin' about any Congress in Eurup.

"But if you call your meeting over there in Eurup a Congress," says he, "I should like to know where you find your authority in the Constitution to make war upon Spain or to go fillibusterin' about Cuba?"

"Why, Uncle Joshua," says I, "we find it in that clause where it says '*I take the responsibility.*'"

"There!" said Cousin Sargent Joel, who had been listening all the time without saying a word; "there, father," says he, "I knew you would find the authority in the Constitution somewhere. That's one of the amendments to the Constitution that was added by Gineral Jackson, you know, and therefore it *must* be right."

Then Sargent Joel turned to me, and says he, "Major, I've been round and notified the whole company of the Downingville militia, and they are all ready, armed and equipped as the law directs, and will be aboard to-morrow at ten o'clock. They are full of grit, and ready to swallow Cuba alive."

I haint got near through my story, Gineral, for I wanted to

tell you more about fitting out the *Two Pollies*, and about the crew, and the sogers, and the marines, and the hoss-marines, and the vigc, but I shan't have room in this dispatch, and the little clipper that's waitin' for me to finish writing, has got a smart wind and wants to be off. If I don't see you standing on the pint of Floriday as we go by, I shall take it for granted

PRESIDENT PIERCE ON THE POINT OF FLORIDA, HAILING THE "TWO POLLIES."

that you have concluded not to go out to see us take Cuba; but if I see a man standing there, and swinging his hat, I shall know it's you, and we'll bear right up with the *Two Pollies* and take you off.

I remain your old friend, and Minister-Gineral at large, and Rear Commodore of the fillibuster fleet,

MAJOR JACK DOWNING.

LETTER LXXIX.

Aboard the Schooner Two Pollies,
Sailin' round Cuba and up the Gulf, September, 1855.

Dear Gineral Jackson :—(There, what an awful mistake I've made ! I meant Dear Gineral Pierce ; but my poor old brains has been runnin' a good deal to-day on that old and true friend of mine, Gineral Jackson, and I s'pose that made the word slip off my pen before I thought of it.)

The truth is, Gineral Pierce, I don't feel satisfied with my treatment, to be left here alone all summer to bear the whole brunt of this fillibuster war, sailin' about in these hot climates, where we light our pipes by the sun without matches, and exposin' our lives all the time ; and two out of our men has died with the yaller fever, and not a soul sent out to back me up, and help me take Cuba—not a single war-vessel, nor a steamer, nor a private fillibuster, nor even so much as Bill Johnson on a pine-log with a fowlin'-piece.

What did you expect me to do ? Was I to pitch into the Moro Castle alone ? The whole English fleet—the greatest fleet in the world—was afraid to pitch into Cronstadt, up there in the Baltic. The Two Pollies is brave and sure fire, but I don't think it's hardly reasonable to match her alone agin the Moro, though I've sometimes almost swore I would do it, hit or miss, getting so out of patience waitin' all summer for re-enforcements. And sometimes I'd have a real time thinkin' of Gineral Jackson, and saying to myself, if Old Hickory was only at the helm—I don't mean the helm of the Two Pollies, but the helm of Government—I guess things wouldn't go on at this rate. There wouldn't be no backin' and fillin' then ; it would be plain sailin', **straight** ahead, and everybody would know where they **was goin' to fetch up.** If Old Hickory put his foot down on fifty-four forty, it would be *there*, and you needn't look for it on forty-nine. If the Spanish folks had a took the Black Warrior steamer under his **Administration, and he had** demanded three hundred thousand dollars to pay **the damages and** wipe out the insult, **the money would have to** be planked right down on the nail, or the hair would fly somewhere. And if he had fairly made up his mind, as our Congress did at Ostend and Ax-le-Shapple, that Cuba was as necessary to our Government as ary one of the States, and **that we couldn't** get along **without it,** and, therefore, "by every law, human and divine, we had the right to take it if we possessed the power," **the** whole business would a been done in three **weeks,** and Cuba marked down on the map of **the** United States. But **a** backin' and fillin' and wrigglin' policy never will fetch anything about; and I don't raily believe we are so near having Cuba now as we was six months ago.

If Mr. **Buchanan** had **only** been at home, I know he wouldn't **have left the whole business on my** hands alone so long without sending me help; but you have kept his hands tied all this time in London, so he couldn't do nothin'. And poor Mr. **Mason,** he's been sick at Paris, and he couldn't do nothin'. And Mr. Souley has had so many other fish to fry, he wouldn't **do** nothin'. **And** as for Sanders and Sickles, I hear they have **gone** off to Russia, to **see** about setting up **a new** Democratic Republic **there,** or else annexin' Russia to the United States. They say **there** is no reason in the world **why** Russia shouldn't belong to us—there is such a good chance to run a telegraph wire across Beering's Straits. So there wasn't nobody left to back me up in this Cuba business but you and the Cabinet. And how have you and they done it? Yes, Mr. President, how have you done it? I must speak plain, for I have had my feelings a good many times badly worked up. I hope there hasn't been any treachery in your Cabinet, and no pullin' the rope over the roof of the house at both ends. But things has looked very dark and foggy to me sometimes. You haint sent me no dispatches, and I've had to keep the run of things by the newspapers that I picked up here and there from vessels goin' back and forth. And when I see Commodore McCauley was coming out with a "force" sufficient to blow every Spanish cruiser to thunder, and knock the Moro into a cocked hat, we had a jolly time aboard the Two Pollies, I tell ye. We threw up our hats and hoorah'd about an hour right out strait.

Wal, arter a week or two, when we got most tired of waitin', the fleet come along. I bore up under the Commodore's lea and hailed him, and asked him where the Two Pollies should hitch on. As soon as he see it was me he was very polite; but he said the Two Pollies better keep dark, and lay low a little while, till he went into Havana and reconnoitered round, and then he should know exactly what to do. So we waited patiently a week or two longer; and then I hailed a Penobscot sloop, Captain Gilman, an old acquaintance, who had been into Havana with a load of lumber, and was homeward bound with a cargo of molasses and sugar.

Says I, "Gilman, did you see anything of Commodore McCauley?"

"See him? Yes, I see him every day."

"Wal, what's he about all this time? Has he took the Moro, and the city, and the war vessels, without giving me a chance?"

"No, I don't think he has took anything," said Gilman, "but the Captain-Gineral has took him."

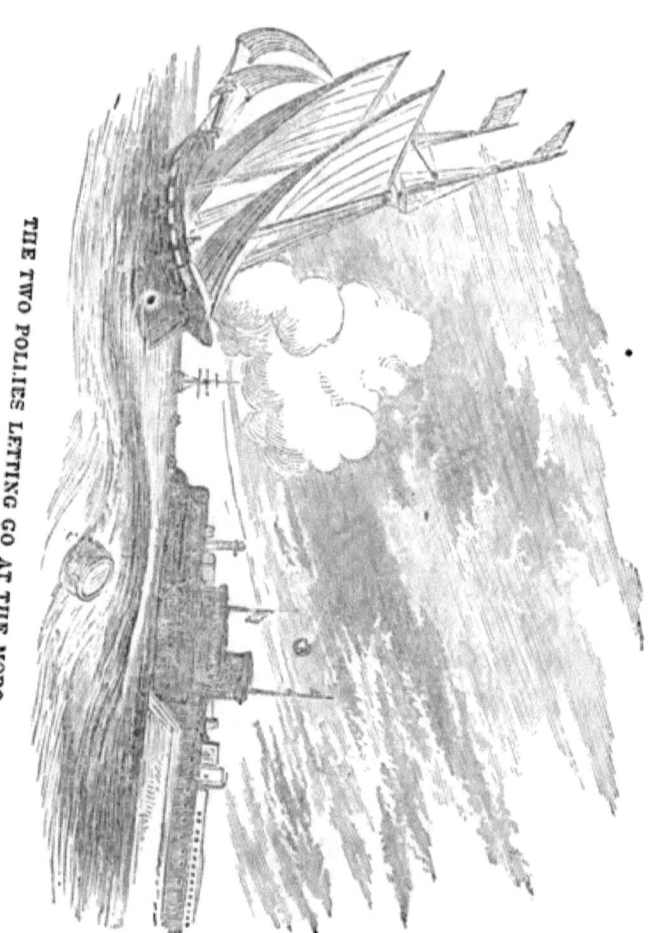

THE TWO POLLIES LETTING GO AT THE MORO.

My dander was right up, I tell ye. Says I, "you don't mean to say he has took our Commodore and shut him up in the Moro? If he has I'll go right in with the Two Pollies and blow the old thunder-jug into the ocean."

"Oh, no," said Gilman, with a little puckery laff creeping round his eyes and mouth; "he's only took the Commodore into his great fine carriage, and I see them most every day riding together, cheek by jowl, and having a jolly time of it."

"Thunder!" says I. "Then somebody's been pulling at the wrong end of the rope, and I won't lay low any longer."

So we up stakes and sot sail agin on our own hook, keeping an eye well to the windward. I felt cross, and told the hands to crack on all sail. I meant to be out of sight and hearing when the Commodore's fleet come out again, for I didn't know but he might take it into his head to enforce the neutrality laws, and I had no idea of being ketched in that trap. I felt sure there was a screw loose somewhere in the Cabinet, and I thought if I could only be in Washington half an hour I could find out where 'twas. But, as things was, there was no other way for me but to take the responsibility, and if I couldn't take Cuba, jest hold on to the slack till something turned up.

Wal, it wasn't a great while before something did turn up that carried our hopes right up to the tip-top rung of the ladder. After scuddin' about a few weeks to keep out of sight of Commodore McCauley, for I had serious suspicions of him, I come back again along the northern side of Cuba, to see if I could pick up any more news. As good luck would have it, a Kennebec brig soon came along, homeward bound. I hailed her, and as soon as the Captain came on deck I see at once it was Captain Drummond, a first rate prying feller, and I knew in a moment if he had been in Cuba a week he would know everything that was going on upon the island.

So I asked him to back his main topsail, and I'd come aboard. We went into the cabin, and he brought on a bottle of old Jamaky. We are both Maine-law folks at home, but out here **we sometimes take** a drop to keep off the yaller fever.

"Now, Captain Drummond," says I, "**how does things stand in Cuba?** I hear Commodore McCauley **has** turned traitor to the cause. Is liberty going to be crushed out there **or not? Or is** there any chance yet for them poor fellers that have been trying so long and **so** hard **to** get their freedom?"

"Any chance, my dear Major?" says he. "Why, the chance never was better; nor half so good before. **The** whole thing is cut and dried, and almost ready to blaze **out** with a brightness that will enable us to spear fish at midnight along the whole coast, from the Kennebec to the Mississippi."

"**Good!** Give us your hand, old boy," says I. "Now prove **that, and I'll** be your humble servant forever."

"Well, it's true as preachin'," **says he.** "Our Government has got a first-rate agent on the island, overhauling the whole business, to see that everything **is in** the right train, **so** there shan't be no mistake and no chance **to** miss fire **again.** He keeps dark, and goes round **among the leading** patriots, and consults about the whole campaign. After he showed his **dockyments,** proving that he was an agent from our Government, they didn't keep anything back, but told him the whole business—how the patriots were all ready to set up **a** free Government, and would very **soon have** everything necessary for that purpose. They told him they **had sent over more** than half a million of dollars to their friends—**the exiled patriots in the** United States—to purchase such things **as** they might need in setting up **their** free Government, and a number of large steamers and other vessels were already chartered and paid for to bring them over; and more than all that, if they

19

should want any help, there was a great Gineral stood ready, with a brave little army all enlisted, to come right over and put his shoulder to the wheel. That's the way the thing

THE CREW OF THE TWO POLLIES CUTTING ON AND DOING JUST AS THEY 'PLEASE.

stands now. The patriots are all right, and our Government's secret agent has been round and seen that they are all right. And now the Government at **Washington is going to** look t'other way, over the **left** shoulder, while the business is doing, so they shan't see anybody violating the neutrality laws."

"That's capital," says I, "Captain Drummond, that's capital, if that agent is all right. Who is he?"

"Oh, he's a fine fellow; he's got the Government dockyments in his pocket. His name, I think, is Davis. I don't know what Davis, but I believe he's from Mississippi."

At that I hopt right up, and slapt my hands together so hard that Captain Drummond jumped half way across the cabin, for he thought I was going to pitch into him; and says he, "What in nature, Major Downing, is the matter?"

"Matter enough," says I. "I verily believe that agent is my old friend, Jeff. Davis, for he's from that part of the country, and he's jest the boy for it. He was out in Mexico with us, and was clear grit. If Jeff. Davis is in Cuba, the thing is done, and no mistake about it."

Upon that we took another drop of Jamaky, and Captain Drummond histed sail, and I went aboard the Two Pollies and told the boys they might crack on and hoorah as loud as they'd a mind to, for the business was all right, and the egg was most ready to be hatched. Finally, I felt so happy, I told all hands they might have a holiday, and cut on and do jest what they liked. And they had a jolly time, I tell ye. I gave them an extra good dinner; and after dinner they sung songs most of the afternoon, and some of 'em scoured the deck by cutting down double shuffle. They sung "Captain Robb," Cousin Sargent Joel's favorite song, five times, in the tune of Yankee Doodle; and every one aboard that could sing Yankee Doodle—soldiers, sailors, marines, and hoss-marines—all jined in and roared it out well. Cousin Joel declared afterwards that before they got through he saw more than fifty delphins shying round the vessel and listening.

If you haven't seen that song, Mr. President, it is raily worth your readin'. So I think I'll send it to you, and here 'tis :

CAPTAIN ROBB.

Air—*Yankee Doodle.*

Says Captain Robb to Farmer Cobb,
   "Your farm is very fine, sir ;
Please give me up your title-deeds,
   I claim it all as mine, sir."
"Pray, how can it be thine?" says Cobb,
   "I'm sure I never sold it ;
'Twas left me by my father, sir,
   I only aught to hold it."

"Nay, Cobb, the march of destiny—
   'Tis strange you can't perceive it—
Is sure to make it mine some day ;
   I solemnly believe it."
"But have you not already got
   More land than you can till, sir ?
More rocks than ever you can blast,
   More weeds than you **can kill, sir ?**"

"Aye, Cobb, but something whispers me—
   A sort of inspiration—
That I've a *right* to every farm
   Not under cultivation.
I'm of the ' Anglo-Saxon race,'
   A people known to fame, sir ;
But you, what right have you to land ?
   Who ever heard your name, sir ?

"I deem you, Cobb, a lazy **lout,**
   Poor, trodden down, and blind, sir,
And if I take your useless **land**
   You aught to think it kind, sir !
And, with my scientific skill,
   I set it down as true, sir,
That I can gather from the farm
   Full twice as much as **you,** sir.

"To be explicit : 'Tis an age
   Of freedom and progression ;

OUT OF THE SENATE.

    No longer, dog-in-manger like,
      Can you retain possession.
    The farm long since you forfeited,
      Because you failed to till it;
    To me it clearly now belongs,
      Simply because—*I will it*.

"My logic if you disapprove,
    Or fail of comprehending,
Or do not feel convinced that I
    Your welfare am attending,
I've plenty more of arguments
    To which I can resort, sir—
Six-shooters, rifles, bowie-knives,
    Will indicate the sort, sir.

"So prithee, Cobb, take my advice,
    Make over your domains, sir:
Or, sure as I am Captain Robb,
    Will I blow out your brains, sir!"
Poor Cobb can only grind his teeth
    And grumble protestations,
That *might* should be the rule of *right*
    Among *enlightened nations*.

But now, Mr. President, I must come to the bitter end of my dispatches, and bitter enough it is. This business needs some explanation between you and me; and the sooner I git it the better. That glorious day aboard the Two Pollies we was all swimmin' in happiness mast-head high. But a few weeks afterward, when we got the next batch of news from home, we was like bein' all down in the dark hold of the vessel, wallowing in bilge-water. Thunder and black snakes! if ever I could swear, it was then. That Davis had turned out to be a very different chap from my old friend Jeff, and somehow or other everything had gone wrong-end foremost. The Cuban patriot cause was all smashed up; their half million of dollars was all scattered to the winds; Gineral Quitman had backed out, and Government was seizing steamers and vessels all along the coast, and making them suffer the delay and expense of lawsuits to prove that they had no notion of going to Cuba. And, more than all this, some of the best patriots in Cuba, men who had opened their whole heart to Davis, men worthy enough to be President of the United States or to command the Two Pollies, had been arrested in Cuba and executed like dogs. Now, Mr. President, where has the blood of them patriots left the heaviest marks? Is it in Havana, New York, or Washington? But how could all this terrible change come about? Was there any awful accident the cause of it, like switching a train of cars on to the wrong track and making a terrible smash-up? I puzzled upon that pint a good deal, and finally come to the conclusion that possibly it was all an accident, and nobody to blame. And the most likely way I could think of that sich a terrible accident could happen was, that Mr. Davis received his secret commission from *one end* of your Cabinet, and, somehow or other, accidentally made his report to *t'other end* of it. But I may be wrong, and shall wait anxiously for your explanation.

Let me hear from you soon, for I don't think I shall hold on here much longer, as things now is, unless I get new orders. I see things is thickening up all round you, and with the troubles in Mexico, and Denmark, and Kansas, and the melting down and mixing up about fifteen political parties all over the country and running them into thirty *new moulds*, you must have your hands full, and will need all your friends to stick by you; and I assure you I am not a man to desert an Administration so long as I hold an office under it.

So I remain your old friend and Minister at Large, and Captain of the Two Pollies,

MAJOR JACK DOWNING.

LETTER LXXX.

To *Uncle Joshua Downing, Postmaster at Downingville, Down East, in the State of Maine.*

Aboard the Schooner Two Pollies,
At anker inside of Sandy Hook, January 21, 1856.

Dear Uncle Joshua :—I have jest got back from Washington, where I have been for the last fortnight watchin' the old ship of State layin' tu in a sort of three-cornered gale of wind. This gale struck her on the 3d of December, and threw her all aback, and the gale holds on yet tight as ever, and there she has been layin' now seven weeks, head to the wind, rolling and pitchin', and hasn't gained ahead a rod. I've seen rough times in the Two Pollies, and long gales of wind, and hurrykanes and whirlpools, and all sorts of weather, but this is the first time I've seen a craft layin' to agin a three-cornered gale for two months upon a stretch, in a choppin sea, worse than the Gulf Stream in a thunder-storm. But don't you be frightened, Uncle Joshua ; she won't go down, but will live through it, and go on her voyage by-and-by all right. Our old ship of State is a stanch craft ; she is built of the very best stuff, and put together in the strongest manner, and there isn't a spar, nor a plank, nor a timber-head in her but what is as sound as a nut. She's the best ship in the world, and the Two Pollies is next. So you needn't be afeerd that any sea will ever swamp her ; and if ever she should be in danger of running ashore, or on the breakers, by the squabbles and foolin' of her officers, she's got a *crew* that will take care of her.

You know, Uncle, I've been sailin' round Cuba and up the

Gulf a good while, tryin' to carry out the plans of our Congress at Ostend and Ax-le-Shappel, to take Cuba, because our country couldn't get along without it; and self-preservation, you know, is the first law of nater. We should got through with that job long ago if our Cabinet hadn't backed out about it. I never understood the home difficulty, but I'm sure there was some hard shuffling somewhere. We was all right abroad; but this backin' and fillin' in the Home Department was what bothered us, and pretty likely has upset the business. First the Home Department told us to go ahead and fix up our Ostend matter the best way we could. But as soon as I and Mr. Bukanan and Mr. Sooley, and the rest of us in the foreign Government, had got things well under way, and was about **ready to take Cuba, the Home Department** turned right round and fit agin **us** tooth and nail. As I said afore, I couldn't account for this home **difficulty, and the** sudden turn-about of the Home Department, unless they was afeard we should get the most of the credit of taking Cuba, and maybe I, or Mr. Bukanan, or Mr. **Sooley,** or Mr. Mason, or Mr. Sickles, or Mr. Sanders might get to be President by it. But such a thought never entered *my* head, and I can pledge myself the same for all the rest. **We was to** work entirely for the country's good, and nothin else. And for the Home Department to get jealous of us and turn agin us in that way was cruel and onkind. It grieves me every time I think of it; for I think like the good Dr. Watts, when he says:

> "How pleasant 'tis **to** see,
> Brethren and friends agree."

I sent dispatches to Gineral Pierce about it more than three months ago, but never got any answer. And finally I got tired holdin' on out there alone, and hearing all the time that the Home Department kept stopping all the re-enforcements from coming out to help me, so I up helm and headed the Two Pollies for Downingville. When we got along in the latitude of New York that terrible 5th of January storm overtook us, and we jest made out to weather the gale, and get inside of Sandy Hook and come to anker. The pilots come aboard and treated us very kind.

Them New York pilots are clever fellows. They brought us lots of newspapers, from which I learnt what had been going on for two months past. When they see the Downingville militia was aboard, and Sargent Joel at the head of 'em, dressed up in his uniform, one of the pilots took me one side and whispered to me that he would advise me, as a friend, not to go up to New York, for if we did the Two Pollies was a gone goose.

"How so?" says I, "what do you mean?"

"I mean," says he, "that Mr. McKeon, the District Attorney, will nab her in less than no time, and condemn her for a fillibuster vessel, and you'll all be put in prison and tried for violating the neutrality laws."

"Let him do it," says I, "if he dares. We are at work for the Government. Our cruise has all been under the direction and advice of Congress."

"If I remember right," says he, "Congress wasn't in session when the Two Pollies sailed for the West India station. How, then, could you be under the direction of Congress?"

"I mean the Ostend Congress," says I, "and it makes no difference which, one's as good as t'other."

"Well," says he, you'll find it makes a difference which when you get up to New York. The District Attorney is death on every vessel that has the least smell of gun-powder, or has anything aboard that bears any likeness to a musket. He has a master keen scent for gun-powder; he often smells it aboard vessels where there isn't a bit nor grain, and it all turns out to be only bilge-water."

"If that's the case," says I, "I'll leave the Two Pollies at anker here, and I'll be off to Washington and see how the land lays."

So I called up Captain Jumper, the sailing master, and told him to keep things all snug and tight while I was gone, and

THE MAJOR IN THE GALLERY OF THE HOUSE.

I told Sargent Joel to take good care of the men, and I'd try, if possible, to be back in a fortnight.

When I got to Washinghton I thought I would jest run in a few minutes and see how Congress was getting along first. I had let my beard grow pretty long, and was dressed so different from what I used to, that I didn't feel afeard of anybody's knowing me ; so I went into the Representatives chamber and took a seat in the gallery. Business seemed to be going on brisk and lively. A man was standing up in front, and reading off, in a good loud voice, Banks, 105 ; Richardson, 73 ; Fuller, 31; Pennington, 5 ; scattering, 4. Then I went out and went into the Senate. But there business seemed to be very dull. I couldn't find out as anything was doing. Some was reading the newspapers, and some was talking a little, and some was setting as calm and quiet as so many bears in their winter den, with nothin' to do but suck their paws. I soon got tired of this, and went back into the House again. I had but jest got seated in the gallery when the man in front got up and read off agin : Banks, 105 ; Richardson, 73 ; Fuller, 31 ; Pennington, 5 ; scattering, 4.

I turned round and whispered to the man who sot next to me, and says I, " That's just the same tune they had when I was in here half an hour ago."

" Exactly," says he ; " they don't play but one tune, and that hasn't no variations."

" Well, what upon airth are they doing ?" says I.

" Oh, they are choosing a Speaker," says he.

" Choosing a Speaker !" says I. " For gracious sake, how long does it take 'em to do that ?"

" I can't have the slightest idea how long," say he. " They've been at it now about six weeks, and if they continue to gain as fast as they have since they begun, I guess it might take 'em pretty near from July to eternity."

" If that's the case," says I, " I'll clear out, for I can't wait so long as that." So I hurried out and made tracks straight for the White House. I rung to the door, and the servant let me in. I told him I wanted to see the President. He said very well, the President was in his private room, and he would take my card to him. I told him he might go and tell

Gineral Pierce that an old friend of his and a fellow-soldier in the Mexican war wanted to see him. Presently he come back and asked me to walk up. I found the President alone, walking back and forth across the room, and looking kind of riled and very resolute. It made me think of Old Hickory when he used to get his dander up about Biddle's Bank, and walked the floor all day, and lay awake all night, planning how he could upset it. The Gineral knew me as soon as I went into the room, in spite of my beard, and shook hands with me, and said he was very glad to see me.

"Well, now, Gineral," says I, "I want to come right to the pint the first thing. I've left the Two Pollies at anker down to Sandy Hook, and I want to know, right up and down, if she's to be nabbed or not. You know how 'tis, Gineral; you know we went out in good faith under the orders of the Ostend Congress; and you know the Home Government backed us up in the beginning of it; but now you've turned agin us, and I understand you've been seizing and overhauling every vessel all along shore that had its bowsprit pointed towards Cuba or Central America; and I was told if the Two Pollies went up to York she'd be served the same sass. Now, I want to know how we stand, that's all. If you don't want the help of the Two Pollies there's enough that does; and if you don't give her a clear passport out and in, she'll be off pretty quick where she can find better friends."

"Why, my dear Major," said the President, and the tears almost come into his eyes, "my dear Major," says he, "you misunderstand me entirely. You and the Two Pollies haven't got a better friend in the world than I am. The fact is, I've been very much tried ever since that Ostend Congress business. It made a good deal of hard feeling in my Cabinet, and as things worked we was obliged to come out agin it.

And then we had to make a show of sticking up very strong for the neutrality laws; and that's why we seized so many vessels. But you needn't give yourself the least uneasiness about the Two Pollies. I pledge you the honor of the Executive that she shan't be touched. And, besides, I'm in a good deal of trouble all round, and I want you and the Two Pollies to stick by me; for, if you don't, I don't know who will."

"Agreed," says I, "nuff said; that's talking right up to the mark. Give us your hand, Gineral; I'll stick by you as close as I did by my old friend Gineral Jackson. Now, what do you want me to do?"

"Well, Major," says he, "I've got a good many ticklish jobs on hand that I don't hardly know what to do with, nor which to take hold on first. You know there's a Democratic Convention to meet at Cincinnati to make the nominations for the next term." (Here the President got up and locked the door, and sot down close to me and talked low.) "The main question is, how to bring things to bear on that Convention so as to make the nomination go right. Marcy wants it, and Buchanan wants it, and Wise wants it, and Dickinson wants it, and perhaps Cass too, though he says he don't, and I don't know how many others, all good Democrats, you know; but we can't all have it; so you see I've got a hard team to pull against. As for Douglas, I think he'll go for me, if I'll go for him afterwards. The Cabinet and I have been tryin' to get things ready before the nomination to give the Administration the credit of being the smartest and spunkiest Administration we ever had. We want, if possible, to go a little ahead of Jackson. You know we've already blowed Gray Town to atoms. We've struck a heavy blow to knock off the Danish Sound dues, and shall be ready for a splendid rumpus there in the spring. We've got a rousin' arthquake kindlin' up between us and England, which will be jest the thing if we can touch it off at the right time. But you know these things sometimes take fire too soon, and do mischief both sides. I feel a little oneasy about this, and wish that stupid Congress would ever get organized so as to take part of the responsibility. Then we've got a quarrel brewin', too, with Colonel Walker, out there in Nicaragua, and have refused to receive Colonel French as his Minister. If Walker chooses to resent it as a national insult, we are ready for him. We shan't give back a hair. Now, Major, what do you think of the chances for the nomination?"

"Wal, Gineral," says I, "I think if you manage right you'll get it. I'll do what I can for you anyhow."

The Gineral shook my hand, and got up and walked the floor. Says he, "The greatest difficulty now is with this confounded stiff-necked, stupid Congress. They won't organize—that is, the House won't—and they seem determined to throw a damper on the Administration somehow or other. Here they've been foolin' away their time six weeks, and lettin' the whole country hang by the eye-lids—war and all. I had to keep my message on hand a month, and let it almost spile, jest because the House wasn't organized. At last I happened to think it was a good chance for me to take the responsibility. So I let drive, and fired my message right in among 'em. Some was quite wrathy; but I didn't care for that. I meant to let 'em know I'd show 'em a touch of Old Hickory if they didn't mind how they carried sail. But here 'tis now goin' on two months, and everything is at a dead stand, because the House won't choose a Speaker. We can't have any certainty of getting enough money to keep the Government agoin' till we get a Speaker, and all our plans is in danger of being knocked in the head. Now, Major, I wish you would shy round among the members a day or two, and see if you can't bring matters to a pint. I don't care much who is Speaker, if they'll only organize."

So I went round among the members two or three days, and did my best. I found 'em all very stiff, and the lobby members were stiffest of any. The third day I went back to the President agin, and says he, "Well, Major, how does it stand now? Does things look any more encouraging?"

"A leetle grain," says I, "but not much."

"Well, how is it?" says he.

Says I, "It is Banks, 105; Richardson, 73; Fuller, 31; Pennington, 5; scattering, 3."

"But that's the same old tune," says he; jest the same that's been for the last six weeks."

"No," says I, "you mistake. Don't you see the scattering has fell off *one*? Isn't that a leetle encouraging?"

The President looked disappointed. Said he, "That's a very small straw for a drownin' man to catch at. But how do they talk? Do they grow any more pliable?"

"Well, the Fuller men seemed to be the most pliable," says I, "of any of 'em. They said *they* was perfectly willing and ready to organize at any time, and the only difficulty was, the Banks men and Richardson men standing out so stubborn."

"What do our true Democratic friends, the Richardson men, say?" said the President.

Says I, "They say they'll stand there and fight till the crack of doom before they'll allow the Black Republicans to get the upper hand."

"Well, that's good spunk," said the President; "but the worst of it is, this business will crack my Administration sometime before the crack of doom. Well, how do the Banks men talk? Is there any hope from that quarter?"

"They say they are in no hurry," says I. "They had as leave vote as do anything else. They've got money enough, and can stand it, and they'll stick where they are till they starve the Administration out."

The President jumped up, and I must say he looked more like Old Hickory than I ever see him before. Says he, "Major Downing, this will never do; we must have a Speaker, by hook or by crook. Can't you contrive any way to bring this business about?"

"Well," says I, "there is one way, I think, the business may be done—and I don't know but it's the last chance—and that is, for me to go and bring the Two Pollies round here, and bring her guns to bear on the Capitol. Then send in word, and give them one hour to organize. If they don't do it, then batter down the house about their ears, or march in the Downingville melitia and drive 'em out, as old Cromwell did the Rump Parliament."

The President stood a minute in a deep study. At last he said, "Well, Major, a desperate disease sometimes needs a desperate remedy. If you think you are right *go ahead*."

So here I am, Uncle Joshua, aboard the Two Pollies. I jest stopt to write this account to you, and if I don't get better news from Washington in a day or two, I shall up anker and make all sail for the Potomac. And if things is no better when I get there you may expect to hear thunder.

I remain your loving nephew,

MAJOR JACK DOWNING.

A POSTSCRIPT.

I have wound up *My Thirty Years Out of the Senate,* and left the Two Pollies at anker down to Sandy Hook, with Sargent Joel and a few Downingville melitia on board to keep guard till we get orders from the Government, or Mr. Bukanan, or somebody else, to *do* something. If Kansas has got through "bleeding," so Mr. Bukanan can get time to look after something else, and thinks it is time to take Cuba, "if we have the power," we are on hand, and all ready to give a lift. Or, if we are to take care of Mexico, and are going to fix up that "protectorate" that they talk about, the Two Pollies will undertake to go out and take care of the castle at Vera Cruz, for her part of the protectorate. She wasn't afraid to pour into the Moro, and I guess she'll have grit enough to handle Vera Cruz. Or if Government hasn't got the Central American question settled yet, and finds it necessary to send out a *force* there, the Two Pollies is the craft to take charge of the business and keep the road open across the Isthmus. Or if the Government should think it best to take in the Society Islands and the Sandwich Islands, away round there in the Pacific Ocean and hitch 'em on to the United States, the Two Pollies would make a first-rate squadron to be stationed round there among 'em, for there aint another vessel in the whole navy that can hold a candle to her in sailin' round Islands—she's been tried, and wasn't found wanting. Or if there should need to be any reënforcement sent to the army that's gone to Utah to whip them beastly Mormons that's got so many wives, Sargent Joel and the Downingville company would be force enough to set things all right there, and the marines and boss-marines could be kept aboard to navigate the Two Pollies. And I want Mr. Buchanan and the Government to understand that we are ready to take hold and help 'em out of their difficulties at any time and in all weathers.

Although I've got through "My Thirty Years Out of the Senate," I aint agoing to sit down and do nothin'—I aint one of that nater; and as it's pretty likely I shall be out of the Senate some time longer, if I live, I shall keep sturrin' round, writin' for the good of the country, or fightin' for the good of the country, as long as I can hold out. My old friend, Colonel Benton, did jest the same thing. When he got through his Thirty Years *in* the Senate he didn't fold his hands and set down and do nothin', but kept on writin' for his country till the last moment, and finally the brave old man "died in harness," as they say, almost with the pen in his hand. I think that's better than to rust out. So when I aint wanted by the Government to go on foreign expeditions, I shall pretty likely keep figerin' away with my pen in somethin' or other. Maybe I can do as much good to the country in that way as any, for I have a kind of a sneaking taste for literature as well as war, after all. And if my name shouldn't appear in the list of contributors to the new Magazine called the "*Great Republic*" *Monthly*, I guess, if the reader looks sharp, he'll see I am at work in it somewhere in an underhanded kind of a way. And if I should happen to go off on a cruise anywhere, I shall, of course, make my reports to the Government and the public through that Magazine.

With the best good wishes for everybody, I remain,

MAJOR JACK DOWNING.

www.ingramcontent.com/pod-product-compliance
Lightning Source LLC
Chambersburg PA
CBHW032001300426
44117CB00008B/856